THE COLLECTED LETTERS OF
KATHERINE MANSFIELD

VOLUME FIVE

1922–1923

Darling Precious Anne

The curse is I cannot possibly start for Paris for a week from today, and that only fixed if the weather permits! So this time we shall not meet again. But Anne, in the spring we are going to Paris to be there for at least 4 months. Surely we shall meet then. We _must_, dearest. See you and they flying there and near with a spyglass on the hotel roof. Oh, Anne, if you knew that I'd give to see you... shall be too happy for words. All because! It's in the spring I am going in for this Russian treatment, chasse des microbes par les Rayons X. What I've done to do is for us to get a small apartment as I have one petite gante with me – in the shape of my cat and I can't expect him to put up with hotels. So spring – let us meet in spring! I shall hold thumbs from now to April. The idea of my coat is very thrilling. We have 6 feet of snow here – that's snow; I think the fertile earth! and I like Paris – and just love you –

Katherine

Postcard to Anne Drey, 18 January 1922
(Alexander Turnbull Library, Wellington)

THE COLLECTED LETTERS OF

KATHERINE MANSFIELD

EDITED BY

VINCENT O'SULLIVAN

AND

MARGARET SCOTT

VOLUME FIVE

1922–1923

OXFORD

UNIVERSITY PRESS

2008

OXFORD
UNIVERSITY PRESS

Great Clarendon Street, Oxford OX2 6DP

Oxford University Press is a department of the University of Oxford.
It furthers the University's objective of excellence in research, scholarship,
and education by publishing worldwide in

Oxford New York

Auckland Cape Town Dar es Salaam Hong Kong Karachi
Kuala Lumpur Madrid Melbourne Mexico City Nairobi
New Delhi Shanghai Taipei Toronto

With offices in

Argentina Austria Brazil Chile Czech Republic France Greece
Guatemala Hungary Italy Japan Poland Portugal Singapore
South Korea Switzerland Thailand Turkey Ukraine Vietnam

Oxford is a registered trade mark of Oxford University Press
in the UK and in certain other countries

Published in the United States
by Oxford University Press Inc., New York

Typeset by SPI Publisher Services, Pondicherry, India
Printed in Great Britain
on acid-free paper by
CPI Antony Rowe, Chippenham, Wiltshire

ISBN 978-0-19-818399-0

1 3 5 7 9 10 8 6 4 2

CONTENTS

INTRODUCTION

Katherine Mansfield's first letter at the beginning of 1922 announced, 'I suppose I am one of those optimists.' She was writing to her brother-in-law Richard Murry in the jaunty, affectionate, sisterly tone she reserved only for him. But towards the letter's end she gives the clue to something rather unexpected. Along with Shakespeare and the Bible, she is reading *Cosmic Anatomy*. Most of the important decisions she took later in the year go back in some way to that now forgotten book, and to the friend who recommended it.

Cosmic Anatomy had been published the previous year, its author identified as 'M. B. Oxon'. Behind the anonymity was the Theosophist Dr Lewis Wallace, who once had lived as a sheep farmer to the north of Mansfield's Wellington, a friend of her early patron and current mentor, A. R. Orage. It is a dated and difficult book to read, an amalgam of psychology and philological insistence, eastern thought and interpretation of myth. It is an attempt to restore unity in the place of the mental confusion and the sense of disparateness that was both Mansfield's personal experience, and that of much of her generation after the collapsed values that followed the First World War. There are sections of *Cosmic Anatomy* which are not so far from what the footnotes to T. S. Eliot's *The Wasteland* directed the reader to consider.

'Nothing of any worth,' Mansfield wrote for her eye alone, 'can come from a disunited being.' Also at the beginning of January, she noted what it was in Wallace's mélange of random historical scholarship and dubious science that so impressed her. 'To get even a glimpse of the relation of things, to follow that relation & find it remains true through the ages enlarges my little mind as nothing else does. It is only a greater view of psychology. It helps me with my writing for instance to know that hot + bun may mean Taurus, Pradhana, substance. No, that's not really what absorbs me, its that reactions to certain causes & effects always have been the same. It wasn't for nothing that Constantia [one of the two maiden sisters in "The Daughters of the Late Colonel"] chose the moon and water – for instance!' (*KMN*, 322, 313.)

Behind these notes is Mansfield's hope, late in the day as it is, that personality and its so apparent vagaries might be both remedied and self-determined. By the time she left Switzerland for Paris and a last-ditch attempt at yet another medical treatment, this personal urgency touches every aspect of her life, her conviction that as well as looking for a physical cure, she must work against her sense of disintegration. The year 1922 becomes a rescue mission for coherence, at a time when her relationship with Murry was deeply unsettled; when her writing did not go anywhere near as well or as fluently as she led her publishers and agent to believe; when her isolation both from other people and normal sensational life impelled her to look harder for what 'community' might mean—while underlying all this was the final ravaging of her disease, and her facing its consequences. And so there is a direct line from her telling Violet Schiff early in the year that 'what saved me finally was reading a book called "Cosmic Anatomy" and reflecting on it' (8 January), to her final months at George Gurdjieff's Insitute for the Harmonious Development of Man at Fontainebleau-Avon at the year's end. It is a line and a conclusion that her biographers and commentators often feel uneasy with, yet it has an inevitable logic, and brought Mansfield indisputable satisfaction. In her last months, she will be contented as she had not been for many years. Even as she tells Murry, 'I don't know which is the ill me or the well me. I am simply one pretence after another', she is nevertheless insistent on what she now has found: 'they are my own people at last. So I feel. Such beautiful understanding & sympathy I have never known in the outside world' (25 October).

Mansfield was clear-sighted on her medical condition. '*Congestion* is quite simple. The lung becomes full of blood, and that means the heart beats too fast & that means one has fever and pain and one puts oneself to bed' (to Violet Schiff, 8 January). This was the life that advanced tuberculosis imposed, and to mitigate it had meant years of seeking out the best treatment, finding doctors she could trust, travelling to climates that afforded relief. The last throw of the dice was a Russian doctor in Paris, with a new treatment that promised much and finally delivered little. But by the time she left the mountains for the city she always preferred, what concerned her as much as her physical decline was how she might improve a personality she so frankly found wanting. It was body and soul, so to speak, that she had in mind as she read Shakespeare early in the year, and lines in *Antony and Cleopatra* leaped at her:

> Like to a vagabond flag upon the stream
> Goes to and back, lackeying the varying tide
> To rot itself with motion. (IV.ii.14–15)

'That is terrible,' she told Murry, 'and it contains such a terribly deep psychological truth. That "*rots* itself" . . . and the idea of "it" returning and returning, never swept out to sea finally. You may think you have done with it forever but comes a change of tide and there is that dark streak reappeared, more sickeningly rotten still. I understand that better than I care to. I mean—alas!—I have proof of it in my own being' (7 February). The image was astutely taken up, its appropriateness so apparent to a woman who for more than five years had believed a change of scene would mean an improvement in her health, and at each change found that hope dashed back. It now applied as well to her drive to better understand herself, to assume control of those vagaries of mood that increasingly distressed her, to face any turn of events and speak of it accurately.

It is rather too glib to assume, as some commentators have done, that had Mansfield hit on a physical cure, then her 'spiritual' insistence correspondingly would have diminished. The facts stubbornly remain. It is more compelling over these last twelve months to note in the more confiding of her letters, in the few stories she completed, and in the notes she wrote only for herself, a mind and temperament striving, against the clock, to wrest meaning and coherence, not from metaphysical assurance but from the reality that inevitably was hers. What one observes is a vivid existential shaping, before such a word or concept was to hand. (Although at that very moment as it happened, Martin Heidigger was formulating existentialism's depth and applicability to contemporary life.)

'The Fly' was written in the same week as that gloss on Shakespeare's lines, an almost clinical case-study of a businessman distracting himself from the memory of his son killed during the war, by slowly drowning a fly in ink—'plucky little fellow', as 'the Boss' describes him. Biography almost directs one to read the fiction as emblematic of fighting against stacked odds. It is not too difficult to fit her father, or even God, into the Boss's role. And it is to the point, surely, that Mansfield frequently referred to her lungs as her 'wings'. Her last story, 'The Canary', written in Sierre in July, and dedicated to Dorothy Brett as a pact of their friendship, took the woman she had watched from her Paris window lavish attention on her birds, and placed them back in her childhood Wellington. The story is a lament for the bird's death, and an intimation that more than mere decease might be drawn from it. At the same time her last poem, 'The Wounded Bird', takes up the same motif and concludes:

> Oh, waters do not cover me!
> I would look long & long at those beautiful stars!
> Oh my wings—lift me—lift me
> I am not so dreadfully hurt...(*Poems*, 82)

Friendship too, and her love for Murry, were under scrutiny in this final year. The insistent presence of Ida Baker remained the trial it had always been. Yet also, as always, Mansfield knew she could not manage the simplest details of daily living without the devotion of her oldest, much imposed-on friend. There was a distinct reprimand of Murry's failures as a caring husband in her tongue-in-cheek advice to Ida: 'But try and believe and keep on believing without signs from me that I do love you and want you for my wife' (14 June); while underlying both her rages and her dependence was one constant fact: 'In the host of indefinite things there is one that is definite. There is nothing to be done for me at present' (21 March).

With Murry, her concerns were deeper; her love for him indisputable. The long months they were together over the Swiss autumn and winter,

and then the dragging weeks in their Paris hotel while she took Manoukhin's treatment, brought home again to Mansfield how at odds their
temperaments were; how Murry's high intellectualism and wilful gloom
went quite against the grain of her own vitality, her sense of fun, and her
delight in the detail and the variety of ordinary things. More recently there
was the widening chasm as she looked to 'alternative' approaches to
experience that Murry found repellent. Most of all, she felt his remoteness,
his confining bookishness, and his caution. As she tried to unravel the
feeling between them, she noted, 'He thinks of you tenderly. He dreams of
a life with you *some day* when the miracle has happened. You are important
to him as a dream. Not as a living reality ... Yet there is a deep sweet
tender flooding of feeling in my heart which is love for him and longing for
him. But what is the good of it as things stand? Life together, with me ill, is
simply torture with happy moments. But it's not life' (*KMN* II. 286).

The strain on their marriage worsened when later in the year Mansfield
threw in the medical treatment Murry by then believed in. What mattered
far more to her was that he look at himself, at her, and at how they were
together, with her own probing clarity. His few letters that survive from
1922 rather miss the point. They are considerate, sentimental, and deeply
puzzled as she moves towards the decision that places them further apart.
Her frankness was wounding as she reminds him of 'the blanks, the
silences, the anguish of continual misunderstanding. Were we positive,
eager, alive? No, we were not. We were a nothingness shot through
with gleams of what might be. But no more. Well, I have to face everything
as far as I can & see where I stand—what *remains*' (11 October). Only
S. S. Koteliansky, among her other friends, was confided in as she told him
what she intended to do. 'The world to me is a dream and the people in it
are sleepers. I have known a few instances of intensity but that is all. I want
to find a world in which these instances are united. Shall I succeed? I do
not know. I scarcely care. What is important is to try & learn to live, and
in relation to everything—not isolated (this isolation is death to me)'
(19 October).

The decision that Murry considered so reckless was for Mansfield both
calculated and consistent, a straightforward choice after months of careful
thought. There was more to one's living, to one's total being, than just
physical health. It was there then, to that larger consideration, she would
attend. 'Dying' she now preferred to see almost as a metaphor for getting
on with life. 'I have to die to so much; I have to make such *big* changes.
I feel the only thing to do is to get the dying over—to court it, almost
(Fearfully hard, that) and all hands to the business of being reborn again'
(to Murry, 11 October). Mansfield's dying is heroic not only because she
did it bravely, but because she refused to accept that her entire being must
be dominated by how close finality was.

What Gurdjieff offered Mansfield when he accepted her at his Institute, rather than hopes of a physical cure or anything remotely like doctrinal certainties, was simply a place that was sympathetic to the 'self-healing' she was set on. The doctor who examined her, and recommended that she be admitted, later spelled out that what Gurdjieff expected of those who came to the former Prieuré at Fontainebleau was 'the intensive practice of self-observation in order to develop the will' (James Carruthers Young, 'Experiment at Fontainebleau—a Personal Reminiscence', *New Adelphi*, September 1927, 80). One of her new Russian friends described the community Mansfield arrived at:

There were doctors, painters, dancers, writers, musicians. All believed that the possibilities of development, knowledge, and achievement are much greater than those already achieved; that interior life—through self-control, through non-identification with the ever-changing states of one's being; through sacrifices, through never-tiring efforts to understand more and do more, through willingness to suffer more when needed—to be made real. (Olgivanna [Mrs Frank Lloyd Wright],'The Last Days of Katherine Mansfield', *Bookman*, March 1931, 6)

'Real' became a word Mansfield liked to use for that drive towards simplicity and truth and delight in everyday life, unimpeded by intellectualism and 'the old mechanical life'. That was the whole point of her entering the Institute in the week of her thirty-fourth birthday. A few days later she would tell Murry 'It's a real new life,' assuring him too that 'only you matter—more and more, if that is possible, for now that I am not so "identified" with you I see the real tie that holds us' (23 October). At the end of December, she would tell him how 'If I were allowed one single cry to God that cry would be: *I want to be* REAL' (17 December).

Mansfield's letters from Fontainebleau are almost childlike in their delight at living on a working farm, among artists and intellectuals who are also physical labourers, with men and women whose approach to each other was considerate and direct, and where watching the Eastern dancing that was central to Gurdjieff's conception of harmony so elated her. Daily life was also demanding; the weather at times miserably cold; the interests of the world she had shared with Murry remote and for the moment of little importance. In almost her last letter, she told her novelist cousin, Elizabeth Russell, 'I am tired of my little stories like birds bred in cages' (31 December).

In the months before her death from a haemorrhage at eleven o'clock on the night of 9 January 1923—the same evening as Murry made his first visit to the Prieuré—there is no detail so poignant and so simply indicative of the life she was attempting to remake, as the list of Russian words and phrases she was trying to learn: 'I was late because my fire did not burn ... The sky was blue as in summer ... The trees still have apples. Apple ... I fed the goats ... I go for a walk ... What is the time. Time' (*KMN*, II, 341).

VINCENT O'SULLIVAN

TEXTUAL NOTE

The text attempts to reproduce what Mansfield wrote as accurately as possible. There has been occasional editorial intervention in providing full stops when this omission was clearly inadvertent; in regularizing single and double inverted commas when these were omitted or mismatched; and in silently emending the very few obvious slips of the pen. When a word or phrase finally resisted attempts to read it, the word 'illegible' appears in italics, within square brackets. When a phrase has been crossed out, the deleted words are enclosed in angle brackets. Any words supplied by way of clarification are in square brackets.

Mansfield's emphases have been rendered in the conventional manner, with words underlined once printed in italics, those underlined twice in small capitals, and further underlinings printed as in the manuscript. The sketches with which she occasionally adorned her letters have been reproduced as they occur in the manuscripts. When these were too small to reproduce, or the originals were not available, they have been briefly described.

When Mansfield did not herself date a letter or provide an address, the date or address supplied is enclosed in square brackets; where the date is uncertain or approximate it is preceded by a query or the conventional '*c.*' for *circa*. The layout of addresses and complimentary closures have been standardized, with vertical rules indicating line breaks. Printed addresses are entered in capitals. Where Mansfield sometimes drew a line between paragraphs or sections of a letter a printed rule has been used.

Because of the difficulty of KM's handwriting the typed transcriptions in the Huntington Library of her letters to Elizabeth, Countess Russell, which do not otherwise survive, contain many gaps and misreadings. However, half a dozen of these letters had already been transcribed, in part at least, by Murry for inclusion in *LKM* II, and from these versions it has been possible to fill some of the gaps and correct some of the errors of the Huntington transcripts. This has been done with the Huntington Library's permission, and each word so supplied or altered is marked with an asterisk.

Important literary figures and personal friends already identified and noted in volumes I–IV have not been annotated again in this volume.

ACKNOWLEDGEMENTS

The editors are obliged to the various institutions and private owners listed under 'Manuscript Sources' who have allowed the use of original letters or transcriptions of letters in their possession.

All unpublished material by Katherine Mansfield is quoted here by permission of the copyright owners of the Estate of Katherine Mansfield. All published material has been corrected when possible against the manuscripts.

In this as in previous volumes, the transcriptions of the letters were made by Margaret Scott. Vincent O'Sullivan is responsible for the annotations, dating, and other editorial aspects of the edition.

The editors are indebted, yet again, to Brownlee Kirkpatrick, Mansfield's bibliographer, to her biographer, the late Antony Alpers, and to the following for their expertise and assistance in a number of ways: Bernard Bosque of Fontainebleau-Avon, Margaret Borshevsky, Margaret Calder, Jim Collinge, Diane Bardsley, Robert Easting, Vic Elliott, Lawrence J. Mitchell, Don McRaild, Anne Mounic, David Norton, Helen O'Sullivan, David Retter, Peter H. Rhys-Evans of The Royal Marsden Hospital, and especially, Peter Russell, Dunstan Ward and Irene Zohrab.

Margaret Scott writes:'I have the warmest memories of the late Dan Davin, the "onlie begetter" of this edition. He it was who envisaged it and got it going. The late Graham Bagnall, Chief Librarian of the Alexander Turnbull Library, was strongly supportive of the project while I was on his staff, and subsequently. I am grateful to the Katherine Mansfield Menton Fellowship committee for giving me, in their first year, an opportunity to track down Mansfield's letters in the Northern Hemisphere, and to form friendships with crucial people such as Ida Baker, Mansfield's two sisters Vera and Jeanne, and Middleton Murry's widow Mary, and brother Richard, all of which friendships have informed the work.'

LIST OF ABBREVIATIONS AND MANUSCRIPT SOURCES

KM = Katherine Mansfield

The following abbreviations and short forms are used in the description and provenance given at the foot of each letter:

MS	autograph original
TS	typescript original
draft	autograph draft
PC	photocopy
TC	typed copy

MANUSCRIPT SOURCES

Institutions

ATL	Alexander Turnbull Library, Wellington
BL	British Library
Bodleian	Bodleian Library, Oxford
Cornell	Cornell University, Ithaca, New York
Huntington	The Huntington Library, Pasadena, California
Newberry	The Newberry Library, Chicago
Society of Authors	Society of Authors, London
Stanford	Stanford University, Stanford, California
Texas	The Humanities Research Centre, University of Texas at Austin
Witwatersrand	University of Witwatersrand, South Africa

Private owners

Bell	Andrew Bell Estate
Cains	Mr Geoffrey Cains, Mittagong, Australia
Lawlor	Pat Lawlor Estate
R. Murry	Richard Murry Estate
Targ	Mr. W. Targ

SOURCES OF PREVIOUS PUBLICATION
and short forms used in the annotation

Adam 300	*Adam International Review*, no. 300 (1963–5)
Adam 370–5	*Adam International Review*, nos. 370–375 (1972–3)
Alpers 1980	*The Life of Katherine Mansfield* (1980)
Bibliography	*A Bibliography of Katherine Mansfield*, by B. J. Kirkpatrick (1989)
CLKM I	*The Collected Letters of Katherine Mansfield*, ed. Vincent O'Sullivan and Margaret Scott, vol. I (Oxford, 1984)

CLKM II	*The Collected Letters of Katherine Mansfield*, ed. Vincent O'Sullivan and Margaret Scott, vol. II (Oxford, 1987)
CLKM III	*The Collected Letters of Katherine Mansfield*, ed. Vincent O'Sullivan and Margaret Scott, vol. III (Oxford, 1992)
CLKM IV	*The Collected Letters of Katherine Mansfield*, ed. Vincent O'Sullivan and Margaret Scott, vol. IV (Oxford, 1996)
De Charms	Leslie De Charms, *Elizabeth of the German Garden* (1958)
Dickinson	John W. Dickinson, 'Katherine Mansfield and S. S. Koteliansky: Some Unpublished Letters', *Revue de littérature comparée*, no. 45 (1971), 79–99
Exhibition	*Katherine Mansfield: An Exhibition*, Humanities Research Center, University of Texas (Austin, Texas, 1973)
Journal 1954	*Journal of Katherine Mansfield*, Definitive Edition, ed. John Middleton Murry (1954)
KMN	*Katherine Mansfield's Notebooks*, ed. Margaret Scott, vol. II (Wellington, 1997)
Lea	*The Life of John Middleton Murry*, F. A. Lea (1959)
LJMM	*Katherine Mansfield's Letters to John Middleton Murry, 1913–1922*, ed. John Middleton Murry (1951)
LKM	*The Letters of Katherine Mansfield*, 2 vols., ed. John Middleton Murry (1928)
MLM	Ida Baker, *Katherine Mansfield: The Memories of LM* (1971)
Murry	*The Letters of John Middleton Murry to Katherine Mansfield*, ed. C. A. Hankin (1983)
Poems	*Poems of Katherine Mansfield*, ed. Vincent O'Sullivan (Oxford, 1988)
Scrapbook	*The Scrapbook of Katherine Mansfield*, ed. John Middleton Murry (1939)
Selected	*The Selected Letters of Katherine Mansfield*, ed. Vincent O'Sullivan (Oxford, 1990)
Usborne	Karen Usborne, '*Elizabeth*': *the Author of Elizabeth and her German Garden* (1986)

The place of publication is London unless otherwise noted.

I
SWITZERLAND — SIERRE
JANUARY 1922

By New Year 1922, KM and Murry had been at the Chalet des Sapins, Montana-sur-Sierre, for almost six months. Some of her most celebrated stories were written during that time—'At the Bay', 'The Garden Party', 'The Voyage', and the uncompleted 'A Married Man's Story'. But life in the chalet was isolated, and the winter months severe. KM reverted to what by now was a familiar pattern, as her delight in new surroundings gradually moved to discontent, and it was apparent that her health had not improved. Through her friend S. S. Koteliansky she had heard of the Russian doctor Ivan Manoukhin, and his new treatment for tuberculosis. By early in the year she had arranged to visit him in Paris, for her last attempt at conventional medical treatment. As well, she was now increasingly determined to remedy a deep personal distress with what she saw as her 'divided nature. All is disunited' (to Murry, 1 February).

To Richard Murry, [2 January 1922]

[CHALET DES SAPINS, MONTANA SUR SIERRE]

Dear Richard,

I suppose I am one of those optimists. If I sit down & think, even, it doesn't remove my conviction (yes, its as strong as that) that the New Year is a most promising infant. I don't know why. It seemed to smile on us. And although we have (please prepare to roll your eyes) seven feet of snow outside our front door, there is a feeling of warmth within–a New Year feeling.

Yes, the snow is terrific. It is like living in the moon. Trees are crashing to earth today & lamp posts are falling & theres no electric light, no little mountain railway. Your brother went forth this afternoon on his immense skis & sped over the tops of fences and walls. I wish you could see him. He wears a blue helmet, you know the kind–airman's helmet, a leather jacket, huge fingerless gloves (the gloves he used to eat a sponge cake in his Go-cart)[1] but of a larger size, breeks, three pairs of stockings, & ski boots. He would earn enormous sums on the pictures in this get up & all covered with snow. I can hear a deep 'A-Ah' go round the dark theatre as he leapt on to the screen. Poor little Wingley is quite confused by this snow. Cant understand it, poor little chap. He went out the other day & began to scratch, scratched, scratched away, SCRATCHED, sat up, scratched his ear, took a deep breath, scratched on & was just rescued by the tip of his quivering tail in time. I suppose he won't come to earth again until next April. When you say you passed Christmas quietly – I see you positively *gliding* by. We had a real pudding, blaging[2] [sic] in brandy and even a tree. Jack *said* he hated trees. But when it came he liked it fearfully. They are curiously beautiful things and this little one, with its burning candles, birds with glass tails, coloured stars, spiderwebs with liqueur chocolate spiders in 'em and presents was a little gem. We are keeping all the decorations for another time, when I hope you will see them, too. After the tree we had *snapdragon* & then played Beat your Neighbour Out of Doors & Old Maid.[3] It's a good thing this only happens once a year...

I think I know that Flower Piece by Van Gogh. Yellow flowers, aren't they, full of life.[4] I noted the Degas show was coming.[5] I hope it's a good one. Tell us more about the pastels WHEN you are in the mood.

I am in the middle of a long story & cant see the end.[6] It will be a very little, small novel if it doesn't stop soon. It is called The Doves Nest. I have been in a black mood about my work lately but some furious reading has pulled me out of the hole, I think. Furious reading consisted of (1) Shakespeare (2) Cosmic Anatomy[7] (3) The Bible.

Its late, dear Richard. I must spare my candle, draw the curtains against the wolves, & go to sleep. Please give my love to Mother.[8] May we meet again before this year is over!

With warm love from
Katherine.

MS R. Murry. *Adam*, 370–5, 31–2.

---

[1] A note of Richard Murry's (ATL) recalled a conversation when Mansfield lived at 2 Portland Villas, Hampstead, and asked him what was the funniest word he could think of. He offered 'go-cart, the name for a small low perambulator' (see *CLKM* IV. 148, n.3).

[2] That is, 'blazing', in the anacoristic language she sometimes used with Richard and JMM.

[3] All card games, usually played by children.

[4] *Sunflowers*, by Vincent van Gogh, which so impressed KM when she saw it in the post-impressionist exhibition at the Grafton Galleries in 1912. As she told Dorothy Brett on 5 Dec. 1921, the painting 'taught me something about writing, which was queer – a kind of freedom – or rather, a shaking free' (*CLKM* IV. 333).

[5] Edgar Degas (1834–1917), whose estate was dispersed in 1918, when the National Gallery acquired major works, and other pieces were bought by English dealers. There was no large Degas exhibition in London in 1922, but Richard may have seen a selection of work at a private gallery.

[6] KM did not finish the story, although she worked on it over the following months, and envisaged it as much longer than what survives in the posthumous volume Murry put together after her death, *The Dove's Nest and Other Stories* (1923).

[7] *Cosmic Anatomy, or the Structure of the Ego*, by 'M. B. Oxon' (1921), was written by Dr Lewis Wallace, Theosophist and friend of KM's early patron and mentor, A. R. Orage (see *CLKM*, I, 97–8). The book profoundly impressed her, as she explained in a notebook entry on 4 Jan: 'I have read a good deal of Cosmic Anatomy – understood it far better. Yes, such a book does fascinate me. . . . To get even a glimpse of the relation of things, to follow that relation & find it remains true through the ages enlarges my little mind as nothing else does. Its only a greater view of psychology. It helps me with my writing for instance to know that hot + bun may mean Taurus, Pradhana, substance. No, that's not really what absorbs me, its that reactions to certain causes & effects always have been the same. It wasn't for nothing that Constantia [one of the two maiden sisters in KM's "The Daughters of the Late Colonel"] chose the moon and water – for instance!' (*NKM* II. 313).

[8] Her mother-in-law, Emily Murry.

To Charlotte Beauchamp Perkins, 2 January 1922

CHALET DES SAPINS | MONTANA-SUR-SIERRE | VALAIS

2 Janvier 1922

Darling Marie,[1]

I am relieved you liked my humble little bag. I was afraid it looked like an offertory bag at the last moment. The handles were so intensely black they almost looked fit for sacred purposes. My mocassins still hang on the willow tree but I shall take them down and dance to the tabors and cymbals ere long. I don't know why I feel so old Testament today. A man came to see us yesterday who had been to church. The flavour must still cling.

Fancy Annie & Jacks departing. I like all changes really when they come – I mean of that kind – don't you? I am all for *clean sweeps* occasionally! especially in the case of servants. One gets tired of the peculiarities of even treasures. No, they are scarce here and poor dumb cattle when you do get them. Mine is honest, good, faithful – sober – in fact she has all the virtues and her ankles are like this ⌡⌐⌡⌐ Poor soul! It is dreadful to have virtuous ankles as well. But thats the worst of very good people. They don't know where to stop.

You never told me who got the ring in the pudding after all. We had a pudding, too, in fact a whole Christmas dinner sent complete from England. And did you get nice presents. I was rich in presents this year – My most surprising however was a cable from Pa. Wasn't it awfully sweet of him. Its the first cable of the kind he has ever sent me. I felt indeed touched.

Do you really expect old V.[2] this month. How I should like a peep at you all. Fancy – it is eight years since I have seen her – I expect it will be eighteen before I do. Do tell me about your meeting! How long is V. staying? We shall be in Paris in April but I expect she will be gone before then – Paris always seems to me a good centre to meet people – with such lots of places to sit down and talk.

Well dear, I envy you your primrose. My room is full of carnations & mimosa & violets at present, titbits left over from the New Year – but Id prefer the primrose.

With much love, darling Marie

Ever your fond
K.

Wingley kisses his paw to Kuri.[3]

MS Newberry.

---

[1] The second of the Beauchamp daughters, a year older than KM, was known in the family as either Marie or Chaddie.
[2] Vera, KM's eldest sister now lived in Almonte, Ontario.
[3] The Maori word for dog.

To Jeanne Beauchamp Renshaw, 2 January 1922

CHALET DES SAPINS | MONTANA-SUR-SIERRE | VALAIS
2.1.1922

Dearest J,

I am so glad the boudoir cap goes with the robes de nuit . . . I hope your party was a success. *My* game always is Musical Chairs, but it is so terribly thrilling that perhaps its better left unplayed. I want to begin screaming when the chairs are being arranged even. Very vivid recollections of being rather good at this game and last *in* with George Nathan![1] I should think you and Marie would give a lovely party. I wish you would ask me one year. Jack is extremely good at lying on the floor and letting people jump up and down on him, also at making faces.

Your weather sounds too good to be true. We have 3 feet of snow here but at present it is pouring with rain. Just the moment for snow pies. It is horrible! But Christmas was fine. We had a tree, an exquisite little thing. There is enough German blood in the Swiss to make them have the most lovely small objects for hanging on trees – birds with glass tails and toad stools with candles in them and spiders webs of silver with liqueur chocolate spiders inside. These last are too realistic for me. Its horrifying to bite into the spider and taste what must be spiders BLOOD.

My poor new book[2] has been so boomed in the press before its born that when it does hatch out I know everyone will be disappointed to find its only a baby small; & will quarrel with its nose. It is terrifying to give birth to books. I wish one could do it in private.

Im still in bed. But I don't care. I defy Life. I shall win the battle after all and then you will be able to say all the cross things you want to without feeling that perhaps when your letter arrives I shall have taken a Bad Turn.

Will you bite me as you used to, little dear? I shant bite back. I feel full of love.

We are expecting our Elizabeth[3] any day now. It will be a joy to have her. Write again. May I say without offence your hand-writing is exactly like a *white kitten's*.

Yours ever
K.

MS Newberry.

[1] One of the children in the Jewish family who lived next door to the Beauchamps in Tinakori Road for the first five years of KM's life. The Nathans became the Samuel Josephs in her story 'Prelude'.

[2] *The Garden Party* would be published in late February 1922.

[3] KM's cousin Mary Annette Beauchamp, known always as Elizabeth. She recently had become much closer to KM, her Chalet du Soleil being a short distance from the Chalet des Sapins.

To Dorothy Brett, 4 January 1922

CHALET DES SAPINS | MONTANA-SUR-SIERRE | VALAIS

4.1.1922

Dearest Brett,

Do you mind shopping for me? If you do please tell me bang out. If you dont would you be a lamb and get me a pair of shoulder straps. Ill explain. Lying propped up so much I have got a bit round shouldered & I want to correct it by wearing straps off and on. Gamage[1] is the place I think. And I heard, once, they had an American pattern very simple which was good. I dont want *buckles* and *canvas* and *bones*, please. But something light, flexible, with elastic, if possible and unobtrusive. The *less* of the contraption the better.

Is this a fearful bore to you, my dear? But Id be so deeply grateful. I really pine for a pair and Switzerland of course is hopeless. Besides here is nothing but snow. We are living in the moon. Its all white, ghostly, silent, eternal, and snow still falls. I hate snow. I could kiss the fertile earth – all this whiteness has a kind of mock mystery about it that I dislike very much. This isn't a *complaint*. Its just the facts.

By the way do you eat porridge? DO. It is good for you – fearfully. But it must be made with a good piece of butter added to it. Then it really does stick to your ribs and make a man of you. Butter I do really believe flies to the brain, also and creates a *glow* – so I wish you a very buttery New Year. I shall never forget how Ottoline, while talking *abstractedly* would pinch my little butter dish draw it towards her with her knife & devour it, whole.

It is strange. I have no faith in you about food. I feel sure you give other people all the best bits & eat the heads and tails yourself. *Dont* do it; it is very bad. Always choose the fish with the fattest eye.

Much love from
Tig

MS Newberry.

---

[1] Gamages was a department store and mail-order service at 116–28 Holborn, Central London.

To Violet Schiff, [c.8 January 1922]

CHALET-DES-SAPINS | MONTANA-SUR-SIERRE | VALAIS

My dearest Violet

I am so happy to know you like my story. It was the most delightful surprise to receive your letter at the end of rather a black day. I had thought At the Bay would pass quite unnoticed and your sympathetic note warms my heart. Thank you sincerely – very sincerely, dearest Violet. I shall not forget your letter. As a matter of fact all that I have written up till now seems to me to have been only... opening the windows, pulling back the shutters... Its only now I feel chez moi and in the work I am engaged in now. I have passed through a state of *awful* depression about work, lately. It had to be. But I see my way now, I think. What saved me finally was reading a book called Cosmic Anatomy, and reflecting on it... That sounds rather funny, doesn't it?

Ah, I do hope we shall meet in the spring. I feel we shall & all will be better than before.

Congestion is quite simple. The lung becomes full of blood, & that means the heart beats too fast & that means one has fever and pain and puts oneself to bed. But I am determined to make an end of all this very soon. I detest the idea of going to Paris at the end of this month but I shant stay – just see my man & arrange to return in the spring.

Snow falls & falls. It is like living in the moon. I *hate* snow. I love the fertile, fertile earth!

Goodnight, chere amie

With my warm love to you both.

I embrace you

Katherine.

MS BL. *Adam* 300, 110.

To Dorothy Brett, [9 January 1922]

CHALET DES SAPINS │ MONTANA-SUR-SIERRE │ VALAIS

Dearest Brett,

This is to catch the post as you say. As far as I know I shall leave for Paris on Monday fortnight; that is to say Monday week when it reaches you. We shant stay for more than a few days & we shall be so busy & the weather so bad that I wouldn't advise you to come. Then in spring we return & if Manouhkin[1] will treat me we'll try for a flat in Paris & spend some months there. Happily our lease of this house is up at the end of May. That will be the time to come to Paris. but its so cold now; we shant stay a moment longer than necessary. And think of that vile Channel in this month! Or rather don't think of it!

I lapped up your letter. The party sounded one of the old kind. Fancy the Puma[2] *still* biting. It seems impossible. She has bitten & wept for years. And why is there always someone on the floor like that doctor? Oh, I do hate such parties. But I like to read about them. They make my eyes roll.

Garsington, too. Isn't Julian[3] a problem? What will she do? I think the trouble with her and Ottoline is that there is absolutely no love between them. There is nearly hate – isn't there? Or is that too strong. Julian will go her way though, in her own time. There is something urgent in her which won't be resisted. She interests me. She did when I saw her in France.[4] I felt – there goes *youth* – with all that it means. I think her real fight will be with Philippo.[5] There I can smell a battle.

But this is all a bit beside the mark... You are right. I think of Man-ouhkin more than anyone can imagine. I have as much faith in him as Koteliansky has. I hardly dare think of him fully. No, I *dare* not. It is too much. But about money I have £100 saved for this *Last Chance* and as soon as I know he can help me I shall make more. Work is ease, joy, light to me if I am happy. I shall not borrow from anyone if I can possibly help it. My family would not give me a penny. But I shall manage. I am not frightened of money for some blessed reason. I know I can make it. Once I am well I can make all I want – I don't want much. In fact my plans go on and on, and when I go to sleep I dream the treatment is over and I am running, or walking swiftly and carelessly by and no one knows I have been ill – no one hands me a chair in a shop. Ah, it is too much!

This awful writing is frozen writing, Brett. I am writing with two icicles for fingers. We have 6 foot of snow here – all is frozen over and over even the birds tails. Is not that hideous cruelty. I have a large table for these precious atoms daily – and the first coconut in Switzerland is the Big Joint. They cant yet believe in the coconut. It overwhelms them. A special issue of the Bird Times is being issued, the bird who discovered it is to be photographed, interviewd, & received at Pluckingham Palace and personally conducted tours are being arranged. What with them and my poor dear pussy – he who got out today & began to scratch, scratched away, kept at it, sat up, took a deep breath, scratched his ear, wiped his whiskers, scratched on, SCRATCHED – until finally only the tip of a quivering tail was to be seen & he was rescued by the gentle Ernestine.[6] He wrung his little paws in despair. Poor lamb! To think he will not be able to scratch *through* until April. I suppose snow is beautiful. I hate it. It always seems to me a kind of humbug – a justification of mystery and I hate mystery. And then there is no movement. All is still – white – cold – deathly eternal. Every time I look out I feel inclined to say I *refuse* it. But perhaps if one goes about and skims over all is different.

How are your Swarees? Is everybody just the same? I am working at such a long story that I still can only just see the end in my imagination – the longest by far Ive ever written. Its called *The Dove's Nest.* Tell me what you are working at? Or are you resting? I hope I shall *see* Marie Loo in her garden of Eden one day – one's mind's eye isn't good enough.[7] But winter is a bad black time for work I think. Ones brain gets congealed. It is v. hard. Goodnight my dear dear Brett. With tender love

Tig

MS Newberry. *LKM* II. 171–2.

---

[1] Ivan Manoukhin, after service in the Ukraine during the First World War, returned to Paris where previously he had worked at the Pasteur Institute, and initiated a revolutionary but medically useless treatment for tuberculosis. Encouraged by her close friend Koteliansky, KM had written to the Russian doctor in December the previous year (see *CLKM* IV. 331–2).

[2] Unidentified.

[3] The fifteen-year-old Julian Morrell was then at loggerheads with her mother, Lady Ottoline.

[4] Julian and her mother had visited KM in Menton in January 1921.

[5] Her father Philip Morrell, Liberal MP 1906–18, and the heir to a brewery fortune.

[6] The cook and general help at the Chalet des Sapins.

[7] A painting of her niece that Brett was working on.

To Elizabeth, Countess Russell, [11 January 1922]

CHALET DES SAPINS | MONTANA-SUR-SIERRE | VALAIS

My dear Elizabeth,

I love my little pelt – its coat is so warm. Thank you *very* much for it. Its such a charming co-partnery, too, between virtue and quelque chose plus gai. And for the Bath Salts which carried my nose straight back to Regent Street. I always had to make a giant swerve past Morny Frere[1] or I went in and was lost. It was delightful to get such a parcel on such a day.

I hope you are warm and happy – It is horrid to think there was no fire to welcome you.

Ah, Elizabeth, what can I do to know that my little figures projected on the bright screen of Time make a "pretty little story" in the Mercury.[2] Good God! How I worked at them and tried to express and squeezed and modelled . . . and the result was a "*pretty* little story"![3]

I sank to the bottom of the ocean after you'd gone and stifled thought by writing another story which wasn't – couldn't be pretty.

It is a very fearful thing to be a writer - - -

John will bring the De La Mare book on Sunday. I hope you will like it. Some of the poems seem to me – marvellous.[4]

I shall pray a double prayer for fine weather now that I know you are there and at work. Work is the only perfect joy, and only blessed state.[5] There is nothing to compare with it.

With very much love.

Katherine.

I am flying to Paris in a fortnight's time.

TC Huntington. Cited Usborne, 242.

---

[1] Morny Freres, a shop specializing in cosmetic products.

[2] 'At the Bay' (*London Mercury* Jan. 1922).

[3] KM entered in a notebook for 11 January, 'In the afternoon Elizabeth came. She looked fascinating in her black suit; something between a Bishop and a fly, She spoke of my "pretty little story" in the Mercury. All the while she was here I was conscious of a falsity. We said things we meant; we were sincere but at the back there was nothing but falsity, I do not ever want to see her or hear from her again' (*KMN* II. 315–16).

[4] *The Veil and Other Poems* (1921).

[5] As she also wrote in her notebook the same day, 'Wrote & finished *A Cup of Tea*. . . . There is no feeling to be compared with the joy of having written and finished a story. I did not go to sleep but nothing mattered. There it was *new* and complete' (*KMN* II.316). 'A Cup of Tea' was published in the *Story-teller* (May 1922).

To Sydney Schiff, [12 January 1922]

CHALET DES SAPINS | MONTANA-SUR-SIERRE | VALAIS

Thursday.

My dear Sydney

I am deeply grateful to you for everything in your last letter. Your criticism of my work is most *precious* to me; there is no other word near enough to describe the feeling. Your understanding, so true and so sympathetic is an encouragement in itself.[1] It would be grief to me to displease you. I hope one day I shall write a book which I may wholeheartedly give to you and Violet – on the title page. But it will be the book after my next – a novel.

I look forward most eagerly to your story. I suddenly put my long story aside and wrote a short one[2] this week which I am tempted to send you. But perhaps it is not worth sending.

I think I do know what you mean by 'friendship'. It is strange I always silently acknowledge the fact that you have one friend. Its as though you carry him with you, within your breast. I think I never see you without being reminded immediately of that other, even though no word has been spoken. This seems to me inevitable.

It is more and more difficult to me to write letters. Once I begin there is so much to say that no *letter* could contain it. I want to answer, too, not only your letter to me but yours to Jack as well. I am very glad he sent you the proofs of his article;[3] I wanted you to see it. I felt you would be in agreement with much he has said.

About Joyce, and my endeavours to be doubly fair to him[4] because I have been perhaps unfair and captious – oh, I cant get over a great great deal. I cant get over the feeling of wet linoleum and unemptied pails and far worse horrors in the house of his mind. Hes so terribly unfein; thats what it amounts to. There is a tremendously strong impulse in me to beg him not to shock me! Well, its not very rare. Ive had it before with men and women many times in my life. One can stand much but that kind of shock which is the result of vulgarity & commonness, one is frightened of receiving. Its as though ones mind goes on quivering afterwards... Its just exactly the reverse of the exquisite rapture one feels in for instance that passage which ends a chapter where Proust describes the flowering apple trees in the spring rain.[5]

But at the memory of that I suddenly long to take your hand and say: "How marvellous life can be. How marvellous!" Ah, Sydney, how can I be thankful enough that Violet and you are on the earth at this time. That we have met & shall meet again. Do you remember one afternoon as we were in the car together you said you would like to go to Sweden? Why on earth should that have been so tremendously important – so infinitely delightful. It often comes back to me and always with the same 'atmosphere' of happiness and understanding between us. But one could go on with such memories – – –

Elizabeth has returned to her chalet. In minute black breeches and gaiters she looks like an infant bishop. When she has talked about London and the literary 'successes' I am thankful to be out of it. I dont want to hear what Hugh Walpole thinks of Clemence Dane.[6] But Elizabeth "fascinates" me, and I admire her for working as she is working now, all alone in her big chalet. She is courageous, very. And for some reason the mechanism of life hardly seems to touch her. She refuses to be ruffled and she is not ruffled. This is incomprehensible to me. I find it devilish, devilish, devilish. Doors that bang, voices raised, smells of cooking, even steps on the stairs are nothing short of anguish to me at times. There is an inner calm necessary to writing, a sense of equilibrium which is impossible to reach if it hasn't its outward semblance. But I dont know. Perhaps I am asking for what cannot be.

I must end this letter. The sun has been out today and yesterday, and although there is about seven feet of snow and great icicles hang from the window frames it is warm, still, *delicious*. I got up today and I feel I never want to go to bed again. This air, this radiance gives one a faint idea of what spring must be here – early spring. They say that by April the snows have melted and even before all is quite gone the flowers begin . . .

With warm love to you both,

I press your hands

Katherine.

MS BL. *LKM* II. 173–4; *Adam* 300, 114–16.

[1] After initial difficulties, KM became friendly with the wealthy art patron Sydney Schiff, who published fiction as Stephen Hudson, and his wife Violet, especially during her time at Menton (see *CLKM* III. 268, n.1). He had now written to her after reading 'At the Bay'. As she wrote in her notebook on 9 Jan., 'A long letter from Sydney. I want to believe all he says about my story. He *does* see what I mean. He does not see it as a set of trivial happenings just thrown together. This is enough to be deeply grateful for' (*KMN* II. 315).

[2] KM interrupted 'The Dove's Nest' to write 'A Cup of Tea' in order to earn quick money once she decided on Manoukhin's course of treatment.

[3] Murry's article 'Gustave Flaubert', which appeared in both the *Dial* (Dec. 1921), and the *TLS* (15 Dec. 1921).

[4] KM's opinion of James Joyce fluctuated considerably after Virginia Woolf first showed her part of *Ulysses* when it was offered to the Hogarth Press in 1918, and she had been impressed by it. See *The Diary of Virginia Woolf*, V, 1984, ed. Anne Olivier Bell and Andrew McNeilie, 353.

[5] The conclusion to Chapter I, in Marcel Proust's *Sodome et Gomorrhe* (1922).

[6] KM had reviewed both novelists in the *Athenaeum*: Clemence Dane's *Legend* with distaste on 5 Dec. 1919; Hugh Walpole's *The Captives* with barbed admiration on 15 Oct. 1920.

To S. S. Koteliansky, [13 January 1922]

CHALET DES SAPINS | MONTANA-SUR-SIERRE | VALAIS

Dear Koteliansky,

What a supremely good piece of translation is this story by Bunin in The Dial.[1] One simply cannot imagine it better done & I am, with everybody else, deeply grateful for the opportunity of reading it.

Bunin has an immense talent.[2] That is certain. All the same . . . there's a limitation in this story, so it seems to me. There is something hard, inflexible, separate in him which he exults in. But he ought not to exult in it. It is a pity it is there. He just stops short of being a great writer because of it. Tenderness is a dangerous word to use, but I dare use it to you. He lacks tenderness – and *in spite of everything*, tenderness there must be . . .

I have been in a horrible black mood lately, with feelings of something like hatred towards "everybody". I think one reason was I wrote a story – I projected my little people against the bright screen of Time – and not only nobody saw, nobody cared.[3] But it was as if the story was refused. It is bitter to be refused. Heaven knows one does not desire praise. But *silence* is hard to bear. I know one ought not to care. One should go on quietly. But there it is.

I am leaving for Paris in a fortnight. A chill and the weather and money have kept me back. But I shall go then. Shall I write to you from there?

Koteliansky – I HATE snow and icicles and blizzards. It is all such mock mystery and a wrestling with the enemy. I love the fertile earth – spring. Wouldn't you like to be now, this instant, in a beech forest with the new leaves just out?

I press your hands

Katherine.

MS BL. *LKM* II. 172–3.

[1] Ivan Bunin's 'The Gentleman from San Francisco' was translated by Koteliansky and D. H. Lawrence in the *Dial* (Dec. 1921).
[2] Ivan Bunin (1870–1953), short-story writer and novelist, recently had arrived in Paris, a refugee from the Bolshevik Revolution. In 1933 he was the first Russian to receive the Nobel Prize for Literature.

To Anne Drey, [15 January 1922]

CHALET DES SAPINS | MONTANA-SUR-SIERRE | VALAIS

Anne,

Can you tell me the name of a Hotel in Paris that has an ascenseur that really does go up & down and isn't too terribly unsympathetic? I simply don't know one, nowadays & shall have to sit on my luggage while someone looks. Last time I stayed at one that Cooks recommended with one of those glass-topped beds and strong tea coming out of the hot water tap. They plucked me to my last pin-feather for these luxuries – I don't mind where it is as long as the lift will go up as well as down – so important that. In Switzerland the lifts only go down. Never up. Its a mystery to me. Id like Fergussons[1] views on it or Blums[2]. K: "How does it happen that this lift never goes up?" Swiss (smiling) "It always goes down Madame". K: ???? Swiss: !!!!

Katherine

MS ATL. *LKM* II. 175–6.

[1] Anne Estelle Rice married the journalist O. Raymond Drey in 1913. When KM first met her in Paris, the American artist was the partner of the Scottish painter J. D. Fergusson.
[2] Leon Blum (1872–1950), distinguished literary critic and journalist, before his career as French politician and Socialist leader.

To Anne Drey, [18 January 1922]

[Postcard carrying the photograph of KM reproduced on the jacket. Under the photograph she has written: 'This is called: "Dreaming of Paris and Anne." The photographer has enlarged it & put it in his windy; people cry so frightfully they have to be just led away. . . . ']

[Chalet des Sapins, Montana-sur-Sierre]

Darling Precious Anne

The curse is I cant possibly start for Paris for 2 weeks from today, and thats only fixed if the weather permits! So this time we shant meet again. But Anne, in the spring we are coming to Paris to be there for at least 4 months. Surely we shall meet then. We *must*, dearest. I see you and Drey flying over and me with a spyglass on the hotel roof. Oh, Anne, if you knew what I'd give to see you . . . I shall be too happy for words. All beams! Its in the spring I am going in for this Russian treatment – chasse des Microbes par les Rayons X. What I want to do is for us to get a small apartment as I have ma petite faute with me – in the shape of my cat and I cant expect him to put up with hotels. So *Spring* – let us meet in Spring! I shall hold thumbs from now to April. The idea of my coat is VERY thrilling. We have 6 feet of snow here – I hate snow; I love the fertile earth and I love Paris – and just *love* you –

Katherine

Postcard ATL. *Adam* 300, 95–6.

To Sydney Schiff, [c.18 January 1922]

[Chalet des Sapins, Montana sur Sierre]

The same evening.

My dear Sydney,

I answer your letter, as you suggest, immediately. Yes, I used the word friendship too lightly. I hang my head. It was *badly* done and you were right to strike me. I do understand. I wince, yes I confess its painful to me to read what you write at the bottom of the second page 'I have not got any friends at all'. And the sentences that follow. At the same time I value the remark immensely. There is a deep separateness in me which responds to it, even though *I* am forever without a complete complement. But it's a strange truth that the fact of you and Violet is not only a joy: it's an extraordinary consolation to believe in you and her as one does. (Violet dearest, speak to me just one moment, will you? I feel sometimes diffident of speaking to you directly. I feel that there are so many others near you who claim your attention. I count on Sydney telling you whatever there is to tell. No, the truth is nearer. I write to you and to him. But you know that.) I agree absolutely – with what you say when you define the forces that go to make friendship and the part played by knowledge. The more one thinks of the image of knowledge as clothing the more valuable it becomes. It is one of the images that delight the mind so much that almost apart from one's *self* one's mind goes on receiving it, turning it to the light, trying it, experimenting with it. Or that is what my mind has been doing . . . proving the truth of it mathematically speaking.

I should like to have friends, I confess. I do not suppose I ever shall. But there have been moments when I have realized what friendship might be. Rare moments – but never forgotten. I remember once talking it over with Lawrence and he said: 'We must swear a solemn pact of friendship. Friendship is as binding, as solemn as marriage. We take each other for life, through everything – for ever. But it's not enough to say we will do it. We must *swear.*' At the same time I was impatient with him. I thought it extravagant – fanatic. But when one considers what this world is like I understand perfectly why L (especially being L) made such claims . . . I think, myself, it is Pride which makes friendship most difficult. To submit, to bow down to the other is not easy, but it must be done if one is to really understand the being of the other. Friendship isn't *merging*. One doesn't thereupon become a shadow and one remains a substance. Yes, it is terribly solemn – frightening, even.

Please do not think I am all for Joyce. I am *not*. In the past I was unfair to him and to atone for my stupidity I want to be fairer now than I really feel . . . I agree that it is not all art. I would go further. Little to me is art at all. It's a kind of stage on the way to being art. But the art of projection has not been made. Joyce remains entangled in it, in a bad sense, except at rare moments! There is, to me, the great distinction between him and Proust. (Take Swann with Odette for instance[1]) or take Richard in Elinor Colhouse[2] . . . . . .

Jones [Ida] is waiting for this letter. I want it to catch the post. I have only begun to say what I want to say. About Paris. I cannot go just at present. I am still in bed and likely to remain there for a time. Congestion is a slow affair, especially at this height. The doctor, like all doctors, is a complete fool. I shall try and put off Paris until May. To meet there in May and to stay there (J and I will be there four months) would be nothing short of wonderful. I hardly dare think of it. Now I know Manoukhine is there I can bear to wait – I think I shall try. Hotels and journeys are a dread prospect in any weather – in this – even more –

Forgive this haste and inadequacy – Read much more in my letters than is there – dear Sydney.

With my warm love to you both
Katherine

MS BL. *Adam* 300, 116–17.

[1] Principle characters in Marcel Proust's *À la Recherche du Temps Perdu*.

[2] Schiff's novel, *Elinor Colhouse*, written under his pseudonym Stephen Hudson, was published late 1921.

To Alfred A. Knopf,[1] 20 January 1922

CHALET DES SAPINS | MONTANA-SUR-SIERRE | VALAIS

20
1
1922

Dear Mr Knopf

Very many thanks for your letter. I am sending you by today's mail a set of corrected proofs of The Garden Party. I think they are in good order. I am only sorry that I did not know before that these proofs could be useful to you; I could have sent them six weeks ago. My reason for wanting proofs was that the London typist to whom I sent *typed* copies of MSS for her to duplicate only, took terrible pity on my spelling, and on the bad grammar used by my little children. I only discovered this when I received my English proofs; the original MSS had gone off to The Mercury.

I fully appreciate all you say about the advisability of English and American editions of the same book appearing at the same time. But I am a little bit helpless personally. If Constable were to delay my book after February it would be swamped in the spring floods. Its only chance is to appear before March; and it has been announced so often that I don't feel I can even suggest a postponement this time. They are bringing out a limited edition of signed copies, too. But that wont affect American sales . . .

I shall see that my next book is submitted to you at the earliest possible moment. But that does not help this one, does it? I am truly sorry. It seems to me the best idea would be to have the American edition published before the English one. I hope this can be arranged with my third book.

With kind regards to you and Madame in which John Murry joins me.

Yours sincerely
Katherine Mansfield

MS Texas. Cited *Exhibition*, 49.

[1] Alfred A. Knopf (1892–1984), one of the leading American publishers of the twentieth century. He founded the publishing house with his wife Blanche in 1915. Knopf published the first American edition of *The Garden Party* in May 1922.

To Dorothy Brett, [21 January 1922]

CHALET DES SAPINS | MONTANT-SUR-SIERRE | VALAIS

Warning. Pages ALL wrong.

Darling Brettushka,

The jumper has jumped & the ribbons fluttered over today. And I can't thank you. It seems feeble just to thank a person for such loveliness. I rejoice in the garment & the exquisite colours beyond words but that is not all. Its your thought in sending them which makes them so precious. I dont see how I am going to keep up with your lovely ways. I shall lag behind & admire. Thank you from my heart. Isn't the jumper an exquisite creature. When I go to Paris I shall wear it to carry you with me in the interview with Manouhkin. It will be my mascot. As for the ribbons. My brother's greenstone[1] looks exquisite hung from one or other of them. If I had been the child of a conjuror I should have eaten ribbons instead of producing them from my hat.

I cant get off to Paris just yet for I am still in bed. Six weeks today with one days interval. I cant shake off this congestion and ALL the machinery is out of order. Food is a horror. But I won't go into it. I feel most frightfully inclined to hold your hand, too, & just let this month & February & March stream by like a movie picture. Then let it be April and all this dark and cold over. Huge fringes of icicles hang from the windows. I know one thing. I must never stay up here for another winter. Evan had a heart of brass. That is why he could stand it. We talked it over together over chops and cabbage in a Pullman one night when he'd just got back. If I can get well enough to go to Paris. Its all I ask. I am fighting for that now...I wish I had got there before this last bout. I was so much stronger than I am now. But this is a bad black month, darling. There is a new moon on the 27th. Look at it & wish. I will look at it & wish for you. I feel so in your mood – listless, tired, my energy flares up & won't last. Im a wood fire. However, I swear to finish my big story by the end of this month. Its queer when I am in this mood I always write as though I am laughing. I feel it running along the pages. If only the reader could see the snail in its shell with the black pen! Don't work too hard just now. Let things be. Let things grow in the quiet. Think of your mind as a winter garden – growing underneath, you know with all the lovely shapes & colours of thrice blessed longed for spring. I think it is good sometimes just to let things be. But what does one *do* on those occasions? I can think of all kinds of plans but they need you near. Tell me about your little house. A queer strange feeling that I cannot explain away tells me I shall see it & know it & stay there once. One is shy of saying these things for some reason. But I feel there is a possibility of a much deeper relationship between us than ever we dream of. I feel a bit like a man about you. I mean by that Id like to make you *feel loved*. There is something I don't like in most of the men you know (I mean those that I know too). They lack delicacy and perception and they do not *give*. I except of course Koteliansky & Tomlinson,[2] both beautiful men. But I would like to try & make you happy, my dear – make you feel *cherished*. I wonder if you know what I mean. We grow in the bosoms of others; we rest there; it is good sometimes to feel carried.

Your still life sounds lovely & I like to think of your bottils, all in a row. They *are* lovely things, even those slender hock bottles. But I see *them* from the 'literary' point of view. They say summer & lunch out of doors and strawberries on a glass plate with gold specks in it...

I have just heard from DelaMare about my little family in The Mercury and from America where another story of the same people is coming out in The Dial.[3] I feel like Lottie and Kezias[4] mother after the letters I have got this month. It is surprising and very lovely to know how people love little children, the most unexpected people –

Heres the doctor stumping up the stairs. No, he has stopped half way to talk to the Mountain.[5]

Elizabeth is here again with a minute sledge on a string wherever she goes. She herself in tiny black breeks & gaiters looks like an infant bishop. Murry & she flew down thousands of feet yesterday – right down into the valley. She is a radiant little being whatever the weather. Born under a dancing star –[6]

He comes. I must end this. Goodbye for now – You know what I think of these gifts. But send me no more, my little artist. You are too lavish. Keep your pennies now.

I embrace you – You must feel that there is in this letter warm tender love. For its there.

Tig

MS Newberry. *LKM* II. 176; *Selected*, 235–7.

[1] A pendant of *pounamu*, New Zealand jade, once belonging to her brother who was killed near Armentieres in October 1915.

[2] Henry Major Tomlinson (1873–1978), journalist, travel writer, essayist and novelist, who worked with Murry on the *Athenaeum*, and remained on as its literary editor until 1923. His impressive writing on the First World War was included in the collection *Waiting for Daylight* (1922). KM noted (20 Jan. 1922), that 'HMT', along with W. J. Dunning, Koteliansky, and Orage, was one of the people she thought of 'every day. They are part of my life' (*NKM*, 318).

[3] The *Dial* had accepted 'The Doll's House', but withdrew publication when the story appeared in the *Nation and the Athenaeum* (4 Feb. 1922).

[4] Two of the children of Linda Burnell in 'At the Bay'.

[5] One of the many disparaging nicknames for Ida Baker.

[6] 'There was a star danced, and under that I was born' (*Much Ado about Nothing*, II. i. 349).

To Ottoline Morrell, [c.24 January 1922]

CHALET DES SAPINS | MONTANA SUR SIERRE | VALAIS

My dearest Ottoline,

That is one thing about our solitary existence. When such a letter as your letter today comes it is done the very fullest justice to. It is reread and read. But oh, how I should love a long talk – anywhere, anywhere out of the silly world of London and the white one of Switzerland.

Its intolerable that you should have had pleurisy! I tremble to think of the time we spend in bed *un*happily. It is out of all proportion. I am fleeing to Paris on Monday next to see if that Russian can bake me or boil me or serve me up in some more satisfying way – I suppose the snow is very good for one. But its horrid stuff to take and there's far too much of it. Immense fringes of icicles hang at our windows. Awful looking things like teeth – And every Sunday the Swiss fly into the forest on little sledges shrieking Ho-jé! Ho-jé positively makes my blood curdle. So off I go on Monday with the Mountain very breathless carrying two large suitcases & begging the suitcases pardon when she bumps them into things. I shall only go to spy out the land and buy some flowers and wallow in a hot bath. But if the Russian says he can cure me M. and I shall go to Paris in the spring and live there for a time. One writes the word 'cure' – but – – but I don't know.

I haven't seen Aldous book[1] and I do not want to. The idea bores me so terribly that I wont waste time on it. The only reviewer who really realised its dullness was Rebecca West.[2] She said just what was right – she shuddered at the silliness of it. But everybody else seems to puff him up. It gets very awkward if young men are forced to feed out of their friends inkpots in this way. In fact I confess it downright disgusts me –

But oh, Ottoline I must ask you if you have read Congreve lately. I have just finished 'The Way of The World'. *Do* read it! For the sake of the character Mrs Millamant. I think she is so exquisitely done when she first appears "full sail" and tells the others how she curls her hair. The maid is marvellous in that little scene too, and the other scene is where [she] decides finally to have Mirabel. That little conversation between the two seems to me really ravishing in its own way.[3] Its so delicate – so gay – But its much best read aloud. What a brilliant strange creature Congreve was – so anxious *not* to be considered a writer, but only a plain gentleman. And Voltaire's shrewd reply "If you had been only a gentleman I would not have come to see you..."[4] I love reading good plays, and so does M. We have such fun talking them over afterwards. In fact the pleasure of all reading is doubled when one lives with another who shares the same books. It is one of the many pleasures of our solitary life. Pleasures we have – ever increasing. I would not change this *kind* of life for any other.

There are moods of course when we long for people. But they pass, leaving no regret, no disillusionment, no horrid remembrance. And one does have time to work. But I wish my new book was a better one. I am *terrified* of it. But it can't be helped now. M. is writing hard, and I am in the middle of what looks like a short novel.

I am so glad you liked The Veil. There is one poem:

> Why has the rose faded and fallen
> And these eyes have not seen...[5]

It haunts me. But it is a state of mind I know so terribly well. That regret for what one has not seen and felt – for what has passed by – unheeded. Life is only given once and then I *waste* it. Do you feel that?

Are there snowdrops yet. It will soon be February – and then the worst is over. By March the first flowers *emerge*, cold, pale as if after the Flood. But how one loves them! And that soft stirring in the trees – in elms especially – and the evening, coming reluctant again. Dearest, I am so glad for your sake that it will soon be spring. I *hate* winter for you. I wish I could come into your room now and say "the lilac is out". Is it only in winter that your dreaded neuralgia is so painful? There's no excuse for winter – none!

I have given M. your messages. He skis everwhere, and skates no more. He looks awfully well. Elizabeth is here, buried in her chalet at work. She is one creature who never has to think of health. She is always well – never even tired and is as active as if she were eighteen.[6]

My dull letter creeps after your winged one – But it is sent with so much love. Love from us both, dearest Ottoline – and may we meet again soon!

Ever yours devotedly
Katherine.

MS Texas. *LKM* II. 176–8.

[1] *Crome Yellow* (1921). Huxley's satire with its wounding descriptions of 'our life at Garsington, all distorted, caricatured and mocked at...horrified....I was filled with dismay' (*Ottoline at Garsington. Memoirs of Lady Ottoline Morrell*, ed. Robert Gathorne-Hardy, 1974, 215).

[2] Rebecca West reviewed *Crome Yellow* in the *New Statesman* (17 Dec. 1921).

[3] 'Here she comes, I' faith, full sail, with her fan spread and her streamers out, and a shoal of fools for tender,' as her suitor Mirabell says of Mrs Millamant's arrival in Act II, Scene ii, in William Congreve's *The Way of the World* (1700). Mrs Millamant then describes how she uses letters from admirers to curl her hair, but 'Only with those in verse, ...I never pin up my hair with prose' (Act IV, scene i).

[4] Voltaire's account of his visit to Congreve, *c.*1726, is recorded in *Letters Concerning the English Nation*, No. XIX (1733).

[5] 'Why hath the rose faded and fallen, yet these eyes have not seen?', the opening line of 'Awake!', in Walter De La Mare, *The Veil and Other Poems* (1921).

[6] Elizabeth was then fifty-five.

To Vera Mackintosh Bell, 26 January 1922

CHALET DES SAPINS | MONTANA-SUR-SIERRE | VALAIS

26.I.1922

My dear Vera,

I had heard via Elizabeth, via Mack[1] that you were in England and how long you were going to stay. I am so sorry to know you have had Flu. What bad luck on arrival! But I expect you will be beautifully nursed and cared for.

I am afraid we shan't be in England for many a long day. I am going to Paris on Monday next. But I expect Paris seems just as far as Switzerland to you.

Yes, its a great joy to us to have Elizabeth back in her chalet. She is a wonderful little being and I love her dearly.

Dont let your Andrew[2] turn into a writer, though, my dear. Take warning by Elizabeth and me! Nip him in the tenderest bud rather than have that happen. All Beauchamp blood ought to be poured into business. Make him a millionaire instead.

My flight to Paris is on business, but its so delightful to look forward to. Paris is much nicer than London.

I hope you have the happiest visit and une belle santé from now onwards.[3]

With much love from

Yours affectionately

K.

MS ATL.

---

[1] James Mackintosh Bell, her sister's Canadian husband.

[2] Vera's ten-year-old son.

[3] On the same day as this letter KM's feelings towards her sisters were more accurately confided to a notebook: 'A letter from Vera and Jeanne. I felt these 2 letters had nothing whatever to do with me. I would not care if I never saw Vera again. There is something in her assumed cheerfulness which I can't bear. I'd never get on with her. And J. – is it fancy – just a touch of carelessness. I feel they are so absolutely insincere' (*KMN* II. 320).

To Dorothy Brett, 26 January 1922

[CHALET DES SAPINS | MONTANA-SUR-SIERRE]

26.1.1922

Dearest Brett

I have taken seats in the puffi-train for Monday and should be in Paris on Tuesday. My address is Hotel Victoria Palace, *68 Rue Blaise Desgoffe, Rue de Rennes*. Write to me there if you can! I hope to see Manouhkin on Tuesday afternoon. It is all rather like a dream. Until it has happened I cannot quite believe it. But I was thinking if Gertler[1] stays in Paris on his way through I wish he would come & see me. Would you tell him? It would be a pleasure to talk to him again. Im deadly tired tonight. I wrote & finished a story yesterday for The Sketch.[2] The day after that happens is always a day when one feels like a leaf on the ground – one can't even flutter. At the same time there is a feeling of joy that another story is finished. I put it in such a lovely place, too, the grounds of a Convent[3] in spring with pigeons flying up in the blue and big bees climbing in and out of the freezias below. If I lived in the snow long I should become very *opulent.* Pineapples would grow on every page, and giant bouquets would be presented to each character on his appearance. Elizabeth was here yesterday and we lay in my room talking about flowers until we were really quite drunk – or I was. She – describing – "a certain very exquisite *rose*, single, pale yellow with coral tipped petals" and so on. I kept thinking of little curly blue hyacinths and *white* violets and the bird cherry. My trouble is I had so many flowers when I was little, I got to know them so well that they are simply the breath of life to me. Its no ordinary love; its a passion. Wait – one day I shall have a garden and you shall hold out your pinny. In the meantime our cat has got his nose scratched beyond words & he's in such a condition that he looks as though he has been taking part in a boxing match up a chimney. He is to have lessons on the fiddle this spring. All the BEST cats can play at least Hey diddle diddle. He *must* learn. The strings of his fiddle will be of wool, of course and the bow will have a long tassel on it. I believe he can play the piano. He sits up & plays with his two front paws:

> Nellie Bly
> Caught a Fly
> Put it in her Tea![4]

This exquisite morceau was in *my* Pianoforte Tutor, words and all. Who can have composed it! However it suits Wingley. Its a subject he can feel sympathy about. He comes down with such a terrific whack on the FLY! He is the most unthinkable lamb, really, and I am sorry if I am silly about him.

But I meant to write about the Flu. You are very nervous of it aren't you? I feel it in your letter; I understand your feeling. But Brett, you can ward it off with food. MILK, my dear. Thats not hard to take. Drink all the milk you can & eat oranges. Oranges are full of these vitamins & they are very rich in some value that milk hasn't, not to speak of their good effect on ones functions. And its half the battle to be rid of any internal poisoning that accumulates in the colon. Milk & oranges. If Mrs. Horne is late drink hot milk & dont get exhausted waiting for her. If you feel depressed lie down & sip hot milk and sugar. Im tired of telling you to eat. I now commend you to drink. Get the milk habit, dearest, & become a secret tippler. Take to drink I implore you. What the devil does it matter how fat one gets. We shall go to Persia where fatness alone is beauty. Besides you'll never be fat; you're too "active".

This isn't a letter. Only an odd note. Goodnight little artist.

Tig

MS Newberry. *LKM* II.178–9.

[1] KM had known the painter Mark Gertler since 1913, but they had not seen each other for some years.

[2] 'Taking the Veil', written on 24 Jan., was published in the *Sketch* (22 Feb. 1922).

[3] St Mary's Convent, Thorndon, close to the Beauchamp family home at 75 Tinakori Road, where KM lived from 1898 until she left for Queen's College, London, in 1903.

[4] A children's rhyme, and presumably a simple musical setting, referring to 'Nellie Bly', pseudonym of the feminist writer Elizabeth Cochran (1864–1922), the first American woman investigative journalist. She was made famous by her travel-against-the-clock exploit, and the book that followed it, *Around the World in 72 Days* (1890).

To Anne Drey, [26 January 1922]

[Chalet des Sapins | Montana sur Sierre]

Dearest Anne

For the Hotel and the dentists I am deeply grateful. The hotel sounds "just the thing" as they say. What an extraorindary quantity of water seems to *gurgle* through it. I shall develop fins and a tail if I am there long. Will you please tell Drey how deeply I am his debtor! I hope to have some very fine specimens of the Cruel Art by the spring. I am taking the puffi train from here on Monday, please tell David.[1] He is le Roi des Puffi Trains, j'imagine. Bless you

Katherine

Postcard ATL. *Adam* 300, 95.

[1] Anne's three-year-old son.

To J. B. Pinker & Son, 26 January 1922

CHALET DES SAPINS | MONTANA-SUR-SIERRE | VALAIS

26.1.1922

Dear Mr Pinker,[1]

Today I received, direct from The Mercury a cheque for twenty-five pounds.[2] I enclose herewith a cheque for two pounds ten which I believe to be the correct percentage. Will you kindly inform me if this is so?

I have written a new story for The Sketch[3] and hope to get it typed tomorrow.

Yours sincerely
Katherine Mansfield

MS Newberry.

[1] James Brand Pinker had been KM's literary agent since she wrote to him in Aug. 1921.
[2] Payment for 'At the Bay'.   [3] 'Taking the Veil'.

To Elizabeth, Countess Russell, [late January 1922]

CHALET DES SAPINS | MONTANA-SUR-SIERRE | VALAIS.

Thank you, dear Elizabeth, for your beautiful letter. It was happiness to receive it. I feel that it has put a blessing on my journey. We are solitary creatures au fonds. It happens so rarely that one feels another understands. But when one does feel it, it's not only a joy; it is help and comfort in dark moments.

For I have far less courage than you grant me, Elizabeth. I faint by the way (although I manage to do my fainting privately.) It is bitter to be ill. And the idea of being well – haunts me. Ever since I have realised *this* possibility I dream of it at night – dream I am alone – crossing streams or climbing hills or just walking. To be alone again. That is what health means to me; that is freedom. To be invisible, not to be offered chairs or given arms! I plan, I dream, yet I hardly dare to give way to these delights . . . (Tho' of course one does) But, if I should become an odious bouncing female with a broad smile *tell me at once, Elizabeth*, and I'll flee to some desert place and smile unseen.

Bill Shakespeare is really past a joke. It's a terrible giveaway for poor Clemence Dane.[1] I'd like to write a potted version with a real great thumping bunch of watercress come hurtling through the window when the Queen throws down her penny. But it's so *cheap*, so vulgar and 'stagey'. Dean with one foot on chair roaring out song, wanton sitting on table (it's always a table) swinging her foot, voices in the distance, she *dotes* on voices in the distance, and Shakespeare with arms outstretched against the wintry sky!! As to the love passages, they are written by your french pear, your withered pear, your true virgin. It smells of the 'performance' I even hear 'chocolates – chocolates' at the fall of each curtain and after Act II almost feel myself passing one of those maddening tea-trays with fingers of ancient plumcake on it and a penny under the saucer.

But enough – more than enough. I am as persistent as *Anne's Voice.*[2] Oh, God!

Elizabeth, on our knees we beg – *write* a new play. Oh, how thrilling it would be to sit by John and watch your play. I reread The Cherry Orchard to take the taste of Clemence Dane away – and the real fascination of the *real thing* shines through it. It's an exquisite play.

I hope your work goes well. I think of you often – This weather is odious. Today was a disgrace to God. Would you lunch with us on Sunday? or any day that suits you – I hope you like dear De la Mare. There is one poem "Why is the rose flowered and faded And these eyes have not seen" – – – I'm not sure of the words. It seems to me almost the best. I hope you meet him one day.

With very much love,

and thank you for everything.
Katherine.

TC Huntington.

---

[1] KM condescendingly reviewed Clemence Dane's novel *Legend* in the *Athenaeum* (5 Dec. 1919), and in a letter to JMM (30 Nov. 1919), described a laudatory review of the novel as 'deplorable humbug – rant – rubbish – tinpot provincial hysterics' (*CLKM* III. 129). Dane's blank verse play *Will Shakespeare: An Invention* was published in 1921. KM refers to the scenes where Queen Elizabeth throws a coin from a window to a hawker selling cress, and where Christopher Marlowe sings in a tavern. Shakespeare stands with arms outstretched at the end of Act I.

[2] In Act I, Anne Hathaway has more lines to speak than Shakespeare.

To J. B. Pinker & Son, 27 January 1922

CHALET DES SAPINS | MONTANA-SUR-SIERRE | VALAIS
27.1.1922

Dear Mr Pinker,

Thank you so much for letting me know that the Nation has taken my *Doll's House*. I enclose the new story for the Sketch. This time I think the number of words is well within the limit of two thousand.

Yours sincerely
Katherine Mansfield

MS Newberry.

To Michael Sadleir,[1] 29 January 1922

CHALET DES SAPINS | MONTANA SUR SIERRE | VALAIS
29 I 1922

Dear Michael Sadleir,

Just in case my book should be out within a fortnight might I have the copies sent to me at the

Victoria Palace Hotel
6–8, Rue Blaise Desgoffe
Rue de Rennes
Paris

And I would be very glad to have half a dozen extra copies charged to my account. I go to Paris tomorrow. I hope Ive not done wrong in writing to *you* about this.

Yours very sincerely
Katherine Mansfield.

MS Targ.

---

[1] Michael Sadleir (see *CLKM* III. 143, n.7), author and scholar, a director at KM's publisher, Constable.

II
FRANCE — PARIS
JANUARY–JUNE 1922

KM began the course of expensive *séances* with Manoukhin at the beginning of February, and for the next four months lived an invalid's life in a hotel near the Luxembourg Gardens. It was here she wrote 'The Fly' during her first weeks in Paris, a succinct and final focusing of what she felt about aspects of her father, about the War and the loss of her brother, and the courage and final hopelessness of struggling to survive. This was her last important story, although a few others were written to fund her treatment. But her interest in the short story form diminished.

During her months in Paris there were meetings with her friends the Schiffs, fleeting contact with James Joyce and Paul Valéry, a chance and awkward encounter with her old lover Francis Carco, and new acquaintances among Russian émigrés. Correspondence as ever was important to her, especially with the rather clinging Dorothy Brett, her new long-distant protégé William Gerhardi, a handful of others who mattered to her, and exchanges with Ida Baker that, as had been the case for years, were both tetchy and tender. But the months were unhappy ones. She was ambivalent about the effectiveness of the treatment she underwent, while her personal dissatisfaction became acute. 'I feel as though I have lived for years – for a whole life time in this hotel. . . . I always want not to be haunted by the idea of Time' (to Ottoline Morrell, 26 May).

To J. M. Murry, [31 January 1922]

[Victoria Palace Hotel, Rue Blaise Desgoffe, Rue de Rennes]
Tuesday morning.

My precious dear,

Although I have not seen Manoukhine yet and am in fact waiting for my bregchick I must write you a little note to be posted in all haste. To tell you what you call news. Bogey – Montana is a *wonderful* place. Since I left I have not once had shortness of breath or a second's trouble with my heart. I am exactly like an ordinary common garden person in that respect. I had to walk at the Gare de Lyon quite a long way and except that my pegs were tired – I have been scoring on paper for so long now (oh it dies hard, my dearest . . . notre jeu[1]) I felt as I used to 5 years ago.

Perfect journey. The hotel is extremely quiet. There is a huge salle de bains. I have a bedroom, hall with private door & this – well its a dressin-groom bathroom for 20 francs a day. I wallowed in a bath on arrival put on clean clothes and am lying down. Its like a dream not to be out of breath & to be alone with ones own sponge again.

Of course numbers and numbers of marvellous things happened on the journey. I am keeping a journal[2] instead of putting them in letters. Its less boring for anyone to read them unashamedly put forth like that. But I suppose my love of you is at the root of everything. Meine Wurzeln sind tauig begiessen with that und mit frischen Bühlen erfüllt. Dear Eckermann and dear Goethe![3] I slept last night in the little hollow in the bed between the two of them. Wasn't that review of Lynd *sickening*.[4] Didn't it make Lynd a sorry worm. There was nothing in the papers (D.N.) but a white satin tea cosy handpainted with flags of the Empire for Princess Mary.[5]

Ida's boots have made a *profound* impression here. I feel she ought to carry a little whip to keep them in order.

But all this is nothing except love. The essence of it is *Love* for you. Ill tell you all tomorrow – if I see M. today. Do let me know about you. I embrace you my dear love, & if this sounds hurried and unimportant forgive it. Its written between 2 stools as it were. Your own

Tig.

MS ATL. *LJMM*, 644–5.

[1] Murry noted (*LJMM*, 644), that KM is referring to cribbage, which they regularly played at the Chalet des Sapins.

[2] KM recorded little about the journey, beyond 'the train shatters one. Tunnels are *hell*. I am frightened of travelling.' But she did note of her last day in Sierre, 'Monday was the first *real* perfect day of the winter. It seemed that the happiness of Bogey and of me reached its zenith that day. We could not have been happier; that was the feeling..... He looked so beautiful too, hatless, strolling about his hands in his pocket.... There was a harmonium in the waiting room. Then I came away, after a quick but not hurried kiss' (*KMN* II. 322).

[3] The name of Johann Peter Eckermann (1792–1854) became linked with that of Johann Wolfgang von Goethe (1749–1832) through the conversations which Eckermann recorded during Goethe's last nine years, and published in 1836 and 1848 as *Gespräche mit Goethe*, a rich compendium about the poet's life, personality, interests and opinions.

The line in German means 'My roots are dewily watered [with that] and filled with fresh blossom-ing.' However, 'begiessen' should be 'begossen', and 'mit frischen Buhlen' is presumably meant to be 'mit frischem Blühen' (with fresh blossoming) or 'mit frischen Blüthen' (with fresh blossoms). While there is no source in Eckermann for this line, and so is probably Mansfield's invention, it is reminiscent of Goethe's short poem 'Gefunden'.

[4] In the *Daily News* (27 Jan.), Robert Lynd reviewed the second of the three volume *The Complete Works of Sir Philip Sidney*, ed. Albert Feuillerat. Lynd found 'The chief interest in Sidney's work as a whole is that it is the work of a paradigm among Christian gentlemen.' And of its author wanting *Arcadia* burned, Lynd thought, 'It would have been no great loss if his orders had been carried out.'

[5] Princess Mary, daughter of King George V and Queen Mary, married Henry Charles George, Viscount Lascelles, on 28 Feb. 1922.

To John Galsworthy,[1] *31 January 1922*

[Victoria Palace Hotel, 6 Rue Blaise Desgoffe, Rue des Rennes]
Paris,
January 31, 1922

Your letter came just as I was on the point of leaving home. How happy I am that you liked *At the Bay* and that Madame[2] likes my little children and the dog! But it is not your praise that I value most, although I am honoured and proud to have that. It is the fact you are watching my work, which is the most *precious* encouragement.

Yes, I have been working a great deal, but in my horrid bed where I've been for the past two months. I hope there are no beds in Heaven. But I managed to finish a long story there and several short ones.

Now I have come to Paris to see a Russian doctor who promises to give me new wings for old. I have not seen him yet – so – though it's still a miracle – one believes. When I have seen him I shall go back to Montana again. After these long months in the mountains it's the flower shops I long to see. I shall gaze into *them* as little boys are supposed to gaze into pastry-cooks...

I hope you are well. It would be very delightful to think we might meet one day. But please remember how grateful I am.

MS lacking. *LKM* II. 179–80.

[1] John Galsworthy (1867–1933), playwright, novelist and author of the enormously popular series *The Forsyte Saga.*
[2] Galsworthy married Ada Nemesis Pearson in 1905.

To J. B. Pinker & Son, 31 January 1922

Victoria Palace Hotel, 6 Rue Blaise Desgoffe, Rue de Rennes, Paris,
31.1.1922

Dear Mr Pinker,
I am very glad that the Westminster has accepted The Garden Party. Thank you for arranging it.

Will it be possible for me to see a proof? I ask because I know there is an error in the typing which makes nonsense of one sentence. In case there is no time for this I enclose a sheet of paper in which I have tried to explain to the proof reader what that error is.

I am in Paris for the next fortnight only. After that I return to Montana.
Yours sincerely
Katherine Mansfield.

MS Newberry.

The Garden Party

At, I think the bottom of page 2 there is a half sentence missed. I have not the MSS with me but as far as I remember it *ought* to run "Laura wished now she was not holding that piece of bread and butter. But there was nowhere to put it..."

Will you please accept this very cursory explanation and put my MSS right for me if there is no time for me to see a proof.[1]

Katherine Mansfield

MS Newberry.

---

[1] The correction was made, although the punctuation was not exactly as KM instructed, when the story appeared in *The Garden Party and Other Stories*, published by Constable at the end of Feb. But the text was extensively cut when it was divided between the *Saturday Westminster Gazette* (4 Feb. and 11 Feb. 1922), and the *Weekly Westminster Gazette* (18 Feb. 1922).

To J. M. Murry, [31 January, 1 February 1922]

[Victoria Palace Hotel, Rue Blaise Desgoffe, Rue de Rennes]
Dearest,

I went to see M. tonight.[1] I found him a tall formal rather dry man (not in the least an 'enthusiast') who speaks scarcely any french and has a lame Russian girl for his interpreter.

He read Bouchage's[2] report & I brought him up to date. He then very thoroughly examined me and reported as follows:

I can promise to cure you, to make you as though you had never had this disease.

You have T.B. in the 2nd degree – the right apex very lightly engaged, all the rest is full of rales (as usual). It will take 15 séances – then a period of repose preferably in the mountains for 2–3–4 months just as you like. Then 10 more. After the 15 you will feel *perfectly well*. The last 10 are to prevent any chance of recurrence. Fees as he stated.

I then explained our 'situation', exactly – what we wished to do, what would be more convenient in every sense, financially & otherwise. He said as follows:

It would be very much better for you to start now. Your condition is favourable. To begin now, to leave Paris in the 2nd week in May, to return in – even September if you liked for the last séances. I do not insist on your beginning now. I do not say you will be greatly harmed by waiting. I do say it is much better not to wait & especially as you have taken a journey not to take another, or to have the re-effort of the altitude, again. Nothing is worse than travelling. He insisted on that and on the great advantage in beginning now. At the same time he said of course he cannot really say anything if we prefer to wait until April. He asked me to write all this to you and to give the answer as soon as possible. His secretary told me he had treated 8000 cases in Moscow, that here in Paris patients in the 3rd & 4th degree – far far worse than I – were now as well as possible. She also said of course do not wait. And especially they kept on speaking of this double journey again. I then left.[3]

What do you think? Will you give me your opinion. The truth is it was a mistake that we did not see him together. It would have been far better. All my inclinations are to come back, not to 'upset' our life. All my wishes are for that. At the same time I must just put it all to you impartially. I said suppose I go for February and come back at the end of March. He said then you must be in Paris in June & July which is *not* good. It is very puzzling. The best thing of course would be for you to see him. But thats no good. Supposing you think I *ought* to take the treatment now I can of course send Ida back for as long as necessary. It is possible we might be able to sub let.

My desire is not to stay. Why? Because of our life. I feel I cannot break it again. I fear for it. If it were possible for you to come 3rd perhaps & just stay a couple of days. Is that a foolish idea? Consider well! Please darling think of this calmly. There is no hurry. I never felt less excited in my life. What do you think, my little King of hearts? Shall I come *bang* back at the end of my fortnight? That is what I want to do. If I am leaving you to decide something hard, then just give me your 'advice'. But don't forget that above all I love you.

Tig

Next day early.

I am going to send Ida out with this at once. I feel this morning perhaps we forget what a difference it's bound to make to us if I was well. It would make our lives very wonderful. And to wait for that longer than we have waited is perhaps foolish. Two things remain. His opinion that I would do far better to start the treatment now – his remark that he did not insist on my starting before April.

Of course, were I alone, I should begin at once. But I am not alone and my life with you is nearly the whole of life. It is so precious that to endanger it by making you unhappy is, I find, equal to endangering my own life. Remember that Ida can do all that is necessary at Montana. And should you decide to come just tell Ernestine simply and leave stamped addressed envelopes with her for the post and some money for her food.

I have learnt, my dear love, that if we act calmly and do not forget our *aim*... it's not so hard. That's why I don't wire, or feel even excited. I refuse to. We must be superior to these things.

Forgive me if I am worrying you my heart's dearest.

MS ATL. *LJMM*, 645–7.

[1] Manoukhin's clinic was at 3 Lyautey in Passy.
[2] Dr Ambroise Bouchage had been KM's doctor in Menton. His medical report on her, written at the end of Apr. 1921, is reproduced in *CLKM*, IV. 360–1.
[3] More frankly, KM wrote in her notebook that evening, 'M. had a lame girl there as interpreter. He said through her he could cure me completely. But I did not believe it. It all seemed suddenly unimportant and ugly' (*KMN* II. 322).

To J. M. Murry, [1 February 1922]

[Victoria Palace Hotel, Rue Blaise Desgoffe, Rue de Rennes]

Wednesday.

My precious

I rested all today, but after sending your letter I wrote one to Manoukhine, saying that before I decided anything I would like to know all there was to know about this treatment, whether one ran any risks, what its effects were on the heart, and so on. I told him that I was very much in the dark, that I could not afford an experiment, and in a word that I would be obliged if he would let me see his french partner & talk it all over. His reply was to ask me to meet them both at 5 oclock at their cabinet medicale. So we took a taxi and I went. The general impression was good, all in the highest degree simple, scientific, professional, unlike anything I have seen before. Manoukhine came & took me in to Donat.[1] He (D) is an elderly man, rather like Anatole France[2] in style, wearing a white coat and skull cap. Quite unaffected, and *very* clever, I should imagine. I told them my difficulties. It was a little bit awkward, especially as Donat has evidently a great regard and admiration for M. But there you were. This matter is serious & past pretending. And they were awfully kind. Donat delivered an absolute lecture; they drew diagrams, described the process, told me of its effects and so on. There is no *risk*. It is, as you know the application of X rays to the spleen. It produces a change of blood. It is a kind of immensely *concentrated* sun action. What the sun does vaguely and in a dissipated way this gently forces. He discovered it while working at typhus & cholera and applied it to tuberculosis. Donat spoke of it always as my colleagues discovery. "Dr M. has taught us". "Dr M. then experimented on so many animals and so on and found such and such results". The whole thing is *new*. That I realised keenly. It is the latest thing in science. That was what one felt. At the same time, there was a very good responsible atmosphere at this place. One felt in the presence of real *scientists* – not doctors. And Donat never says a fantastic word. He is dead straight. One does feel that. Its what I always imagined a Pasteur institute[3] to be. Donat agreed I could be cured. He has healed an englishman in the 3rd degree who after 12 applications has no more bacillus at all in his sputum ... He asked me about Montana. He & Manoukhine said that if I had been anywhere really healthy & led a quiet life free from worries I would have had the same amount of benefit. But in their united opinion Montana was too high for my heart in its present state. If I stayed absolutely still in bed there – bien – but to make a continual effort of that kind is not and cannot be good. One is living on l'energie nerveuse. He ended by saying "It is easy to see you are not a little ill. You have been ill for a long time. One has not an endless supply of force. You ought to get well. L'air de Paris et les rayons de Doctor Manoukhine will make you well. Of that I am confident."[4] I then came away.

I am glad I saw this man as well as the other. But isn't it strange. Now all this is held out to me – now all is at last *hope* real *hope* there is not one single throb of gladness in my heart. I can think of nothing but how it will affect 'us'.

Dear love, dont worry about me though. The food in this hotel is excellent. I have such a nice airy room with a comfortable chair. It could not be better in all those ways & I rest. I take my evening meal in bed.

In all things though you are my first thought – You know it. Remember Ida asks for nothing but to manage everything for us, and at all times. Your own Wig.

MS ATL. *LJMM*, 647–8.

---

[1] Dr Louis Donat (b. 1868) was attached to a community tuberculosis clinic in the 13th Arrondissement of Paris, where Manoukhin was sent by the Institut Pasteur to demonstrate his method of irradiating the spleen of TB patients with X-rays. Donat and Manoukhin, both at the clinic and privately, began using the treatment together in June 1921.

[2] Anatole France (1844–1924), French novelist, short-story writer and critic, admired for his erudition and biting irony. He received the Nobel Prize for Literature the previous year.

[3] The Pasteur Institute in Paris, known for its research as well as its treatment of diseases. Manoukhin had worked there before the First World War.

[4] But that evening KM made the notebook entry: 'I have the feeling that M. is a really good man. I have also a sneaking feeling...that he is a kind of unscrupulous imposter. Another proof of my divided nature. All is disunited. Half boos, half cheers' (*KMN* II. 322).

To S. S. Koteliansky, 1 February [1922]

Victoria Palace Hotel | 6 Rue Blaise Desgoffe | Rue de Rennes
February 1st

Koteliansky

I have seen Manoukhine. Yes, one has every confidence in such a man. He wishes me to begin the treatment at once. I am taking steps to try to do so, but it is not quite easy to arrange. It will cost me *much* money. I have £100 saved but I must make not only another £100 but enough to live on here and for special food and so on. Also I have Ida Baker to keep as well until I am strong enough to walk about and so on. It is all difficult, and for some reason I find it hard to accept all its difficulties, as one must. Perhaps for one thing it is not nice in a city. I had forgotten how women parade about, idle and unworthy, and how ignoble are the faces of men. It shocks me to see these faces. I want more than anything simply to cry! Does that sound absurd? But the lack of *life* in all these faces is terribly sad.

Forgive me, my dear friend. Let me speak of something else for a moment. While I was waiting at the clinique tonight the doors were all open & in the doctor's cabinet people were talking russian. They talked all together. Doctor M's voice was above the other voices, but there was a continual *chorus* – all speaking. I cannot tell you how I love Russian. When I hear it spoken it makes me think of course always of Tchekhov. I love this speech. I thought also of you, and I wished you were with me.

Send me a note here. Not a letter. I don't expect you to write. If I get well you will let me help you with the people you help, won't you? Now a bell is striking as though it turned over in its sleep to strike. Its very late.

Goodnight.

I press your hands

Katherine.

MS BL. *LKM* II. 180–1.

To Dorothy Brett, [2 February 1922]

[Paris]

Begin treatment tomorrow. Tig.

Telegram Texas. *Exhibition*, 49.

To J. M. Murry, [3 February 1922]

[Victoria Palace Hotel, Rue Blaise Desgoffe, Rue de Rennes],

Friday.

My precious Bogey

Your telegram came yesterday as a complete surprise – a very very marvellous one – a kind of miracle. I shall never forget it.[1] I read it, scrunched it up, then carefully unscrunched it and put it away "for keeps". It was a very wonderful thing to receive. I agree absolutely it is best that I start now & I telephoned the same moment to M. whose sole reply was "deux heures". (But before I speak of my time there I want to say your two letters my dear one are simply such perfect letters that one *feeds* on them.[2] I don't know. You have become such a wonderful person – well, you always were – but the beams are so awfully plain now – on se chauffe at every word you write. And there is a kind of calmness which I feel, too. Indeed I feel we are both so changed since the days before Montana – different people. I do feel that I belong to you, that we live in our own world. This world simply passes by – it says nothing. I do not like it but thats no matter. It is not for long. Do you realise that ɪꜰ the miracle happens we May Go to England This Summer Together? Thats just an idear of what the future holds. May it make you a hundredth part as happy as it makes me!)

I went to the clinique today and there the French doctor with Manou-khine went over the battlefield. Really it was the first time I have ever been 'examined'. They agreed absolutely after a very prolonged examination that I had *no* cavities. Absolument pas de cavernes. They tested & tested my lungs & always said the same. This means I am *absolutely curable*. My heart, rheumatism, everything was gone into and noted & finally I passed into another room & had a séance.

I want to ask you something. Do you really believe all this? There is something that pulls me back the whole time and which wont let me believe. I hear, I see. I feel a great confidence in Manoukhine – very great – and yet – – I am absolutely divided.[3] You know how, to do anything well, even to make a little jump, one must gather oneself together. Well, I am not gathered together. A dark secret unbelief holds me back. I see myself after 15 goes apologising to them for being not cured, so to speak. This is very bad. You realise I am in the mood now when I confess to you because I want to tell you my bad self. But it may be its not me. For what is bad in me (i.e. to doubt) is not bad in you. Its your nature – If you do feel it – please tell me – please try and change. Try and believe. I know Manoukhine believes. I was sitting in the waiting room reading Eckermann when he came in, quickly, simply and took my hand and said "vous avez décidé de commencer. C'est très bien. Bonne santé!" But this was said beautifully, *gently*. (Oh, Bogey I do love *gentleness*.) Now I have told you this I will get over it. It has been a marvellous day here, very soft, sunny and windy, with women selling les violettes de Parme in the street. But I could not live in a city ever again. That's done – that's finished with. I read Shakespeare (I am with you as I read) and I am half way through a new story. I long for your letter which follows mine. Oh, those precious birds at the coconut. How I see and hear them! And E's fig pudding. You write the word fig in such a nice way that all your precious darling self walks in the word. Goodbye for now, my blessed one. I feel a bit mysterious, full of blue rays, rather like a deep sea fishchik.

YOUR
Wig.

MS ATL. *LJMM*, 648–50.

[1] Murry's telegram does not survive.

[2] Murry's letters of 1 and 2 Feb. (Murry, 347–50).

[3] KM's notebook entries continued to touch on a far more personal struggle than her letters made evident. She wrote on 2 Feb.: 'Nothing of any worth can come from a disunited being. It's only by accident that I write anything worth a rusk and then its only skimming the top – no more. But remember the Daughters was written at Menton in November when I was not as bad as usual. I was trying with all my soul to be good. Here I try and fail & the fact of my consciousness makes each

separate failure very important – each a *sin*. If, combined with M's treatment I treated myself, worked out of this slough of despond, lived an honourable life, and above all made straight my relations with L.M. I am a *sham*. I am also an egoist of the deepest dye – such a one that it was very difficult to confess to it in case this book should be found. Even my being well is a kind of occasion for *vanity*. There is nothing worse for the soul than egoism. Therefore . . . ' (*NKM* II. 322–3).

To Dorothy Brett, 3 February 1922

[Victoria Palace Hotel, Rue Blaise Desgoffe, Rue de Rennes]

iii [February]

Dearest

Your letter has come. Now I have worried you after all. Stop! All is over. I wired you yesterday that I had decided to stay. I should not have written then – I should have waited. For, as so often happens, after waiting I saw daylight. And I knew that whatever might happen I must take this chance. Now I have written to my agent about money. I shall manage it. Dont ever send me money, Brett! I mean that. Please don't. I am that kind of man!! I haven't yet heard from Murry but I wrote to him fully. You mustn't say that about thrashing him for it makes me sorry I told you.[1] I *understand* Murry awfully well; its only I cant bear to make him unhappy or to make him feel he is having to make sacrifices.

As soon as I decided about the treatment I phoned Manoukhin and had my first treatment today. And its only now this minute, in bed, with a warm spring like wind at the window that Im beginning to feel perhaps it *may come true.*

But now all goes smoothly, dearest. Ill stay at this hotel which suits me in every way. The Mountain will go back to Montana and settle everything there. I expect Murry will join me here a bit later. All goes well – awfully well. Dont come for a few weeks. Wait until about the 5th week when I shall be able to walk a bit and laugh without coughing. Then come for a weekend. We'll be merry – really merry – two small crickets chirruping away – and there will be buds on the trees.

So

From now

Don't lets talk any more about Tig for the present. She is done with – settled in Paris and so full of blue rays at this moment that she feels like a deep sea fishchik. Thank you for your precious sympathy. Let it be an exclusive film about you. Your work – your house – your plans – *how you are* – everything. Have you worn your new buff dress yet? That is important, too. And what about that *milk*? And your house. May I plant a lavender bush in your garden – a very big one – with long blue flowers?

What funny Ms you make. They are very nice. They are like foxes. I always want to give them eyes. But you must put the name of this hotel on

your envelope or I shant get your letters, and I don't want to lose them.
Victoria Palace.

It seems a nice place – Letters simply fly here. Yours was only posted yesterday evening & it was on my supper tray tonight. It was still warm. I want to tell you heaps of things, but first I want to hear about you. So curl your little head into my shoulder & talk to me – You don't feel sad do you? Dont be sad! Next month is March & then there is no stopping the spring – I always feel winter is over in February even. The Dogs Mercury is in flower, so I read. But what is Dogs Mercury? And does the dog know? Its all a great puzzle – Perhaps he is *very* pleased or perhaps he just looks at it and bolts it. Oh, I do hope not. Life is so wonderful – very wonderful. Let us be happy in it. Above all let us not *waste it.*

I am thinking of you with tender love.

Tig.

MS Newberry.

---

[1] KM's earlier complaining about Murry does not survive.

To S. S. Koteliansky, 3 February 1922

Victoria Palace Hotel | 6 Rue Blaise Desgoffe | Rue de Rennes | Paris

III Fevrier 1922

Koteliansky

There is no answer to this letter. But I wanted to tell you something very good that happened today. Yesterday I decided that I must take this treatment and I telephoned M. I was sitting alone in the waiting room of the clinique reading Goethes conversations with Eckermann when M. came in. He came quickly over to me, took my hand and said simply "Vous avez decidé de commencer avec la traitment. C'est très bien. Bonne santé", and then he went as quickly out of the room saying 'tout de suite' (pronounced '*toot sweet*' for he speaks very little French). But this coming in so quickly and gently was a beautiful act, never to be forgotten, the act of someone *very good.*

Oh, how I love gentleness, Koteliansky, dear friend. All these people everywhere are like creatures at a railway station – shouting, calling, rushing, with ugly looks and ways. And the women's eyes – like false stones – hard, stupid – there is only one word corrupt. I look at them and I think of the words of Christ "Be ye therefore perfect even as your Father in Heaven is perfect".[1] But what do they care? How shall they listen? It is terribly sad. Of course, darling Koteliansky, I don't want them to be all solemn or Sundayfied. God forbid. But it seems there is so little of the spirit of love and gaiety and *warmth* in the world just now. Why all this pretence? But it is true – it is not easy to be simple, it is not just (as A.T.' s [Anton Tchekhov's] friend used to say) a sheep sneezing.[2]

It is raining. There is a little hyacinth on my table – a very naive one. Heaven bless you. May we meet soon.

Katherine.

MS BL. *LKM* II. 181.

[1] Matthew 5:48.　　　[2] Untraced.

To J. M. Murry, [4 February 1922]

[Victoria Palace Hotel, Rue Blaise Desgoffe, Rue des Rennes]

Saturday.

Ref. No. Letter X.[1]

My darling Bogey

Your letter came as a surprise to me but I absolutely agree with every word of it! It is far and away the best plan.[2] I understand perfectly your feeling about your work and here is an opportunity. I, too, shall put in a great deal of work. I feel this year must float our ships if we are going to bring any cargo home. Goethe has filled me with renewed longing to be a *better writer*. No, I have no other idea to offer at all. Except – wouldn't it be far less unsettling if instead of you coming down for that week I got Brett over while Ida went up there. Shed come like a shot. In fact she begged me to let her come for a weekend. You know what energy a journey takes. We have nothing to talk over, darling that can't be done by letters. And then when you come in May all will be so different. I think wed better leave the Oiseau Bleu[3] in the air – in flight – until we are certain we shall want to go there – But I hope you will agree with the Brett suggestion. Nothing is gained by you coming here for a week and you would lose a great deal by the geographical change. I don't think anyone can realise *how* different a city is until they come right into it. It makes a most extraordinary impression. I have a definite aim and hope in being here so I can ignore the effect – but for you at present in the middle of your novel it would be bad.

It seems to me there is no more to say about it all. You see when Ida comes back she can settle everything and then when you come down in May she can go up again (its like a see-saw, isn't it?) and finish up the Chalet des Sapins. By the way coconut II is *under* the house. Ida saw it fall. Near the bathroom . . . I am so glad E. [Ernestine] is improved. I thought she would be all right on her own. Shes an honest creature and Wingley makes it proper there being 2 gentlemen in the house instead of one. What wretched *posts* are arriving. I am glad about Pinker and Massingham.[4] I must get Alice Jones[5] to find me an English typist. She sent me the Lancet[6] today with Manoukhine's article in it. Shall I send it to you?

The only thing I don't quite understand in your letter is your "breaking the back of your years work" and so on. Its all right – isn't it? Youre not working in secret at something I know nothing about? It sounds so very appalling.

Well, I shall end this letter here for I want Ida to send it at once. Its Saturday night. Im afraid it may not reach you until Tuesday. Please reply at once about the Brett idea. And thanks most awfully for sending the letters – Will you go on sending them? I long to see the Tchekhov books, too when you have finished with them.

Your loving Wig.

MS ATL. *LJMM*, 650–1.

[1] JMM identified his letter in this way, to prevent confusion at a time when he and KM corresponded almost daily.

[2] In reply to KM's letters telling him of her visits to Manouklin, Murry wrote: 'You must do what M. says, begin the treatment now, come back here for the summer in May and go back and finish the treatment in September.' As for his own plans, 'What I feel is – I want to stay here. If I come and try to live in a hotel in Paris, I shan't really be able to work. I can't have my books and I shan't be able to settle down to the regular grind of my novel....I've got masses of work to do and I want to get it done. Moreover, we've paid the rent here' (Murry, 351).

The disappointment KM did not reveal in her letter is evident in her notebook on the same day: 'Heard from M. saying he prefers to remain in Montana. All his letters now the same. There breathes in them the relief from strain. It is remarkable. He does not believe a word about Manoukhine & talks of coming to "fetch" me in May. Well, if I am any better there will never be any more *fetching*. Of that I am determined. The letter kept me awake until very late' (*KMN* II. 323).

[3] A chalet near Montana they considered renting when the lease on the Chalet des Sapins expired.

[4] KM's agent had written to say *Cassell's Weekly* had bought 'A Cup of Tea' for ten guineas, and her old acquaintance, the journalist and editor H. W. Massingham, assured her that the *Nation and the Athenaeum* would accept regular stories from her.

[5] The secretary at the *Nation and the Athenaeum* office, 10 Adelphi Terrace, The Strand.

[6] Ivan Manoukhin, 'The Treatment of Infectious Diseases by Leucocytolysis Produced by Rontgenisation of the Spleen', *Lancet* (2 Apr. 1921, 685–7).

To Anne Drey, 4 February 1922

Victoria Palace Hotel | 6 Rue Blaise Desgoffe | Rue de Rennes
4 ii 1922

Darling Anne,

Just a mot to say how grateful I am for the address of this hotel. Its just what I wanted, and it simply flows with hot baths. I have a heaven-kissing room au 6ième with a piece of sky outside and a view into the windows opposite – which I love. Its so nice to watch la belle dame opposite bring her canary *in* when it rains and put her hyacinth *out*. I have decided to stay in Paris and not go back to that Switzerland. There is a man here – did I tell you about him? (It sounds rather an ambiguous beginning, by the way) But enfin there *is* a man here who treats my maladie with the X rays and I am going to him for this treatment. I had the first yesterday & I feel at this moment full of des rayons bleus – rather like a deep sea fish. But he promises to cure me by the summer. Its hard to believe it. But if it is true I shall take a puffi to your very door and come and have tea with David out of a very little small teapot... The only fly in the ointment is the terrific expense. Its 300 francs a time. However, I have been fortunate with my work lately and Ill just have to do a double dose of it until this is paid off. Money is a bore but I never take it *dead* seriously, and I don't care if I havent a sou as long as I can leap and fly alone.

You know darling I really do expect you in the SPRING. I feel the winter is over already and I read in the Daily Mail yesterday that the Dog's Mercury is out. But what *is* the Dogs Mercury? And does the Dog know? I hope hes very pleased but I expect he just looks at it and bolts it and goes on with a kind of "so that's that" air. Sad for the Dog's Mercury – don't you think?

Well dearest, I feel a bit weak in the pen this morning & inclined to laugh at rien – you know the feeling? Do send me a little note here when you are not too busy. Its a fool of a day here – sunny & windy. Fat old men lose their hats & cry houp-là as they stagger after them.

Heaven bless you.

Your devoted
Katherine

[P.S.] A kiss for David on the pussy's little derrière.

MS ATL. *LKM* II. 182.

To William Gerhardi,[1] *4 February 1922*

Victoria Palace Hotel | 6 Rue Blaise Desgoffe | Rue de Rennes | Paris iv. ii. 1922

Dear Mr Gerhardi,

Wont you let me know what has happened about your novel. I have so often wondered. I hope you will write and tell me when it is going to be published.

Another thing. Do you know Lady Ottoline Morrell who lives at Garsington? Would you care to? She is a *personality* and her house is exquisite and one meets there people who might 'interest' you. Im thinking of the literary point of view as well as the other.

I have come down from my mountains and am living in Paris until May. Oh, the flower shops after nothing but snow and pine trees! It is devilish not to be rich enough to go inside them. I stand and stare like a little boy in front of a pastry cooks.

Yours very sincerely,
Katherine Mansfield.

MS ATL.

---

[1] While an undergraduate at Oxford, and before he added the final 'e' to his name, William Gerhardi had written admiringly to KM in June 1921 (see *CLKM* IV. 248–9). Unable to find a publisher for his first novel *Futility*, he asked KM's help, and she successfully put him in touch with Richard Cobden-Sanderson.

To Charlotte Beauchamp Perkins, [5 February 1922]

Victoria Palace Hotel | 6–8 Rue Blaise Desgoffe | Rue de Rennes | Paris
Sunday.

Darling Marie,

Do send me a line and say how you are. As you see I have left my mountains. I came here to see a specialist and I shall stay here until the second week in May taking a course of X ray treatment. A Russian doctor here has discovered a method of treatment of consumption by X raying the spleen (which lives next door to your heart my dear & in the same street with your liver.) It sounds very wonderful. It is terribly expensive. Each treatment costs *300 francs*. But I was doing no good in Montana really and I have been ill nearly 5 years now. Anything rather than go on with a sofa life. Besides which it is my only chance, which makes a great difference towards what one can try to afford. By the way (a strictly family question, my dear) do you know a good depilatory. I wish you would tell me. I foresee the day is not far distant when I shall have to start using one.

But above all *do* let me hear from you. Its like spring in Paris — so mild. Always your devoted sister

K.

MS ATL.

To Alice Jones, 5 February 1922

Victoria Palace Hotel | 6–8 Rue Blaise Desgoffe | Rue de Rennes
Paris
V II 1922

Dear Mrs Jones,

Thank you very much. The Lancet turned up in record time. And now
I am going to ask you if you would kindly forward any letters that arrive at
the office for me to the above address. I am staying in Paris for the course
of treatment and shall not return to Switzerland. Will this be troubling you
too much? It would be simpler if you entered the postage expenses etc. to
J M M s account and I will settle (or try to get out of settling) with him.
He is staying up in the mountains with his beloved little black and white cat
to bear him company.

Yours very sincerely
Katherine Mansfield Murry.

MS Texas.

To J. B. Pinker & Son, 5 February 1922

Victoria Palace Hotel | 6–8 Rue Blaise Desgoffe | Rue de Rennes | Paris
v.ii.1922

Dear Mr Pinker,

My husband forwarded to me your letter of January 31st telling me he
had corrected and returned the proofs of The Garden Party to save time.
I hope that will be all right and that my note did not complicate matters.

I am glad to hear Cassells have taken A Cup of Tea. I shall try and send
another story of the same *genre* to you in the course of a week or so. I enclose
a letter from Mr Massingham. I hope it does not matter that I wrote to him
without consulting you suggesting I should supply a regular story to The
Nation once a month or once every six weeks, at their usual rates of pay.
They will take work that it is difficult to place elsewhere and it seems to me
a good idea for a short story writer to make a regular appearance in one
paper. I hope you agree. I will send you the stories as they are written – if
you will kindly send them on.

I am not returning to Switzerland for the present. The above will be my
address until next May.

Yours sincerely
Katherine Mansfield

MS Newberry.

To Michael Sadleir, 5 February 1922

Victoria Palace Hotel | 6–8 Rue Blaise Desgoffe | Rue de Rennes
Paris
V II 1922

Dear Michael Sadleir,

I am not returning to Switzerland, so the above will be my address until May next. I would be very glad if you would send me a line at your convenience telling me if my book is to appear this month. Its not mere curiosity that prompts the question!

With best wishes

Yours ever,
Katherine Mansfield.

MS Targ.

To Elizabeth, Countess Russell, [c. 5 February 1922]

Victoria Palace Hotel | 6 Rue Blaise Desgoffe | Rue de Rennes.

Dear Elizabeth,

Let me write what is in my heart – will you? But don't let it worry you or disturb your work. It is as I thought – the Russian Doctor wants me to begin the treatment at once – now – and not to go back to Montana until May when he says I will be "perfectly well". I'd have to come back here in the Autumn for another ten weeks of treatment but that is all. He strongly advises me not to take another journey. He says "But why delay? You have been ill so long. Why lose any more?"

And I don't feel a single throb of joy. Now that this wonderful chance has come I am torn in two. John hates the idea of a city, loathes hotels, is happy now as he never has been. I see him up there, hatless, well, on his skis, or sitting at peace in his little brown room that is like a nut. And now I must disturb him, tear him up, stop his work, ask him to do all the things he *hates*. The man here says I ought not to wait until April. John would like me to wait until then. *Then* all would be arranged; he would be ready; the subject would be familiar. But its no good, I shall have to stay and send the faithful one back to leave all in order. Or shall I not?

Love is a difficult thing. I love John a shade too much, I think. I want to spare him everything. When I was with him and discussed the possibility of this very thing happening, because it made him wretched and because he didn't want to face it I refrained. And now I'm in a worse case. But that sounds as though I am wailing. No, Elizabeth dear, I'm not. But its rather awful now that the prison door is open to realise one hesitates, – after all – knowing that John would rather I stayed there a little longer! Fantastic horrid positions! The city is horrid, too, *dark* and people look glum. Life is only given once. I wish we were all happier. And this outpouring is not a very cheerful one. But I yielded to temptation. Forgive it and me. With very much love.

Ever your
Katherine.

TC Huntington.

To J. M. Murry, [6 February 1922]

[Victoria Palace Hotel, Rue Blaise Desgoffe, Rue de Rennes]

Monday.

Darling Bogey,

I have just received your Friday-Saturday letter – full of snow. The whole of Switzerland according to the papers is snowing. It must be horrid! I hope it is over. No, its not been really bad weather here and April-mild until yesterday when it froze. But today the sun is in-and-out again.

Will you send me the Lit. Sup? And the Dial? Id be very glad of both if its not too much bother.

Ida is arranging to return on Friday, leaves here Friday night, that is. Don't feel any doubt about *not* coming here. Id far rather you didn't come. Theres no point in it and it would unsettle us both. Hotels are odious places for two. If one is alone one can work and forget but thats not so easy à deux. No, let the red peg and the white peg[1] meet in May – not before...

Have you read that Goethe – Eckermann? I shall give it to Ida to return to you. But I mean to order a whole one for myself. That taste has given me *such* an appetite. Its a mystery to me that so fascinating a book should be so little talked of. In fact its one of those books that once discovered abides for ever. Its such a whole (even in part as I have it). These two men live, and one is carried with them. The slight absurdity and the sentimental bias of Eckermann I wouldn't have not there! Delightfully human – one smiles but one cant help smiling always tenderly. And then outside sounds come in – the bells of Weimar ringing in the evening, the whisper of the wheat as the friends walk together, the neighbours little children calling like birds.[2] But all this human interest (ah! how it draws one!) apart there is Goethe talking, and he did say marvellous things. He was great enough to be simple enough to say what we all feel and dont say. And his attitude to Art was noble. It does me good to go to church in the breasts of great men. Shakespeare is my Cathedral but Im glad to have discovered this other. In fact, isn't it a joy – there is hardly a greater one – to find a *new book*, a living book, and to know that it will remain with you while life lasts!

How is your novel?[3] Does it go easily? I write slowly here because it takes time to abstract oneself. I feel I have a terrible amount to do, though. I hardly dare look out of this story because of all the others. They are in rows in the waiting room. But one would not have it otherwise.

Ive read Anthony & Cleopatra again last week and upon my word it is appaling to find how much one misses each time in Shakespeare – how much is still new. Wonderful play! But Bogey you remember " *'Tis one of those odd tricks which sorrow shoots out of the mind* ".[4] That is familiar enough but it still leaves me gasping. There is something over and above the words – the meaning – all that I can see. It is that other language we have spoken of before. I feel that as I am – I am not great enough to bear it. The image that for some reason comes into my mind is of an old woman in a cathedral who bows down, folds herself up in her shawl, mournfully closes herself against the sudden stirring of the organ. You know when the organ begins & it seems to ruminate, to wander about the arches & dark altars as though seeking some place where it may abide . . .

I must get up. I hope you have my letters, and that, Wingley is a good little pussy-wee.

Your loving
Wig.

MS ATL. *LJMM*, 651–2.

[1] As in her letter to Murry on 31 Jan., KM refers to the pegs used to tally scores in the card game cribbage. She had written in 'Prelude', section XI, how 'The cribbage pegs were like two little people going up the road together, turning round the sharp corner, coming down the road again.'

[2] While several conversations with Goethe recorded by Eckermann took place during their walks together (e.g. 22 Mar. 1824), no single walk includes the different impressions KM here evokes.

[3] Murry was then working on his novel *The Things We Are*, published by Constable later in the year.

[4] *Antony and Cleopatra*, IV. ii. 14–15.

To Dorothy Brett, [6 February 1922]

[Victoria Palace Hotel, Rue Blaise Desgoffe, Rue de Rennes]
Monday

Dearest Brett,

Your letter about the little still life has come. I cannot express to you what I feel at the beauty of your letter. IT is indeed such a still life that I shall keep it in my breast forever and never never forget that it was you who gave it to me. My dearest Brett you are very very rich that you have such gifts to give away, such treasure to unclose. Do not let us ever be less to each other than we are now. Let us always be more. I shall repay you one day with all that is in my power. In the meantime put this letter down & just feel for one moment that I love you. No more – no less.

Now I want to fly off at a tangent at once and say that we must spend the summer (part of it) together. Is it agreed? If – if – if I get better let us go off alone to Perpignan and lie on the beach & walk in the vineyards. I am serious. You can paint, I shall write. We shall both wear very large hats and eat at a table under a tree with leaves dancing on the cloth.

No, I *dare* not look out of prison at these delights. They are too much. And yet I do nothing else in bed at night when the light is out. I range the world over. It is just what prisoners must do when their time is getting short. I must write a story one day about a man in prison. Murry has answered my letter. He does not want to come to Paris. He feels it would do his work harm. So he is staying in Switzerland. But he says he will come and "fetch" me in May. By that "fetch" I know he hasn't the slightest faith in Manouhkin. Indeed, after saying "what terrific news" he never mentions it. I might have picked up a shilling. Men are odd creatures. But he is very happy and well looked after. In fact he sounds perfectly blissful. So there it is.

This isn't a letter dearest, just a word to answer yours. I dreamed last night Ottoline had taken to painting & gave an exhibition out of doors – at Garsington. One immense canvas was a portrait of Philip called "Little Pipsie head-in-air". I can see it now. What fools our dreams make of us! But Ottoline was delighted with her work. She kept wandering about saying "such lovely *reds*, dont you think so? *So* warm!" I must get up. I have a whole story to finish. Ive got a job on the Nation to write a story a month for them & *Cassells* want some more and *The Sketch*. What places to let ones poor little children go wandering in. It cant be helped. They are like waifs singing for pennies outside rich houses which I snatch away & hand to Manouhkin.

God bless you

Tig

Im worse at present in every way but then I shall be for 3 weeks. Its a kind of reaction.

MS Newberry.

To J. M. Murry, [7 February 1922]

[Victoria Palace Hotel, Rue Blaise Desgoffe, Rue de Rennes]

Tuesday.

My darling Bogey

I have had no news from you today yet (3 p.m.). I expect it is the snow. Arctic conditions prevail in Switzerland, so the papers say. I hope you manage to keep warm and that Wingley's tail is not frozen.

Advise me – will you? I am looking for a tiny flat – very small – a mouse's hole just big enough to nibble a pen in. If I find anything suitable I shall take it until the end of May and Ida will look after it to save money on servants and so on. But (this is where I want your advice) to whom can I apply for a reference? They are sure to ask me for at least two – can you think of anybody? I wish you would answer this as soon as possible, Bogey. A card will suffice, as they say. Its rather urgent. Flats are so scarce here and I want to be settled as soon as possible once something is found. Of course it may all be a wild goose's chase. Ida has gone off to an agent this afternoon. But there it is!

I have started a new Shakespeare notebook. I hope you will let me see yours one day. I expect they will be legion by that time. And reading with the point of view of taking notes I begin to see those marvellous short stories asleep in an image as it were. For instance

> ... 'Like to a vagabond flag upon the stream
> Goes to and back, lackeying the varying tide
> To rot itself with motion.'[1]

That is terrible, and it contains such a terribly deep psychological truth. That '*rots* itself'... And the idea of 'it' returning and returning, never swept out to sea finally. You may think you have done with it for ever but comes a change of tide and there is that dark streak reappeared, more sickeningly rotten still. I understand that better than I care to. I mean – alas! – I have proof of it in my own being.

There are awful good oranges to be had in Paris. But theres nothing else good that I know – nothing *fresh, sound,* or *sweet.* But mines a partial view, of course. I have done with cities for ever. I want flowers, rather sandy soil, green fields and a river not too deep to paddle in, also a large number of ancient books and a small but *very* pretty cow. In fact I should like the cow to be strikingly pretty. I shall put it in the advertisement. 'No plain cows may apply'. No, I cant do that. Its too cruel. But its an airy-fairy herd for a long time, Im afraid. How is your work going? If I am very dull for five weeks you must remember that for 5 weeks this treatment makes me rather worse. After that you will have to snatch my letters (like snapdragons) all blaging out of the postman's bag.

Your loving
Wig.

MS ATL. *LKM* II.183–4.

[1] *Antony and Cleopatra*, I. iv. 45–8.

To J. M. Murry, [8 February 1922]

[Victoria Palace Hotel, Rue Blaise Desgoffe, Rue de Rennes]

In reply to your telegram.

My darling Bogey,

I do not "understand" why you have sent this telegram,[1] so my reply is rather in the dark. Still, I must send it. Please do not come here to me. That is what I wish to say, and I say it deliberately. It is not *easy* to write so to you. I will try and explain my reasons. I want you to have your freedom as an artist.[2] You asked for it at Menton. I thought it was a mistake – that you did not mean it and only wrote under influence. But then after I left Montana you asked for it again. You were willing to join me *if I wanted you* – you were prepared, like a shot *to be of help to me*. (But that is exactly like saying to a person if you want to borrow money, borrow from me, or Fathers telling me I could count on him up to £50 if the necessity arose. It is not the gesture of people who deeply understand each other.) On the other hand your own personal feeling was not that at this most critical of all moments in her life I could not leave Wig. Golly – no! It was my work – May would be too late – my novel – and so on. Reverse the positions, darling. *Hear* me saying that to you!

It is no good. I now know that I must grow a shell away from you. I want, 'I ask for' my independence. At any moment in the future you may suddenly leave me in the lurch if it pleases you. It is a part of your nature. I thought that it was almost the condition of your working that we were together. Not a bit of it! Well, darling Boge, for various reasons I cant accept this. And now that I am making a bid for health – my *final bid* – I want to grow strong in another way, too. Ida is leaving here on Saturday. She will be with you on Sunday. Tell her what you want her to do, if you intend leaving Switzerland. And write to me about everything. But my very soul rebels against when its fine you prefer your work & your work is more urgent than this affair in Paris has been. When it snows you might as well be playing cribbage with me! And also that remark "Moreover the rent is paid here!"

No, darling, *please*. Let me be alone here. This queer strain in you does not, for some extraordinary reason in the very least atom lessen my love for you. Id rather not discuss it. Let it be! And I must work now until May. These 'affairs' are 1000 times more disturbing than 1000 train journeys. Pax, darling. You will see Ida on Sunday. But for the last time I ask you not to join me. I cannot see you until May.

Your loving
Wig.

Please just accept this. Its awfully hard having '*it*' to fight as well as my other *not* dear Bogies!

Later.

Dearest Bogey

I have just opened my letter to say your Sunday & Monday ones have come – about the snow, about Elizabeth, about your staying there. If the weather is fine by now I dare say your doubts will have taken wings, too. But for my part – I would rather stay here alone. I have seen the worst of it by myself i.e. going alone to Manouhkin, having no one to talk it over and so on. I want now intensely to be alone until May. Then IF I am better we can talk things over and if I am not I shall make some other arrangement. There's no need to look ahead. But that is my very *calm collected* feeling. So if you do want to leave the chalet before May – let us still be independent of each other until then – shall we?

I hope that horrible weather is over. Don't we get dreadfully few letters I am going to see a little flat tomorrow which I hope will be suitable. Here – I cant stay longer than necessary.

Your loving Wig.

P.S. We haven't read *The Schoolmaster*. Have we? Are you certing?[3] Don't bother to send the D.N. about Bibesco.[4]

MS ATL. *LJMM*, 654–5.

---

[1] JMM's telegram saying he would come to Paris if needed, does not survive.

[2] His letters of 5 and 6 Feb. (see Murry, 354–6).

[3] JMM would review *The Schoolmaster and Other Stories*, translated by Constance Garnett, in the *Nation and the Athenaeum* (8 Apr. 1922).

[4] Murry offered to send on Rose Macaulay's review of Princess Bibesco's *I have only myself to blame*, from the *Daily News* (2 Feb. 1922), which described the stories as inferior Mansfield. The memory of Murry's flirtation with the Princess a year before still rankled (see *CLKM* IV. 199–200).

KM sent this letter express. When Murry received it the next day, he wrote back: 'I deserve the letter. It's the most awful one you've ever sent me. . . . Don't say I was "claiming my freedom as an artist" – such an idea never entered my head. . . . I don't want, never have for a year now even dreamed of wanting "freedom".' He explained how over the past four years he had been 'petrified with fear' of life, and that 'There's only one thing greater than my fear – that is my love' (Murry, 361–2). He left that evening to join her in Paris. KM later pasted his letter into her copy of Shakespeare.

To Elizabeth, Countess Russell, 8 February 1922.

Victoria Palace Hotel | 6–8 Rue Blaise Desgoffe | Rue de Rennes
Paris
8.II.1922

My dear Elizabeth,

Thank you so much for your letter. But what horrid snow. There must be too much of it. I hope it now settles down and the sun shines warm. It seems impossible that I missed you at Randogne. You were in my thoughts as we waited at the station & I tried to catch a glimpse of your chalet. I hate to think I did not see you.

It served me right about John. After my agonies as to what would become of him – *relief* breathed in the poor boy's letter. He was like a fish off a line, swimming in his own element again, and never dreaming really of coming here. He made me feel like a very stuffy old Prospero who had been harbouring a piping wild Ariel.[1] I hope he does stay where he is. It would be much the best plan. Poor John! Its horrible to think how I have curtailed his freedom. In my silly innocence I felt certain he couldn't bear not to know what this Russian man said and so on. But not a bit of it. He is hand in hand with his new novel – I see them rather like the couple in Donne's Ecstasy.[2] But I *do* hope he wont change his ideas now. Bad weather and no posts are a trial which he hasn't experienced yet in solitude. He would repent of coming to Paris Im sure while he is seething with work which will out. Id much rather be alone until May, too, now that I know his sentiments.

Its literally years since I have been in a city. Hampstead[3] was only my room – it wasn't any more of London. But in an hotel one is plunged into the very housemaid's pail of it, and odious it seems to me. There is nothing sweet sound fresh except the oranges. Paris looked at through a taxi window has its grave beauty. It *is* a lovely city! But the people. Did people always look so . . . impudent? And I used to think *all* the women were pretty in a way. And now I think they are bold, stupid hussies and the men awfully like dogs. Is it because I do not leap and fly myself, Elizabeth? As to the flowers – I haven't had a flower yet. Tulips are 1.50 each. The F.O.[4] can't find anything sweet and reasonable. And it had been my plan to send you a basket the very first thing. Nothing but my horrid poverty stops that basket arriving. Manoukhin says that by the second week in May Ill feel perfectly well. Its exactly like being in prison and hearing somehow that there is a chance you may be let out. *Now* I know what a prisoner's dreams must be. I feel inclined to write a long story about a gaol bird. But I shouldn't know how to end it.

I wonder how your novel is going?[5] I am hard at Shakespeare again, tapping away at him like the birds tapped at my half coconut on the window sill.

The F.O. has been looking for *small flats*. Yesterday she found one — "*very* nice", where five girls with bobbed hair lived with their uncle. It was, she confessed rather full of beds at the moment. But when the girls, who were from the country had gone the beds would be whisked away. And the concierge was most agreeable. The house very quiet. It seemed to me rather a strange menage but I went to see over it today. Really the F.O. is like Una in the Fairy Queen.[6] She is too innocent for words to express. That flat! Those bobbed haired girls! 'Uncle' had departed but two cigars remained to *prove* as F.O. murmured to me "that a man lived there". And the BEDS. Merciful Powers! There was something horribly pathetic about it in the pale afternoon light, in its attempts at gaiety, at real flowering. But the whole place will haunt me for ever. I said to the F.O. as we left "But its a bawdy-house." And after a long pause she said "Dear me! I had never imagined such a thing. But I quite see what you mean!"

This letter must end.

With *much* love dear Elizabeth

Yours ever
Katherine.

MS BL. *Selected*, 243–5.

[1] The elderly and banished Duke of Milan, the creative force in Shakespeare's *The Tempest*, and his spritely but obligated assistant – a wry comment on KM's relationship with Murry.

[2]
                                 Sat we two, one another's best.
                                 Our hands were firmly cimented...

John Donne, 'The Extasie', written before 1615, published 1633. A glancing jibe at Murry's 'intellectual' fiction, the thought, as in Donne's poem, standing in for the deed.

[3] KM and Murry had lived at 2 Portland Villas, East Heath Road, Hampstead, from early Sept. 1918 to Sept. 1919, and again from the end of Apr. to Aug. 1920.

[4] The Faithful One, another nickname for Ida Baker.

[5] Elizabeth was working on *The Enchanted April*, published later in the year.

[6] Una represents fidelity and true religion in Book I of Edmund Spenser's *The Faerie Queene* (1589).

To William Gerhardi, 8 February 1922

Victoria Palace Hotel | 6–8 Rue Blaise Desgoffe | Rue de Rennes | Paris.
8.ii.1922

Dear Mr Gerhardi,

I can't tell you how honoured I am by your asking me to be Godmother. I have the warmest feelings towards your little nouveau né and shall watch its first steps with all the eagerness a parent could desire.[1] I cast about in my mind as to what to send it. Not a silver mug. No, not a mug. They only tilt them over their noses and breathe into them. Besides, the handle of mine, being silver was always red hot, so that I had to lap up what was inside, like a kitten... The matter I see demands time for consideration. But very seriously, I am most happy Cobden-Sanderson liked your book. I am sure it will be a success. And I look forward to reading it again and making other people read it. All success to you and many thanks.

Please do not praise me too much. It is awfully nice to be praised but at the same time it makes me hang my head. I have done so little. I should have done so much more. There are these rows of stories, all waiting. All the same, I cant deny that praise is like a most lovely present, a bright bouquet coming to one (but gently! I hope) out of the air. Dont imagine for one moment though, that I think myself 'wonderful'. That is far from the truth. I take writing too seriously to be able to flatter myself. Ive only begun. The only story that satisfies me to any extent is the one you understand so well 'The Daughters of the Late Col.' & parts of Je ne parle pas. But Heavens! what a journey there is before one!

By the way, for proof of *your* being a writer you had only to mention a bath chair & it crept into your handwriting. It was a queer coincidence. I had just been writing a bath chair myself and poor old Aunt Aggie who had lived in one & died in one, *glided* off, so that one saw her in her purple velvet steering carefully among the stars and whimpering faintly as was her terrestial wont when the wheel jolted over a particularly large one.[2] But these conveyances are not to be taken lightly or wantonly. They are terrible things.

No less.

I hope if you do come to Paris at Easter you will come and see me. By then I expect I shall have a little flat. I am on the track of a minute appartement with a wax-bright salon where I shall sit like a bee writing short stories in a honeycomb. But these retreats are hard to find.

I am here undergoing treatment by a Russian doctor Ivan Manoukhin, who claims to have discovered a cure for tuberculosis by the application of X rays. It is a mystery. But it sounds marvellous. And at present I am full of wandering blue rays like a deep sea fish. The only real trouble is its terribly expensive. So much so that when I read the price I felt like Tchekhov wanted Anna Ivanovna to feel when she read his story in a hot bath[3] – as though someone had slung her in the water & she wanted to run sobbing out of the bathroom. But *if* it all comes true it means one will be invisible once more – no more being offered chairs and given arms at sight. A close season for ever for hot water bottles and glasses of milk. Well people dont realise the joy of being invisible – its almost the greatest joy of all. But Ill have to write at least a story a week until next May, which is a little bit frightening.

Oxford, from the papers sounds very sinister. And why when people receive anonymous boxes of chocolate do they always wait to hand them round until friends come to tea. What ghouls they are, to be sure! Professor X who saved the lives of Doctor and Mrs F. sounds *profoundly* moved.[4] I should feel very tempted were I in Oxford to – hm – hm – better not. No doubt the secret police has steamed this letter over a cup of warm tea...

Goodbye. We will leave Lady Ottoline then. Perhaps if it is a very good strawberry season you might one day much later care to go over – she is not at all fierce. I must tell you, Mr Gerhardi, that you write the most delightful letters.

Yours very sincerely
Katherine Mansfield.

My new book I am terrified to say comes out on the 23rd. I had wanted to send you a copy; I shall not be able to. When I am rich I shall send you a copy *at once*.

MS ATL. *LKM* II. 184–6.

---

[1] Gerhardi's first novel, *Futility*, was soon to be published.

[2] In 'Mr and Mrs Williams', an incomplete story which Murry included in *The Dove's Nest* in 1923, there is the brief mention of 'Aunt Aggie's happy release.... After fifteen years in a wheelchair passing in and out of the little house at Ealing she had, to use the nurse's expression, "just glided away at the last."'.... One saw her, in her absurd purple velvet, steering carefully among the stars and whimpering faintly, as was her terrestrial wont, when the wheel jolted over a particularly large one.'

[3] A story KM may have heard from Koteliansky, a reference almost certainly to Anna Ivanovna Souvorina, the second wife of Aleksei Souvorin, Chekhov's friend and publisher.

[4] The *Daily News* (6 Feb. 1922), reported how a box of chocolates containing an unnamed powder had been sent to Dr Farrell, Vice-Chancellor of Oxford University. A visiting professor advised that the chocolates be examined rather than eaten.

To J. B. Pinker & Son, 8 February 1922

Victoria Palace Hotel | 6–8 Rue Blaise Desgoffe | Rue de Rennes
Paris
8 ii 1922

Dear Mr Pinker,

Many thanks for your letter. I will try and write another story for The
Sketch[1] as soon as possible. I am undergoing treatment here which will
make work rather difficult for the next few weeks.

I sincerely hope that many of your writers do not give you so much trouble
with correspondence. I am ashamed that you should have to write to me so often.

Yours sincerely
Katherine Mansfield

MS Newberry.

[1] No other story was written for the *Sketch*.

To J. B. Pinker & Son, 9 February 1922

Victoria Palace Hotel | 6–8 Rue Blaise Desgoffe | Rue de Rennes
Paris
9 ii 1922

Dear Mr Pinker

I beg to acknowledge with my grateful thanks the cheque for £12.2.11
received by me today.

Yours sincerely
Katherine Mansfield

Ms Newberry.

To Charlotte Beauchamp Perkins, 10 February 1922

Victoria Palace Hotel | 6–8 Rue Blaise Desgoffe | Rue de Rennes
Paris
10 ii 1922

My darling Marie,

You *do* write the most satisfactory letters! One seems to get so much out
of them; they've such a flavour, if you know what I mean. All the difference
between very dull cold mutton and very excellent lean beef with chutney &
a *crisp* salad! I start with an appetite and end with one.

It must be fun to be shopping. Its rather hard to realise that 'V' doesn't care a great deal about clothes. I should care if I were on a desert island & had to try on my hats & see the effect in the lagoon. Perhaps, though, Mack doesn't take them very seriously. That makes a difference. Jack is like a brother in that respect: I mean he talks them over and criticises them just as a brother does. Poor Ida has been flattening her nose against the windows in the Rue de la Paix and is completely demoralised for the moment. She can only talk about garments that appear to be moulded on, with heavy embroidery, russian backs & the fascinating new boleros. Fancy boleros coming back! Its such an absurd word too, isn't it. I expect by the time we are old dolmans will be all the rage again and I shall meet you – where? – flashing with jet bugles.

Yes, I do miss the chalet. Hotels are odious places, and I hate restaurants. But with this hope of getting better I can put up with anything. I don't *dare* look ahead, Marie. I feel just like a prisoner must feel who's been told there is a chance of his release. Its too much happiness to think of walking along by myself with nobody handing me a chair or offering me an arm or coming to meet me with a hot water bottie in one hand and a glass of milk in the other! If you have a small private God, say a prayer for me!

I wish I had seen J.B. It would have been a pleasure. I hope you will run across in April. Paris is no distance. One is at Charing X at ten oclock & here for dinner. My friend Anne Rice whose baby is my godson is coming over in March for a long pow-wow and Brett is coming over for the weekend. But don't ever feel you *must* come my dear. Its awful to do things for that reason.

Many thanks for the address. I shall send to Canada as I feel sure one couldn't get the preparation here. Its strange how difficult it is to find anything; it seems to be always "wrapt in mystery". I wish I did know a cure for chilblains. The worst of it is I am always reading infallible cures, deciding to remember them in case I know anyone who wants one, and then forgetting. They must be agonising things. Doesn't it mean that one's blood needs a tonic? I am sure they ought to be tackled from within. By the way I *have* discovered the most marvellous secret of growing hair where one *wants* it to grow. And that is – damp the head with rose water every night and fan it dry. I have twice the amount I had a few months ago.

Well, darling, I must end this letter. Forgive the writing. My block has no back and its against my knee. I hope this treatment is one of the marvels of X rays. If its not I shall go and hide among mountains for the rest of my short days.

I enclose two little bits of 'goo'. Do you ever see the Saturday Westminster? I have a serial in it, but its only going for 4 weeks – a small run.[1] My book comes out on the 23rd.

Give my love to little J. and big V. with very much for yourself.

Ever your devoted
K.

MS Newberry. TC cited *Exhibition*, 49.

¹ See p. 34, n.1

To Michael Sadleir, [12 February 1922]

Victoria Palace Hotel | 6 Rue Blaise DesGoffe | Rue de Rennes | Paris.

Monday.

Dear Michael Sadleir,

I hear from Jack, who has just joined me here, that he wrote to you asking you to send the copies of my book to Adelphi Terrace. This was a mistake on his part. Will you kindly have them sent to me here? Im so sorry to bother you.

Yours ever
Katherine Mansfield.

MS Targ.

To Ida Baker, 14 February 1922

[Victoria Palace Hotel, Rue Blaise Desgoffe, Rue de Rennes]

14.II.1922

Dear Ida,

I am writing to you so that you shall have a letter and because I want one from you. We have heard nothing from Mrs Maxwell about subletting. I think you'd better not even make enquiries until we do hear with Doctor H. on the spot to report to her.¹ It is annoying. We shall look v. silly if she says 'no' . . . A devil of a day here, a London fog outside the windows. Not a gleam of light. Perhaps to compensate immense meals have been served by the hotel. Whole eels with rings of potato round em, chickens in beds of rice. It doesn't bear thinking about. My laundry came home. Deciding that if I were sick I could afford to pay for it they charged me 5 francs for my pantalons & 5 for my camisoles. I should think they would charge for my pyjamas by the leg. What grasping devils these frenchies are. And I have just spilt lashings of ink on one of their old sheets and theres no Ida to run off cheerfully to get me citric acid as if it grew in her garden.

Jack is a tremendous shopper. There is a new teapot, bowls, terrine de foie gras, little brown loaf that looks as though it ought to have little brown legs to run away on. It is remarkable – more – how such a dreamy nature can care for another as he looks after me. He even brushed my hair last night. It was rather queer brushing but there it was.

By the way: will you send the Mercury with my story[2] in it to Romer W?[3] And will you buy another coconut for the birds? I cant bear to think they look in vain.

What has E. done with the newspapers? She has not sent on *one* & Jack asked her to. I suppose she has just thrown them away. Make her look after you properly. Please write and tell me how you found things and so on and what was the *feeling* of the place. I am longing to hear about everything. You mustn't be so silly as to imagine because I am such a horrible creature I don't love you. I am a kind of person under a curse, and as I don't and can't let others know of my curse you get it all. But if you knew how tenderly I feel about you after one of my outbreaks. You do know. I cant say 'nice' things to you or touch you. In fact I behave like a fiend. But ignore all that. Remember that through it all I love you and *understand*. That is always true.

Take care of yourself, ma chere

Katherine,

MS BL. *MLM*. 177.

[1] Mrs Maxwell was the owner of the Chalet des Sapins, her son Bernard Hudson a doctor and expert on tuberculosis.
[2] 'At the Bay'.
[3] Romer Webster, a friend suffering from severe tuberculosis.

To Dorothy Brett, 14 February 1922

[Victoria Palace Hotel, Rue Blaise Desgoffe, Rue de Rennes]
St. Valentine's Day

My dear Lamb,

As soon as I am in full possession of my legs again I shall have to walk abroad with a purse of gold and buy you presents. Even then I shan't be able to catch up. But Ill do my best. Ribbons – the last two are perfectly *celestial* – I really am beginning to feel flow out of your hat with white rabbits, canaries, and tight little rose buds. But here is this little book. It charms me beyond words! Im going to make it a Little-Great-Men-Book, an ever permanent note book. And coming on St. Valentine's very day. I always remember St V's Day. Its in one's diary, too. But it has a fascinating sound. Who was St. V?[1] A ravishing person, no doubt, young, very young, with a glorious voice... But this is true. How *ever* much you may think these lovely gifts mean to me they mean ever... so...much...more... I shall not forget them.

Now I want to answer your letter. I do hope your tooth is better. Why have we got teeth. Or why haven't we brass ones. I cling to mine but I feel they will all go one day, and the dentist is such a terrifying animal. I hate to think of you in the clutches of that chair. I always think of dear Tchekhov in Nice, with toothache, where he says "I was in such pain I crawled up the wall".[2] That just describes it. It is maddening and exhausting to have toothache; I do hope yours is over.

About Easter. Its a perfect plan. Its just the right time for Paris – April. Everything is still new-green and the sun is really warm and the first shadows of the new leaves (unlike all other shadows, so soft, so tender) are fluttering over the tables and on the grass. I think it is an excellent idea, too, to be here for May and June. For selfish reasons I like it too. We really shall have time to talk, and in Paris or anywhere outside England as far as I am concerned there is never that queer feeling that one is tied to the clock hand. One can go easily, in a leisurely way bask, take the air . . . Oh, Brett, let us look forward to this.

Where *is* your little house! It is somewhere – but where. Sometimes I think it must be in the branches of a tree. Do let me know. I think you are very wise not to take a large one. Little houses are always best. A house is like an ark – one rides the flood in it. Little ones bob over the waves and can rest on the extreme tops of mountains much better than great big ones. Can I be official godmother to the garden? I should like to STARTLE you with the most superb things and to send for seeds from far corners of the earth and have a boronia plant below the studio window. Do you know the scent of boronia? My grandma and I were very fond of going to a place called McNabs Tea gardens[3] and there we used to follow our noses and track down the boronia bushes. Oh how I must have tired the darling out! It doesn't bear thinking about.

I am amazed that the Hannays[4] have bought Thurlow Road. I thought they were penniless. But these penniless people always manage to afford what they want. I suppose we all do, more or less. Brett, I am so glad you know Koteliansky. I think he is one of the best human beings alive. He is *real* and not a coward and he has such fine feelings. One can always be absolutely safe with him. Perhaps that feeling of safety is almost the most precious of all. It means so terribly much. I hope Gertler's show goes off well.[5] Its not a very good moment for selling pictures or so I should think. There is an unrest in everyone. Its between light and dark, between winter and spring. People are neither open or closed. The moment to catch them is just a little later. I think the time for a picture-show or to publish a book is in the first days of real spring or just at the beginning of autumn. We are more alive then than at any other time. We are in the mood to receive. It seems to me one ought to link up all one's projects as much as possible with the earth's progress. The more I know of Life the more I realise it is profoundly influenced by certain laws. No matter how many people ignore them. If we obey them our work goes well; we get our desire. Its like studying the tides before we put out to sea in our fishing boat. We are all sailors, bending over a great map. We ought to choose the weather for our journey.

Murry is here. After an awful week last week of letters and telegrams (for when I said I thought it a good plan of his to stay in Switzerland he hated the idea of staying) he came last Saturday. It takes M. time to realise things and to find out what he does want. But two days was enough to disgust him with Switzerland. He will stay here now, and at the end of March we are going into a flat which we have found – awfully nice – high up – but absurdly furnished, like the Arabian Nights by Poiret.[6] Very sumptuous and exotic. When you come to see me a little black boy with a pineapple on his head will open the door. The Mountain is at Montana, settling up the house & looking after the pussy. This is an excellent hotel. We have two rooms at the end of a passage, cut off from the rest of the hotel with a bathroom and masses of hot water. Rooms cost from 13 francs a day. There is a lift of course and one can eat on the premises. If I were you Id come here at Easter. All rooms have hot and cold water. After 7 months in that cleanliness I feel water and soap are the great necessities. M. and I have settled down according to programme, as we always do. We work, play chess, read, make our tea and drink it out of nice small bowls. I can do nothing but get up and lie down, of course, and Manouhkin says in three weeks I shall have a real reaction & then be able to do even less than that for the next three weeks. Its rather like waiting to have an infant – newborn health. My horrid time ought to be just over by Easter.

I must begin work. Seven stories sit on the doorstep. One has its foot inside. It is called *The Fly*.[7] I must finish it today. This is a hard moment for work – don't you feel? Its hard to get *life* into it. The bud is not up yet. Oh spring, hurry, hurry! Every year I long more for spring.

Its a pig of a day – a London fog outside the windows and I have to pull my stockings on. Think of pulling ones stockings on like winking – without noticing even. Can that happen to me again?

Of course I will seize the first chance to speak of your ears.[8] My plan is to ask Manouhkin to the flat. At the clinique he is so busy and never alone for a moment. But Ill have a shot there, all the same. Its difficult too because he speaks hardly any french. Goodbye dear precious little artist. Ever your loving

Tig

MS Newberry. *LKM* II. 186–8.

[1] A Roman priest martyred *c*.269 AD.

[2] The appalling dentistry in Nice is described in a letter from Chekhov to his sister M. P. Chekhov, with the Russian expression 'to crawl up a wall in pain' (22 Feb. 1898).

[3] During KM's childhood, a popular tea-rooms, ornamental gardens and zoo at Lower Hutt, a short distance from Wellington city.

[4] Brett's landlords at 28 Thurlow Road.

[5] Mark Gertler's show at the Goupil Gallery confirmed him as a leading English painter.

[6] Paul Poiret (1879–1944), French couturier famous for modernizing and simplifying fashion for 'the new woman' before the First World War. As a designer for the Ballet Russes, he was influenced by vibrant oriental taste. His ensemble designs and extravagant parties drew on stylized motifs from translations of the Arabic classic, *The Thousand and One Nights*.

[7] 'The Fly', published in the *Nation and the Athenaeum* (18 Mar. 1922).

[8] Brett suffered from severe deafness.

To Ida Baker, 16 February 1922

[Victoria Palace Hotel, Rue Blaise Desgoffe, Rue de Rennes]

16.II.1922

Dear Ida

If the boxes are going to take such a long time (i.e. three weeks) to arrive I see no point whatever in sending them. They had far better come with you as your personal luggage even if you don't return for a month. I *can* manage more or less with what I have here. And Id rather do that than pay vast sums to have my clothes sent by post. I shall send you the keys today. But don't send the boxes. Let them wait until you are ready to leave Montana.

I don't think I care what Dr H. thinks of the climate of Paris . . .

Please try and sell the notepaper.

Yours

K.M.

Everything is quite all right here. But why repeat such *stupid* remarks about the climate of Paris. Its hard enough to have to bear it without being told so and so doesn't at all approve of it. What tactlessness! Dont you feel it! Please repeat to me NOT ONE word about what he says of the Manou-khin treatment. Id rather not hear.

My dear Ida

I open my letter to acknowledge yours.

(1) *Of course* we must have references! It is absolutely essential for many reasons.

(2) Ill post my keys tomorrow. Send as little as possible at that price (15 francs).

(3) Will you try the Palace[1] for selling skis. If you can get nothing they had better be stored as you suggest.

(4) Blow the old crepe de chine jumper. I shall never wear it again.

(5) No, *why* should Mrs M's letter come there?

(6) Why didn't you send the D.N? [*Daily News*]

(7) Why *not* give the address to the P.O. at once?

Mysteries!

It is serious about references, though. We are *sub*letting. The house isn't ours even. We have to account for everything to Mrs M. What mugs we would be to find all so "simple and satisfactory".

Thats all.

(8) Please call me K.M. – not K. I never feel like K.

(9) Jack must have the parcel from Collins *at once.* It is proofs![2] UNpack parcel & send as *printed matter* & chuck out Jacks original copy. He only wants the PRINTED PROOFS – not what is cut out of papers. Love to Wingley.[3]

MS BL.

[1] The Palace Hotel in Montana, a medical clinic as well as an hotel, where KM stayed overnight when she consulted Dr Hudson.

[2] Of *Pencillings*, a collection of Murry's reviews published by Collins in 1922.

[3] Ida Baker explained the background to these exasperated letters. 'I returned to Switzerland in mid-February expressly to deal with the chalet, for there were five months left of our tenure. . . . My first thought was to find another tenant . . . another possibility was to stay and take paying guests; but everything was surrounded by thorns made fierce by my poor knowledge of French. How could I find out about the cheapest way of sending Katherine her belongings? . . . What to do when faced with the law that one could not take in paying guests? How to get goods to the station, the post? It was all a nightmare!' (*MLM*, 176).

To Ida Baker, [18 February 1922]

[Victoria Palace Hotel, Rue Blaise Desgoffe, Rue de Rennes]

Saturday

Dear Ida,

Can you tell me (1) what my boxes would cost to send by rail and (2) how long they will take. I have been thinking it over. It seems from your card today there is a chance the chalet may not be let as soon as we had thought. In that case I can't do without my clothes. In fact I feel the need of them very much, so perhaps they had better come along as soon as you have the keys. Yes, that's best. They had better be sent at once.

If the chalet is not let I have been thinking what had better be done. These last few days have made me feel I don't want any flat before May. I prefer to stay here. Its simpler and it would be cheaper in the end – of that I am *certain*. Here one can tell what all costs to a $\frac{1}{2}$d – là-bas there is food, servant, concierge and all the unforeseen expenses . . . It is not very gay here but its clean and one is independent; one soon gets into a routine and is free to work. Its a good hotel and the people are decent. But if the chalet remains unlet it will mean a loss of about £50 and that is horrible. In fact I can't easily meet it. Also we shall have to keep it open and warmed and cared for. Here is a suggestion. What about you staying there until, May, keeping Ernestine, and taking in a married couple as pensionnaires? At not less than 32 francs a day the pair. Does the idea revolt you? As far as I can make out one would then pay for the heating, lighting, E's wages, your keep, and youd make a profit of £10 a month (that is allowing £1 a day for all expenses, i.e. food, heat, light, laundry). Id put them in the top double bedroom of course and *ask* 35 francs. Tell me what you think of this idea. It would be a terrific help if it could be done *easily*. No help at all, in fact a horror if you don't care about the idea or if it sounds difficult. It is indeed only a suggestion – an in case – to be answered as such – to be taken "lightly".

As I write I am conscious I exaggerate a bit and that is not fair to you. If I have to drop that money on the chalet – well I must drop it, that's all. But I want to tell you its a little bit hard to do so. The first fortnight here I spent in all £50. And I cant earn to keep up with it. This 'plan' would save your fares down and up again. There is that to consider. It would also give you your £8 a month clear and perhaps a little over. I want you to believe I am not just making use of you. I am treating you as my friend, asking you to share my present *minuses* in the hope I can ask you to share my future *pluses*.

Talk it over with me – will you?

Yours ever
Katherine

If my MS will not go into the box *in* Esher,[1] will you take it out of Esher & pack it separately at the bottom of the box. It would go then, I think. I must just 'risk' losing it. But don't let go of my shawl.

[On back of envelope] grey flowered silk off blue skirt. Would you make it into 'top' for me? *Lower* neck etc. ditto blue charmeuse sans lining.

MS BL. *MLM*, 177–8.

---

[1] Presumably a trunk once belonging to Dorothy Brett, whose father was the formidable Reginald Baliol Brett, 2nd Viscount Esher, eminent civil servant.

To Dorothy Brett, 18 February 1922

[Victoria Palace Hotel, Rue Blaise Desgoffe, Rue de Rennes]
Dear Brett,

The pink cyclamen has come and is in front of my vanity table. I am so very happy to have it. It will hang in my room wherever I am. Eventually I shall pay you back with a story. And even then I'll still be in your debt. I love cyclamen.

Forgive this card. I am desperately tired but I had to let you know at once. I will write again in a few days. But for the next week or so I shall be a fearfully dull [?]

But a loving one.

Tig

MS Texas.

To Charlotte Beauchamp Perkins, 19 February 1922

Victoria Palace Hotel | 6–8 Rue Blaise Desgoffe | Rue de Rennes | Paris

19 ii 1922

Dearest Marie,

I am so sorry to have had to send that wire.[1] To think you might be here now! But for the first week or two I did not have much reaction from these X rays. Now I do. Ten minutes after a séance I am so dead tired I feel as if I had swum across Wellington harbour in the wake of the Duco.[2] And that feeling goes on until Saturday evening. It is a mysterious business and my doctor (whose name is Ivan Manoukhin) says it will go on getting worse for five weeks. After that one begins to get better and by May he promises one will feel quite well! I feel as though I were about to faire un enfant. All my plans begin in May. But if it does all come true it will be little short of a miracle after these nearly *five* years.

When you come over in May you could not do better than come to this hotel. It is excellent. Very clean, very quiet, with boiling water day and night. And one can eat on the premises – which is a point – if one wants to. Jack and I seem to have been here for months. We always drop into a routine. That is the best of having regular work. One has to arrange ones life round it. Ida is back in Switzerland trying to sublet the chalet *and* looking after Wingley. I foresee that Wingley's travelling days are not over. Poor little chap! He will have to write his Memoirs later on.

Has V. returned to Canada? Is it this summer she thinks of bringing her boys over? Woodhay[3] must be quite a family seat. Are the bulbs up yet? Do tell me how your garden grows. Every year I feel *more* impatient to hear that the crocuses are really out and that the daffys are lifting their spears. I read in the paper the Dog's Mercury is in flower. But what is Dog's Mercury. And does the dog know? Is he pleased about it or does he just look at it and bolt it stem and all. Ask Kuri from his aunt Katherine.

I have been cosseting four yellow tulips all this last week and they are still radiant. Oh, how I love flowers! People always say it must be because I spent my childhood among all those gorgeous tropical trees and blossoms. But I don't seem to remember us making our daisy chains of magnolias – do you?

Well darling I have to finish a story for the good old Sketch[4] before tea. They have asked me to write them a series. The Sketch always reminds me of the morning room at '47'[5] . . .

With so much love

Ever your

K.

MS Newberry.

[1] The telegram asking her sister to postpone her visit does not survive.
[2] The steamer which sailed between Wellington city and Days Bay, on the other side of the harbour.
[3] The house in Surrey which Harold Beauchamp had bought for his widowed daughter.
[4] 'Taking the Veil', the *Sketch* (22 Feb. 1922).
[5] 47 Fitzherbert Terrace, the last Wellington home KM lived in, from May 1907 until she sailed for England in July 1908.

To Jeanne Beauchamp Renshaw, [19 February 1922]

[Victoria Palace Hotel, Rue Blaise Desgoffe, Rue des Rennes]

Paris. *Very* Sunday afternoon.

Jeanne dearest

Many thanks. It is rather funny we should have to send all the way to the li'l Canadian village from London and Paris! Almonte[1] must be a most useful spot to have beyond one's park walls. I shall be deeply grateful for the little pot and shall abide by your instructions. Its a mysterious operation – isn't it. Unhappily I shall have no one to roll their eyes at the marvellous result. But it can't be helped.

I am so awfully sorry to have put off you and Marie. Do come in May – Paris is perfect then and we shall be able to walk about and do a little (what Jack always calls) nose flattening. As far as *he* has flattened he says the shops are marvellous, especially the china shops. I have a special passion for china shops. Have you? He has bought already a very light grey teapot covered with tiny blue flowers for 1/6 which pours perfectly and would have cost *at least* 7/6 in Heals,[2] my dear! So save your pennies for May.

There is a whiff of some kind of exciting secret in your letter. Or do I dream it? I feel certain there was something in the air. Perhaps its only spring. And I do feel too that this year is going to be a lucky one. It has begun well which is half the battle. Yes, I am terrified to say my book is due on the 23rd. It is like waiting in the wings to come on to the stage. I wish I could learn my part all over again, but there is no time.

I am so glad you like DelaMare. He is a wonderful person as well as poet. Do you know his book The Three Mullar Mulgars?[3] It is the story of three monkeys – very nice monkeys – not like the ones in McNab's gardens. I am awfully fond of it.

Forgive this groggy writing. My fountain pen has failed me. Why do fountain pens always die so early. As soon as one has become really attached to them they curl up their nibs and spit their last. It is very sad.

Your devoted

K.

(I shall not forget Tuesday).

MS ATL.

---

[1] Her sister Vera lived in Almonte, Ontario.   [2] A store in Tottenham Court Road.
[3] Walter De La Mare, *The Three Mullar-Mulgars* (1910).

To Ida Baker, [20 February 1922]

[Victoria Palace Hotel, Rue Blaise Desgoffe, Rue de Rennes]

Monday.

Dear Ida

I am sorry you have had a cold. But what a good thing to have it away from me so that you could indulge yourself a little and be looked after. I expect you will grow healthy up there again with good air and no surprises for your nerves. I hope so.

Jack is posting the keys this afternoon. Send the boxes! I am longing for my clothes. It is too warm here for this heavy under-clothing. He has gone today to try and wrench away from the post the parcel you sent from Montana. Devilish difficulties! And I cant understand why. I had clothes sent from England & so on without a murmur. But here I must go in person to Heaven knows where between 9 & 11 only and so on. However, I refuse. We shall see what happens.

Tell anyone who asks my book is to be 'out' on Thursday the 23rd. I dont want to lose one single purchaser. Its no secret, you know.

Ive no idea what the paper cost. I would ask 25 francs for it. But there again I have not seen how much remains – haven't been to the drawer for months.

Its a glorious spring day here – quite warm. By the way your Mme de Maris[1] is a fraud, I think. What utter rubbish about moving her daughter 10 yards if the daughter suffers so from the noise and discomfort of that other house! I am afraid she tried always to talk big to you. I wonder if that champagne was real at Christmas or lemonade with savon fouetté. And – why don't you learn to ski? Jack wonders, too. What a chance!

Is the cat a pretty cat again? And my birds – are they there?

K.M.

MS BL.

---

[1] An acquaintance of Ida Baker's in Montana.

To Ida Baker, 21 February 1922

[Victoria Palace Hotel, Rue Blaise Desgoffe, Rue de Rennes]

21.II.1922

Dear Ida

I had a letter from you today written on Monday. I hope you have heard from me by now. The keys were sent off at long last today; I had to send them all as I didn't know which was which. What horrible weather you are having. Here it is fine and not fine – dull, silvery, not bad.

About the chauffage. Isn't it best to use electricity during the morning & part afternoon & to heat the chalet as from about 4 oclock onwards through the night. I can't help feeling it would be cheaper and of course you must get in more coal, and keep not too big a fire. *Warm* you must be.

Would you post Jacks M.S.S. in a registered envelope? What a man he is! The extraordinary thing is there will always be someone to find these things for him & to look after him. He is born like that. Many men are and many women are *not.*

Mrs Maxwell has sent more bills to pay i.e. for rates, taxes, servage and so on. I have never in my life heard of tenants who take a furnished house paying these things. I think her bills are a try on. I shall copy out the card she sent and ask you to take it to your friend Mr Nantermot and ask him if it is the custom for these things to be paid by us or by her. Make him say it is her job, but please be sure to tell me as we must write to the old lady.

The blue frock has been excavated. I have it on. Its a comfort to have it but I feel a bumpkin all the same.

I am v. glad little Wingley is calmer. Nothing short of that amount of snow would keep him at home. How is your cold? I wish I had some money for you. Do you want some? Tell me. We are quite settled down in this hotel and might have been here for months.

There are 3 spelling mistakes in your letter, Miss. One I must tell you. To lose a thing French 'perdre' has only one o; to loose a thing – to make it free has two o's. You never get this right. Its such a common mistake that you ought to avoid it. Chaddie always makes it.

You and Woodifield[1] seem to be having quite a courtship. Its a pity – but Ive said that before – –

K.M.

MS BL.

---

[1] A friend of KM's in Montana. As on several occasions in the past, she seems to resent the possibility that Ida Baker should encourage close friends or admirers on her own account. She recently had taken the name 'Woodifield' for a character in her story 'The Fly'.

To Elizabeth, Countess Russell, 21 February 1922

[Victoria Palace Hotel, Rue Blaise Desgoffe, Rue de Rennes]

21.II.1922

Most dear Elizabeth

It rains and rains here and then the sun shines and its silvery. Big drops hang along the balcony. John goes out and comes back with four anemones and a handful of leaves bright with rain. Its like spring. The woman in the room opposite has a wicker cage full of canaries. How can one possibly express in words the beauty of their quick little song rising, as it were, out of the very stones . . . I wonder what they dream about when she covers them at night, and what does that rapid flutter really mean.[1] And there sits the woman in her cage peering into theirs, hops down to the restaurant for her seed, splashes into a little too short bath. It is very strange.

We speak of you so often. John, after his beating at chess has had the satisfaction of teaching me. If he wallops me absolutely he remarks "A good game. You're getting on." If it is a draw he exclaims "My God, Im a complete idiot. Ive lost my head completely." This strikes me as very male. The gentle female would never dare to be so brutal. There is a look of Bertie about the knight – don't you think? And John Conrad[2] can be a little pawn attending.

We have settled down, shaken into this life as if we had been here for months. That is one blessed thing about work. It prepares a place for one everywhere. And though it would be awful to live in a hotel indefinitely, while we are waiting for the 'arrival', so zu sagen, its not too bad. I feel exactly as though I were going to have an infant in May. Everything dates from then. I am sure if the Faithful One were here she would begin making little caps. But she is not here, and the horrid fact is one is thankful. Of course I do, I must, feel undyingly grateful but oh the joy it is not to be watched! Men, in my experience, however much they may care for you, they do not watch you, they don't want to share your very shell in the way a woman does. One can issue forth and retire at will. But there is something about the persistent devotion of women (I expect its very noble) which is stifling! Or am I wrong.

John tells me there is a chance – just a chance – that we may meet in the summer in Bavaria. Elizabeth, it would be happiness! Warmth, flowers, long evenings, the smell of grass, the shadow of leaves on a table and funny things that make one laugh happening. Will it come true.

No, please let all the pride be mine that you are *my* cousin. If you knew how I feel it. I should like to write one story really good enough to offer you one day. Which reminds me that my unfortunate book is due to come on Thursday. When you open the parcel there will sound a squeak of terror!

I hope it is fine; I hope you are warm and that your work is going quickly. John is immersed in Plutarch's Lives.[3]

Accept my love

Katherine.

MS BL.

[1] A question that ends her last story, 'The Canary', written in early July, where the observing narrator concludes, 'But isn't it extraordinary that under his sweet, joyful little singing it was just this – sadness? – Ah, what is it? – that I heard.'

[2] Bertrand Russell's son John Conrad was then three months old.

[3] Plutarch (AD 45–125), Greek historian known mainly for his *Parallel Lives*, pairing the biographies of Greek and Roman historical figures.

To Ida Baker, [22 February 1922]

[Victoria Palace Hotel, Rue Blaise Desgoffes, Rue de Rennes]

Wednesday

D.I.

Please do not on any account send me any more clothes by letter post. Another notification has come this morning for a second parcel & it means all the trouble of going off to the bureau again. But apart from that I never imagined you would send me anything by letter post. It is far and away too expensive, in fact its a most shocking waste of money. I thought you intended to send whatever you did send by *parcel* post. Now I understand at last why you were asked 15 francs...

Yours
K.M.

Postcard BL.

To J. B. Pinker & Son, 22 February 1922

Victoria Palace Hotel | 6–8 Rue Blaise Desgoffe | Rue de Rennes
Paris
22 ii 1922

Dear Mr Pinker,

I enclose my new story for the Nation and The Athenaeum. Would you kindly forward it to Mr Massingham?[1] I send you a second copy in case you may care to try it in America.

Yours sincerely
Katherine Mansfield.

MS Newberry.

¹ Editor of the *Nation and the Athenaeum*, where 'The Fly' was published (18 Mar. 1922).

To Alice Jones, [22 February 1922]

Victoria Palace Hotel | 6–8 Rue Blaise Desgoffe | Rue de Rennes
Paris.

Wednesday

Dear Mrs Jones,

I am so very sorry to hear what a bad time your brave little Hugh is having. It must be an anxiety to you! Must he really have another operation for adenoids and tonsils on Saturday? I wonder if you have heard of the great success of a hospital in Chelsea¹ where children are treated for both without operating. I read a good deal about the whole subject recently in the Daily News but unfortunately I did not keep the letters. They made a strong case for *not* operating. But you must know a great deal more about these things than I do. I do hope that, in any case, Hugh will soon be better. Its warm and sunny again here; I hope it is in London. I shall try and get out and send him a little Easter gift.

With our very best wishes to you both

Yours sincerely
Katherine Mansfield Murry.

MS Texas.

¹ The Victoria Hospital for Children in Chelsea. Even in the 1920s, recurrent tonsilitis without antibiotics was a serious childhood condition, with a significant mortality rate. The only non-surgical method attempted was by the use of diathermy, radium or X-rays, each of them liable to serious complications.

To Ida Baker, [24 February 1922]

[Victoria Palace Hotel, Rue Blaise Desgoffe, Rue de Rennes]

Friday.

Dear Ida

Your Tuesday and Thursday letters have come. From them it seems you are waiting to hear from me *still* about the boxes. But your wire said you were sending them by G.V.¹ unless you heard. I naturally kept quiet, which meant SEND. Do please get them off at once! Anyway – Grande – Petit – as long as they are here.

We had better have all the bills, too, and settle them up. Yes we have decided to stay here and have entirely given up the idea of a flat. As a matter of fact I have begun to like being here in this hotel. It suits very well and the people are nice. I can work here, and am more independent than I have been for a long time. Even if the chalet were let I would not change.

No, don't turn my nightgowns into pyjamas. They'd better stay as they are, thanks awfully.

Its the first I have heard of E's 'character'.[2] But I will send her one.

You must think over the pension idea, won't you? I do *not* want you to do it if it is in the smallest degree distasteful to you. I feel I rather forced your hand and that was bad. My whole idea was to tide 'us' (you and me) over until May. Once this treatment is over I shall be able to give you some more money. I mean enough for you to live on. Until then its a little difficult. It seemed to me, it still seems, the best way out of a difficulty *all round*. I have just heard from Hudson too, and little Doctor Watts; they must be paid as I am no longer there.

I am thankful the coconut is back, and to hear that Wingley is turning into a respectable cat again. Why *does* he go out! I suppose, as you put Keatings[3] on him you have been bitten again. Have you? Tell me. It would clear the mystery up. I have had no sign of a bite. What a little devil he is. He brings them back in a matchbox and lets them loose.

Keep the chauffage going. See that second F? Its big, on purpose.[4] I gather from the way you speak you have been very ill indeed. Get better now & keep well. Eat and sleep. Sleep is the more important of the two because it helps ones mind equally with ones body.

Yours ever
K.M.

If there is enough of any of the wools in the house to make you a jumper give it to your Aylesburys[5] – won't you? Its such an opportunity to get a new good one. The *tan* thin wool would make stockings if it wasn't thick enough for a jumper. Take any of the wool you want. I can always replace it. Its a pity you cant knit yourself a complet – little cap with a pom-pom and all.

But you might make something for your little neffy,[6] surely, out of some of it.

Later.

I have broken open this letter to say after two mornings spent at the Post Office we have managed to get second parcel & found it contained 1 belt, 1 pr stockings. If it wasn't comic it would be too much of a good thing. Its a sight to make the evings themselves look down. There was a letter from you, too. I don't believe in your shivering & shaking because of my barks. That is fantastic. If you don't yet know the dog I keep you never will – –

Glad to know – very glad – about the birds. Why should it be extravagance. Buy another coconut if you like. I shall look at the bills & reply in the next letter. I am 'off' bills for today. My boxes – mythical, tantalising boxes, I 'note' are packed to perfection. But oh – why don't they come. You torment me – show them to me, & whip them away again. I freeze, I burn for my kimono, my Anne coat.[7] Tell Wingley to wriggle & stamp[8] until you take them to the post.

Roger sounds *very* nice. All the more reason you should knit him something. I don't care for John. I feel he was ill on purpose too, to get his parents attention away from R. That is natural enough, however.

I don't want your old money if you do keep a pension. The whole point is – it should pay for the house & E. and then pay you.

Thats enough of letter writing. My hand shakes because I have been writing very fast. Its not paralysis or the family wasting.

The Lord be with you.

K.M.

MS BL. *MLM*, 179.

[1] Grande Voiture, a fast postal rate.
[2] A reference to be written for Ernestine.
[3] A powder for fleas on animals.
[4] A reprimand to Ida for yet another spelling error.
[5] Young friends of Ida Baker in Montana.
[6] Roger, the son of Ida's sister in Rhodesia.
[7] A coat given to KM by Anne Drey.
[8] As Ida Baker explained, 'A quotation from Walter De La Mare's story *The Three Mullar-Mulgars*, 1910, about a tribe of monkeys burning down their own house to be warm and rejoicing in the great fire quite forgetting that in fact they would be much colder' (*MLM*, 179).

To Dorothy Brett, [26 February 1922]

[Victoria Palace Hotel, Rue Blaise Desgoffe, Rue des Rennes]

Sunday.

Cherie,

I must answer your letter at once because I like it frightfully. What is it doing in London today? Here it is spring. For days past it has been warm, blue & gold, sunny, faint, languishing, soft, lovely weather. Isn't it the same over there? The reckless lift boy says "dans un mois il serait plein été". That's the kind of large remark I love the French for. They have very nearly hung out their sun blinds; they have quite turned the puddings into little ices in frills. But why cant I send some of this weather over to you? Can't it be done? Look in the glass. If there is a very bright gay sunbeam flittering over your hair I sent it from Paris, expres. At any rate you *are* putting out new leaves, crepe de chine ones & baby ribbons ones. The craving for a new hat is fearful in the spring. A light, crisp, fresh new curled spring hat after these winter dowdies. I suffer from it now. If I had one I should wear it in bed! But the barber is cheaper. He came yesterday and gave a coup de fer to my wool. Now its all waves on top. (I have a *great* tendre for barbers[1].)

I not only know where your new house is. But I have been there & looked over one of three little houses in Pond Street. Three lambs they were – years and years ago before Anrep[2] was even born. I shall call you the little Queen B. when you are in yours, which is a kind of mixture of *you* & Queen Anne. Its much better to have a tiny wax bright hive. Everything will shine there. And then suppose you want to shut it up for a time you can just pop your thimble over the chimbley and all's hidden. No good leaving those great barracks to stare house breakers in the face and shout 'Look at *me*'...
(Do you realise I am working through your letter as I write)

About painting. I agree. Good as Gertler is I shall never forget seeing a ballet dancer of his – it was the last thing I saw of his – at his studio. A *ballet* dancer. A big ugly nasty female dressed in a cauliflower![3] I don't mean to be horrid; but I do not and cannot understand how he can paint such pictures. They are so dull they make one groan. Hang it all Brett – a picture must have *c h a r m* – or why look at it? Its the quality I call *tenderness* in writing: its the tone one gets in a really first chop musician. Without it you can be as solid as a bull & I don't see whats the good. As to Ethel Sands[4] – (isn't her name a master piece, *wouldn't* it be Ethel) her painting is a kind of 'dainty' affair which it doesn't do to think about. You feel that ultimately where, of all places, she ought to be a woman she is only a very charming satin bow. Forgive my coarseness but there it is! Talking about feeling. I had a shock yesterday. I thought my new book would enrage people because it has too much feeling – & there comes a big review talking of the 'merciless analysis of the man of science'. It's a mystery. If you do see my book read a story called The Voyage will you? Keep it if you like it...

See Elliot[5] has been to your Thursdays.[6] Yes he is an attractive creature; he is pathetic. He suffers from his feelings of powerlessness, He knows it. He feels weak. Its all disguise. That slow manner, that hesitation, side long glances and so on are *painful*. And the pity is he is too serious about himself, even a little bit absurd. But its natural; it's the fault of London, that. He wants kindly laughing at and setting free.

Yes, I love Koteliansky – no less.

(Look here – darling – what can I give you? Tell me. What is the great difficulty? Show it to me. Or – can't you... Don't you trust me? You *are* safe. You are wrong if you do not trust me. And why wait until we meet? Even this moment will not return. I have given up the idea of Time. There is no such person. There is the Past. That's true. But the Present and the Future are all one –)

Once I have settled down for a few months you must know De la Mare. He is a very wonderful man – beautiful. Now I have arrived at the word "primroses" & I see them. Delicate pinkish stems, and the earthy feeling as one picks them so close to the damp soil. I love their leaves too, and I like to kiss buds of primroses. One could kiss them away. They feel so marvellous.

But what about bluebells. Oh dear! Bluebells are just as good. White ones, faint blue ones that grow in shady hollows, very dark blue ones, pale ones. I had one whole spring full of bluebells one year with Lawrence.[7] I shall never forget it. And it was warm, not very sunny, the shadows raced over the silky grass & the cuckoos sang.

Later. I then got up had a big blue bath & rather a horrid lunch. Then played chess – rested for a couple of hours, had tea & foie gras sandwiches and a long discussion with M. on "literature". Now the light is lighted, outside theres a marvellous deep lilac sky and I shall work again until dinner. Its strange how nice it is here. One could scarcely be more free. The hotel servants are just a little bit impudent and that's nice, too. There is no servility. I meant to tell you the barber was in raptures with your still life. I think that's a great compliment, don't you? It grows before ones eyes said he, "il y a de la vie. Un movement dans les feuilles." Excellent criticism. He, good man, was small & fair & like all barbers smelt of a violet cachou and a hot iron. He begged, he implored me to go to a cinema near here. Downstairs it was a little mixed but upstairs on the balcon there were armchairs of such a size and beauty that one could sleep in them . . . Oh Brett, how I like *simple* people – not all simple people, some are simple pigs – but on the whole – how much more sympathetic than the Clive Bells[8] of this world. Whatever else they have – they are alive. What I cannot bear is this half existence, this life in the head alone. Its deadly boring.

I think my story for you will be about Canaries. The large cage opposite has fascinated me completely. I think & think about them – their feelings, their *dreams*, the life they led before they were caught, the difference between the two little pale fluffy ones who were born in captivity & their grandfather & grandmother who knew the South American forests and have seen the immense perfumed sea . . . Words cannot express the beauty of that high shrill little song rising out of the very stones. It seems one cannot escape Beauty – it is everywhere.

I must end this letter. I have just finished a queer story called *The Fly* about a fly that fell into the ink pot and a Bank Manager. I think it will come out in The Nation. The trouble with writing is that one seethes with stories. One ought to write one a day at least – but it is so tiring. *When* I am well I shall live always far away in distant spots where one can work and look undisturbed. No more literary society for me *ever*. As for London – the idea is too awful. I shall sneak up to Pond Street every now and again – very rarely indeed & Ill beg you not to let a soul know. Its no joke my dear to get the letters I do from people who want to meet one. Its frightening!

Don't leave me too long without letters. I have grown to look for you now and I cant do without you. Youre my friend. I miss you. See? Oh, one thing. When I *do* come will you ask the children to tea? I have had serious thoughts of adopting a little tiny Russian lately. In fact it is still in the back of my mind. It's a secret, though.

Easter this year is April 16th. That is March and a bit away. Come
April. Isn't it a divine word – and in all languages its so exquisite – Avril,
Avrilo. What a name for a book – April!

Forgive my writing. My hand is always stiff with work. Can you read it?
Yours ever, dear little artist.

Tig.

MS Newberry. *LKM* II. 188–90.

[1] There is a sympathetic portrait of a bereaved young barber in KM's story 'Revelations', published in the *Athenaeum* (11 Jun. 1920), then collected in *Bliss*.

[2] Brett would move at Easter into 6 Pond Street, Hampstead, next door to the Russian Boris Anrep (1883–1969), a sculptor and artist now best remembered for his mosaics in the National Gallery, London, and Westminster Cathedral.

[3] A painting KM had seen at Gertler's Penn Studio, Hampstead, in 1918.

[4] Ethel Sands (1873–1962), a wealthy American painter, one of the founders of the London Group.

[5] KM had met T. S. Eliot in 1917, and admired his poetry. Eliot however did not care for her, regarding her as 'a dangerous WOMAN' (see *CLKM* III. 292, n. 1).

[6] There were regular Thursday evening discussion groups, 'usually male', at Brett's house. 'At one time Brett was allowed to preside . . . because, as she said, she was too deaf to intervene' (*Mark Gertler, Selected Letters*, ed. Noel Carrington, 1965, editorial note, 185).

[7] KM passes over the strain when she and Murry shared a house with the Lawrences at Higher Tregerthen, near Zennor, Cornwall, from April to June 1916 (see *CLKM* I. 259–68).

[8] KM met Clive Bell, art critic and husband of Virginia Woolf's sister Vanessa, in 1915. He epitomized for KM the intellectualism and insincerity of what she called the 'Bloomsberries'.

To Michael Sadleir, 26 February 1922

Victoria Palace Hotel | 6/8 Rue Blaise Desgoffe | Rue de Rennes
Paris

26.II.1922

Dear Michael Sadleir,

Very many thanks for sending the copy of Bliss to Chapman & Hall.[1] I am
sorry the moment was an awkward one; I hope your strike will soon be over.

My books have come. The printing and general appearance is delightful, I think. I think its a little pity that the jacket is pink and can't help
feeling more hands would have reached it down from the shelves if it had
been citron yellow or a good blue.[2] Pink always makes me think of Lives of
Napoleon. But thats horribly ungracious – and please believe I am very
very sensible of the way 'Constable' has treated me.

I am glad there is to be no large edition.

Yours ever
Katherine Mansfield.

MS Targ.

[1] A London publishing house.

[2] The jacket was changed to red for the second edition, blue for the third.

To Ida Baker, [28 February 1922]

[Victoria Palace Hotel, Rue Blaise Desgoffe, Rue de Rennes]
Dear Ida

If I were you I would give up all idea of letting the chalet & if you are inclined to try the other scheme try it bang off. I feel sure the chalet will not let. Isn't the other scheme best anyway?

I am sure you are being too careful about money. Theres a false carefulness in your letters. I ∴ send you £2.2.0 which I don't want to hear of again. Don't put it down on a list! Spend it and don't tell me what you have bought. Also – are you having enough food? I mean by that decent meals – not bread or pudding. It is essential! You may shirk feeding properly just to torment yourself and me. Try not to. Remember what illness is like. You really have seen enough of it to impress even you. When you said you thought I might consider it "wicked extravagance" to buy another coconut for the birds you were being unfair, you know. That was a make-up out of your tormented past. Thank goodness I don't 'recognise' the remark as mine but neither do you really. Try not to give way to these feelings.

Have just had your Saturday letter. I am glad it is proved about the fleas. What a young monkey he is! Yes, stay there for a bit if you can stick it; I am sure it is the best plan. I smiled at your asking about the distressed gentlewomen. I am only waiting for *my* boxes to come to fall on them & *weed out*. But I have lost my poor distressed gentlewomen. Dear knows where I can send my bundil. I thought of asking the Daily Mail. One thing is certain – I must get rid of everything that I do not use. I cant go on carrying things all over the world that I never wear. Away with them all! But the danger is that if I do find a charity to take them I shall only be left with what I stand up in. Thats my mood today. A clean sweep of everything!

What a shame about Ernestine. Who was the woman. How dreadful. Poor good creature, I hope she has recovered. Please give my compliments to anyone – to the trees if you like. About the blue charmeuse top – quite! I agree absolutely! Most satisfactory! Quite! (That is not ingratitude. But my eyes can hardly read those directions. Take out, fill in, cut, leave, baste. I feel gizzy as Campbell[1] used to say.)

If you can stick it up there until the thaw and early spring I think you may be even a little bit happy. Yes, all goes well here – very well. The weather is lovely, but so warm. Those cursed long sleeved combinations! One feels like linen and ribbon bows.

I must work.

Yours ever
K.M.

Would you send me a Swiss stamp for 40?

MS BL.

[1] The Irish barrister Charles Henry Gordon Campbell, 2nd Baron Glenavy, and his wife Beatrice, became close friends of KM and Murry when they met in 1913.

To Dorothy Brett, 28 February 1922

[Victoria Palace Hotel, Rue Blaise Desgoffe, Rue de Rennes]
Tuesday

The pussy willows have come and they are lovely beyond words. Thank you very much indeed, please.

Tig

MS Texas.

To Charlotte Beauchamp Perkins, [late February 1922]

[Victoria Palace Hotel, Rue Blaise Desgoffe, Rue de Rennes]
Dearest Marie

In case you should think I am rather a little pig of a sneak not to send you a copy of my new book – its because I can't get copies over here for the moment – I mean extra copies. All I have had I have been obliged to send to journalists. Thats why.

Would you pass this first review on to Pa? It sounds very powerful, doesn't it. But it is rather my eye. *I* thought people would say I was rather sentimental!

What is the weather like in England. Here it is Spring – really Spring, sunny, absolutely warm and the kind of weather that makes one long to put out new leaves at any rate *one* new leaf in the shape of a hat. Don't you know that mood when you keep on imaging spring hats – curled and crisp and light after these substantial winter ones?

Forgive writing. I am in bed & my back has no backbone. I feel so much better – its almost frightening. Tell J. not to forget me.

Ever your devoted
K.

MS ATL.

To Sarah Gertrude Millin, [? early March 1922]

Permanent Address | c/o The Nation and | The Athenaeum | 10 Adelphi Terrace W.C.2 | London
March.

Dear Mrs Sarah Gertrude Millin[1]

Your letter makes me want to begin mine with "Do write again. Don't let this be your last letter. If ever you feel inclined for a talk with a fellow-writer summon me." I cannot tell you how glad I am to hear from you, how interested I am to know about your work. Are you really going to send me a copy of Adam's Rest² when it comes out? It would give me great pleasure to read it.

Now I am walking through the third page of your letter. Yes I do think it is "desolate" not to know another writer. One has a longing to talk about writing sometimes, to talk things over, to exchange impressions, to find out how other people work – what they find difficult, what they really aim at expressing – countless things like that. But there's another side to it. Let me tell you my experience. I am a 'Colonial'. I was born in New Zealand, I came to Europe to "complete my education" and when my parents thought that tremendous task was over I went back to New Zealand. I hated it. It seemed to me a small petty world; I longed for "my" kind of people and larger interests and so on. And after a struggle I did get out of the nest finally and came to London, at eighteen, *never* to return, said my disgusted heart. Since then Ive lived in England, France, Italy, Bavaria. Ive known literary society in plenty. But for the last four–five years I have been ill and have lived either in the S. of France or in a remote little chalet in Switzerland – always remote, always cut off, seeing hardly anybody, for months seeing really nobody except my husband and our servant and the cat and "the people who come to the back door". Its only in those years Ive really been able to work and always my thoughts and feelings go back to New Zealand – rediscovering it, finding beauty in it, re-living it. Its about my Aunt Fan who lived up the road I really want to write, and the man who sold goldfinches, and about a wet night on the wharf, and Tarana Street³ in the Spring. Really, I am sure it does a writer no good to be transplanted – it does harm. One reaps the glittering top of the field but there are no sheaves to bind. And there's something, disintegrating, false, *agitating* in that literary life. Its petty and stupid like a fashion. I think the only way to live as a writer is to draw upon one's real *familiar* life – to find the treasure in that as Olive Schreiner⁴ did. Our secret life, the life we return to over and over again, the "do you remember" life is always the past. And the curious thing is that if we describe this which seems to us so intensely personal, other people take it to themselves and understand it as if it were their own.

Does this sound as though Im dogmatising? I don't mean to be. But if you knew the numbers of writers who have begun full of promise and who have succumbed to London! My husband and I are determined never to live in cities, always to live 'remote' – to have our own life – where making jam and discovering a new bird and sitting on the stairs and growing the flowers we like best is – are – just as important as a new book. If one lives in literary society (I dont know why it *is* so but it is) it means giving up one's peace of mind, one's leisure – the best of life.

But Im writing as if to beg you to unpack your trunk, as if you were on the very point of leaving South Africa tomorrow. And that's absurd. But I am so awfully glad you have Africa to draw upon.

I am writing this letter in Paris where we are staying at [i.e.till] May. I am trying a new Xray treatment which is supposed to be very good for lungs. Its early spring, weather very lovely and gentle, the chestnut trees in bud, the hawthorn coming into flower in the Luxembourg Gardens. I can't go out, except to the clinic once a week but my husband is a very faithful messenger, He reports on it all for me, and goes to the Luxembourg Gardens every afternoon. We work hard – we are both very busy – and read a great deal. And both of us are longing to be back in the country. If this treatment succeeds at all we'll be gone in May. But its hard to write in a hotel. I can only do short things and think out long stories. Do you have anemones in South Africa. I have a big bowl of such beauties in this room. I should like to put them into my letter, especially the blue ones and a very lovely pearly white kind –

It is late – I must end this letter. Thank you again for yours. I warmly press your hand –

Katherine Mansfield.

MS Witwatersrand. *Selected*, 257–9.

[1] KM noted, 8 Feb., 'Heard from Sara Millin' (*KMN*, 324). She had warmly reviewed the South African writer's first novel, *The Dark River*, in the *Athenaeum* (20 Feb. 1920), praising its 'sudden view of a country and an experience', and urged Murry to print Millin's story, 'A Pair of Button Boots', in the *Athenaeum* (3 Sept. 1920). They had exchanged letters at that time (see *CLKM* IV. 8).

[2] Millin's third novel, published in 1922.

[3] An 'invented' name for an aunt in Wellington. 'Tarana' is the fictitious name she sometimes used for Tinakori Road, where she was born and spent her first five years, and where she lived again from 1894 until her early teens. Several of her relatives and family friends lived there or in neighbouring streets.

[4] Olive Schreiner (1855–1920) left South Africa for England in 1881, for a career as novelist and feminist. Her most celebrated work, *The Story of an African Farm*, was published in 1883.

To Charlotte Beauchamp Perkins and Jeanne Beauchamp Renshaw, 1 March 1922.

[Victoria Palace Hotel, Rue Blaise Desgoffe, Rue de Rennes]
Paris.

March 1st.

Darling Marie & Jeanne,

Will you accept a double letter this time? I can't tell you how I appreciated yours. Praise from other people is all very well but it is nothing compared to ones family. And you always have believed in me so generously Marie that I am more than glad I have repaid a little of that belief. It *is* only a little – a drop in the ocean. Ive got an awfully long way to go before I write a book that counts. I marvel at the kindness of the papers. But I expect some are saving up to give me a whacking.

So old V. has gone back to Canada. I wonder if I shall see her and her boys. She feels further away from me now that she has been over here and we have not met. Has she changed much? But thats hard for you to say for you have been seeing her during these years; we haven't met since John was new-born.[1] Elizabeth says Mack is very prosperous. I always thought he would be. I hope V. has her share of it – I mean *takes* her share. She always erred on the too generous side.

Your crocus border fills me with envy. How I love them! Its strange we should all of us Beauchamps have this passion for flowers. I shall never forget the large glass vase of sweet peas in my bedroom at Woodhay when I spent that weekend with you nor the easter lilies in the drawing-room. They sit in my mind, fresh and lovely for ever. At the moment I have a large bunch of the good old fashioned marigolds on my table, buds, leaves and all. *They* take me back to that black vase of ours at 75[2], one that you used to like to put mignonette in. It was a charming vase and well in the van of fashion, wasn't it. By the way do you remember the brown china bear on the top of the black what-not? I can see it! *And* I happened to read in the Daily News the other day that the "latest fashion" was a china mustard pot – very chic in the shape of a tomato. This was one of Aunt Kittys wedding presents at Clifton Terrace.[3] So wags the world.[4] I expect all her mustard pots have been sterling silver long ere now not only with the lion on them, but shaped into roaring lions with their tails for spoons. Oh dear, having got so far I do wish I could go further *and* find myself with you two dears, in your own home. I hope your weather has improved. It is still warm here. All the puddings have changed into little ices in frills and I was quite glad of the electric fan playing on my fried whiting at lunch! We shall have very special tea parties when you come in May. Jack has discovered a marvellous shop for cakes. Not those fat Jewish cakes with a bird's nest in icing on the top and a chocolate bird sitting on plaster of Paris eggs but short crisp delicious tiny ones – all kinds, little whiffs. These with his pate de foie sandwiches are a tea for the Duchess of Devonshire.[5] But I keep on planning what we shall do in May. I am so glad this hotel is so good. You and J. can have a very large double room with your private bathroom etc. for 25 francs a day. A most sumptuous bathroom and ones own little hall door shutting one off from the outside world. Such a point in an hotel. I do hate the feeling that everybody is running past ones very toes as one lies in bed. I am sure you will love Paris. It is a beautiful city. So airy, on such a noble scale. The taxi drivers range like lions seeking whom they may devour.[6] But the way to avoid that is to get into a taxi yourself and there you sit singing like Jonah (who must have been an optimist at heart) in the tummy of the whale.[7] I must end this letter, my dears. I am so busy and the old rays are working hard in my joints and bones. Would you let me have Papa's frisco address[8] on a card? Jack wants to write to him. So do I. I look forward to the little pot. Thank you J. dear.

With very much love to you both

Ever your devoted grateful

K.

[P.S.] Dear little mother's birthday month;[9] I thought of it when I woke this morning.

MS Newberry.

[1] Her sister Vera's son John was born in Feb. 1914.   [2] 75 Tinakori Road.

[3] Edith Dyer, known as Aunt Kitty, was the sister of KM's mother.

[4] 'Thus we may see,' quoth he, 'how the world wags.' *As You Like It*, II.7.26.

[5] Rather than a reference to the contemporary Duchess, KM seems to have in mind an elaborate Devonshire Tea, a traditional name for tea with scones, jam and cream.

[6] '... your adversary the devil, as a roaring lion, walketh about seeking whom he may devour' (I Peter 5:8).

[7] Praying, rather than singing (Jonah, 2: 1–9).

[8] Harold Beauchamp was then sailing to England.

[9] Annie Burnell, who died in Aug. 1918, was born on 24 Mar. 1864.

To Michael Sadleir, 1 March 1922

[Victoria Palace Hotel, Rue Blaise Desgoffe, Rue de Rennes]
Paris
1.III.1922

Dear Michael Sadleir,

I enclose this letter from *the Sketch*. By the same post I received one from the literary editor of *The Nation* saying that he had been sent no review copy but had had to telephone specially for it. This is indeed worrying especially in the case of two papers which, it stood to reason, would give the book a 'show'. And there is a Miss Evans, London Correspondent of the New Zealand Associated Press, 85 Fleet St E.C.4 who has written to me asking for a review copy. I think it would be of the greatest advantage to the book to let her have one.

Yours ever
Katherine Mansfield,

I think its very important that the weekly illustrated papers like The Sphere, The Tatler, Vogue etc. should have prompt review copies of my book. I fancy they do more good to the sales than any others. They gave me such long reviews last time.

MS Targ.

To Ida Baker, [2 March 1922]

[Victoria Palace Hotel, Rue Blaise Desgoffe, Rue de Rennes]
Send this cutting back – will you. I thought you might care to see the kind of thing they are saying.

My dear Ida

Your Saturday-Sunday letter gives me the impression that you are unhappy and restless. Is that so? Tell me! What do you do now. I suppose I hope and trust the 'settling' of the chalet is over. All is in order? And Ernestine capable of doing all that is to be done. Do you see your girls? Do you find people to talk to? How do you spend your days. I should be very interested to know. Dont *focus* on Wingley, tho' he is a nice cat. You have books in plenty and wool. But books & wool don't make life. I don't want you to feel stranded up there – cast away. 'At any rate' here is March. If you feel you can't stick it just take someone until the chaffauge is no longer necessary and then shut all up. If it must be so – it must. All is well here. I have lovely marigolds on my table. Flowers are cheap now. Reviews of my new book are pouring in. They are extremely favourable so far – much more so than Bliss. This is indeed surprising. I have not sent you a copy because I have not got one to send. The second 'batch' has never turned up. I had 2 letters today from *Father* enclosing letters from my cousins who live down the Sounds – all about hay and crops as high as the fences and perfect tirades about the spots on butterflies' wings and the colour of foxgloves. One of these letters was from a woman who has nine children – my uncle Stanleys[1] wife. The other from a woman who has about £150 a year all told to live on with her husband. Such people are the salt of the earth. The longer I live the more I realise that any life but a life remote, self-sufficient, simple, eager, and joyful, is not worth living. Cities are ashes. And people know it. They want the other thing; they feel their own 'poverty' in their several ways. It is sad. However the only way to help others is to live a good life oneself. Its a roundabout way but I see no other. But these Beauchamps down the Sounds are right. They are inheriting the earth. How I wish I could drive off in a little spring cart & have tea and scones with them & hear about Norman and Betty and Jess and the rest.[2] I hope your May doesn't go in for town life and trying to be a social success in Bulawayo. I hope Roger[3] gets a real chance. Youll have to gallop off there one day and look after him if you love him. Dont you feel that?

This is just a little chat with you. Now I must work. I have masses to do. Keep well!

Yours ever
K.M.

'Industrials' continue to inform me that your shares are 30/6. If its a trouble to find that book say so *at once*. Its just Jack's dreaminess – typical. But just send a card saying it cant be found. Nothing is simpler.

MS BL. *MLM*, 180.

¹ Aunt May, the wife of Stanley Beauchamp, Harold's younger brother.
² Beauchamp cousins, the children of Uncle Stanley.   ³ Ida's sister and nephew.

To Ida Baker, [3 March 1922]

[Victoria Palace Hotel, Rue Blaise Desgoffe, Rue de Rennes]

Friday

Dear Ida

Your Ash Wednesday letter is rather ashy. I confess it makes me feel impatient. Will you in reply to this speak out. Say exactly what you want. I can't tell. I must know.

(1) We can afford £2.10.0 to £3 a week quite well. I would greatly prefer the chalet *not* to be left. If it costs a little more it would be far better than leaving the keys with anyone.

(2) No. While you are there please keep Ernestine. That is final. So for heaven's sake don't go on about it. Rubbish! I must say it all sounds dreadfully ineffectual and vague & foolish. If a pensionnaire did 'turn up' as you say what about your servant? You must have one. In any case theres no need for E. to go. And no earthly need to work miracles at keeping down the chauffage. Ugh! I think its extremely ungracious about the cheque. However, if you feel like that you must act like that. Its not good or right or splendid. If you had said: 'How nice to get the cheque. I shall have a small spree on the spot.' I should have been delighted and warmed. As it is I dont feel at *all* warmed! Please take things a little more lightly. There is no need to go on 'worrying'. This is what happens when you burrow undergound & suggest and think and so on. Why? Its so unworthy! Please just say out what you mean. You know what I think now and its final. I cant write every day about it.

And I am sorry I can't send the reviews. I must keep them at present in case I need them for America.¹ I shall not throw them away however & later on if you care to see them I will send them to you then. If I get duplicates you shall have them.

But *cheer up*.

Yours ever

K.M.

Did you know Captain Bernhard² at the Palace is dead of influenza?

MS BL. *MLM*, 180–1.

[1] The first American edition of *The Garden Party* would be published by Alfred A. Knopf, New York, in May.
[2] An acquaintance at the Palace Hotel, Montana, a close friend of Elizabeth.

To William Gerhardi, 3 March 1922

[Victoria Palace Hotel, Rue Blaise Desgoffe, Rue de Rennes]
Paris
3. iii. 1922

Dear Mr Gerhardi,

I meant – only the first chapter – not the 'confession'.[1] No, I don't think thats a bit too 'tragic'. I can assure you I never stick pins into my cat; he's far more likely to stick pins into me.

And the reason why I used the 'florid'[2] image was that I was writing about a garden party. It seemed natural, then, that the day should close like a flower. People had been looking at flowers all the afternoon, you see.

Thank you for your delightful letter. I shall write en quelques jours. Just for the moment Im having rather a fight with the rayons X.

Yours ever
Katherine Mansfield.

Postcard ATL. *LKM* II. 190–1.

[1] References to the original version of his novel, *Futility*, which KM had read before recommending a publisher.
[2] Gerhardi noted (*LKM* II. 191), 'I had written jokingly to K.M. of a criticism [of the *Garden Party*] overheard on that score.'

To Richard Murry, 3 March 1922

Address safe till May   Victoria Palace Hotel | 6/8 Rue Blaise Desgoffe
Rue de Rennes | Paris
3.III.1922

Richard

I wrote to you a few days ago and now I cant remember if I sent that letter or if it disappeared. This is very bad. In case it didn't go I shall send this note for I am thinking of you. I wish you could see the marigolds on our table. They are like little stars in their own firmament – Jack bought them. They are good flowers to buy. Remember them when you set up house. They last well and are always so full of life. There is also, little painter brother, a fine sky this afternoon – big rolling clouds. In fact its spring here – and has been for days. Its quite warm. Once February is over there is no stopping it. All the same it seems almost too good to be true. I hardly dare to look ahead and think of what is in store for *all* of us. And I always have the feeling that there may have been other springs but wait till you see this one. Think of lying under a tree again or paddling in a sunny river or just feeling the air is enough.

Its nice here. It would be splendid if you managed to come across at Easter time. Jack and I seem to have settled down very easily. We have two good rooms and a bathroom at the end of a corridor down a little passage of our own. And its as private as if we were in a flat. We work, play chess, read, Jack goes out, we make our own tea and work again . . . and its all easy and pleasant. If this treatment is a success we shall spend the summer in Germany, in some small place. Richard I couldn't *live* in a city again, or I feel I could not. There seems no point in it. As for meeting people and so on Id rather see them just now and again, rarely, in intervals of work. Parties, and literary society – I flee from the very idea. And it seems to me one cant write anything worth the name unless one lives – really lives. Talk and all that kind of thing is a kind of frittering away. Perhaps that is old age. But the whole secret of doing anything is *to gather oneself together* and to live in a way that makes that as easy as it can be made. I don't see how it is to be done without solitude and a simple way of living. Do you agree? Tell me if you think its the beginning of my grey hairs.

Jack is very well. I think the change is really deep in Jack since he left London. He really is happier. If you come over I like to think of you both trundling off to look at pictures together.

I ought not to be writing this letter. I have a brain like a sawdust[1] this afternoon. But I wanted to just greet you – just wave as you go on your way. Give my love to Mother. *For*give my dullness.

I press your hand

Katherine.

MS R. Murry. *Adam* 370–5, 33.

---

[1] A phrase passed on as a family joke, from when an exasperated milkman told a persistently querying young Richard, 'You've got a brain like a sawdust' (Richard Murry note, ATL).

To J. B. Pinker & Son, [3 March 1922]

[Victoria Palace Hotel, Rue Blaise Desgoffe, Rue de Rennes]
Paris
3 iii 1922

Dear Mr Pinker

Many thanks for your letting me know that The Nation has taken The Fly. If you do not hear from Constable in the course of the next few days would it be possible to remind them of the cheque due on publication?.

Yours sincerely
Katherine Mansfield

Postcard Newberry.

To Ottoline Morrell, [4 March 1922]

[Victoria Palace Hotel, Rue Blaise Desgoffe, Rue de Rennes]

It's a joy to know that *The Garden Party* has given you pleasure and especially that you like my poor old girls, the 'Daughters'. I shall never forget lying on that wretched little sofa in Mentone writing that story. I couldn't stop. I wrote it all day and on my way back to bed sat down on the stairs and began scribbling the bit about the meringues.[1]

But your beautiful letter is too generous. I can't pretend praise isn't awfully nice! And especially as I have not heard one word from anyone whom I know personally since the book appeared. Reviews there have been and a few notes from strangers. But that's not at all the same. I didn't expect to hear and yet my 'subconscious mind' has been intensely interested in whether there are any letters or not! I don't think it's bad pride that makes one feel like that. It's the "You feel that too? You know what I was trying to say," feeling which will be with me while life lasts. Or so I feel. I treasure your letter, even though my *Garden Party* doesn't deserve it.

Brett sent me a couple of pages from *Vogue* with reproductions of Gertler's paintings.[2]

I cannot say what is happening. I believe – just blindly believe. After all illness is so utterly mysterious that I don't see why one shouldn't recover as mysteriously. I have a sneaking feeling all the time that Coué is really the man and Coué[3] would only charge 3d where this man squeezes three hundred francs a *time* out of me. Happily I have saved £100 so I can pay. But if it is all my eye at the end I shall look awfully silly and dear knows what will happen. But anything, anything to be out of the trap – to escape, to be free. Nobody understands that "depression" who has not known it. And one cannot ever explain it. It's one's own secret. And one goes on rebelling. Yes, I do, too. But don't you think we do feel it more than other people because of our love of life? Other people really don't care so much. They have long periods of indifference, when they almost might as well be ill. But this poignant, almost unbearable feeling that all is passing. People who are well do not and cannot understand what it is....

We have not seen one French person to talk to. We live here like hermits in our two caves at the end of a long dark passage. We work, play chess, read, M. goes out and does the shopping; we make tea and drink it out of dove-blue bowls. For some reason, it's all very nice. I should hate to live in a city – in fact I could not, but this is only to last till May. And out of my window I look on other windows and see the funny things people put on the window sills, a hyacinth, a canary, a bottle of milk, and there's a large piece of light, pale sky and a feeling of Spring. Real Spring. Yesterday on my way to the clinic I saw new leaves on one little tree. It's quite warm too and sunny. We have planned to go to Germany or to Austria this summer if – if – IF. . . . .

MS Texas. *LKM* II. 191–2.

[1] In Section VIII, 'The Daughters of the late Colonel'.
[2] An unsigned article, 'Mark Gertler', with the sub-title 'A Painter Who Knows How to Record the Natural Quality of Things', *Vogue* (late Feb. 1922, 68–9). Among the illustrations was his portrait of Koteliansky.
[3] Emile Coué (1857–1926), whose works and courses on self-mastery through mind control KM already had discussed with Ottoline Morrell, and referred to in a letter in late Dec. the previous year (*CLKM* IV. 357). Coué's *La Maîtrise de soi-même par l'autosuggestion consciente* was published in 1921.

To J. B. Pinker & Son, 5 March 1922

Victoria Palace Hotel | 6–8 Rue Blaise Desgoffe | Rue de Rennes | Paris
5 iii 1922

Dear Mr Pinker,
I have to thank you for a cheque for eighty-nine pounds fifteen shillings and sixpence, which I have received yesterday.[1]

Yours sincerely
Katherine Mansfield

MS Newberry.

[1] The first royalty payments for *The Garden Party*.

To Elizabeth, Countess Russell, 6 March 1922

[Victoria Palace Hotel, Rue Blaise Desgoffe, Rue de Rennes]
Paris
6.III.1922

Most dear Elizabeth,
Your letter about my Garden-Party was almost 'too good to be true'. I could not believe it; I kept taking peeps at it all day. I know of course you

are far too generous to me. But oh, dear Elizabeth how you make me long to deserve your praise. My stories aren't half good enough yet; I shall try with all my heart to make the next book better.

Its rather hard to work just now. I am at the moment when one feels the reaction. After five doses of Xrays one is hotted up inside like a furnace and one's very bones seem to be melting. I suppose this is the moment when real martyrs break into song but I can think of nothing but fern grots, cucumbers and fans, and they won't mix in a story. However this stage does not last.

I am glad you are going back to England – to spring. There is new green on some of the trees already and even those that are still bare have a hazy, *thoughtful* look. John brought me a bunch of daffodils yesterday, the little half wild kind that smell sweet – far lovelier than the others, I always think. Garden daffodils are so plump and self-contained, rather like ducks. I feel I shall never look at a bud or a flower again without thinking of you, and that there is an extra reason for saying – as one does – Praise Him – as one smells the petunias. I still 'in vacant or in pensive mood'[1] go over those bunches you brought last summer – disentangle the sweet peas, marvel at the stickiness of the petunia leaves, come upon a sprig of very blithe carnations and shiver at the almost unearthly freshness of the nasturtiums. What joy it is that these things cannot be taken away from us. Time seems to make them fairer than ever.

Did you receive a mysterious letter from Sir Henry Lunn asking for the pleasure of your company this summer.[2] He told me, in the letter you forwarded that he had asked us *both*. For a moment I saw us arriving with little bags at the foot of those beetling mountains and being met by a body of Lunn's Tours. How terrifying! But I should call myself 'the Rev.' if I did go. I am sure the lecture would open with a prayer and Mrs Arnold at the harmonium.

I want to say how sorry I am about Major Bernhard. Its such a violent change of subject – but then Death always is. I felt I knew him; I used to ask Dr H. about him and the last news was 'much better'. And now May will come and he won't get up and feel the sun – poor man!

We both send our loves

Katherine.

MS BL.

---

[1] William Wordsworth, 'I wandered lonely as a cloud' (1807).

[2] Sir Henry Lunn, father of Murry's friend, the biographer and critic Hugh Kingsmill (1889–1949), established the Lunn Travel Agency, an early organizer of cruise ships and group tours. He had invited KM and Elizabeth to speak as 'celebrities'.

To Ida Baker, [7 March 1922]

[Victoria Palace Hotel, Rue Blaise Desgoffe, Rue de Rennes]

Told you your shares are now 32/6.
Tuesday. Warm, thundery weather.
Is your red dress a success?

My dear Ida

Thats the kind of letter for me! Now keep that in mind as your ideal, 'focus' on it and Ill never be cross again. I cannot tell you how relieved I am to know what you are doing and that you are happy doing it. Thats the important thing. At four oclock this morning I had decided to write to you again and really tell you what I thought of you for keeping me for so long without any detailed news. Nothing but chauffage and money! When I wanted to know what you were doing, thinking, feeling. However, this is a noble effort and so I say no more Betsy.[1]

Alas for the Distressed Gentlewomen. How can I get this vast parcel across? I shall have to write to the English clergyman in Paris if I can find his address somehow. But there is so much that they (the poor) would call fancy dress – little jackets and so on. As to woven combinations (the very height of fancy dress) I seem to have collected the things or they have bred. They are my horror and my box was stuffed with them like peas in a pod. Away they *must* go. All my things looked rather as though they had been washed through the customs – they are very much exhausted. But even a change is such a relief that I fully expect a low hiss of admiration when I go to lunch today in different shoes. I suppose your Miss Yates[2] would not know of a worthy charity in Paris that would call for a bundle? Is it worth asking?

Yes, large towns are the absolute devil! Oh, how glad I shall be to get away. The difficulty to work is really appaling. One gets no distraction. By distraction I mean the sky and the grass and trees & little birds. I absolutely *pine* for the country (not English). I could kiss the grass. Its true there is a jampot & a jug in my room full of small daffodils. But exquisite though they are they keep on making me wonder where they grow. Its wickedness to live among stones and chimneys. I keep on thinking of lying under a tree in some well hidden place (alive not dead.) But this is not a complaint. It may have the ghost of a moral in it, a "dont settle in a town whatever you do". But I don't think you will. Do let me see Olive's letter.

I hope your 3 girls[3] turn up & not the family. I wish you could stay up there for a bit if you like it. It seems to me *right* for the moment. You felt the place suited you spiritually when you just got to know it & that was the right feeling, I believe. I wonder if the Palace[4] would be tolerable? Another small barbed thrust "I saw you in the Palace mood . . . " I don't care. I do think it might be very interesting. Hudson is an extraordinary decent man – really he is. I have had quite remarkably simple nice letters from him here. He may be stupid but all doctors are that. And I always rather took to that matron. However – its a long way off. Wingley I presume would be a kind of Red Cross *scout*. Which reminds me. After I had unpacked the boxes I had all the symptoms of terrific bites. They have gone off this morning. But I was certain last night that Wing had carefully put in a flea for a surprise for me. Have you ever found one of the biters? Are they fleas or what?

Yes, I was glad to hear from Pa. I began of course to plan a visit to N.Z. with Jack – to start this autumn, late, to return at the end of March. I wish I could work it. I should like it more than anything in the world. It would be the compensation prize of prizes. I dream of driving out to Karori in an open cab & showing Jack the Karori school.[5] But I'm afraid it will stay a dream. Father will be over here in June. My 'success' makes a difference to him, naturally.

I feel you don't want to jump to Rhodesia just now. Well, there's no hurry is there. You can wait & be godmother to Roger's first. But try to keep in touch with him whatever you do. May is – all she is – I don't know – but you can give him a great deal that she has no idea of & never will. I see her John[6] is going to be a Vera's John. He too is ugly and beyond words second fiddle to Andrew. Its very hard on the children. But warm blooded women have a passion for their first born, and always have had.

I have had letters from Elizabeth, Chaddie Waterlow[7] about the book which are a great joy. Letters from strangers, too, and 'my' undergraduate[8] (*pages* from him) & Clement Shorter the 'Sphere' man who asked for a portrait for publication and has ordered 12 stories to be ready in July. This is no less than staggering. I enclose the Times review.[9] Please return it.

Jack, who read my card to you, said off his own bat hed order you a copy to be sent direct from London. He also said off his own bat "Of course she won't believe it was I who did it." Well, it was. Thank you for the grey satin top with all its little blanket stitches. They make me smile. My writing case looks excessively sumptuous here. It reminds me of the Ida I love. Not because of what it cost. *No.* But the 'impulse' – the gesture – what you call the 'perfect thing'. It carries me back back to Isola Bella.[10] Oh, memory! And back I go to the Casetta and the olive tree before and cotton vine along the twisted fence and the red roses and big starry-eyed daisies. Menton seems to hold years of life. How hard it is to escape from places. However carefully one goes they hold you – you leave little bits of yourself fluttering on the fences – little rags and shreds of your very life. But a queer thing is – this is personal – however painful a thing has been when I look back it is no longer painful, or no more painful than music is. In fact it is just that. *Now* when I hear the sea at the Casetta[11] its unbearably beautiful.

I must begin working. Ill never be a Wealthy Woman. I write like this because I write at such a pace. I cant manage it otherwise. Here is some money. Be well! Be happy! Eat! Sleep!

Yours ever

K.M.

MS BL. *MLM*, 182–4.

[1] An affectionate nickname used for both Murry and Ida.

[2] Another friend of Ida's.

[3] Susie de Perrot, a daughter of the Suchard chocolate maker, and two Irish sisters, the Aylesburys, came to share the chalet with Ida as a 'group of friends' and not as '*pensionaires*' (*MLM*, 182).

[4] The Palace clinic and hotel. Ida had worked there for a time.

[5] KM's first school in Wellington, when she lived at 'Chesney Wold' at the end of the Karori valley from Easter 1893 to mid-1898.

[6] Roger and John, the sons of Ida's sister May.

[7] Charlotte Beauchamp, Elizabeth's elder sister, was married to George Waterlow, heir to Waterlow and Son, City Stationers.

[8] William Gerhardi.

[9] No review appeared in *The Times*. KM must mean that in the *TLS*, unsigned, by A. S. McDowall (2 Mar. 1922).

[10] The villa at Menton she shared with Ida from Sept. 1920 to early May 1921.

[11] KM was at the Casetta Deerholm, Ospedaletti, from Sept. 1919 to Jan. 1920.

To Clement Shorter,[1] *7 March 1922*

Victoria Palace Hotel | 6–8 Rue Blaise Desgoffe | Rue de Rennes | Paris

7 iii 1922

Dear Mr Clement Shorter,

I felt the very least I could do was to send you my book as a small token of my gratitude for your generous encouragement. And now I am to have the pleasure of working for you again! I shall be delighted to write the stories as you suggest.[2] If I send you the first six in June and the second in August – would that be satisfactory?

I wish I could look forward to visiting England this summer. But it is a remote possibility. I have left Switzerland and come to Paris to try an X ray treatment which promises new wings for old. But it is all promise for the moment.

This little Swiss photograph is the only one I have. I hope it will be of use.

Believe me to be

Yours very sincerely – very gratefully

Katherine Middleton Murry.

MS ATL.

[1] Clement King Shorter (1857–1926). In a long career as literary journalist, Shorter had founded the *Sketch*, the *Tatler*, and in 1900, the *Sphere*, which he edited until 1926. He was also an authority on the Brontes. His uncompleted *C.K.S: an autobiography*, ed. J. M. Bulloch, was published in 1927.

[2] Seven of KM's stories, 'The Singing Lesson', 'Sixpence', 'Mr and Mrs Dove', 'An Ideal Family', 'Her First Ball', 'The Voyage', and 'Marriage a la Mode', appeared in the *Sphere* in 1922. Shorter paid her at the handsome rate of ten guineas a story. None of the work promised here for later in 1922 was delivered.

To Dorothy Brett, 9 March 1922

[Victoria Palace Hotel, Rue Blaise Desgoffe, Rue de Rennes]

9 iii 1922

Dearest Brett

I was v. glad to hear from you though you sounded rather 'distracted'. Who is Valentine?[1] And if she interferes with your painting why is she there? And why should not intellectuals love? What a queer idea! Whose is it? As for the Bloomsburys[2] I never give them a thought. Do they still exist. They are rather pathetic in their way, but bad people to think about or consider – a bad influence. And what have I to guard against? It sounds very frightening. As to my being humble – oh dear. Thats between me and my God. I should retire behind 500 fans if anyone ever *told* me to be humble! You don't imagine that reviews and letters and requests for photographs and so on make me proud – do you? Its a deep deep joy to know one gives pleasure to others but to be told that increases ones store of *love* not *pride*. Also what has it got to do with ones work? I know what I have done and what I must do, nothing and nobody can change that.

A whiff of London came from the last pages of your letter – a whiff of years and years ago, a kind of ashy feeling. Oh, I shall never go back to England again except en passant. Anywhere anywhere but England! As I write theres a sound of sweet scolding from the pigeons outside. Now it rains, now its sunny. The March lion is chasing the March lamb but not very seriously – the lamb doesn't mind much. They have an understanding. I was reading La Fontaine's Fables in bed early. Do you know them? They are *fearfully* nice – too nice for words. What a character the ant is – a little drop of bitterness and fury and slamming her door in everyone's face; and the frog – I am so sorry for him. He had a sister, too, she should have warned him. Instead she stood by and gloated.[3] La Fontaine must have been an adorable man – a kind of Fabre,[4] very distrait very amorous. He didn't even know his own children. He *forgot* their faces and passed them by in the street. I don't expect they cared.

France is a remarkable country. It is I suppose the most civilised country in the world. Book shops swarm in Paris and the newspapers are written in a way that English people would not stand for one moment. There's practically *no* police news. True, they did write about Landru's[5] execution, but so well it might have been de Maupassant![6]

They are corrupt and rotten politically, thats true. But oh, how they know how to live! And there is always the feeling that Art has its place, is accepted by everybody, by the servants, by the rubbishman as well as by all others as something important, necessary, to be proud of. Thats what makes living in France such a rest. If you stop your taxi to look at a tree the driver says "en effet cet' arbre est bien jolie" and ten to one moves his arms like branches. I learned more about France from my servant at Menton than anywhere.[7] She was *pure* French, highly highly civilised, nervous, eager, and she would have understood anything on earth you wished to explain to her – in the artistic sense. The fact is they are always *alive*, never indifferent as the English are. England has political freedom (a terrific great thing) and poetry and lovely careless lavish green country. But Id much rather admire it from afar. English people are I think superior Germans (10 years hard labour for that remark). But its true. They are the German ideal. I was reading Goethe on the subject the other day. He had a tremendous admiration for them.[8] But all through it one felt "so might we Germans be if only we knocked the heads of our police off." Its fascinating to think about nations and their significance in the history of the world. I mean in the spiritual history. Which reminds me Ive read lately 2 amazing books about present day Russia – one by Merezhkovsky and Zinaida Hippius[9] and the other by Bunin. It is a very extraordinary thing that Russia can be there at our back door at furthest, and we know nothing, pay no attention, hear nothing in English. These books were in French. Both were full of *threats* – "You may think you have escaped. But you have not escaped. What has happened to us will happen to you. And worse. Because you have not heard our prayers." The ghastly horror and terror of that life in Petrograd is impossible to imagine. One must read it to know about it. But English people, people like us, would never survive as some of these Russian intellectuals have survived. We would die of so many things – vermin, fright, cold, hunger, even if we were not assassinated. At this present moment Life in Russia is rather like it was four centuries ago. It has simply gone back four centuries. And anyone who sympathises with Bolshevism has much to answer for. Dont you think that the head of Lenin is terrifying? Whenever I see his picture it comes over me – it is like the head of something between an awful serpent and a gigantic bug. Russia is at present like an enormous hole in the wall letting in Asia. I wonder what *will* happen, even in our little time.

Yes, Princess Mary's wedding seems to have been no end of a wedding. Even the French papers were flooded with it. I don't think I believe that about the chairs. The same thing has been said about every such occasion. Its always said. I think its the kind of joke they make up on the Stock Exchange and dirty minded Bank Managers enjoy – a *City* joke. Perhaps its true. No, it doesn't give me the creeps...

But do you really feel all beauty is marred by ugliness and the lovely woman has bad teeth? I don't feel quite that. For it seems to me if Beauty were absolute it would no longer be the kind of Beauty it is. Beauty triumphs over ugliness in Life. Thats what I feel. And that marvellous triumph is what I long to express. The poor man cries and the tears glitter in his beard and that is so beautiful one could bow down. Why? Nobody can say. I sit in a waiting room where all is ugly, where its dirty, dull, dreadful, where sick people waiting with me to see the doctor are all marked by suffering and sorrow. And a very poor workman comes in, takes off his cap humbly, beautifully, walks on tiptoe, has a look as though he were in church, has a look as though he believed behind that doctor's door there shone the miracle of *healing*. And all is changed, all is marvellous. Its only then that one sees for the first time what is happening. No, I don't believe in your frowsty housemaids, really. Life is, all at one and the same time, far more mysterious and far simpler than we know. Its like religion in that. If we want to have faith, and without faith we die, we must *learn to accept*. Thats how it seems to me.

How is your big still life, dearest? Dont let those people 'worry' you. Are there daffys in London yet. My pussies lasted & lasted and were a *perfect surprise*.[10] I embrace you.

Tig who loves you.

MS Newberry. *LKM* II. 192–5.

---

[1] Valentine Dobrée (1894–1974), who as Gladys Brooke-Peche studied at the Slade School of Art with Brett, and would later achieve a modest reputation as both painter and writer. She was married to the literary scholar and essayist Bonamy Dobrée (1891–1974).

[2] KM's dismissive term for the artists and intellectuals of the 'Bloomsbury Group', some of whom, especially Virginia Woolf, she had once been close to.

[3] Jean De La Fontaine (1621–95), prolific poet and fabulist, whose celebrated *Fables* appeared in three volumes. KM refers to two fables in Livre I of the first volume (1668), 'La Cigale et la Fourmi', and 'La Grenouille qui se veut faire aussi grosse que le Boeuf'.

[4] Jean-Henri Fabre (1823–1915), poet and scientist whose ten-volume study of insect life, *Souvenirs entemologiques*, was valued as literature as well as science. KM quoted his verse in a letter to Murry (3 Feb. 1918); (see *CLKM* II. 52).

[5] Henri Landru, the witty and urbane French con-man who, during the First World War, seduced then murdered ten women and profited from their finances. He was executed in Feb. 1922.

[6] Guy de Maupassant (1850–93), journalist and novelist, at his most original in short stories.

[7] The widow Marie, whom KM described as 'a most *remarkable* type. . . . Oh, how I love people who feel deeply. How restful it is to live with them even in their 'excitement'.' After several months, however, she had become 'The serpent in the kitchen', and a considerable trial (see *CLKM* IV. 59, 196).

[8] The *Gespräche mit Goethe* includes numerous admiring references by Goethe to the English. KM's comments refer to the entry for 12 Mar. 1828, where he expresses his approval of the self-confidence and naturalness he found in young Englishmen visiting Weimar.

[9] Dmitri Merezhkovsky (1865–1941), religious philosopher and editor, and his wife Zinaida Hippius (1867–1945), symbolist poet, novelist and essayist, emigrated to Paris in 1919. They were part of the same Russian émigré circle as Manoukhin, through whom KM came to read Merezhkovsky's *Le*

Règne de l'Antéchrist, and Hippius's *Mon Journal sous la Terreur*, translated from Russian and published in French in one volume, 1922.

[10] Brett noted on the letter, 'The pussies were a bunch of Pussy Willows I sent over. Afterwards I found Paris full of them!'

To Michael Sadleir, 9 March 1922

Victoria Palace Hotel | 6/8 Rue Blaise Desgoffe | Rue de Rennes | Paris
9.III.1922

Dear Michael Sadleir,

When things are more settled may I have that second half dozen copies of The Garden Party sent to me?

Dont you think an extract from the D. News review coupled with that of Time and Tide would make a good ad?[1] I wonder what I have done to the T. and T. lady to make her so fierce. Its frightening.

Yours ever
Katherine Mansfield.

MS Targ.

[1] An admiring review by R. Ellis Roberts, *Daily News* (27 Feb. 1922), and a severely aggressive one by Mary Agnes Hamilton, *Time and Tide* (3 Mar. 1922).

To Violet Schiff, [? early March 1922]

Victoria Palace Hotel | 6/8 Rue Blaise Desgoffe | Rue de Rennes

My dear Violet

I have just received your letter which was posted on to me from the office. Will you forgive me but I cant see anybody before May at earliest. I am trying a new treatment and until I know whether its in the least successful or not I simply cant see anyone. That sounds horribly ungracious. I wish I had not to write it. Murry would be delighted to see you both. Do let him know when he may come and call upon you. I hope you'll find Paris agreeable. When its fine its very very fine.

With love to you both.

Yours ever
K.M.

MS BL.

To Ida Baker, [11 March 1922]

[Victoria Palace Hotel, Rue Blaise Desgoffes, Rue de Rennes]
Dont send Js letter back.
Dear Ida

Thank you for the letters. I return them in case you want them back. Olive[1] sounds very happy – a proper little wife. She might have married a young Pilgrim Father in 1624.[2] 'Diana' is rather a painful name, isn't it – awful name in fact when there are so many simple ones. But I expect by the time she gets to her youngest she'll be thankful to take plain Anne or Lucy. Her pride in the 2 stitches amused me, too. She might have been having them once a year for the past 10 years. However, she sounds content, and how much better than wheeling the pram to Selfridges![3]

John Suttons[4] letter was 'nice', too. Honest, decent – letter of a plain man. Wherever you go children seem to crop up like mushrooms. Your old age will be black with children. If you marry you will have three at a time to serve you right for having waited so long. Why is this?

About the clothes. I am afraid my bundle would not do for a jumble sale. Old combinations, knickers etc could never be displayed before the curate. You cant have a jumble sale without a curate. If the A. [Aylesbury] girls really do want a large unwieldy parcel about the size of a large pillow they are thrice welcome. But warn them – really warn them! And wouldn't they perhaps bring that blue slip & post it in Paris? It would get here more quickly. My shawl mustn't go through the post unless necessary. Its too valuable. Perhaps later on someone whom you know would deliver it here ... The slip is just what I want, thank you. I wear it *outside* with my blue serge marine coat and skirt.

Tell me: Does E. still want her character? I must send it. Is she happy? Do you need money? Please reply to these questions.

Yes, I sent you a card the day before I wrote to you last about the keys of my boxes. I suppose it went astray. I feel letters must have gone astray from that end, too. But perhaps not.

This letter which I send from J. speaks for itself![5] I had a terrific adventure with her dipilatory. It certainly does remove hair. It would remove anything – I think it is gunpowder. However I shall try again. I had an afternoon when I thought I was disfigured for life and should have to paint my whole face navy blue to match my upper lip. Its awful stuff to get off. What a curious, secret life one does lead to be sure!

I heard from Elizabeth yesterday that the weather was wretched. She leaves for London today.

You asked me about my health and so on. Ida, I find it so hard to write about such things. It disgusts me to talk about my health – it seems unnatural always & always will. Well – let – me see – I am in the middle of the 'grande réaction' which comes after the 5th seance. So for one fortnight I shall be more ill in every way, as I *am*. I get up for lunch but thats all. Everything is very satisfactory, in every way. It could not be better. We seem to have rediscovered all our old shops – Ferguson's bread shop, Conté for petits fours – and so on. Jack prides himself *very* much on his shopping and on his tea. I must say we have excellent tea – the real old fashioned kind.

The weather is dark, thundery, with squalls of wind & rain, then its sunny again. Very big raindrops, like stars. Pigeons scolding sweetly on the roofs, and someone playing Chopin beyond words. That is March here. So glad you see poor Woodifield. Im afraid he is really very ill, and I *know* he is frightened. How are you off for SHOES? What are you wearing on your feet? Are there nails in your boots? Why not? Be well. Be happy.

K.M.

MS BL.

[1] She, and others mentioned in the first paragraph, are presumably Rhodesian friends or family in the letters Ida sent on.

[2] The English Puritans who founded the colony of Plymouth, Massachusetts.

[3] A large department store in Oxford Street.

[4] The husband of one of Ida's English friends.

[5] KM's sister Jeanne had sent details on how correctly to use a depilatory cream.

To Charlotte Beauchamp Perkins, 11 March 1922

[Victoria Palace Hotel, Rue Blaise Desgoffe, Rue de Rennes]
Paris
11 iii 1922

Should you ever need it
Tel. address here is
Victorpal Paris.

Marie darling

After sending off that wire I remembered you had the telegraphic address of this hotel. It was too late to do anything. I feel horrified at my carelessness and especially when I received your reply... Please accept these five shillings and forgive me. I think my letters to you must have been storm bound & as I was particularly anxious to catch Pa at Frisco it seemed to me a wire was the best idea.

Please thank J. for her letter & cuttings. I was much amused to read of the Silver Weddin'.[1] What grandeur! I saw it all, especially Franks button-hole. Fancy Uncle Sid (from Napier) there and old Aunt Aggie.[2] It was too marvellous. Lulu's letter too in the paper made me laugh. Her comment re the hotel late dinner "no trouble with servants here". I suppose she was thinking of *Maud*.[3] Phoebes appearance, uncurled feather, crystal drop earrings and all. What a picture! I always think of her with curling pins, red flannel dressing gown and jockey club perfume. Its a queer world. I suppose you saw no sign of them at Buckingham Palace, did you? I wonder Lul's didn't book a young Prince...

I am in the throes of my two worst weeks. After that the improvement really begins. I seem to have taken very powerfully which is all to the good. Two weeks only while one feels like a worm and then one creeps up on deck and smells land again! Jack is looking after me so beautifully. He really is a marvellously unselfish and sympathetic 'companion'.

Well, I must finish this and put the kettle on.

With warmest love to you both

Ever your fond
K.

MS Newberry.

[1] The 'Social Gossip' column, *New Zealand Free Lance* (18 Jan. 1922), reported the fiftieth wedding celebrations of KM's maternal uncle, Frank Dyer, and his wife Phoebe.

[2] Other relatives on her mother's side.

[3] Lulu Dyer, Uncle Frank's daughter, had just returned from a visit to London, where she was presented at Buckingham Palace. Presumably she had written a letter to the press comparing servants in England with those at home. Maud may have been a family servant in Wellington.

To William Gerhardi, 11 March 1922

[Victoria Palace Hotel, Rue Blaise Desgoffe, Rue de Rennes]
Paris

11.iii.1922

My dear Mr Gerhardi,

Please do not think of me as a kind of boa-constrictor who sits here gorged and silent after having devoured your two delightful letters, without so much as a 'thank you'. If gratitude were the size and shape to go into a pillar box the postman would have staggered to your door days ago. But Ive not been able to send anything more tangible. I have been – I am ill. In two weeks I shall begin to get better. But just for the moment I am down below in the cabin, as it were, and the deck, where all the wise and happy people are walking up and down & Mr Gerhardi drinks a hundred cups of tea with a hundred schoolgirls is far away. But I only tell you this to explain my silence. Im always very much ashamed of being ill; I hate to plead illness. Its taking an unfair advantage. So please let us forget about it...

Ive been wanting to say – how strange how delightful it is you should feel as you do about The Voyage. No one has mentioned it to me but Middleton Murry. But when I wrote that little story I felt that I was on that very boat, going down those stairs, smelling the smell of the saloon. And when the stewardess came in and said "we're rather empty, we may pitch a little" I can't believe that my sofa did not pitch. And one moment I had a little bun of silk-white hair and a bonnet and the next I was Fenella hugging the swan neck umbrella. It was so vivid – terribly vivid – especially as they drove away and heard the sea as slowly it turned on the beach.[1] Why – I don't know. It wasn't a memory of a real experience. It was a kind of *possession*. I might have remained the Grandma for ever after if the wind had changed that moment. And that would have been a little bit embarrassing for Middleton Murry... But don't you feel that when you write? I think one always feels it. Only sometimes it is a great deal more definite.

Yes, I agree with you the insulting reference to Miss Brill would have been better in French.[2] Also there is a printer's error 'chère' for 'cherie'. Ma petite chère sounds ridiculous...

And yes, that is what I tried to convey in The Garden Party. The diversity of life and how we try to fit in everything, Death included.[3] That is bewildering for a person Laura's age. She feels things ought to happen differently. First one and then another. But life isn't like that. We haven't the ordering of it. Laura says "But all these things must not happen at once" and Life answers "Why not? How are they divided from each other." And they *do* all happen, it is inevitable. And it seems to me that there is beauty in that inevitability.

I wonder if you happened to see a review of my book in 'Time and Tide'. It was written by a very fierce lady indeed.[4] Beating in the face was nothing to it. It frightened me when I read it. I shall never dare to come to England. I am sure she would have my blood like the Fish in Cock Robin.[5] But why is she so dreadfully violent; one would think I was a wife beater, at least, or that I wrote all my stories with a carving knife. It is a great mystery.

Is it Spring yet in Oxford? Here, as the taxi hurls me to the clinic and back I look everywhere for signs. But the March lion is still prowling after the March lamb and now it rains now its sunny. When I go down in the lift and its raining the little lift-boy says 'C'est l'hiver encore' but when I come up and theres a gleam of sun he cries 'Dans un mois il serait pleine été.' I like the French for these large remarks... They are specially comforting after the cautious Swiss.

Please forgive a dull letter. As soon as I am really 'up' again I shall write another. But this goes with my warm, sincere thanks, dear Mr Gerhardi, for your wonderfully generous praise – Ill try & deserve some of it one day.

Yours ever
Katherine Mansfield.

MS ATL. *LKM* II. 195–7.

¹ Details from 'The Voyage', a story in *The Garden Party* based on KM's childhood memory of sailing between Wellington and Picton with her paternal grandmother.
² The unkind remarks the elderly spinster overhears from the young lovers beside her on a park bench, in the story 'Miss Brill'.
³ The death of a young working-class husband that undermines the gaiety of the middle-class garden party.
⁴ KM had twice scathingly reviewed the novelist, scholar and Labour Party activist Mary Agnes Hamilton in the *Athenaeum*, her *Full Circle* under the heading 'The Easy Path' (6 Feb. 1920), and *The Last Fortnight*, with several other novels under 'Ask No Questions' (22 Oct. 1920). Now, in *Time and Tide*, (3 Mar. 1922), Hamilton conceded that '"At the Bay" and 'The Garden Party" will stand comparison with Tchekov, in rendering the sort of impression for which the medium chosen is perfectly adjusted', but she also found the collection 'unrelentingly cruel. . . . beyond what is bearable or legitimate; there is something almost rancid about it. . . . The world would be a madhouse if Miss Mansfield's picture were a wholly true one.'
⁵ The second stanza of the anonymous children's rhyme 'Who Killed Cock Robin':

> Who caught his blood?
> I, said the fish,
> With my little dish,
> I caught his blood.

To Orlo Williams,¹ 11 March 1922

Victoria Palace Hotel | Rue Blaise Desgoffe | Rue de Rennes | Paris.
11
March
1922

Dear Mr Orlo Williams,

I cannot say how happy your generous letter has made me. Thank you from my heart. It is too generous. You say nothing, or almost nothing, about the big black holes in my book which I must mend next time. But I know they are there. In fact I am so conscious of them that its awfully pleasant when a fellow-writer ignores them for a moment and says he liked the rest.

It is a relief to me that you realise that my heart was with William in Marriage à la mode and with old Mr Neave and young Mr Dove. It makes me gasp when reviewers think I am jeering at them and poking cruel fun. When one has been away from people for so long – I have only seen glimpses of people for five years now – that is positively frightening... I had meant to convey that I loved them – especially the Doves. I have often wondered about their married life.² How nice it is you should single out just that story! Nobody else has.

Murry and I have left Switzerland. I am trying a new X ray treatment here which promises wonders. It is all promise as yet but we believe implicitly in it – perhaps for that reason – and have planned to walk into Germany this summer. Its strange to be in a city again. I do not see much of it – only what shakes past the taxi windows as we are hurled to and from the clinic once a week. We are like hermits and have seen nobody. Murry went to a Punch and Judy show today in the Luxembourg

Gardens (Front Seats 2d) and enjoyed it *very* much. I don't know whether
he screamed. Everybody else screamed and one little boy was overcome
and had to be led away.

It would be delightful to meet you again and to talk over this mysterious
business of story writing. There is so much to say, but letters wont do . . .

I wonder if you will be seeing my cousin Elizabeth; she returned to
London this week.

Murry asks me to send you his love.

With my grateful thanks once more

Yours very sincerely
Katherine Mansfield.

MS Cains.

[1] The civil servant, fiction writer, and parliamentary historian, to whom KM had written in Jan.
1921 (see *CLKM* V. 163–4).
[2] Characters in stories in *The Garden Party*.

To Harold Beauchamp, 13 March 1922

[Victoria Palace Hotel, Rue Blaise Desgoffe, Rue de Rennes]
Paris. 13.III.1922

Dearest Father

I only send these few reviews as it is tiring to read many. They are – I may say –
representative of the reviews I have had so far. I thought May's and Chaddie
Waterlow's[1] letter might interest you! My letter under separate cover.

Your ever loving
Kass.

MS ATL.

[1] Her cousin Elizabeth (christened May Annette) was known in the family as May, and her older
sister Charlotte as Chaddie.

To Ida Baker, 13 March 1922

[Victoria Palace Hotel, Rue Blaise Desgoffe, Rue de Rennes]
13.III.1922

Dear Ida

These cuttings must go to America next week. So will you have a squiz
and send them back quickly? They are just a job-lot. But if you lose them

Miss there will be the d – l to pay. I hear from Constable the book is well in its 2nd edition which is not bad as there is a 'warehouse' strike on & supplies are difficult to get. I am *still* waiting for mine. Reviews & letters are all I get.

Elizabeth writes that it is snowing hard. She was just 'off' in a cow sledge and had to spend a night in Sierre, as the funicular had more or less promised not to run the day after – her real going-away day. Did I tell you Sir H. Lunn asked her and me to go to Muren[1] next summer as his guests & lecture there with readings from our Works. Its a picture isn't it? Elizabeth says "the idea of you & me going over those beetling mountains hand in hand with our little books under our little arms made me laugh for a week." So it did me. I had decided to call myself The Very Rev. Katherine Mansfield & E. was to be The Dean. The list of lecturers was thick with Bishops; I felt we would be too dreadfully out in the Swiss cold otherwise ... I also saw *At the Harmonium* Mrs Arnold Lunn – and Lunns Tours chasing us while we were there in immense yellow cherry-bangs like the one in Baugy. Its a marvellous world.

Chaddie wrote yesterday she had been gathering daffodils in the *fields* all the afternoon. It is a marvellous year for wild daffodils & pussy willows. I 'note' also that the rooks are building, the elm trees are in flower, theres a remarkable show of white crocuses in Kensington garden, the bird-cherry is out in the hedges, the fields are bright with colts foot, the male & female catkins are out, violets are in bloom, primroses, and bluebells are pushing up – All that was in the paper last week – distributed over the week.[2] As far as I can see the one good of newspapers is that kind of news. I wish they published a morning & evening paper devoted exclusively to such things. Really well run, well staffed, with good photographs, with no war news except the wars of the roses. How much more thrilling to read of the marriage of a Queen B. rather than a Princess M.

I did happen to see one other thing which pleased me *very* much. In China the kettles are made with four very thin pieces of iron fastened with an air space between to the nearly flat bottom of the kettle. So that when the water heats the bubbles of steam through these slits cause the kettle to sing not like English kettles sing, but a plaintive, sweet faraway song.[3] No house in China is complete without such a kettle.

I hope its fine again with you. It's a glorious day here – still, sunny, warm – cats sun – the basking kind. There are some very wicked bad little children in this hotel – one about 2, one about 4. They throw their bread on the floor, eat with both ends of the fork & stand up on their chairs when they want to drink. The head waiter is extremely nice to them & writes them out each a separate bill. They are lambs.

Be well. Be happy.

K.M.

MS BL.

[1] Murren, a holiday resort in the Bernese Oberland in Switzerland.
[2] Details gleaned over the past week from the gardening and other columns in the *Daily News*.
[3] From a paragraph in the unsigned 'My Notebook' column, *Daily News* (11 Mar. 1922).

To Ida Baker, [14 March 1922]

[Victoria Palace Hotel, Rue Blaise Desgoffe, Rue de Rennes]

Tuesday.

Please give this character to E. with mes mille remerciments et mes meilleurs souvenirs. Better put it in an envelope, if you will.

Dear Ida

I have just received your Sunday letter. Don't apologize for writing what you feel. Why should you? It only means I have to cry 'De rien de rien' each time and that's silly. Heavens! What a journey it is to take one anywhere! I prove that to myself every day. I am always more or less marking out the distance, examining the map, and then failing to carry out my plans. Its rather nice to think of oneself as a sailor bending over the map of ones *mind* and deciding where to go and how to go. The great thing to remember is we can do whatever we wish to do provided our wish is strong enough. But the tremendous effort needed – one doesn't always want to make it, does one? And all that cutting down the jungle and bush clearing even after one has landed anywhere – its tiring. Yes, I agree. But what else can be done? What's the alternative? What do you want *most* to do? That's what I have to keep asking myself, in face of difficulties.

But you are saying 'what has this to do with our relationship?' This. We cannot live together in any sense until we – *I* – are am stronger. It seems to me it is my job, my fault, and not yours. I am simply unworthy of friendship, as I am. I take advantage of you, demand perfection of you, crush you. And the devil of it is that even though that is true as I write it I want to laugh. A deeper self looks at you and a deeper self in you looks back and we laugh and say 'what nonsense'. Its very queer, Jones, isn't it? Can you believe – that looking back upon our times in Italy and Garavan – even the afternoon when you were raking the garden and I was proving our purely evil effect on each other I keep on remembering that it was a lovely day or that the button daisies were ducks. How nice, how very nice it would be to bowl along in one of those open cabs with the wind ruffling off the sea & a smell of roasting coffee & fresh lemons from the land.

Oh dear! Oh dear! And do you remember standing at your window in your kimono one morning at five oclock while I sat up in bed behind the mosquito curtains and talked of decomposition? No, we can't simply live apart for all our lives from now on. We shall have to visit at least. How can we live? What is the best plan? The future is so wrapt in mystery. Until

I am well its foolishness for us to be together. That we both know. If this treatment 'succeeds' I shall go to Germany for the summer, then to Elizabeth at Randogne and then come back here in September or October. If all goes well I shall then go back to Germany for the winter – or Austria or Italy. Then – I have not the remotest idea . . . Jack wants to take a little house in the English country in Sussex and put all our furniture in it and so on and have a married couple in charge. I feel it is my duty to spend 6 months of every year there with him. The other six October to March I shall spend in either the South of France or Italy and I hope and imagine that if he has his house, Arthur, his books, his married couple, a little car, and friends coming down, Jack will not want to come with me. They will be my free months. That's all I can see. Now my *idea* is that we should spend the foreign months together, you and I. You know by that I mean they will be my working months but apart from work – walks, tea in a forest, cold chicken on a rock by the sea and so on we could 'share'. Likewise concerts in public gardens, sea bathing in Corsica and any other pretty little kick-shaws we have a mind to. But here is a brick. Money. If I can manage to pay for those months can you get a job for the others? That's the point. And of course the 'arrangement' is only in case you care to, are not in Rhodesia, are not married or living with some man. Tell me what you think. If you say 'what the dickens could I do for six months?' I reply 'why not the Universal Aunts[1]. Why not try them? See what kind of jobs they have . . . ' But don't fly off and cry 'this is very kind of you to arrange for and dispense my life like this merci pour la langouste.' Im not doing it. Im only talking in the dark – trying to keep you – yes, I will own to that, and trying to make things easy, happy, good, delightful. For we *must* be happy. No failures. No makeshifts. Blissful happiness. Anything else is somehow disgusting. I must make those six months with Jack as perfect as I can make them and the other six ought to be fearfully nice. But I know any form of life for Jack you & me is impossible & wrong. (There is all the [illegible] if this treatment does not succeed but I pass it by.)

Now the immediate future for you. It seems you are not going to get P.Gs. [Paying guests] Can you stay there until its time for the chalet to be shut? Do you want to? And then – what do you want to do? Will you go to the Palace this winter? But this is all far away and uncertain. And I must stop writing and begin to work. The great point is – if you can – think of happiness, work for happiness, look for it. I should like to ask you, every day between sleeping and waking, i.e. before you go to sleep & before you get up to practise this. Breathe *in* saying I am and *out* saying hap-py. Your subconscious, Miss will then take note of that fact and act according. However miserable you will be that has a quite definite counteraction. I suggest you teach Wing on the same principle to say 'I like – stopping at home . . . '

Goodbye for now. You say don't write letters and you lead me a terrific dance writing them. Thus it will always be –

Yours ever
K.M.

MS BL. *MLM*, 185–7.

---

[1] A firm providing professional domestic help.

To Ida Baker, [15 March 1922]

[Victoria Palace Hotel, Rue Blaise Desgoffe, Rue de Rennes]
Wednesday.

Touching photographs of Wingley. They look as though they were taken on the deck of the steamer on the way to Rhodesia. Prophetic, perhaps . . . Would you photograph the chalet & a room or two if the weather is fine & you are not busy! I don't think I shall have a parcel for the As. Many thanks all the same for their offer. Most grateful if they bring shawl. Please ask for me – anytime after midday. Re my letter yesterday. Did I make it clear that I should not be '*free*' until this autumn twelve-month, at earliest. i.e.1923 . . . I think you left a page of your letter out.

Yours ever
K.M.

Just tell the As I have made other arrangements about the clothes in the meantime.
LATEST. FINAL DECISION. Yes, please ask them to call for parcel.

Postcard BL.

To Dorothy Brett, 15 March 1922

[Victoria Palace Hotel, Rue Blaise Desgoffe, Rue de Rennes]
15 iii 1922

My lamb

I never felt less like going back into my shell in my life. And please please don't not tell me things. That would be a punishment. I wish you would trust me a little bit more. It is my fault that you cant. I will try and mend it. And I wish you were here, this minute, in this room with me. Writing is all very well, but we could understand each other at a glance if we were together. Brett! Now I am holding your hand. Now I am talking to the solitary you and you are talking to the solitary me. We're sitting under a yellow sun umbrella on a big clump of rocks overlooking the sea. Wild lavender & rosemary grows in the rocky crannels and the sea sounds & where the wave lifts its that wonderful gold radiant colour. But we've got our backs to the world for now. Brett! When you sit down to write to me feel that I am near and that I am your secret friend who loves you. But take me! If friendship means anything it means we must be important to each other, we must make each other happy and above all we must *feel sure*. People who say that love and friendship depend upon the feeling of ultimate uncertainty, of danger, are all wrong. They depend on exactly the opposite feeling. Its only promiscuous, light human beings who need such a big pinch of spice to keep them going. But then so few people even want to try for love or friendship. Substitutes suit them better. Talking of this always reminds me of Lawrence who said, talking of friendship, "We must make a contract and feel it is as binding as the marriage contract, as important, as eternal." I agree, and I believe in friendship with all my soul. I like to look ahead and see you and me being friends all our lives. Years ahead, meeting and talking and enjoying a treasure of memories and counting on each other and having a very fine collection of things that make us laugh. But above all feeling, as soon as we are together, *warmth*, joy, lightheartedness! Oh Brett, how I believe in happiness! Its only happiness that gives that ease, joyful freedom, which is essential to life. And the end of all this is – will you please once and for all believe I do not suspect you and whatever you say you do not 'disgust' me –

If you were here, as it happens you wouldn't have listened to a word of what Ive been saying. Your eyes, green with envy would have been fixed on, hypnotised by two very old apothecary's jars on my dressing table. Murry who is a *very* good nose flattener has been gazing at these for days and yesterday he bought them. They are tall milk-white jars painted with a device in apple-green, faint yellow and a kind of ashy pink. They have gold tops. On one in exquisite lettering is the word *Absinthii* on the other *Theriaca*. We intend to keep pot pourri in them during our lives and after our deaths we intend to put our ashes in them. Im to be Absinthii and M. Theriaca. So there they stand our two little coffins on the dressing table & Ive just sent M. out for some fresh flowers to deck them out with as Ive no pot pourri. But if I am well enough to nose flatten at Easter, darling, you and I must go off with our little purses in our little hands and glare!

Are you aware that there is an extremely fine Punch and Judy in the Luxembourg? In a theatre of its own. Stalls 2d, pit 2d too. The audience screams frightfully and some are overcome and have to be led out. But there it is. We had better buy some comfits from the stall under the chestnut tree and go there too. I believe there is a one-eyed thief who comes in, rather, looks round a corner who really *is* awful. M. said he "let out a yell ⟨⟩ himself" & the little boy next to him roared. You know the kind of eye. ⟨⟩

Oh, I do not like Dot![1] Her name is good. It always reminds me of a wooden rocking horse and that is just what she sounds like. I hope she goes away soon. Your Scotch girl is very beautiful. Tell me about her will you? Tell me as much as you can. There is something so fascinating about that little photograph. And the look of youth – ah, how lovely that is – young hands, young lips. Is she living in London? Is her little boy with her? Who is she? What is her Christian name? I feel Koteliansky would admire her face tremendously.

The weather is glorious here. Warming, sunny, so mild. One hears the voices of people in the open air – a sound I love in spring and all the windows opposite mine stand wide open so that I see at one the daughter sewing with her mother, at another the Japanese gentleman, at another two young people who have a way of shutting their bedroom window very quickly and drawing the curtain at most unexpected moments... I can't go out though, not even for a drive. I am and shall be for the next ten days rather badly ill. In fact I can only just get about at all. But Manoukhin says the worse one is at this time the better later on. So there's nothing to be done but be rather dismally thankful.

Later. M. has come in with 2 bunches of anemones, two small tea plates and a cake of rose thé soap. We have had *our* tea and Im going back to bed. What is a nuisance is I can*not* work for the moment & Shorter has ordered 13 stories – all at one go – to be ready in July. So they are in addition to my ordinary work. I shall have to spend a furious May and June. The chestnuts are in big bud. Don't you love chestnut buds. I shall have a look at them on Friday. I think they are almost the loveliest buds of all.

Oh, your cinerarias. I wish I could see them. Do you know the blue ones, too? And the faint faint pink kind? Mother loved them. We used to grow masses in a raised flower bed. I love the shape of the petals – it is so delicate. We used to have blue ones in pots in a rather white and gold drawing room that had green wooden sun blinds. Faint light, big cushions, tables with "photographs of the children" in silver frames, some little yellow and black cups & saucers that belonged to Napoleon in a high cupboard and someone playing Chopin – beyond words playing Chopin... Oh, how beautiful Life is. How wonderful!

A knock at my door. The maid has come in to close the shutters. Thats such a lovely gesture. She leans forward, she looks up & the shutters fold like wings.

Goodbye for now, my little artist. I cant *bear* to think you make Gertler's[2] bed & carry water jugs. It is very ugly and wrong of him. It is shocking that he should be so uncivilized. It gave me a pang of horror. Don't do it for him.

Take care of yourself. Write as soon as you can.

God bless you *ever* your loving

Tig.

MS Newberry. *LKM* II, 197–8.

---

[1] Valentine Dobrée.
[2] Brett gave the frequently hard-up Mark Gertler free lodging at 28 Thurlow Road.

To S. S. Koteliansky, [15 March 1922]

[Victoria Palace Hotel, Rue Blaise Desgoffe, Rue de Rennes]
Dear Koteliansky

– A delicate question. Is it not possible for Gertler to be made to understand that when Brett is without a servant he must make his own bed and carry his own water jug. To do less is to be an uncivilised being. Brett never complains to me but the facts show through her letter tonight, and they are not pleasant. Could you tell Gertler (in the form of a good solid parable) that such things must not be. Please do not think I am impertinent, dear friend. But it is sad when there is such a small band of decent people in the world that they should not be able to teach other how to live.

I have read recently a book by Merezhkovsky and Hippius and another by Bunin (stories with a preface). All were about present day conditions in Russia. They are so terrible that there is nothing to be said. It is strange. I fear Lenin, even personally, to such an extent that I am frightened to look at a picture of him.[1] It is not simply the head of a devil – No, better not to speak about it.

I wish I could be with you for a little.

I press your hands

Katherine,

MS BL. Dickinson, 90–1.

[1] Vladimer Ilyitch Lenin (1870–1924), as a leader of the Bolshevik movement and first Premier of the Soviet, was a despised and greatly feared figure among the émigré Russians KM met in Paris.

To Ida Baker, [16 March 1922]

[Victoria Palace Hotel, Rue Blaise Desgoffe, Rue de Rennes]
Thursday.
Dear Ida

Did you pack my File – a cardboard, concertina arrangement with a cloth strap round it. I had thought it was in 'Esher'. Jack says it was on my shelves. Please tell me by return of post whether you packed it. If not please send it on *at once*. And if you can find the small green Tchekhovs make them into a parcel & send them to me will you? I need them badly.

K.M.

Postcard BL.

To Richard Murry, [16 March 1922]

[Victoria Palace Hotel, Rue Blaise Desgoffe, Rue de Rennes]

Paris. Thursday

Dear Richard,

I must have sounded an unsympathetic and selfish creature in my last letter to you. Forgive me! It was too bad of me to crow so loudly being out of the wood (more or less) myself while my little bruvver is still tangled up in the branches. I wish I could help you a bit. Perhaps you and Jack, above a long glass of something cool under a chestnut tree in the Luxembourg Gardens will find out a way. Yes, old boy, I see your point about Art Schools. I can imagine what I should have felt with Max Pemberton telling me to "cut the cackle and come to the osses."[1] Which is what would have happened. And I understand too why you would rather not pitch your tent in the camp of Brett and Gertler.[2] Its difficult. But I pin my flag on Easter. And by my saying that don't think I mean to interfere or that I want to solve anything that is after all your own affair. No. I imagine you are like Jack. Jack tells me things because its a relief to tell them. But he knows he doesn't deliver himself into my hands by doing so. It stops at that and he's safe and can either tell me more or not mention it again as he likes. This I understand.

Shall we really meet next month? Richard, *what larks.* I can't realise it. If spring goes on at the rate its going just now it will then be nearly full summer. Everything is coming out. Chestnut buds have burst, its warm, almost hot, and theres such a good sound when I put my head out of the window – the sound of people talking out of doors again – one of the surest signs of spring. Talking at their leisure, you know, in the open, without an enemy ready to pounce, without old winter round the corner. I don't know – it seems to me that winter is a bad business in every way. There's no excuse for it.

Jack, who is a very fine nose-flattener has bought two old apothecary's jars which will make you green with envy. They are tall, rather slender jars painted with a device in apple green, pale yellow and a kind of ashy pink. One has *Absinthii* written on it and the other *Theriaca* in very beautiful lettering. They have tops with gold knobs. Fearfully nice. We mean to keep pot-pourri in them during our life time and to put our ashes in them after our death. I shall be Absinthii – no – I can't even make a joke about Jack not being alive. Lets all live for ever instead.

By the way. Look here. I don't agree with you about women knocking off works of art at thirty or round about and men not until fifty. Or rather I don't agree personally. I'm 33; I feel I am only just beginning to see now what it is ... I want to do. It will take years of work to really bring it off. Ive done one or two things, like the Daughters of the Colonel which were the right kind. But *one* or *two*! Oh Richard, to be *sincere* I could groan at all there is to do and the tiny beginning I have made. Not a groan of misery but of impatience. Why don't I get down to it more. I must this year. But if you are right about most women I don't feel its true about me. Im one of the slow ones . . .

Have you seen Jack's book on Style?[3] I don't like the squiggles in the lettering. The size and shape are nice, and its well printed – very. Its a highly professional looking book. Im always deeply impressed by '*see note*'. Rather aspire to it myself. I hope it gets a good press. Its time Jack did. The critics have a way of taking him for granted, it seems to me.

I am glad you liked my Garding Party. I am still waiting for copies as I want to send one to Mother. There's a strike on (well, of course you know that) but it has put Constable very much out of joint.[4] Ive just sold a continental edition to Collins. It seems successful, so far. I am *very* dissatisfied with it myself. But its no good. One must just go on & try and get nearer the real thing.

Our present plans are to stay at this hotel until the end of May and then go to Germany or Bavaria for the summer. Then I have to come back here in the autumn for 8–10 weeks to finish this treatment. At present I am just at the 'reaction' stage which is pretty awful. But it will be over in a little over a week and then according to Manoukhin one begins to go up the hill in leaps and bounds. Ida Baker doesn't live with us any more, and she won't be living with us again. We live like two hermits here. Only Jack, who goes out every day to the Luxembourg Gardens meets numbers of very small children and has silent conversations with them. He went to a Punch & Judy show last Sunday (Best Seats 2d Worst Seats 2d) in a little theatre with green canvas sides. The audience ranged from about 1 year to 6 years. They screamed frightfully when le voleur came in. Jack says he nearly did himself. He had one awful eye – you know the kind.

Goodbye for now old boy. This letter is written lying down; thats why (or I like to think thats why) the writing is so bad. Let us know more about your Easter plans when you are able.

Ever your loving
Katherine.

MS R. Murry. *Adam* 370–5, 34–5.

---

[1] Sir Max Pemberton (1874–1950), prolific writer of mystery and detective fiction. KM is suggesting that the advice given to Richard at the Slade Art School, where he was enrolled to study painting, would be like Pemberton advising her on how to write.

[2] The possibility that the nineteen-year-old Richard might board with Gertler and Brett was abandoned.

[3] *The Problem of Style*, Murry's six lectures given at Oxford the previous May, had just been published by Oxford University Press.

[4] A warehouse strike was delaying distribution of the stories.

To Ida Baker, [17 March 1922]

[Victoria Palace Hotel, Rue Blaise Desgoffe, Rue de Rennes]

Thanks for letters today. I am amazed that you are still waiting to hear from England. Why not fix the other arrangement immediately. And with regard to that make it a business arrangement. Dont go on the principle you must give them all that you gave me. The point is *to save money*. As it is we have to pay out £4 a week for the rent and we cant afford any more.

Are you sure about the butcher not being included. Please look again. It seems impossible that we missed out so large an item. It came over me today that Switzerland is still costing us nearly £7 a week. It is a great deal.

K.M.

Postcard BL.

To Harold Beauchamp, 18 March 1922

Victoria Palace Hotel | 6–8 Rue Blaise Desgoffe | Paris

My darling Father,

I can't express to you my feelings when I read your letter. How you can possibly find it in your heart to write like that to your undeserving little black sheep of a child only God knows. It wrings my heart to think of my ungrateful behaviour and I cannot understand how I have been the victim of my fearfulness and dread of misunderstanding. You have been – you are – the soul of generosity to us all. Then how – loving you as I do – feeling your sensitiveness and sympathy as I do – can I have made you suffer? It is a mystery. I sometimes wish that we could have been nearer to each other since I have been grown up and not the intolerant girl who returned to New Zealand with you years ago.[1] But fate has willed otherwise.

Believe me, I am not, and never shall be, unmindful of what it must have cost you to write that letter to me. Perhaps one day I shall be able to express my gratitude and love.

My darling, it is such a joy to think we may meet this year. My letters from the girls at Wood Hay are full of your coming and the preparations for it. Everything they do seems to have the same end – Chaddie's last batch of marmalade. And they seem to have done wonders with their garden.

My plans for the immediate future are very uncertain. I knew that in spite of the considered opinion of the Swiss doctors, Montana was too high for my heart. My lungs appeared to improve, but my heart got so much worse that I could do nothing whatever except lie in a chaise longue.

However, I decided the only thing to do was to give the Swiss treatment a good trial. But with the advent of the snow I went to bed and there I remained. If I got up I'd be attacked by congestion at once and I don't think I should have seen the winter through.

For some months previously we had been hearing of a new treatment for tuberculosis — an X ray treatment which was practised by a Russian doctor in Paris. It was endorsed by the Lancet:[2] we heard of definite cures. And as my Swiss doctor had promised to do no more than patch me up on the best showing, I decided to make all enquiries re the X ray man and I did so. The more I heard the more satisfactory and "sound" it seemed to be. Finally, in January, I came to Paris and saw the doctor, who promised me a full and complete cure. After – as you may imagine – a great deal of consultation, I decided to put myself in this man's hands. Jack fully agreed. The course of treatment is to last until May, then there is a break of two–three months, and then I must have ten more "treatments" in the Autumn. According to this doctor, and to his partner, I shall then be as well as ever. It sounds rather too much to believe. The method is to X ray the spleen. This doctor, who has been working for some years at the Pasteur Institute, Paris, has discovered that the spleen is the spot where the blood changes – that if the spleen is fed with X rays the blood is likewise fed. What a frightful bother, isn't it, darling? I don't think I'll go into the question. I'll supply you with literature if you are inclined to know more about it. But the fact is my spleen is lapping up these X rays and I have gained four lbs., and have never had fever since I started. So the future looks rosy. Its too early in the day to say more. We are living in a quiet very satisfactory hotel. Jack looks after me in every way. He is very keen on this treatment; so am I. But I have had so many disappointments that I can't quite believe fully until I am further along the road.

The girls, who stayed in England for Vera's sake, hope to come over to Paris in April and see the sights under Jack's escort. He is a very powerful guide.

I have found it almost impossible to do any work so far, as the treatment is exceedingly tiring. But my new book has been a success and that is a comfort. It went into a second edition after a fortnight's publication and I really must have had nearly a hundred reviews and notices. They are still coming in. It is to be published separately in America, Africa, Sweden and the Continent.[3] It is extraordinary the letters I receive from strangers – all kinds of people. I have certainly been most fortunate as a writer. It is strange to remember buying a copy of The Native Companion[4] on Lambton Quay and standing under a lamp post with darling Leslie to see if my story had been printed.

I was so interested in the letters from Aunt May and Ethel Anderson.[5] What a good letter Aunt May's was. She seemed to be leading such a satisfactory life, too, with her growing children and the farm. The more I see of life the more certain I feel that its the people who live remote from cities who inherit the earth. London, for instance, is an awful place to live in. Not only is the climate abominable but it's a continual chase after distraction. There's no peace of mind – no harvest to be reaped out of it. And another thing is the longer I live the more I turn to New Zealand. I thank God I was born in New Zealand. A young country is a real heritage, though it takes one time to recognise it. But New Zealand is in my very bones. What wouldn't I give to have a look at it!

Chad sent me two cuttings you had sent her – one describing Miss Lulu Dyer's sensations in the Suez Canal – the other Mr. and Mrs. F. Dyer's reception. I was amazed at the richness and splendour of the latter – all described down to Phoeb's earrings. The only thing missing was Frank's buttonhole. Can't you see Uncle Syd's frock coat, too, and Aunt Aggie's parasol. I had such a laugh over it all. I wonder Phoeb didn't capture one of the young Princes at the Royal Garden Party for Lulu.

Well, my dearest, dearest Father, I could go on talking for pages more. I hope you are having a really favourable voyage and enjoying the rest and change. I look forward with all my heart to our meeting this year, either on the Continent or in England.

Jack, I know, has written to you. He and I are equally interested in the Bank of New Zealand reports you send us.[6] In fact, Jack seems to have adopted my country more than I have adopted his.

God bless you, darling,

I am, ever your loving and grateful child,

Kass.

TC ATL. *LKM* II, 199; Alpers 1980, 360–1.

---

[1] KM was the one Beauchamp daughter who, as a teenager, challenged parental decisions. Harold Beauchamp later had reservations about Murry as a provider for his daughter, and there was additional strain when KM heard of his low opinion of her writing.

[2] 'Reported' rather than 'endorsed' would be more accurate. See p. 43, n.6.

[3] For an account of early editions of *The Garden Party*, see B. J. Kirkpatrick, *A Bibliography of Katherine Mansfield* (1989, 22–6), and its section on 'Translations into Foreign Languages'.

[4] Mansfield's earliest publications were a series of prose poems and sketches in the Melbourne periodical, *The Native Companion* (Oct., Dec., 1907).

[5] The daughter of her uncle Cradock Beauchamp and KM's godmother, aunt Harriet, lived with her husband Grimsdale Anderson at the entrance to Kenepuru Sound.

[6] Her father sent on his annual reports, assessing New Zealand's trading and financial position, for KM's perusal.

To J. B. Pinker & Son, 18 March 1922

Victoria Palace Hotel | 6–8 Rue Blaise Desgoffe | Rue de Rennes | Paris
18 iii 1922

Dear Mr Pinker,

Strangely enough I wrote to you yesterday on the subject of Bliss. As far as I know the Scandinavian rights are available. I shall be greatly obliged if you will negotiate them for me.

Sincerely yours
Katherine Mansfield

MS Newberry.

To Alfred A. Knopf, 18 March 1922

Victoria Palace Hotel | Rue Blaise Desgoffe | Rue de Rennes
Paris

Dear Mr Knopf,

Many thanks for your letter and for the copy of your Spring list which looks delightful. What a fine blue you have used for the cover: one cannot look away from it when it is on the table.

I am sending you a few of my first reviews of The Garden Party. It has been successful so far. I think its possible the tide has turned in favour of short stories. But perhaps that's the optimism of one who loves that form.

With kind regards

Yours sincerely
Katherine Mansfield

MS Texas. Cited *Exhibition*, 50.

To Dorothy Brett, [19 March 1922]

[Victoria Palace Hotel, Rue Blaise Desgoffe, Rue de Rennes]

My little Golden Bee,

Ill simply indulge myself and write to you before answering all these letters. My bed is a battlefield of letters and press cuttings. I cant move a toe without a rustle of *dead leaves*. Oh, what a joy it will be to get to some remote place again where posts come only once a day! But – put all that away. It is all away. Let me think about April & Easter, and *your* letter, dearest. Ill answer the questions first. About coming here. This hotel is a bit expensive I imagine for Arthur and its not Gertler's *kind*. Its very big, families come. The cheapest room is 13 francs and you are obliged to take some of your meals here – lunch *9* francs, dinner *10*. It wouldn't weigh on me at all to know you were all here. But I don't think either A. or G. would care for it. And there is this to think of. I cant see anyone before midi. I have to stay in bed until then and rest i.e. not talk much. Murry wont see anyone before midi. Wild horses wont drag him from his table before then. It seems to me you'd do better at your Pantheon Hotel.[1] You'd feel freer and spend less and its more at the real centre. Its much less of a big hotel with concierge, porters and so on (I imagine) than this one. When Gertler and Arthur go back perhaps you could move here? I wouldn't choose here if I were well. I wouldn't be here if I were you. Its not got the right *spirit*. It suits us because – I am as I am for the present.

Oh I am so longing to get over this last crisis and begin to climb the hill so that by the time you come I shall not be such a Job-in-the-ashes.[2] Manoukhin says in eight days now the worst will be over. Its such a queer feeling. One burns with heat in one's hands & feet and bones, then suddenly you are racked with neuritis, but such neuritis that you cant lift your arm. Then ones head begins to pound. It's the moment when if I were a proper martyr I should begin to have that awful smile that martyrs in the flames put on when they begin to sizzle! But no matter – it will pass... I wish I knew what was happening to Manoukhin, though. The atmosphere of that clinique is terrible. Yesterday he simply would not and did not speak to his partner. He was so agitated that he could not speak French at all. The apparatus went wrong as usual (its always going wrong) and he banged the doors so terribly that one trembled. It seems imbecile to be in the same room with someone and to be as dumb as cattle. It seems *wrong* that one cannot help. I shall never get used to this – never!

It is real spring here – really come. Little leaves are out. The air is like silk. But above all beyond all there is a kind of fleeting beauty on the faces of everybody – a timid look, the look of someone who bends over a new baby. This is so beautiful that it fills one with awe. The fat old taximan has it and the fisherman on the Pont d' Alma that I passed yesterday and the young lady at the office with her scent and her violet cachou and her shoes like beetles. All – all are the same. For this alone one is thankful to have lived on the earth. My canaries opposite are of course in a perfect fever. They sing, flutter, swing and make love. Even the old clock that strikes over the roofs says one – two no longer, but drowsily, gently, says spring – spring...

Yes, paint the Luxembourg gardens! Do paint a new tree, a just come out chestnut – wouldn't that be good to paint? When the leaves are still stiff they look as though they have sprung out of the buds. Chestnut trees are marvellous. But so are limes and acacias and umbrella pines. I cant say I like firs awfully, though. If you had lived among them as we did in Switzerland you would have found them *stodgy*. By the way the Mountain is *living* in Switzerland. Strange she should have found her ancestral home so to speak. She may be there for years. And that reminds me. Dearest could you bring me over some fine linen from Robinson & Cleavers?[3] I don't know how heavy linen weighs. I mean is 8 yards terrific? Don't bring a snip more than you can comfortably carry. Its for pantalons. I can't get it here, not fine or good enough. I don't know what it costs. I haven't an idea but Ill send a cheque as soon as you send me the bill. Please tell the man it must be a really fine quality that will wear well. Words can't express the price they charge here for crepe de chine and charmeuse pantalons and tops at the laundry. And I have three very fine linen camisoles that I want these to 'go' with. I shall get the Mountain to make them. I'd *like* too a box of chaminade bath tablets from Morny frères. Theyre not far from Robinson & Cleaver are they? But leave them if they are a bore.

Oh what shall I say about your Easter egg. And what *can* it be! I burn to know. You know I do and you're just torturing me – rustling the paper and then hiding it away. I have an idea of what I shall give you. But I shant breathe a word until I know whether there is any possible chance of getting *another*. You're not to guess what it is on pain of death.

Forgive my writing. I am lying down. My precious little artist, look after yourself. Boil only one egg for Gertler, no more. Tell me what the Grosvenor man[4] says. Im having a book published in Scandinavia & Ive just sold the Continental rights of the Garden party (North Africa included). Do you see the black ladies making curl papers of it? I do!

God bless you. My warm warm love.

Tig

MS Newberry. *LKM* II. 199–200.

[1] Brett regularly stayed at the Hotel des Grands Hommes, Place du Pantheon.
[2] After his trials, and before his lamentations, Job sat in an ash heap (Job 2:8).
[3] A quality drapery store in Regent Street.
[4] The Grosvenor Gallery in Albemarle Street, Mayfair.

To Vera Beauchamp Bell, 20 March 1922

Permanent address which always finds me: c/o The Nation and the
Athenaeum | 10 Adelphi Terrace W.C.2 | London.

Paris 20.III.1922

My dear Vera,

Yes, I was sorry, too, that we did not meet. It was a very close shave. For I wrote that Id be in Paris in a fortnight – not a week – and at that time my X rays were not having any horrid effects. We might have seen each other and rediscovered each other. But it was not to be! I feel its a toss up whether we shall ever meet now; I am such an impermanent movable and so are you. And theres always the very good chance of a person with consumption moving off for a grim journey where she certainly wouldn't wish to be followed. But I mustn't freeze your blood, my dear, by talking about such subjects.

Dear Marie and little J – they are a remarkable little pair, aren't they. I wonder why they don't adopt a baby each? Do you think that would interfere with their chances of matrimony?[1] Well – not Jeanne – but Marie. A baby would be far greater fun than Kuri and Im sure if she caught one young enough she would feel it was her own. Short of marriage Im sure to be a mother is the happiest life for women who have not a profession. Perhaps Id better say a foster mother in case my Canadian sister thinks Im approving of immorality.

What a horrid crossing you must have had! I have such memories of bad times shared at sea. But I was always in such a furious temper then and you were an angel.[2] I should like to hop across to America one day; we have many friends there. It must be a ghastly country to live in. Canada is attractive because of its back-country life and its size. Do you feel you are a Canadian now? I expect you do.

We intend to stay in Paris until May. Then, if this treatment has been a success we shall go to Austria or Italy for part of the summer and to Elizabeth for the rest. Then I have to come back here for 10 more applications. And that's as far as I can even dimly see. But its all vague, for the treatment is experimental, at present. If its a failure I shall go to Nancy[3] and try the new psychotherapeutics which are rather on the lines of our stepmother's subconscious mind treatment. Im a desperate man now; I cant be ill any longer.

Ida has remained in Switzerland. Its her spiritual home, I think. Its just her size and build. She is very happy there, living in our chalet until the lease is up in June. After that I want, if I can possibly manage it, to send her to Rhodesia. Im under such immense obligation to her that I feel its the least I can do. But I don't see my way at present, I confess.

Jack and I are as usual awfully busy. We never seem to have enough time. There is so much business correspondence and so on connected with writing, and although I have a very good agent I seem to be never at an end with it. But Im not complaining. I love my work and Ive had such good fortune. My new book has been far more successful than the others even. I sent Father some of the first reviews to 'Frisco.

Weren't you delighted to be *home again*. Will your boys stay at boarding school now that you are back? I wish I knew them. Boys are such darlings at that age. Give them my love even though Im a wraith-like aunt to them. I could recommend Jack as an uncle with all my heart if he were nearer.

Much love, dear, from your affectionate sister

K.

MS ATL.

[1] KM's sister Marie (Chaddie) had been widowed in 1916, and would remarry in 1932; Jeanne married in Oct. 1922.

[2] KM and her sisters travelled together to England in Jan. 1906, and returned to Wellington in Oct. 1908.

[3] Where Emile Coué practised the psychotherapy known as Coueism, based on the subconscious effect of the repeated mantra, '*Tous les jours à tous points de vue je vais de mieux en mieux.*'

To Ida Baker, [21 March 1922]

[Victoria Palace Hotel, Rue Blaise Desgoffe, Rue de Rennes]

Tuesday

Dear Ida,

I have been waiting for an answer to my last letter, I think, before I wrote to you. It happened on the night I sent it I had a peculiarly odious and typical dream about '*us*', and though that did not change my feelings, au fond, it made me feel that perhaps I had been premature in speaking so definitely about the future. You felt that too? Rather you were wiser than I and simply did not look so far. I think that is right. I think its best to leave the earth alone for a bit, i.e. plant nothing and try to stop cultivating anything. Let it rest as it is and let what is there either grow or die down or be scattered or flourish. By the earth I mean the basis the foundation of our relationship – the stable thing. Let it rest! Depend on me, though even when I don't write. Don't get fancies, will you? I am just the same whatever is happening.

In the host of indefinite things there is one that is definite. There is nothing to be done for me at present. And whenever we do meet again let it be in freedom – don't do things for me! I have a horror of personal lack of freedom. I am a secretive creature to my last bones. Whether that is compatible with asking you to make me some pantalons in April I don't quite know. Brett asked me what Id like for April – Easter and I said some fine linen. But if you feel it is not part of our compact for you to sew for me from afar I must go about with a paper ham frill on each leg instead.

Its a glorious day here – cold again but sunny, fresh, the day when one wants to be living in rather a small seaport and watching a large French sailing vessel come riding into the harbour. The climate of Paris is very remarkable. The air is really good and its nearly always dry – not like that disgusting London. Try not to gravitate towards London. I have a real horror of it – I feel its a bad dangerous place – a plague spot and nothing would get me there. I think I hate everything about it.

By the way *tell me* if you'd like to go to Rhodesia any time. I could get the money if you tell me early enough. What would a 2nd class fare cost? And you'd want £20 for clothes before you went.

I hope your pensionnaires turn out well. It seems devilish little to pay – less than the Valpini[1] even. They are in clover in one of the best chalets in Montana for 13.50 and I suppose you will give up every moment of the day & ½ the night to caring for them. I can't see how you can do it at the price – but you know best.

I must get up. These last days have been very busy. So many letters to write & so much business to attend to. Ive sold the Scandinavian rights of the book & the Continental & North African of this new one – and it all means agreements and so on – cursed business! However, according to plan this is my last really bad week. After this next Friday I begin to go up the hill again. This has been that second bump on the switchback.

I feel more at home in this hotel than I ever did in Switzerland. One blessed thing about Jack is he does ignore one completely – in a *good* way – in a way that is necessary if one is a writer. He is there and not there. Give me warning of the Aylesburys won't you? Their parcel grows & grows. I mentally put on another brand for the burning each day. I shall be left stripped to my last leaves.

Oh, how I am longing to be in the green country though – with a block and a pen! Oh, for that German village in its nest of green and the hay meadows and the lilac bushes. I shall leave here the first moment I can!

Goodbye for now. Forgive an odd letter. Im in bed still & rather vague.

Love from
Katherine.
K.M.

Every letter I forget about the small electric iron. Can you send it? Jack has decided to do his and my small washing & burns to do some fine ironing.

Im glad my book has turned up. Please note the little *b*. Otherwise I feel youre talking about the Bible. How is Woodifield? I have a bad presentiment about him. Isn't my name in the file? In large letters? Is Wingley behaving?

This letter is colder than I mean it to be. I have read all your letter. I understand what you mean. Look upon it, our time apart, as something that never is permanent. Its just like a long interval between the acts. It had to be. The irony is I should never get well with you who wish me well more than any other being could. But you were always ready to help and the consequence was I didn't have to make those efforts which tire one and at the same time drag one back into the *normal* world. I don't know – its difficult and mysterious. But having tried the one way and found it a failure one must try the other way. We gave the one way a good run nearly four years – over four years in fact.

About where my writings appear – *really* they are not worth digging out. I'll send you a couple of stories. But I'll have to ask for them back as I have no other copies. Sorry for the blots.

MS BL. *MLM*, 187–9.

---

¹ The Valpini, a small hotel in Montana.

To Michael Sadleir, 21 March 1922

Victoria Palace Hotel | 6/8 Rue Blaise Desgoffe | Rue de Rennes | Paris

21.III.1922

Dear Michael Sadleir,

The last ½ dozen have turned up safely, thank you. I think the others must have been lost in the post. As Pinker is my agent I have asked him to look after Bliss for me. Would you therefore write direct to him if it should be necessary and pay any monies to him if or when they may be due to me.

I am glad the G.P. is selling. I only hope it goes on. Should a 3rd impression be necessary would it be impossible to have a white or a grey or a blue or a yellow jacket instead of the red?

Yours ever
Katherine Mansfield.

MS Lawlor.

To Ida Baker, [22 March 1922]

[Victoria Palace Hotel, Rue Blaise Desgoffe, Rue de Rennes]

Wednesday.

Dear Ida

I have received your letter & the one for Mrs M. [Maxwell] I shall send it on. I am simply astonished that you should consider such a woman as our tenant. My dear Ida! I asked you to stay up there in our interests because I did not trust the people to know what kind of tenant would be suitable. You say to me a 'horrid coarse dirty looking woman who might leave the house in a disgusting state'. To Mrs M. 'I didn't much like her.' But consider what a horrible breach of faith & even decency that is with Mrs M! What are you thinking of? As to my not being responsible – nonsense! Of course I am by any honourable canon responsible . . . 'Not even gentlefolk' & knowing that little woman you entertain the idea of letting them have it.

I feel too bitterly ashamed to write about it any more. I would not have believed it. Either your letter to me is a greatly exaggerated account or yours to Mrs M. is a shamefully understated one.

You have NOTHING to do with letting the house for a year, or selling it. Your one affair was to let it to SUITABLE tenants until June 27th. Thats your whole concern. You are not there as Mrs Ms *agent*. Nothing else is any concern of yours.

The Swiss affair is simply maddening. What have they to do with us? We are not responsible after June. Why worry about them & whatever they may intend. Its simply confusing. *Again* I say if you can get P.Gs leave it at that. If you cant get them you'd better leave the place as soon as the chauffage can be left safely rather than make these muddles.

K.M.

No, I return your letter to Mrs M. And you must write direct to her and tell her the *real truth at once*. You have made this muddle, by considering these horrid Belgians, you must try & put it right. I cant explain to Mrs M. The affair of subletting until June had nothing to do with Mrs M. It was my affair purely. & unsuitable tenants cannot be considered. You do understand that the Belgians are to be refused AT ONCE & FINALLY on my behalf.[1] I have asked Jack to write this for me.

We are responsible for the chalet till June 27. We want to find a suitable subtenant until then; with what happens after we have nothing whatever to do.

You are acting in our interests, not in Mrs Maxwell's. You ought to have said to the de Perrots that the house was, as far as you knew, to let only till June 27. For anything after that they must address Mrs Maxwell directly.

You should have said the same thing to the Belgians.

It is not in our interest that the chalet should be let from June 1. It does not profit us in the least, but only Mrs Maxwell.

We are *morally* & *legally* responsible for the character of any tenant who takes the chalet up to June 27.

You should have told the de Perrots that we had no interest in letting the house from June 1–June 27 and that naturally in our own interests we should prefer a tenant who would take it now or very soon. That would have been quite clear & straightforward and would have avoided all these unnecessary complications in which we have no interest, and for which, unless you are very careful, you will engage our responsibility.

K.M.

MS BL.

---

[1] From this sentence to the end of the letter is in Murry's hand.

To J. B. Pinker, 22 March 1922

Victoria Palace Hotel | 6/8 Rue Blaise Desgoffe | Rue de Rennes
Paris

22
iii
1922

Dear Mr Pinker

I have this day written to Constable asking them to address all further communications etc relative to Bliss, direct to you.

Yours sincerely
Katherine Mansfield.

MS Society of Authors.

To Elizabeth, Countess Russell, 24 March 1922

[Victoria Palace Hotel, Rue Blaise Desgoffe, Rue de Rennes]
Paris.

24
III.
1922.

My Dear Elizabeth,

I have been on the point of writing to you for days. And now – merciful Powers! – it's winter again with real live snow, and I've not been out of this hotel once since I arrived in Paris eight weeks ago except to go to the clinic and back. Oh to be on grass – fed again after all this hay and dry food. I've read Michelet[*1] and Madame d'Epinay[*2] and Remy de Gourmont[3] (exasperating old stupid as often as not) and I cling to Shakespeare. But even Shakespeare ... It's awful. However the Russian promises that after this week I really begin to mend, so have no right to make moan.

But cities are the very devil, Elizabeth, if one is embalmed in them. And here's this postcard of the Chalet Soleil in summer in all its ravishing loveliness, with two perfect guardian angels, large, benign, frilly ones, in full leaf, behind it. I think they are oaks. I cherish, embedded in Twelfth Night a sprig of mignonette from the bush that ran wild in its second generation by the front door. And do you remember smelling the geraniums in the late afternoon in the hall? It seemed just the time and the place to smell those geraniums – I can't even imagine what going back there would be like; it would be too great happiness. But I shall remember that day for ever.

Oh, I've just remembered that you asked me about Ernestine. She is not a breaker, faithful, honest, almost terrifyingly clean. And the F.O. has taught her to cook quite well. I mean she makes excellent omelettes, soups, egg-dishes, pastry, and so on. She never sings except when a pig is being killed afar off and then she breaks into a kind of lustful crooning... At present she and the F.O. are still at Montana. The F.O. thinks of going to the Palace in the winter as a V.A.D.[4] I am beginning to find where I miss her. The ribbons run out of one's chemise and pantalons so fast and I never have time to run them back again. I shall soon be doomed to walk abroad with a paper ham frill round each leg.

How are you – dear Elizabeth. Oh, how nice it would be to see you, to hear you. Lucky people in London!

My book has died down. Mrs. Hamilton (Bertie's friend) tore my hair out beyond words in Time and Tide. How awful such reviews are. One's whole world trembles. John's book is just born.[5] (Speaking confidentially to you alone) I wish I could be enthusiastic about it. It's a horrid fate. Have you read anything very good? Is your tour beginning soon?

With both our loves – much love

Yours ever,
Katherine.

TC Huntington. *LKM* II, 201.

[1] Jules Michelet (1798–1874), vastly prolific historian whose *L'Histoire de France* is considered the high achievement of romantic narrative history. He also wrote the seven-volume *La Révolution française*, and works on natural science.

[2] Louise-Florence D'Épinay (1726–83), educationalist and celebrated letter writer, whose autobiographical novel, *Mémoires*, records the literary society of her time.

[3] Remy de Gourmont (1858–1915), critic, essayist, and novelist. There is no evidence for which books by these authors KM may have been reading.

[4] Voluntary Aid Detachment, a term used during the First World War for auxiliary nurses. Ida already had worked as a nurse aid at the Palace Clinic in Montana.

[5] Murry's second and last novel, *The Things We Are.*

To Mrs. Oliver Onions,[1] *24 March 1922*

[Victoria Palace Hotel, Rue Blaise Desgoffe, Rue de Rennes]

March 24, 1922

What a letter you have sent me! If I could hope one of my stories had given you one moment of the happiness you have given me I would feel less at a loss how to thank you. I have sat here, looking at the pages, and thinking "So she felt like that about *The Stranger*, she notices Florrie the cat, she understood my poor old Ma Parker and Miss Brill..."

For it's not your praise I value most (though, of course, one does like praise) it's the fact that you have so beautifully, so generously seen what I was trying to express. It is a joy to write stories but nothing like the joy of knowing one has not written in vain. I have lived too remote from people for the last four years seeing nobody except my husband for months on end – And that makes one a little bit frightened sometimes lest one has lost touch with life. But a letter like yours is such encouragement that the only way I can thank you is by trying to write better... You say scarcely anything about the big black holes in my book (like the servant's afternoon out.[2]) But I know they are there. I must mend them next time.

How glad I am that you did not listen to the person who said you had "much better not." One does not *expect* such letters – how could one – few people are rich enough to be able to afford to give such presents.

MS Lacking. *LKM* II, 200–1.

[1] Bertha Ruck (1878–1978), the pen-name taken by the fiction writer Amy Roberta Onions, wife of novelist and ghost-story writer, Oliver Onions (1873–1961), who wrote as George Oliver. For all the compliment of the first paragraph, it is unlikely that KM thought much of Bertha Ruck's low-brow popular fiction.
[2] Section VIII of 'At the Bay'.

To J. B. Pinker & Son, 25 March 1922

Victoria Palace Hotel | 6–8 Rue Blaise Desgoffe | Rue de Rennes

Paris

25 iii 1922

Dear Mr Pinker,

Thank you for your letter telling me you have sold the Swedish rights of Bliss and The Garden Party.[1] I am delighted – –

Yours sincerely
Katherine Mansfield.

MS Newberry.

[1] *Bliss* was published in Swedish in 1922, *The Garden Party* in 1923, both translated by Marta Lindquist.

To Ida Baker, [25 March 1922]

[Victoria Palace Hotel, Rue Blaise Desgoffe, Rue de Rennes]

Saturday.

Dear Ida

Your letter has come. But first, Ive just made £20 out of the blue so tell me how money is – send me the bills that remain & Ill let you have a cheque. Do, please!

I felt after I had sent you my letter that perhaps I had not explained enough. I was fearfully busy and rather indisposed. Im glad you have given the Belgians – will give them – their congé. No, its not that I think you foolish. I still absolutely and entirely disagree that the behaviour of such a woman as you described & said even E. didn't think she would work for could be put right in a few days. That may be because you don't think imaginatively of what she could do to the *linen*, the *carpets*, the few kitchen things, Mrs M's china – and so on and so on. On your showing any tenant is a possible tenant – 'all can be put right'. But that really is not true. Its childish, surely. You know a dirty coarse untidy woman can ruin a house in a week – or you ought to know such things by now. It makes me feel despairing that I have to write these things to you. Do you think I like writing them? I *hate* doing so with all my heart! Must I go on and say a dirty carpet is a damaged carpet, a broken breakfast set can be replaced – true – but at what a cost! Oh, its all infinitely boring and unpleasant. And don't you see that if Mrs M. knows you are there, she will accept the woman as much because you have seen her and not really objected as because of her references. No, I still think as I did! And I still feel from your letter that I am beating the air as you alone can make me feel. Its so exasperating that I cant get past it. I can only go on. When I think of you, imagining you saying "But if the expense is so dreadful to you surely it doesn't matter much what the Belgians do. You won't be *paying* any more." And again I read in this letter, "untidy rather dirty QUITE uncared for" – only that and nothing more. Thats quite enough for me, however, Id rather pay till the last day of June than act as if I were morally irresponsible. This doesn't mean that I am not intensely anxious to be rid of the expense. Please understand that – I am.

Ill write again in a day or two and say no more about it. My fatal habit of not being able to forget and ignore as I should is still a habit.

By the way why don't you use the writing paper in the house? There's heaps of it. Why not use it?

Dont worry about your young P.Gs! I didn't realise your young people were so young. What a horrid man Muralt[1] must be. But was one a boy? And was he attached to the girl? How mysterious! In that case perhaps Muralt was right. A boy and a girl alone in a chalet doesn't sound a good idea at all. In a first floor apartment Rue de Pasle, Avenue Suffort, a woman who has just taken a flat there has been found dead in the kitchen with her head cut off. The magistrate said it was an endroit (the rue) where people went to find a place for the night. A nice escape that! Well, let this blow over. Do be moderate in your desires to let the chalet! Is it clear now that the tenants must be gentlefolk – quiet, clean, decent? NO OTHERS WILL DO.

Yours ever
K.M.

Of course Jack entirely agrees with you that the one thing is to let. He was all for your Belgians, and in spite of all you said wanted them taken on at once. £10 would cover damage. This makes it *very* nice for me as I have 'dropped' £50 according to him!

MS BL.

---

¹ Another doctor KM knew in Switzerland.

To Ida Baker, 25 March 1922

Victoria Palace Hotel | 6/8 Rue Blaise Desgoffe | Rue de Rennes | Paris
March 25th 1922

Dear Miss Baker,¹

I am delighted to let the little chalet to you, Madamoiselle de Perrot and your friends for four pounds (£4) a week, for as long as you may wish to have it. I hope you will be comfortable. It is a charming convenient little home.

Yours very sincerely
Katherine Middleton Murry.

I understand the arrangement is to date as from March 27th.

MS BL.

---

¹ The letter to be shown to the landlady, Mrs Maxwell.

To S. S. Koteliansky, 25 March 1922

[Victoria Palace Hotel, Rue Blaise Desgoffe, Rue de Rennes]
Paris
25.III.1922

Dear Koteliansky

No – no – hara-kiri is wrong. Why not be a moralist then? But is it to be a moralist – simply to tell someone who does not know what must be done? To share one's discoveries? Even if they don't agree it seems to me you are bound to tell them what you have found best to do. But I know there is an objection to this, and I have been called an 'interfering schoolmistress' for it. I dont care; I shall go on being one. Of course there must be no violence and no tub-thumping. The other person must *think* they are having tea with jam. It is however, all rather difficult.

Manoukhin says that after this week I shall begin to get better. You know there is a grosse reaction after the 5th seance which lasts for about 3 weeks when one is worse in every way. I am at the end of the 2nd week. I long to be better. 8 weeks in a hotel bedroom, never going out once except to the clinic is very deadly. He won't even let me go for a little drive yet. But its not long now.

Yes I knew M. & H. [Merezhkovsky and Hippius] were liars about Gorki. There was a black stain of malice on every page that had his name.[1] Hippius, too, for a woman of imagination, told awful bangers about her 'cahiers'.[2] She only had the one, you remember, and after it was filled she wrote on the cover and the lining and under the lining and so on. But no cahier on earth could have been big enough for all she wrote. She would say "I have just found a place for a few lines more" and then followed pages and pages with even quotations, of poetry! This is very inartistic.

Goodbye dear precious friend.

Yours ever
Katherine.

MS BL. Dickinson, 91.

---

[1] The offensive remarks about Gorki were made only by Hippius. Maxim Gorky (1868–1936), politically radical novelist who left Russia in 1921, but returned in 1928, and contributed to the implementation of Socialist Realism. KM and Koteliansky would work together on translating him later in the year.

[2] "Le Cahier Noir", one section of *Mon Journal sous La Terreur*, is much too long and detailed to be written as spontaneously as Hippius claimed.

To Michael Sadleir, 25 March 1922

Victoria Palace Hotel | 6/8 Rue Blaise Desgoffe | Rue de Rennes | Paris

25.III.1922

Dear Michael Sadleir,

Many thanks for your letter. About In a German Pension. Even if it did sell moderately well it would antagonise people – and rightly – to such a degree that my next book would stand a very poor chance. Its *awfully* bad. There's a kind of odious smartness about it which would make any decent critic or reader writhe. No amount of revision would make it presentable. Id much rather sit tight on its grave.

Yes, the curly blue hyacinth blue of Jack's cover made me groan for envy. It is most beautiful. Its very kind of you to say I may have my red jacket changed if the G.P. should reach a third impression.

What a curse this strike must be!

Yours
Katherine Mansfield.

MS Targ.

To Charlotte Beauchamp Perkins, 26 March 1922

[Victoria Palace Hotel, Rue Blaise Desgoffe, Rue de Rennes]
Paris
26.iii.1922

My Darling Marie

One blessed thing about Paris is there is a Sunday post. It brought me your most welcome letter today, and I am answering bang off because I particularly enjoy a chat with you on Sundays. I don't know why, exactly. It seems the day for it. Perhaps its a reminiscence of the old '47' days. We have been having just the same due East weather – too fierce for words. Snow, hail, a bitter wind and that quite peculiar wet slate pencil coldness which I hate above all other varieties. I am waiting until the weather changes before I show any new leaves. As soon as I do I'll let you know, dear. But this temperature keeps me very tied up. A great bore. Marie I love domestic details in a letter. After all one tells the other items of news to the outside world. But when you say you've just made your second batch of marmalade I feel as though I had run in & were watching you hold the bottle up to the light, or waiting to see the result of a fresh cooking experiment! Its as though we still shared part of our lives and that is a precious feeling to me.

Rosie's[1] letter was a gem of the first water, my dear! When I came to the bee stinging her leg I jumped up and down in bed like a baby in its pram. It was too pa[2] for words. And the bit about all the washing put away except the starched things. I read it aloud to Jack who thoroughly appreciated it too. He has adopted all my memories of people to such an extent that its quite hard to believe he does not really know the people. I hope your little maid turns out a success. Why do all little maids have their moments of *stupidity.* Never shall I forget my Cornish Hilda whom I used to discover in the kitchen just looking at the kitchen table – dazed – at times. Never shall I forget the sight of her leaping over the stiles either on her way home with legs that took ones breath away. I am sure tho' its a good idea to catch em young if possible.

I had a letter too from old V. written in the Freight sheds while waiting for her luggage to be put through. Poor child! Wasn't that typical. Fancy the strength of mind that must have needed to 'concentrate' as she would say at such a moment. Did you like Mack more this time? Do they have fun together? I mean – does he love her as much as she loves him? Its poor fun otherwise. I am so glad you made her buy some charming clothes. But what a trip across. Its awful to think such an experience still lies in wait for travellers. One feels that by this time the sea ought to have been tamed – and not allowed to run wild any more.

Im sending you a few cuttings. But the best shoots have gone to my foreign publishers and some to Pa. I have had at least twice as many and as long reviews this time and my book went into a second edition in a fortnight. Ive also sold the Swedish, Continental and African rights as well as the American. But best of all are the letters from unknown people – not from my friends though I cherish those, too. But other people write just as though it was all real – talk over the stories just as though they had happened. This is such a joy. But I have so much work to do as a result of all this that I shall have to spend a very secluded summer somewhere. Its almost impossible to write anything long in a hotel. I can't. One feels so conscious of people round one – don't you know.

Fancy Elizabeth and I were invited to lecture this summer with readings from our works. It might have been very amusing, but I should have got the giggles, Im afraid.

I can't believe Papa is on his way. I hope he has a happier visit this time – finer weather. Its bound to be happier though because he'll so tremendously enjoy Woodhay. I can see him looking at the vegetables and feeling that he mustn't make you both too proud – he mustn't show his admiration too much. Can't you?

By the way do coloured anemones do well with you? One never seems to see them in English gardens and they are so decorative and last so well when they are cut. I have beauties in my room now and they are a week old. I should think they'd grow well in your climate – where its warm and sheltered.

Well darling, this pow-wow must end. I send bad reviews as well as good ones to give you an idea. I hope they will amuse you and dear little J. Give her my love. Yes, I thought of you both, first thing, on Mother's birthday. I am sure that Mother's spirit lingers, so lovingly, so content, over Woodhay.

Bless you both, my precious sisters.

Ever your own
K.

MS Newberry.

[1] Not identified.
[2] A word much used in the Beauchamp family for behaviour that was quirky, old-fashioned and endearing (see CLKM I. 32, n. 3).

To Ida Baker, [28 March 1922]

[Victoria Palace Hotel, Rue Blaise Desgoffe, Rue de Rennes]

Dear Ida

I had a letter from you today. Its winter here, too – devilish weather. Am prepared for the As, [Aylesburys] with a whopping great parcel.

Glad to know your Plans are settling again. Thats an obscure way of saying it.

When and How do you send the Tchekhovs. File received but no books.

Yours ever
K.M.

Postcard BL.

To Ida Baker, [29 March 1922]

[Victoria Palace Hotel, Rue Blaise Desgoffe, Rue de Rennes]

Wednesday.

Dear Ida

Your As have just been and gone. I thought they were nice girls. What skin hair teeth the young one has! Youth itself is beauty – *and* health. Theres no other beauty I feel after feasting on that smiling creature in her white felt hat and big coat. They delivered the parcel. I was v. thrilled by the oatmeal bags & the honourable wounds in the stockings were miracles of fine surgery. I feel *most* rich. I shall be able to change my stockings once a fortnight now instead of once a month. And where did the knickers come from? Such good quality too. The blue slip looks very pretty & nice. I'll put it on when winter goes again. The girls babbled away about that strange person called Miss Baker. She'd been with them to the station, sat on their boxes, packed them, got her P.Gs and was ever so pleased to have them. They thought she might *stay* up there. She liked it so. And spring had come & gone & they'd had to give away $\frac{1}{2}$ pots of jam and whole coat hangers at the last. It was a dear little flat – it was indeed! But the mosquitoes in Venice were awful. One saw nothing but woke a fright. And the Mystery was the girl with us wasn't touched. Picnics in the summer were also very nice but Edith wasn't there then. And it seemed from her letters she had a little second hand shop. If you had a jumble sale there was such a rush from miles around you had to have the police. *Very* fond of Wingley. And the balcony was lovely, too. Doctor Muralt had even asked what her age was. Well – not *personally*, but he had asked. There was no room the first night but Miss Yates sent them to a quiet little hotel and it was cheap at all events . . . I could go on with this indefinitely. I spent weeks & weeks with them in 20 minutes. They had just *had* tea thank you very much. And they didn't care in the least about carrying the big parcel. Paris wasn't Dublin, after all.

Yours ever
K.M.

MS BL. *Selected*, 253–4.

To Richard Murry, 29 March 1922

[Victoria Palace Hotel, Rue Blaise Desgoffe, Rue de Rennes]
Paris
29.III.1922

Dear Richard,

Your letter came last night. There's something extremely good in that drawing. Jack, who pinned it up on the wall, on the wardrobe, against the curtain to get a good light said it was because the head's set so well on the shoulders and there's a kind of brooding feeling in it. His remark was "Hm! He's certainly got on with this drawing business." But you know Jack's tone when he says that & goes on to say "Keep it, won't you. Don't lose sight of it." I have therefore kep' it and would have done anyway.

Yes, I too was very interested in Sullivan's review,[1] though I didn't agree with it all. For instance his quotation from Tolstoi "There are no heroes only people".[2] I believe there *are* heroes. And after all it was Tolstoi who made the remark who was – surely – a large part of a hero himself. And I don't believe in the limitation of man; I believe in "the heights". I can't help it; I'm *forced* to. It seems to me that very feeling of inevitability that there is in a great work of art is a proof – a profession of faith on the part of the artist that this life is not *all*. (Of course Im not talking of personal immortality as we were taught to imagine it.) If I were to agree with Sullivan Id have to believe that the *mind* is supreme. But I dont – not by a long long chalk. The mind is only the fine instrument its only the slave of the soul. I do agree that with a great many artists one never sees the *master*, one only knows the slave. And the slave is so brilliant that he can almost make you forget the absence of the other. But it is only really *living* when one acknowledges both – or so it seems to me – and great art is achieved when the relation between these two is perfected. But its all very difficult.

About religion. Did you mean the 'study of life' *or* Christ's religion "Come unto me all ye that labour and are heavy laden and I will give you rest."[3] The queer thing is one does not seem to contradict the other – one follows on the other to me. If I lose myself in the study of life and give up SELF then I am at rest. But the more I study the religion of Christ the more I marvel at it. It seems almost impertinent to say that. But you understand...

To turn from these subjecks to another. I had a letter from Brett yesterday in which I felt she did not want to come to Paris at Easter. She said it was on account of me (and of course she believed it was) but I think the real truth is she wants to get into her new little house first. Im writing to her to say that as far as I am concerned it is O.K. but she must do as she

thinks best. In any case her plans will not affect you, will they? Jack
suggests, if she does *not* come that he meets you at the station of course
and that you stay at our hotel. We are not going to take a flat. We shall stay
on here for as long as we're in Paris. I hope you will come at Easter, dear
Richard, not only for my own delight in seeing you again. But Id like to
think you took Jack about with you and gave him a rest from K.M. and a
change of scene. You know what I mean. Not that we are tired of each
other – far from it, we seem always to get happier & happier (on the Coué
system) but all the same *in confidence* I'd like Jack to have a good time and a
change with his little bruvver.

I reread Jack's novel these last few days. Ever since I first read it
I have thought that you will understand it better than anyone else,
without exception. Its badly printed, isn't it, but the jacket is a lovely
blue. Not like my awful red – dining room red – hateful colour. They
have promised to change it for this third impression. Ive been lucky with
that book. I suppose Ive had 50 reviews at least and sold the Swedish
and Continental rights. But its the letters I get from strangers who don't
care a button about technique but talk about the stories as if they had
happened that I value most. Oh – we are looking forward to cutting
away deep into the country at the end of May and getting down to work
again!

I wish you read German. *Goethe's conversations with Eckermann* is one of
those books which become part of ones life and whats more enrich one's
life for ever. Our edition is in two tomes. We lie in bed each reading one –
it would make a funny drawing.

Goodbye for now, dearest Richard.

With love
Katherine

The Constable p.c. is exquisite.[4] It is put into my Shakespeare with
the Rubens you sent me before. But you feel in the Constable the trees
are there for the sake of the cathedral & the cathedral for the sake of the
trees.

Do you know Marquet's work?[5] Jack wants to go to his studio one time.
We have a small book of reproductions. I shall try & get you one. He seems
to me *very* good.

MS R. Murry. *LKM* II, 202.

[1] J.W.N. Sullivan had written an appreciative, unsigned review in the *Nation and the Athenaeum*, 25
March 1922.
[2] The quotation from the review simplifies Tolstoy's sentence: 'For a historian, from the point of
view of the influence that a person exerts in relation to a certain aim, there are heroes; for the
artist...from the point of view of the relationship of a person to all aspects of life, there should not
be any heroes, only people' (trans. Irene Zohrab from the essay, 'A Few Words about the Book "War
and Peace"', 1868, Tolstoy's *Collected Works*, Moscow, 1955, vol. 16, p. 57).

[3] Matthew 11:28

[4] Richard had sent a postcard of 'Salisbury Cathedral from the Meadows,' painted by John Constable in 1831.

[5] Albert Marquet (1875–1947). Although associated with the Fauves early in the twentieth century, his palette was more subdued, and his use of perspective remained traditional.

To Eric Pinker,[1] *29 March 1922*

Victoria Palace Hotel | 6/8 Rue Blaise Desgoffe | Rue de Rennes | Paris.

29.III.1922

Dear Mr Pinker,

I am so very sorry that I did not hear of your father's death before now. Please accept my sincere sympathy. I do trust that my ignorance did not pain you, but I live remote from people at present and I hear little of what has happened.

I shall be most grateful if you will continue to look after my work.

Yours sincerely
Katherine Mansfield.

Ms Newberry.

[1] Following the death in early Feb. of James Brand Pinker, the first and most significant literary agent in London, his son Eric took over his father's business, but not his probity. He was later imprisoned for financial misconduct.

To Eric Pinker, 30 March 1922.

Victoria Palace Hotel | Rue Blaise Desgoffe | Paris, 6ème

March 30 1922

Eric Pinker Esq.
London.

Dear Mr Pinker,

Many thanks for your letter.

First, in regard to the novel – I may and I may not write one. But in any case it is so uncertain that I should greatly prefer that it should not be mentioned in any negociations. I know myself well enough to assure you that the only safe moment for mentioning a novel by me is when you have the MS of it actually in your hands.

Second, as to leaving Constables. Constables have treated me well enough; but I am under no sort of obligation to them. As I am largely dependent on my work, I naturally wish to go to the publisher who will pay me best. But I should like Constables to be given the refusal of my next book of stories at the best price offered for it by anyone else.

Third, with regard to the serial rights of my next book of stories I have already promised the British serial rights of... a sequence of twelve short stories to Mr Clement Shorter for the "Sphere". This sequence will (according to my present plans) form the principal long story in my new book, and be a third part of the 'story' which began with "Prelude" and was continued in "At The Bay". I have already mentioned something of this to you, I believe. I mention it again because it seems that it may be a hindrance to your offering the serial rights and the book rights of my next volume of stories together to the same publisher.

I hope this will give you a clear idea of my position.

Yours sincerely,
Katherine Mansfield

TS Newberry.

To Dorothy Brett, [30 March 1922]

[Victoria Palace Hotel, Rue Blaise Desgoffe, Rue de Rennes]
Darling Brett.

I see your point about Easter.[1] As regards *me* it wouldn't tire me at all for I feel we know each other too well now to tire each other. But its true the weather will be more settled in May and warmer. There is a chance still I may be able to get about and sit in the Gardens and so on and I shouldn't be able to do that in Easter. And then Ill know my plans more in May – everything is up in the air now... Also I can't help thinking it would be a thousand times more satisfactory if you were already in your little house and no longer homeless. Oh you poor lamb! I think your friends are – to put it at its kindliest – terribly lacking in imagination. Why don't any of them give you a real room and a fire with trimmings. To think of you – frail little creature that you are – blowing along the streets like a leaf in this devilish East weather, and catching cold, and having to take a room in – of all depressing places – Paddington Green! It is all very wrong and horrid. Couldn't you afford a nice warm stuffy hotel like the Langham?[2] There at least one is tucked in and the bath water is hot and theres someone to run messages and so on. Will that nurse look after your cold properly? And I wish I didn't see your days dotted with buns. You need the Bes Food when youre moving. It takes such masses of energy and good humour out of one. The weather here is nothing short of horrible. Its almost dark all day, it rains and snows, drizzles with snow. I cant go out yet. I feel I shall soon come out in satin wallpaper stripes – after these eight weeks in one stuffy room. It has been terrible. Better not talk about it. The worst of it is I am not one atom better so far. – Theres no talking to Manoukhin. He either does not listen or does not understand but shouts across one about his other cases to his partner. So soothing! I get to the point of thinking he has no other cases & that they are both living on my 300 a week in the meantime. But it may turn out better than one imagines. Perhaps this is that famous "darkness before dawn" ...

And the big ray of light is I am fearfully lucky with my writing. In fact my agent wants far more than I can do. But the greatest pleasure is all the letters I get from strangers who know nothing whatever about technique but who go through all the stories and say how sorry they are for William and how they understood why Anne laughed at Reggie and so on.[3] I value these letters far more than any review. Its marvellous to feel these people care like that. And its amazing to find how generous they are. Fancy bothering to write all that! I had a wonderful letter from H. G. Wells[4] yesterday, too. He is another incredibly generous man! I shall have to find a green place in the summer & just stay there fixed and work. Then if this has all been not successful I think Ill try and go to Nancy and have a go at the new pyschotherapeutics. What confusion! Thats the result of hotels. AND poor Murrys excitement this morning. He lost his pocketbook. This to ordinary people doesn't matter much. I – at any rate – am so careless about money that even if I lose it and can't afford to I don't mind. I can't mind. There it is. One can always sell something to get along with. But for M. it is really the deepest most terrifying tragedy. He goes white as paper. He is hopeless at once. He drifted out of my room back into his, turned over everything, pulled everything out of the waste paper basket, made my writing table a haystack, banged the doors, smiled like a person on the stage, pulled the bed about, just didn't shake me by the heels. And his gloom is so dreadful that really one feels deadly sick – its as though one were hanging over a cliff. Finally after about half an hour in my room I got up, threw on my kimono and went off to his. And *I* started while he declared "No, it was no use. It was gone. Hed looked everywhere. The thing was hopeless."

In about five minutes it was found. He looked like an angel as he clasped it or some saint visited by the Lord. Such is the effect of heredity! I suppose for years his family has felt like that, his mother suffered like that while she carried him and so passed it on. Devilish grind of life! But why do those people let themselves be ground. How I thank Heaven that there were a few rascals in my family. Its the rascals who save one from the peculiar tortures that M. suffers from.

I keep an eagle eye on the place where the parcels are put but no egg has arrived yet, darling. As for mine – don't scorn it. It will be the best I can do in the circumstances. Ill buy you a really good egg in May. Do you remember those rose buckles you gave me? They are really very lovely. I thought of having them mounted on a piece of black velvet & each of us wearing one for a bracelet. They are *so* charming. And the idea is nice, I think. How it would make peoples eyes pop if they had seen yours and then saw mine. Tell me if you agree ...

No, I don't miss the Mountain for buttons. I miss her for tidying. I hate leaving my room in disorder or letting any of my personal things get out of place, and its tiring to do it oneself. Still Id far rather do it than have it done by the Mountain. It was always a false position.

How is your little house? And who is helping you with it A very good moving firm is Popes Hammersmith. They clean and sweep one as well & they are cheap. Have you got a servant? If I were a well strong person I would come over & offer my services. I like to think youd accept them & we would make each other cups of tea and drink it sitting round a packing case. That is nice, too.

Goodbye for now, my precious little artist.

Always your
Tig.

Forgive writing. Am lying down & the book has no backbone.

MS Newberry. *Selected*, 254–6.

---

[1] Easter Sunday fell on 16 Apr.
[2] The Langham Hotel, in Langham Place, where KM's father usually stayed when visiting London.
[3] William the mocked husband in the story 'Marriage à la Mode', Anne and Reggie in 'Mr and Mrs Dove'.
[4] The novelist H. G. Wells (1866–1946) had written congratulating her on *The Garden Party*.

To Violet Schiff, [c. 1 April 1922]

[Victoria Palace Hotel, Rue Blaise Desgoffe, Rue de Rennes]
Violet dearest

You may imagine how much I dislike proving to you and Sydney how insupportable a creature I am. But I am now in bed with a violent cold. I caught it somehow on Wednesday in these corridors and there it is in all its vileness. This means of course that again I shant be able to see you. I am tired of being governed by the Furies; I think its time they left me alone a little. But the moment I am better may I telephone you and come and see you?

I was so distressed that Sydney stayed such a short time on Wednesday. But Joyce[1] was rather... difficile. I had no idea until then of his view of Ulysses – no idea how closely it was modelled on the Greek story, how absolutely necessary it was to know the one through and through to be able to discuss the other. Ive read the Odyssey and am more or less familiar with it but Murry and Joyce simply sailed away out of my depth – I felt almost stupified. Its absolutely impossible that other people should understand Ulysses as Joyce understands it. Its almost revolting to hear him discuss its difficulties. It contains *code words* that must be picked up in each paragraph and so on. The Question and Answer part can be read astronomically or from the geological standpoint or – oh, I don't know! And in the midst of this he told us that his latest admirer was *Jack Dempsey*.[2]

No, I really believe there is no reason Civilisation should go. There is still a chance of saving it in spite of everything and Im against the destroyers...

But oh, how much Id like to talk and not write this! Its just on the point of raining again. M. is standing over me waiting for this. Goodbye my dear Violet — Sydney dear

Your loving regretful
Katherine.

MS Cornell. Alpers 1980, 357–8.

[1] Sydney Schiff had taken James Joyce to visit the Murrys in their hotel on 29 Mar., as a preliminary to Murry's writing 'Mr Joyce's "Ulysses"', in the *Nation and the Athenaeum* (22 Apr. 1922). KM's letter was sent on to Wyndham Lewis on 4 Apr., whom Violet told 'J. [Joyce] told us last night that Mrs Murry seemed to understand his book better than her husband which would have surprised her' (see Alpers 1980, 357–8); Alpers however mistakenly assumes that Joyce visited Murry as a result of the review).

[2] Jack Dempsey, the Irish-American boxer who won the world heavyweight championship in 1919. Alpers suggests, 'A quaint mistake on Katherine's part. Joyce must have mentioned George Stanislaus Dempsey, his English teacher at Belvedere College, Dublin, who had kept in touch with him' (Alpers 1980, 358).

To Ida Baker, [2 April 1922]

[Victoria Palace Hotel, Rue Blaise Desgoffe, Rue de Rennes]
Sunday,

My dear Ida

Your full house may be amusing but where are you sleeping? I hope the de Perrot girls do not stay. Five is too many for comfort. I cannot see where they all are. Besides feeding five and so on must be a bore in that little house. Dont forget stuffed nouilles and plats like that, they go farthest and are easy to make.

The weather is still devilish here. Friday was fine but now it pours again. However one cant get over the fact that its April. Once it is fine it will be very very fine. And all early spring plants and so on are extremely hardy. It is not they who come to harm. Bitterest cold, east wind, and storm won't hurt violets or hawthorn buds or daffodils or primroses. They seem to have some special resisting power in these months. Even half open leaves can stand snow. Or so Beach Thomas[1] tells me – and he's a very fine honest naturalist, Tomlinson's great friend. Its a relief to know this.

If you want to know how I am my grande réaction will go on for another week. Then Manoukhin says peu et peu I shall begin to get better.

My book is in a 3rd large edition which is more important, & the reviews still roll in – still the same – *and* letters. Do you remember Mrs Belloc Lowndes?[2] Wrote me at Baugy? Shes coming over in May for "ten days talk". So are Chaddie & Jeanne, so is Brett, Anne, Drey, Richard. The Schiffs are *here*. But I wrote saying I couldn't see them. I shan't see the others either if I can escape in time. I have a horror of people at present. As it *is* one never has enough time to oneself.

If you can manage without the money – good! For my teeth are beginning to give me gyp. I shall have to start with Heppwell in May. And if I don't get my hair washed next week I shall commit suicide. There is a good shop in the rue de Rennes that specialises in henna. I shall go there and come out shining like a chestnut, I hope.

I am very insincere in my horror of people for the Russians here, writers like Bunin, Kuprin, Merezhkousky and his wife [Hippius] and so on I am longing to meet. Manoukhin has asked me to his flat to see them. It will be really thrilling. But it's the English and French 'crowd', always the same, so ashy, so gossipy, so tiring that I don't want to see. Horrible ingratitude I know!

Forgive a dull letter. I ought to be working. But I wanted you to know I was thinking of you. All goes very well here. Have you really time to sew? And have you patterns of my knickers and nightgowns? In case Brett sends the stuff?

Yours ever,
KM,
Love to little Wing – the sweet boy!

MS BL. *MLM*, 190–1.

[1] William Beach Thomas (1868–1957) established his reputation as one of the few British journalists permitted to file heavily censored front-line reports during the First World War, when he wrote for the *Daily Mail*. After the war he wrote widely on foreign affairs, and contributed a weekly nature column to the *Observer*, which KM regularly read.
[2] KM had written several times to the novelist Marie Belloc Lowndes in April–May 1921 (see *CLKM* III. 204–5, 209–10, 241–2).

To Eric Pinker, 2 April 1922

Victoria Palace Hotel | 6–8 Rue Blaise Desgoffe | Rue de Rennes | Paris
2 IV 1922

Dear Mr Pinker,

I have received your letter but the forms were not enclosed. As soon as I receive them they shall be signed and returned to you. With regard to my last letter I confess that thinking it over I feel I might do better with a change of publisher. This book on the strength of its reviews (it has been most

extensively reviewed) ought to have sold more if it had been more advertised. It had a chance of going really well, I fancy, but it seems to me
Constable did not make the use they might have of their opportunity.
I have received numerous letters, too, from the kind of people who comprise
the reading public which prove it had a chance of popularity. (I haven't any
desire to be fashionable and exclusive or to write for the intelligenzia only.)

But these are of course the opinions of a 'layman'. The real point is
I shall have to make as much money as I can on my next book — my path
is so dotted with doctors.

Yours sincerely
Katherine Mansfield

MS Newberry.

To Dorothy Brett, [4 April 1922]

[Victoria Palace Hotel, Rue Blaise Desgoffe, Rue de Rennes]

Tuesday

Dearest

I sent my last letter to Thurlow Road. Did the Hannays impound it –
horrid thought! This I shall send to Pond Street and hope that the painters
wont light their fires with it. Shall I in future always send your letters there?
It's a very nice address. One sees it pond and all. But what I want to say first is.

Do come on the 18th. You will? You are coming? Im to expect you then?
Don't put it off till May. I feel we shall be freer then for I dread to say who
wont be in Paris in May. As it is the Schiffs have arrived. I haven't seen
them though and am not going to for a week or so, though Im awfully fond
of both of them. But we must be alone – that's flat. We must feel a bit free.
Another reason. When I went to the clinique on Friday Manoukhin said
that I should be on the turn in another week. *Now* he says it is from the 5th
to the 10th one feels so ill and Ive had my 10th whack so I ought to be well
on the turn by the 18th. I was rather in despair last Friday but suddenly
just as I was getting on to the table Manoukhin began to talk about
literature – about a story of Bunin's and one of Kuprin.[1] This was such
a joy that after that nothing mattered and I believed in everything.
We began to rejoice over what was so fine in Bunin's work and – all was
well. There is nothing on earth more powerful than love of work.

I hope for the sake of your cold you are not having this weather. Cold,
dark, lashings of rain, strong wind – a general blast in fact. Nothing
matters except the dark. Its that that gives one colds. Take care of yours,
my lamb, and if you do go junketting, make yourself into a parcel.

Im interested in what you say of Wyndham L.[2] Ive heard so very very
much about him from Anne Rice and Violet Schiff. Yes I too admire his

line tremendously. Its beautifully obedient to his wishes. But its queer I feel that as an artist in spite of his passions and his views and all that he lacks a real *centre*. Ill tell you what I mean. It sounds personal but one can't help that: we can only speak of what we have learnt. It seems to me that what one aims at is to work with ones mind and one's soul *together*. By soul I mean that 'thing' that makes the mind really important. I always picture it like this. My mind is a very complicated, capable instrument. But the interior is dark. It *can* work in the dark & throw off all kinds of things. But behind that instrument like a very steady gentle light is the soul. And its only when the soul *radiates* the mind that what one does matters... What I *aim* at is that state of mind when I feel my soul and my mind are one. Its awfully terribly difficult to get at. Only solitude will do it for me – But I feel Wyndham Lewis would be inclined to call the soul tiddley ompom. It's a mystery, anyway. One aims at perfection – knows one will never achieve it and goes on aiming as though one knew the exact contrary.

By the way do you know Marquet's work well? I have a book of reproductions I will show you. He's not a very great painter but hes most awfully good sometimes. What a bore! As I write about him he suddenly seems very small beer. And the reproduction of a picture by *Nain* (in the Louvre) Le Repas de Paysans[3] which is four-pinned on my wall is miles and miles better than all Marquet's kind of thing.

Ive masses of things to tell you, my little artist, but I must finish my story for the Nation[4] and I must get up. Murry is going to lunch with the Schiffs. Its nice to think I shall be alone. The funny truth is I like solitude 1000 times more than he does. He thinks he does – but he is much more restless mentally than I. Im restless physically and he not at all. That reminds me of another thing. If I get *well* Ill have to live 6 months of the year in England. I see that. He will never be happy without a real English HOME. But from October till May I shall go South and work. If my work goes on as it is going I hope to be able to get a small house at the back of Bandol, in the mountains there – to get an ancient and her mari in it. My plan is – some years you & I will sneak off for a winter & early spring together. There's no real winter. But I shall make it my working house. Can't work at all properly in England and never shall be able to. So off we'll go – alone – work, walk, have picnics, sit on the terrace & look at the moon, have very huge wood fires when the sun goes in. All so remote, my dear, far away, beautiful, gentle, like a land of faery.

But we'll talk of that this month. *Tell* me you are coming as soon as you get this letter. A card will do. I hope Arthur comes with you. Make him carrier-in-chief.

I've begun to listen for your knock already. Warm warm love my precious little friend.

Ever your
Tig

MS Newberry. *LKM* II. 203.

[1] Alexander Kuprin (1870–1938), whose story 'Ribnikov', in Koteliansky's translation of *The River of Life and Other Stories*, provided the name for a doll KM kept with her for several years. She had reviewed his short story collection, *The Garnet Bracelet*, in the *Athenaeum* (26 Dec. 1919).

[2] Wyndham Lewis (1884–1957), satirist, novelist, painter and combative critic, had studied at the Slade School of Art, and was the founder of Vorticism, a literary and artistic movement derived from Cubism.

[3] Louis Le Nain (1593–1648), best known for his depictions of peasant and family life, whose 'Le Repas Paysan', painted in 1642, KM had seen in the Louvre.

[4] 'Honeymoon', published in the *Nation and the Athenaeum* (29 Apr. 1922).

To Violet Schiff, [c.4 April 1922]

[Victoria Palace Hotel, Rue Blaise Desgoffe, Rue de Rennes]

Dearest Violet,

Your sweet letter – I feel a brute. Let me explain. After ten weeks without going out of this hotel except to the clinic Ive lost my nerve for the present. And then this wretched coughing and this not being able to reply to "how are you?" But your letter makes me long to see you and Sydney. And since I wrote to you I have seen my doctor again and he declares the 'réaction' will be over this week. These last weeks have been simply hell . . . Its so humiliating, so shameful to be always more or less ill. Its such a terrible bore for other people. But if we can ignore it – *do*, Violet dearest, forgive what looks like horrid ungraciousness and let me come and see you both on Sunday or Monday – or whenever you are free . . . If you would just tell Murry.

With love to you both

Yours ever
Katherine.

MS BL.

To Ida Baker, [5 April 1922]

[Victoria Palace Hotel, Rue Blaise Desgoffe, Rue de Rennes]

Dear Ida

It is no use writing to you when you are too tired to reply. And please do not write to me after 10.30 o'clock p.m. You know what I think about your incredible folly in sitting up after midnight. Its more; it really will *ruin* your mind and memory and understanding. But you only do it to attract attention to yourself. Even to attract yourself *to* yourself. Nobody admires it.

I send back Mrs M's letter as I daresay you have not made a note of the address. No, I shall not write to her. Why should I? She has not written directly to me.

Yours ever
K.M.

Wednesday.

MS BL.

To Ida Baker, [8 April 1922]

[Victoria Palace Hotel, Rue Blaise Desgoffes, Rue de Rennes]

Saturday

Dear Ida,

You have missed my point. Where do you sleep? When do you go to bed? These two important questions you hedge away from. If you omit to put the time why the devil should that put my mind at rest. It doesn't in the least. I still hear midnight strike through the pages. You are a peculiarly maddening character to have to do with.

(1) Now I will answer your letter. I enclose the note you asked for in case Dr M. continues his annoyance. Would you like Jack to write to him direct, very briefly, merely asking him to 'discontinue his intereference with our subtenants?' Reply to this. Jack can write a very cool letter, very on his dignity, if you'd like one.

(2) What about *giving* Wingley for always to the de Perrots. If they would take him would it not be a good plan? As regards Jack and me we shall not be settled anywhere for over a year. I hate to think of the cat being pulled about from pillar to post. He'd be much happier with kind friends – the dear. I'd rather not have him than have him after an interval of suffering. I think it would be in the long run kinder to destroy him than to let him be with strangers. Jack's Mother would be perfectly gentle with him, but Jack's Father might kick him. Or so I feel. Will you decide this? Dove that he is I feel I have said goodbye to him, and that it would be very cruel and sentimental to deprive him of a good home if the de Perrots would like him –

When you wrote Thursday with icicles it was warm, really hot here and sunny. I had a most extraordinary afternoon. Got ready to go to Cooks & lost my cheque book. Spent an hour with Jack turning the whole room into a haystack. No sign. Went off to Cooks to stop all cheques. I had to wait to explain to see my entire account, to go to the intelligence department where my name 'Mansfield' was cried like a vegetable & finally escaping prison by a hair we went off to the Bon Marché[1] to buy a very simple light hat. Have you been there? Its one of the wonders of the world. Having fought to the lift we got out on to an open gallery with about 5,000 hats on it, 10,000 dressing gowns, and so on. But the gallery looked over the entire ground floor & the whole of the ground floor was taken up with untrimmed 'shapes' & literally hundreds & hundreds of women – nearly all in black – wandered from table to table turning & turning over these shapes. They were like some terrible insect swarm – not ants more like blowflies. Free balloons were given away that day & fat elderly women with little eyes & savage faces carried them. It was exactly like being in hell. The hats were loathesome. Jack as usual on such occasions would not speak to [me] and became furious. If I said 'Do you like that?' he replied 'No. Horribly vulgar!' If I timidly stretched out a hand he hissed 'Good God!' in my ear. We got out of the place at last. Then while waiting for a taxi a woman tried to commit suicide by flinging herself at his umbrella with which he was prodding the pavement. *She* was violently angry. I ran away to where a man was selling Easter chickens that cheeped when you blew a whistle. The taxi came & Jack had by this time lost me. Finally both of us raging we got in, drove to the hotel, got out, got in again, and drove to another hatshop. "Get this damned thing over!" was Jack's excuse. There [was] a quiet shop we both knew. We found only about 25 people and hats flying through the air. One woman put on another woman's old dead hat with the pins in it & walked off to pay the cashier. The owner dashed after her with a face of fury & snatched it off her astonished head. My one stipulation was I didn't mind what kind of hat I bought but it must have no feathers. And I finally decided on a little fir cone with 2 whole birds on it! So now you know what city life is like.

Pour changer un peu. The little tight chestnut buds that Jack stole from the Luxembourg Gardens have, in warm water and salt, swelled, abusted of themselves & turned into the most exquisite small dancing green stars. Too lovely for words.

I went to the clinique yesterday. Since I came here I have gained 5 pounds; we begin dining downstairs on Monday. I simply do not dare to think this is going to be a success – or rather I cant write it. Dont mention it. It makes me so terribly – frightened. But so far all has happened exactly as Manoukhin said. The reaction is over. From now on I am supposed to get 'better & better'. I'll tell you as much as I can. I am beginning to go for short walks. But I get terribly tired and breathless. Thats natural however: its my legs that get tired because its so long since I have used them. However . . . in another 2 weeks Ill know much more.

Yours ever
Katherine.

P.S. Re chocolate shop & tea room. I believe theres an awful lot to be made out of a *good* tea room at the seaside, with morning buns after bathing and so on. But Id make it really very original, *very* simple, with a real style of its own. The great point is to be 'noted' for certain specialities & to make them as good as possible. That means ever so much less work and it's far more interesting. If you go in for chocolates, have the very latest thing in chocolates, and so on. As you realise I could write a book on such a scheme. But when you are in the mood tell me your plans. Your shares dropped to 29/3 and are at 30/6 at present. The revolution in Johannesburg[2] had a very bad effect on all African trade for the time.

Excuse writing. I am in the devil of a hurry as usual, with a story to send off today. But I thought you'd better have a chat with me or you'd be beginning to make me feel guilty.

K.M.

MS BL. *MLM*, 191–2.

[1] Au Bon Marché, on rue de Sevres, the first and most famous of the large nineteenth-century department stores in Paris. It inspired Émile Zola to write his novel *Au Bonheur des Dames*, 1883.
[2] The Rand Revolt, a three months' strike by white miners, which led to repeated clashes with the government of General Jan Smuts, who used air and land forces to break the strikers. Around 150 are thought to have died in these events.

To Charlotte Beauchamp Perkins, [8 April 1922]

[Victoria Palace Hotel, Rue Blaise Desgoffe, Rue de Rennes]
Paris.
Saturday.

Darling Marie,

I was so delighted to hear from you. Fancy your leaves not out. We are as green as can be in Paris – no – not really 'out' but all little crumpled new born leaves – most lovely. And we had that fine day you spoke of. It was a joy after the fierce ones there have been lately.

I am so wondering if you and little J. are coming in May. Are you? We both *hope* so. I must say it seems as though my reaction is over and for the last three days I am marvellously better. I don't dare to say too much about it. But Ive been out, walking, bought a sweet-pretty-hat for a song, had my hair cut and altogether I feel absolutely a different human being. I shall be able to tell more in another week. But the doctors at the clinic were delighted yesterday and since I came to Paris I have gained 5 pounds! But if things go on at this rate, my darlings, we ought to have fun in May. The hat shop I found is a treasure – *very* cheap and very original. Tomorrow we are lunching with the Schiffs – South of France friends – and I shall cull addresses from Violet Schiff who always looks exquisite, in case you do come. You would really like this hotel immensely. Double room with private bath 25 francs a day – without food. Meals to be had on the premises – too much meat and not enough trimmings but we might dodge out for our meals in May. Its so warm then and the evenings are so exquisite in Paris. I want to *lure* you across. Brett and Jack's brother are coming for Easter, but only staying for a week. Of course you will have to be on the spot for Papa. Perhaps you'd rather wait until after his coming (it sounds as though he was a celestial person out of the prayer book.) Of course, in spite of my saying *do* come – you know don't you that I would understand perfectly if you didn't, if it was in the least inconvenient. Dont ever feel bound in any way as far as I am concerned. Jack says of course he will send you a copy of his book but he is afraid you won't like it. He doesn't think much of it himself. His next will be much better. And I hesitate to send you mine because you may think it 'personal' – like old V.did.[1] Thats so difficult to explain. You see the Daughters of the Late C. were a mixture of Miss Edith & Miss Emily, Ida, Sylvia Payne,[2] Lizzie Fleg,[3] and 'Cyril' was based on Chummie. To write stories one has to go back into the past. And its as though one took a flower from all kinds of gardens to make a *new* bouquet. But this is a thing which no amount of talking can change. One either feels it, or doesn't feel it . . . About writing a novel – I am going to write a kind of serial novel for The Sphere this summer – to start in August. You [are] right, my dear, one is kept *very busy*. But one wouldn't have it otherwise.

My love to little J. and to you.

Ever your devoted
K.

MS Newberry.

[1] KM's relatives continued to feel that the family were misrepresented in several of the Wellington stories.
[2] Sylvia Payne, a cousin of KM's, and her closest friend when she first came to Queen's College, Harley Street, in 1903 (see *CLKM* I. 7, n.l).
[3] A childhood friend in Wellington.

To Dorothy Brett, [8 April 1922]

[Victoria Palace Hotel, Rue Blaise Desgoffe, Rue de Rennes]
Saturday

Brettushka,

I wish I knew whether my letters arrive or not. If you get this one do please send me a card on the spot. Are you coming on the 18th. I went out today Miss and bought myself a sweet-pretty-hat-it-was-indeed, and walked away in it carrying my dead one in a paper bag. Which is to say:

That this reaction seems to be nearly over. I do feel much better. Manoukhin is very pleased, was yesterday.

Oh, Brett I cant say what its like! I still dont dare to give myself up to believing all is going to be quite well. But all the same.

God bless you darling.

Your
Tig

MS Newberry. *LKM* II. 203–4.

To S. S. Koteliansky, [8 April 1922]

[Victoria Palace Hotel, Rue Blaise Desgoffe, Rue de Rennes]
Saturday.

My dear Koteliansky

I feel better. I went to the clinic yesterday and Manoukhin says all is going according to plan. The reaction is practically over. I have gained

5 pounds! If this 'succeeds' really I hope and believe I shall be able to do much for Manoukhin. It is extraordinary: he is simply *not known*. In a week or so I am going to meet Bunin and Kuprin at M's flat. To think one can speak with somebody who really *knew* Tchekhov.

You know Koteliansky darling, when I write about myself I feel it is selfish and heartless because of all that is happening to the world that you have known. Forgive me!

I press your hands. Do you remember "God sent the crow...a piece of cheese".[1]

Yours ever
Katherine.

MS BL. Dickinson, 92.

---

[1] The title and the first line of a well-known fable by Ivan Krylov (1769–1844).

To the wife of a French friend, [11 April 1922]

Victoria-Palace Hotel | Rue Blaise-Desgoffe | Paris 6ème
le 11 avril 1922

Chère Madame,

Je vous remercie de votre lettre. Je regrette beaucoup de ne pas avoir eu le plaisir de voir V.; mais j'espère que je serai encore à Paris quand il revient du Midi, et qu'il sera tout à fait rétabli par le beau soleil. J'ai un si bon souvenir de ma soirée chez vous, Madame,[1] que l'idée même d'une autre me donne un rouge vif aux genoux. Vous souvenez-vous du moment quand vous avez versé sur mon pantalon gris-perle la petite tasse de chocolat et ma reponse en vous frappant (façon anglais) avec ma porteplume? 'Helas mon passé: Òu est-il passé?' comme disait votre soi-disant mari.

Avec un de mes fameux baisers sur la joue,
    Croyez-moi chère Madame,
      Votre Boule-Dogue le plus fidèle,
      John Middleton Murry.

MS lacking. *LKM* II. 204.

---

[1] Murry's note explains (*LKM* II. 204): 'The part in italics was written by J.M. Murry. It was, in fact, the beginning of an ordinary, polite social letter to the wife of a French friend. He left it unfinished on his writing table and went out. When he returned he found it completed for him.' During these months in Paris Murry saw something of his friend the poet and critic Paul Valéry (1871–1945), and the 'V' referred to in Murry's portion makes it possible at least that the letter was addressed to his wife, Jeannie Gobillard (1877–1970), whom he married in 1900.

To Violet Schiff, [13 April 1922]

[Victoria Palace Hotel, Rue Blaise Desgoffe, Rue de Rennes]

Thursday.

Dearest Violet

Once again I have to send my regrets – not because I am ill this time. But I have to go to the clinic early to have a séance extraordinaire. They want to take photographs and so on, and I dare not go out to lunch beforehand. Its damnable! I only heard from M. this evening. But this is positively my last seance. After tomorrow I shall become a reasonable human being. Forgive me once again.

My exquisite dip into life with you & Sydney has given me a longing for all kinds of things out of reach. Yes, money can buy very much. Your rooms, too! The peace of them and the subdued light. I did not realise such rooms existed in an hotel.

With so much love to you both

Katherine.

MS BL.

To Eric Pinker, 16 April 1922

Victoria Palace Hotel | 6–8 Rue Blaise Desgoffe | Rue de Rennes | Paris

16 IV 1922

Dear Mr Pinker,

Please excuse me for not having acknowledged your cheque for £27.8.2 sooner. Thank you very much. I enclose a second copy of my five-weekly story for The Nation.[1] The other copy I sent direct to be in time for next week's issue. Can you dispose of these second copies in America?

And would you kindly send me those forms to sign? I hope they have not been lost in the post.

Yours sincerely
Katherine Mansfield.

MS Newberry.

---

[1] KM contributed only three stories to the *Nation and the Athenaeum* in 1922: 'The Doll's House' on 4 Feb., 'The Fly' on 15 Mar., and the story she refers to here, 'Honeymoon', on 29 Apr.

To Dorothy Brett, [17 April 1922]

[Victoria Palace Hotel, Rue Blaise Desgoffe, Rue de Rennes],

Easter

My dearest Brett

I look at my list and there are eleven letters to write this morning. But you shall come first; I have so much I want to say to you its hard to begin. First – the Easter egg did arrive on Saturday. It took nearly another day to get it through the customs. I am quite overwhelmed by it and can't utter a word. I certainly never would have guessed *that*. But you must have paid so much, too. That makes me feel uncomfortable. It must have cost a fearful sum. It is too noble a gift; I shall have one day to give it back to you. But I can't for the life of me speak about it. Overwhelmed is the only word. But I wish you hadn't spent so much, especially as you need money now. And I cant help feeling you bought it for yourself and sacrificed it. I shall only keep it for you. Thats the only way I can.

Its a good thing on the whole dearest that you are not coming this month after all – May will be better. I was a little imprudent last week, or I suppose I must have been, and ever since I last wrote Ive been . . . as before. It will pass away again. Manoukhin said last Friday I must not walk more than 10 minutes yet but drive everywhere. So thats what I am doing. The rest of the time I lie down again and write. But its only a li'll bit of a downfall. In a week or two Ill be up again.

Brett how dare you even breathe the idea of *scrubbing*. If you ever take a scrub brush in your hand I hope it will sting you and run after you like a beetle. Dont work any more than you can possibly help! Its cheaper by far to employ slaves for those jobs. I hope your servant is a good creature and will really look after you. I wish I knew more about your house and its fixings but its tiring to write such things. You'll tell me when you come over. Im sure we shall be in Paris until the middle of June for once Manoukhin is over I must get my teeth seen to before we go off again. Then we think of making for Austria or Bavaria, and perhaps our old love, Bandol[1] for the winter. Thats what we *want* to do. I foresee I shall have to pick up a young maid in Bavaria. I cant do without somebody – not a Mountain – but a maid. Who takes ones gloves to be cleaned? Looks after ones clothes, keeps them brushed and so on – and then there's ones hair and all that. It takes such a terrific time to keep everything going. There is an endless succession of small jobs. And then one wants little things bought – new sachets and toothpaste – all those things to keep renewed. I can't keep up with it not if I was as strong as ever. There's too much to write and too much to read and to talk about. I can't for the life of me understand how women manage. Its easier for men because of the way they dress and so on. Also they aren't dependent on small things like we are. No, a little nice Bertha or Augusta is my ambition.

We nearly saw Ethel Sands last week. Murry quite saw Iris Moffet.[2] Met her in the street. Has she been ill? He said she was so changed he hardly knew her. Something has happened to her skin. But perhaps it was only temporary. I have been seeing my Schiffs after all. They are wonderfully kind and sensitive. There are some people whom one delights in for most complicated reasons – by delights in I mean *enjoys*. I suppose the pleasure is nearly all literary. The Schiffs are a perfect feast to one in that way. I could watch, listen, take in for days at a time. And then I admire Violets appearance very much – do you? Everything is so definite – her lips, her eyes, nose, teeth, and that air of radiance. She has a lovely throat, too – very full, and her gaiety is very very rare.

By the way I have discovered something interesting about the Russian colony in Paris – I mean Manoukhin and his friends. They are intensely religious. Before the revolution they were all sceptics – as far from religion as the English intelligenzsia. But now that is changed. They go to church perpetually, kneel on the cold stones, pray, *believe*, really, in religion. This is very strange. Last Good Friday at the clinic Manoukhin was late and his partner, Donat, a handsome white bearded man with a stiff leg, talked to us about it. They have become mystics, said he. Mystic! That strange word one is always touching the fringes of and running away from . . .

Forgive this letter – all is scraps and pieces. I am shamefully tired and only fit for business communications. I try to whip myself up but its no good. The spirit is there all right, dearest. Please read between the lines and I promise in another week or two I shall send a better different letter. Write to me when you can in spite of my little scrappy yelp of a reply. Ive a new story coming out in the Nation called *Honeymoon*. Read it if you have the time – will you? Id like to feel you had seen it. Are you working? Can you work with all the chairs standing on their heads? How soon will it be over – your move? Do you really thrill at the thought of the little house? I'd like to fly over & talk. A man was at lunch yesterday who had left Croydon at 11.30! Goodbye for now, my little artist. I embrace you.

Ever your own
Tig.

MS Newberry. *LKM* II. 205–6.

[1] Where KM and Murry were at their happiest together, from Nov. 1915 to Apr. 1916. She stayed there again from Jan. to May 1917, in very different circumstances, as her health declined and being alone with Ida Baker became intolerable.
[2] A friend of Brett and her circle, wife of the London decorator Curtis Moffat.

To Ida Baker, 19 April 1922

[Victoria Palace Hotel, Rue Blaise Desgoffe, Rue de Rennes]

19.IV.1922

Dear Ida

I was v. glad to hear from you today. I had begun to wonder how things were going. When you write again tell me – will you? about money. What is the situation.

We have had awful weather lately, with the exception of Vendredi Saint. I have not been well for the past ten days as a result, I expect, and work has accumulated to such an extent that Im afraid Im no good as an advisor to you about your T House. If not Brighton, I'd try Eastbourne long before Sheringham (which is a most horrid place). But I have heard of a place called *Frinton,*[1] very chic – Winston Churchills,[2] Gladys Cooper,[3] *Sir* Gerald du Maurier[4] & Dora Morley[5] and family. I know nothing more about it but I should imagine it would be more your affair.

About a name. I don't think the title is at all a good idea. People with ozone appetites don't care a button if its Lady Diana Manners[6] or plain Jane who satisfies them. In any case I doubt if it ever pays to pander to snobs.

But you'll bring this off much better on your own, you know. When Im in England Ill come and admire.

Don't bother to send me flowers. Ill look at them from afar. What a beautiful feast Easter is. There is not another to compare with it. Its very ancient, of course. The Christians only adopted it. In fact it dates back as far as anything does. There is a deep mystery in it.

Forgive a short note. Ill write again. But just at present Im hard at it with rather a difficult story.

Give my love to that spoilt little cat.

Yours ever
K.M.

MS BL.

---

[1] Frinton-on-Sea, Essex.

[2] Winston Churchill (1874–1965), after a career as writer, and politician with both Conservative and Liberal Parties, including First Lord of the Admiralty and serving on the War Council during the First World War, at this time was Colonial Secretary. He had married Clementine Hozier in 1908.

[3] Gladys Cooper (1888–1977), a stage and screen actress who became a pin-up star for troops during the First World War. She returned to the London stage in the 1920s, but from 1930 most of her life was spent in the United States.

[4] Gerald du Maurier (1873–1934), popular actor who first created the role of Captain Hook in J. M. Barrie's *Peter Pan* (1904). He was a neighbour of KM's when she lived in Hampstead, and was knighted in 1922.

[5] Lady Dorothy Hope Morley (1891–1972), daughter of the 7th Earl of Buckinghamshire, wife of Hon. Claude Hope Morley.

[6] Lady Diana Manners (1892–1981), daughter of the Duke and Duchess of Rutland, famous for her good looks, married in 1920 the diplomat and politician, Alfred Duff Cooper. In 1922 she took the leading role in *The Glorious Adventure*, a Hollywood film that did not succeed.

To Elizabeth, Countess Russell, [23 April 1922]

Victoria Palace Hotel | 6/8 Rue Blaise Desgoffe | Rue de Rennes
Paris.

23
IV
1922.

Most dear Elizabeth,

I have kept on putting off writing to you until I could say that I was quite well. But that's silly. For I think of you, wonder where you are and if you have started your journey, long to know, and miss the joy of your hand-writing on the envelope. Oh dear, it would be nicest of all to see you and to hear you talk. I shall always miss you as one misses someone very near and dear. It would be too lovely if John and I might come to the Chalet in August – too thrilling. I dip into the idea and put it away again – as one does a beloved book.

About John's novel. I felt very much as you did when I read the Times review – almost as though the reviewer had been reading another book . . . "A later and a loftier Annie Lee."[1] It has been very well reviewed on the whole. Don't you think that perhaps he lays bare the secret of many many men – the desire to walk away from their solitary job, solitary cottage loaf and marmalade and find an ideal pub with a cosy landlady. I don't know. I had much better hold my tongue. John is by no means puffed up. He looks upon it as an experiment and having written it feels he can now swim in the deep end of the bath without fear. We are both longing to get away to that small Bavarian village and to work. I feel I have spent years and years at this hotel. I have eaten hundreds of wings of hotel chickens and only God knows how many little gritty trays with half cold coffee pots on them have whisked into my room and out again. It doesn't matter. Really one arrives at a rather blissful state of defiance after a time when nothing matters and one almost seems to glory in everything. It rains every day. The hotel window sills have sprouted into very fat, self-satisfied daisies and pitiful pansies. Extraordinary Chinamen flit past one on the stairs followed by porters bearing their boxes which are like large corks; the lift groans for ever. But it's all wonderful – all works* of the Lord – and marvellous in His sight. John and I went for a drive in the Bois the other day. Elizabeth, it was *divine*. That new green, that grass; and there were cherry trees in flower – masses of adorable things . . .

But how are you? Are you enjoying London? I don't know why I rejoice so to hear of Bertie's happiness and his wife's dimple.[2] But I do. The dimple is very important. No wife ought to be without one. But she sounds so pretty. I love bright eyes. How satisfying it is to write about pretty creatures. Your Lucy[3] was so lovely, her slender legs as she lay asleep by the fire – her long lashes.

Are you working? I won't[*] ask you what you are reading. Do you sometimes get tired of books – but[*] terribly tired of them. Away with them all! It being a cold night, lately, John and I slept together and there we lay chaste in one bed, each with an immense Tome of Eckermann's Conversations with Goethe perched on our[*] several chests. And when my side of the bed began to shake up and down

J: "What in God's name are you laughing at?"
K: "Goethe is so very very *funny*!"

But it hadn't[*] 'struck' John.

This shamelessly long letter must cease. I shall have no right to begin looking for one from you. But . . . no – it's a curse to know one is expected to answer.

Goodbye for now
With much – very much love

from us both,
Katherine.

(I still hope to be well in May. But it only wakens the Furies to speak of one's health until one is out of their reach)

TC Huntington. *LKM* II. 206.

---

[1] 'Freud among the Fairies', an unsigned review of *The Things We Are*, (*The Times*, 1 Apr. 1922). The 'Annie Lee' reference is KM's, and not in the review, and her point is obscure. It may refer to Tennyson's long poem, *Enoch Arden* (1864), in which the shipwrecked protagonist returns after many years to find his early love, Annie Lee, happily married, and so does not reveal his identity.
[2] Bertrand Russell was Elizabeth's brother-in-law. He married his second wife, Dora Black, in 1921.
[3] The attractive young wife in Elizabeth's novel *Vera* (1921).

To Ida Baker, [24 April 1922]

[Victoria Palace Hotel, Rue Blaise Desgoffe, Rue de Rennes]

Monday afternoon.

My dear Ida

The Flowers arrived in the most perfect condition – so fresh they might have been gathered $\frac{1}{2}$ an hour ago. I have made a most exquisite 'garden' of the moss, little violet roots, anemone roots & crocus blades. Its like a small world. The rest are in a jug. They are surpemely lovely flowers. But please do something for me. I *beg* you. Tell me (1) where they grew (2) how they grew (3) was there snow near (4) what kind of a day was it (5) were they among other flowers or are they the first? Don't bother about description.

I only want *fact*. In fact if you can send me a kind of weather & 'aspects' report as near as you can you would earn my deep deep gratitude. By aspects I mean the external face of nature.

If E. [Ernestine] had anything to do with the gathering mille remerciments. If W. had a paw in the matter pull his tail for me.

K.M.

Postcard BL. *Selected*, 259.

To Elizabeth, Countess Russell, [25 April 1922]

[Victoria Palace Hotel, 6–8 rue Blaise Desgoffe, Rue de Rennes
Paris]
Tuesday

My dear Elizabeth,

It was a small miracle to receive your letter this morning when I had only cast mine on the waters yesterday. Oh dear, what an enchanting way you have of filling your letters so full that there are little side flower-beds as well and tufts of sweet-smelling delicious things tucked into the very corners! I revel (decently and modestly, I hope) in every word.

But it's horrible to think of you facing castor oil. And the worst of it is C.O. is such a jealous God. Every dose puts one into grimmer bondage. Thou shalt have none other gods but me.

May I as an old campaigner suggest that a large wine-glassful of Saint [ ] Water sipped *slowly* an hour before breakfast and followed by an apple or an orange is very 'helpful'. Another glass of Saint [ ] sipped slowly during the day completes the cure, I find. Old [ ] who had the inside very much to heart used to swear by spinach at the evening repast, eaten *very hot*. The whole secret lay in that.

I wish you would see Doctor Sorapure. He is a great lamb and an extremely intelligent one. In fact he is a unique human being. His address is 47, Wimpole Street. His telephone number is 3146 Mayfair.

TC Huntington.

To Eric Pinker, 27 April 1922

Victoria Palace Hotel | Rue Blaise Desgoffe | Paris 6ème
April 27 1922.

Dear Mr Pinker,

I thank you for your letter of April 22.

You are right in thinking that my next book of stories will contain about 60,000 words, of which the English serial rights of 24,000 are already sold to "The Sphere".[1] In addition to these there are four stories which have already appeared serially, which I intend to include in my next book. This disposes of a further 8,000 words, say 30,000 in all, leaving 30,000 words still undisposed of serially. As far as I can foresee – it is extremely difficult to be definite about work that is still unwritten – these 30,000 words will be composed of 8 stories – 3 of about 5000 words, 3 of 3–4000 words, and 2 short ones of 2000 words.

If Messrs Constable enter into this arrangement and buy the serial rights of these unsold 30,000 words at £8 a thousand, I should be content with £100 in advance on the book rights. If, however, the arrangement falls through and they do not buy the serial rights at this price, I should not consider £100 adequate. But, as you say, £8 a thousand is a better price than I have hitherto received for serial rights, and that would compensate for the rather small advance on the book royalties.

With many thanks for your care of my interests,

I remain,

Yours sincerely,
Katherine Mansfield
[Signature in JMM's hand]

TS Newberry.

---

[1] No further stories were written for the *Sphere*.

To Dorothy Brett, [29 April 1922]

[Victoria Palace Hotel, Rue Blaise Desgoffe, Rue de Rennes]
Saturday

Dearest Brett,

Many many thanks for your letter. Ill answer it first. About Joyce. Don't read it unless you are going to really worry about it. Its no joke. Its fearfully difficult and obscure and one needs to have a really vivid memory of The Odyssey and of English literature to make it out at all. It is wheels within wheels within wheels. Joyce certainly had not one grain of a desire that one should read it for the sake of the coarseness, though I confess I find many a "ripple of laughter" in it. But that's because (although I dont *approve* of what he has done) I do think Marian Bloom & Bloom are superbly seen at times. Marian is the complete complete female. There's no denying it. But one has to remember she's also PeneIope, she is also the night and the day, she is also an image of the teeming earth – full of seed, rolling round and round. And so on and so on.[1] I am very surprised to hear a Russian has written a book like this.[2] Its most queer that its never been heard of. But has Kot read Ulysses? Its not the faintest use considering the coarseness except purely critically.

I am very interested that Koteliansky thinks the German Russian treaty good. Manoukhin and all the Russians here say it means war in the *near* future – for certain, for certain! It is the beginning of Bolshevism all over Europe. The Bolsheviks at Genoa are complete cynics. They say anything. They are absolutely laughing in their beards at the whole affair, and treating us as fools even greater than the French. The French at least have a sniff of what may happen but we go on saying "let us all be good", and the Russians & Germans burst with malicious glee.[3] I was staggered when I heard this. Manoukhin's partner here, a very exceptional French-man, started the subject yesterday, said why did not we English immedi-ately join the French and take all vestige of power from Germany. This so disgusted me I turned to Manoukhin & felt sure he would agree that it simply could not be done. But he agreed absolutely. So they declare, the Russians here, we are in for another war and for Bolshevism partout. Its a nice prospect – isn't it!

I must say I have never in my life felt so entangled in politics as I do at this moment. I hang on the newspapers. I feel I dare not miss a speech. One begins to feel like Gorky feels that its one's duty to what remains of civilization to care for these things and that writers who do not are traitors.[4] But its horrible. Its like jumping into a treacle pot. However, perhaps tomorrow one will stop reading the papers or caring a fig.

> A B C
> Tumble down D
> The cats in the cupboard
> And cant see me.[5]

I send back your Father's letter. Its cold – very. But after all you live a life he disapproves of absolutely and he gives you £500 a year. One can't expect more from ones parents. And Im afraid, my dear, you don't treat him *cleverly*. If you really tell him "dealers are fools" you only give him a weapon to beat you with. Of course he doesn't believe it. He believes they know their job and if they bought your pictures he'd still believe they knew their job. Then he complains you write him 'insulting' letters. I suppose that is really 'unfriendly'. Well, if you do you can't expect him to help you more than he does. There is nothing on earth like an appearance of discontent and failure to harden the hearts of men like your father. It cuts deeper than you imagine. It hurts their pride and they refuse to attempt to help. Yet I feel equally certain that if you had gone the right way about it you could have won your Father. He would have seen your rare qualities and admired them. If Im not mistaken in many ways your Father fascinates you. You enjoy him, appreciate him immensely for some qual-ities he has. But something prevents you from making the best of each other. Its a pity. Perhaps you will say its another case of your childish memories and surroundings. But Ah Brett, we cant plead them – We simply cant! It means the end of all personal freedom if we do. We have to simply get over them, stifle them, no – root them out and fling them over the wall like weeds so that our own flowers can grow. *They* all bear the same flower and its got a smell that will destroy everything else – self-pity. Fatal! Fatal weed! One must be hard and just have done with it – thats all.

I must end this letter. Dont take it for a real letter. Its written from bed where I lie with influenza for tumpany. I am sure Im over the worst of it today. But I still feel very boiled and put through the wringer. You see the weather here is simply beyond words. It rains and rains & its cold and it hails & the wind whistles down the corridors. Only frogs and mushrooms being noseless could refrain from catching things. Influenza puts the fear of God into me. The very word has a black plume on its head and a trail of coffin sawdust. But I hope to get up and go out next week. Don't think I am discouraged. Not a bit of it. On the contrary if a puddinghead could sing – I would. M. comes in every afternoon with a fresh victim to tell me of. Everybody has got it – woman at milk shop, woman at library, bread woman. Where does all the rain come from? And the channel is rough every day. When you come in May if I were you I'd fly. So simple. No horrid old changing from boats to trains and diving into cabins and along gritty station platforms. Flying seems so clean – like cutting out ones way with a pair of sharp scissors.

With much love, dearest

Ever
Tig.

MS Newberry. *LKM* II. 208–10.

[1] James Joyce's *Ulysses* was published in Paris in February 1922. Two of its central characters are Leopold Bloom and his wife Marian, whose long monologue concludes the novel. The episodes of *Ulysses* roughly parallel certain characters and events in the *Odyssey*.

[2] A likely reference to the experimental Andrei Bely novel *Petersburg* (1916). A reworked second edition appeared in 1922.

[3] The German–Russian Agreement (the Treaty of Rapello) was signed on 16 April, a surprise response to French pressure on the Soviets to honour Tsarist debts. The Bolshevik refusal to accept pre-revolutionary debts represented, to French commentators, the loss of both French honour and money. The Treaty emerged as a side-line to an Allied-Russian-German conference at Genoa in 1922. It was widely thought that the likelihood of war was enhanced by Germany's thus securing a peaceful Eastern Front.

[4] A letter from Maxim Gorky to Lenin, written in Mar. 1920, and widely circulated, appealed for the release of Russian scientists and writers who had been imprisoned. 'I stand on their side and I prefer arrest and imprisonment, rather than participation – even silent or passive in the destruction of the finest and most valuable strengths of the Russian people.'

[5] One of many variations on an eighteenth-century rhyme originally used to teach children the alphabet. See Iona and Peter Opie, *The Oxford Dictionary of Nursery Rhymes* (1951, 51).

To Ida Baker, [30 April 1922]

[Victoria Palace Hotel, Rue Blaise Desgoffe, Rue de Rennes]

Sunday

Dear Ida

Thank you very much for answering my card so carefully. It was just what I wanted to know. The flowers, by the way, died at once but the moss & the violet plants in my little terrine is – are – fresh as ever. I think the violet plants are growing.

About the chalet. As soon as your girls[1] leave would it not be a good idea to close it? Put it in order, have Mrs M's agent go over it with you & 'certify' as to its condition and then leave it – with E. to go in once a week and air it until our tenancy is up. In that case I must have notice at once & would you kindly have boxes made for the books by your carpenter. He must come & measure for them. And all being packed they had better be dispatched to Popes Hammersmith where our other furniture sleeps. They can be sent of course by the longest way round. It doesn't matter if they take a year getting there. Can you see about this? Then when I hear from you as to money Ill send a cheque settling everything with £10 for yourself. Or tell me what you need and so on? Will you go to Esmond R.[2] until you start the T. room? It would be a good idea if we met on your way to England and talked over this money business. And again what about Wingley once you get to England? I suppose he'd better go to a vet. He can't then be left with the de P's? Its very confusing. But we must thoroughly discuss money. That is most important. Suppose I give you £10 a month until your T. room pays? Or until you are in a paying job. Would you be able to manage on that? Or would you prefer a lump sum of £50. I ought to get that from America soon & I could hand that over to you instead. Answer me quite frankly please. There is no emotion in all this. My position is as always. Im hard up for the moment because of the expense here. I am living (with the treatment) at not less than £12 a week. Its terrible. As soon as the treatment ends I begin the dentist. Also Im in Paris; I must buy a dress for outdoor wear and so on. I hope to recover some of this money by going to Germany this summer & living more cheaply, however. But I can start giving you £10 a month as soon as you need it. Don't hesitate to be as frank with me as I have been with you, will you? It worries me not to know how your affairs are and you say so little.

Since I wrote you that last letter Ive had flue. The weather has been really appaling, never the same for ½ an hour. I feel better today however and shall get up for lunch. Im rather glad to have had influenza; it has been such a dreaded thing to me.

My agent has sold every single story of my new book in advance & I have not written one. That's pleasant! But once we get away we shall be able to work without end. My book has been a complete success, really. It has made it possible for me to publish stories anywhere I like, it seems. I even get column reviews from the Tribuna[3] – the Italian 'Times'. I intend, next spring, to go to London, take the Bechstein Hall[4] and give readings of my stories. Ive always wanted to do this and of course it would be a great advertisement. Dickens used to do it.[5] He knew his people just as I know old Ma Parker's voice and the Ladies Maid. I heard from Connie.[6] Poor little Alice fell down those marble steps at the Louise,[7] double fractured her thigh and put her backbone 'out' – I think it was – something like that. Of course "we have done ALL we can – X-rays, Le Beaux & Rendall[8] (as though other people would have only had the gardener to help her) but she is not well YET. Jinnie[9] & I find it so "*surprising*" that she has not healed!" Poor little Alice, how our Lord loves her! Connie had seen a photograph of me in The Court Journal[10] & the Queen.[11] Which accounted for the letter.

Elizabeth has never recovered from that toboggan ride to Sierre. She says her insides have turned against her and she has to live on castor oil. I have begged her to go to Sorapure. We shall both be at the Chalet Soleil in August – tell Ernestine. Rally[12] had been spending a long evening with Elizabeth who said "Your fame has soaked through even to him & he speaks of you with awe." I tell you this nonsense to amuse you and because you know the past, not because I am puffed up. On the contrary. Ive just read a new story in The Nation[13] & feel disgusted.

Well, if Im going to get up for lunch up I must get. Another gritty, heavy tray on this bed and I shall scream. Terrible lessons in patience are needed to be ill in an hotel. But the people mean to be so very kind. They are certainly a remarkable set of servants – I shall always come back here with pleasure. They will do anything for one and one can keep canaries or cover the walls with pictures or have 113 vases of flowers as one little Chinaman has (according to my maid) and the servants like it!

Goodbye. Write again when you have a mind to. I am always astonished you write so seldom. But I think you do it with intent. It seems to you best. That first long gap including Easter amazed and worried me. I couldn't believe it of you, after I had so earnestly begged you to keep in touch. I nearly wired Hudson in my anxiety. And then along came your letter with the days fly by & painted eggs and so on. After that *no* silence will surprise me. So never feel bound to write. Letters aren't everything, but I have always found it a trifle difficult to understand how people keep in touch without them. But people do. I expect you'd have a "spiritual" reason.
Ever

K.M.

My deep sympathy with the little wounded lion.

MS BL.

¹ The de Perrot sisters.   ² Not idenitified.
³ A full column review signed 'Il Tarlo', *La Tribuna* (14 Apr. 1922).
⁴ The Bechstein Hall on Wigmore Street, London, which later became Wigmore Hall. In her early years in London KM already had firm ideas on how stories might be recited (see *CLKM* I. 84, 86n).
⁵ Charles Dickens, in the later years of his life, gave acclaimed dramatic readings from his novels.
⁶ Her cousin Connie Beauchamp in Menton.
⁷ Alice, the maid at the Villa Louise, Connie's large handsome house behind the smaller Isola Bella which she had let to KM.
⁸ A doctor in Menton whom KM herself had consulted.
⁹ Jinnie Fullerton, her cousin's companion.
¹⁰ The *Court Journal: Court Circular and Fashionable Gazette* (24 Mar. 1922), carried an unsigned paragraph on *The Garden Party*, describing its author as 'probably the first short story writer we have today'.
¹¹ *The Queen, the Lady's Newspaper and Court Circular* (25 Mar. 1922), published a full-page review by Edward Shanks.
¹² Elizabeth's brother Ralph.
¹³ 'Honeymoon', *Nation and the Athenaeum* (29 Apr. 1922).

To Ida Baker, [April 1922]

[Victoria Palace Hotel, Rue Blaise Desgoffe, Rue de Rennes]

Dear Ida

Will you find one of my photographs of Jack (preferably the one which has a merry look – *not* the one reading) and, having enclosed a card with 'A photograph of Mr Middleton Murry'
on it send it to

The Editor
The Bookman¹
St Pauls House
Warwick Square
E.C.4

Thanks most awfully. Please register it. The Tchekhovs have turned up.
Love from
K.M.

Postcard BL.

¹ Under 'News Notes' in the *Bookman* (May 1922, 73–4), an interview with Murry discussing his recent novel was accompanied by the photograph Ida Baker sent on.

To S. S. Koteliansky, [late April 1922]

[Victoria Palace Hotel, Rue Blaise Desgoffe, Rue de Rennes]

Koteliansky

I am terribly angry. What a swindle! There, on my breakfast tray was the thick envelope. There inside, two miserable letters for Mr and Mrs!! And why bother you with such a stupid affair. I shall write immediately to the Manager & ask them if they have another sixpence for me to send it c/o The Nation. I flashed about in bed like a fish in a net with rage. Basta!

Ever since Easter I have been thinking of you. Easter was wonderful this year. It reminded me of how Tchekhov used to spend the night walking about listening for the bells. And then I always remember this story Easter Eve about the monk at the ferry.[1] It is one of my favourites; it is a marvellous story. And I don't know why, I am so often imagining that you will come to Paris. Do not contradict this imagining. If you do not come – there it is. But let me go on thinking that one day we shall sit in the Bois and talk. It is such a pleasant *dream*.

It was dangerous to write to you as I did while the Antagonist was still living with me. He immediately started another réaction, then a chill, then influenza. What a fearful lodger! But all this will pass. It is strange. I feel perfectly well in spirit but my body will not obey. I do not see how this can be. But there it is.

It is very good to know you have translated Bunin.[2] I look forward to this book immensely. Now I must put off seeing Bunin again for a week or two.

How nice it will be to leave this hotel. Not to see any more wings of hotel chickens, or any more gritty little trays whisking in and out of the room. Yet, in spite of everything, I am glad to have been here. But I long to go into the country, a little village near a river, with fields and orchards. I think I shall go to Germany. Besides there is so much work to do. I have sold every story of my new book in advance, to pay for this treatment, and I have not written one! Six must be ready in June.

It is raining. It always rains now, every day. I notice a change in people's voice a kind of 'quack-quack', and there is a terribly frog-like look about the men. Umbrellas are growing enormous too. It is marvellous growing weather for them.

Goodbye, my precious friend.

Katherine.

MS BL. Dickinson, 92–3.

[1] Chekov's story 'The Student' (1894).
[2] *The Gentleman from San Francisco and Other Stories*, trans. D. H. Lawrence and S. S. Koteliansky (1922).

To Anne Drey, 1 May [1922]

[Victoria Palace Hotel, Rue Blaise Desgoffe, Rue de Rennes]
Paris
May 1st

Dearest Anne,

I have just been through that déchirante experience – two lovely young creatures from the Chemiserie with little frocks "pour essayer seule-ment

Madame". Im sitting, fringe straight again at last writing to you in the one they forced on me – a kind of plum grey – tout droit, with buttings on the hips and no trimming at all except a large embroidered lobster bien posé sur la ventre!!! Shall I ever wear it again? Its beginning to look [more] extraordinary every moment. The little creatures twittering chic-chic-chic would have made me buy a casserole for a chapeau with two poireaux in the front. That is the worst of living as I do far from the female kind. These moments come and Im lost.

Yes, darling Ill be here first week in June for sure. Do come then. Otherwise I don't know where I shall be off to. Ive got a wandering fit on. Anywhere, anywhere but England! The idea would be to have a small permanent niche in Paris and another in the South and then a small car, and so on, ma chère. Very nice – only one thing is missing to make it complete. However, I never care much about money. I always feel sooner or later it will turn up – one will find it somewhere, in the crown of ones hat or in the jam pot.

I was horrified to realise David is old enough to make jokes. Heavens! Do keep him a nice small little boy for a little bit longer. Does he know about the 'Three Little Kittens who Lost their Mittens'[1] and rhymes like that? I think there is nothing to beat those very silly but awfully funny nonsense rhymes and when you are small they have a meaning that we forget later. Oh, Anne I saw such perfect lambs of little boys in the Bois the other day. They made me wish wish wish that you and David were there too. The Bois is simply too beautiful just now. Jack Murry haunts the Luxembourg Gardens however and is to be seen creeping into the back row of the 2d guignol. No one else is there over four. But he says when the VOLEUR appears with a most terrific eye – you know the kind 🔶 – he cant help letting out a yell himself. If only it would stop raining – large spots of rain as big as mushrooms fall every day – Paris would be perfect just now. I dont see much of it for I have still two weeks of my X ray 'cure' to go. But after that I shall really begin to prowl. I can't say much about the cure till its over. I dare not. But I feel very different already.

Im so sorry to hear of your servant débacle. If I go to Germany this summer (we've almost settled to go) I mean to find a good sober German & keep her attached to me for ever. Shall I look out one for you? Germans are the ideal servants, I think, and they are so lasting. They don't ladder at once like the English kind. I want to get a very nice one with a pin-cushion in the shape of a strawberry pinned on her Buste and one who will catch my ribbons when they run out of my chemises and run them in again and be a comfort. Thats what one really wants. A Comfort. They ought to be bred specially.

Im sick to death of this hotel. Ive eaten hundreds of wings of hotel chickens & God knows how many gritty little trays have whisked in and out of my room. But its a marvellous spot to know of. I can never be grateful enough. Its so simple, as they say, and all the servants are pleasant. But I want to be off where I can work more – I can't work in cities. And Ive already sold every story of my new book in advance – and have 12 to deliver in July. Im afraid I am absolutely 'booked up' for this year with work for here and America. But if we could meet next spring, Anne, & do a book then. I mean – make a small spring Tour & write a book on it. I think that would be a perfectly adorable idea.

Weve seen nobody in Paris – Joyce came one day for a talk but thats all. Im a bit too old, or I feel too old for cafés, even if I were well enough to go to them. I don't like that crowd – Nina Hamnet[2] and Co. Can't get on with it. Life is too short. Or perhaps this is old age.

J.M. who is an excellent nose flattener has bought two lovely old apothecary jars decorated in green and pink and yellow. I wish you could see them as they are now full of anemones.

About my old book, Anne. Yes, it has been a success – more than the other was, on the whole. As soon as I get some more copies across I'll very gladly send you one, dearest. I'd like you to read 'Ma Parker'.

Please give my love to Drey. And kiss darling little David for me.

Je vous embrasse, amie, de tout mon coeur.

Darling precious Anne

I am
Katherine

 for David.

MS ATL. *LKM* II. 207–8.

[1] Verses sometimes credited to the New England writer of children's books, Eliza Follen (1787–1860).

[2] The writer and painter Nina Hamnett (1890–1956), was known as 'The Queen of Bohemia'. KM knew her through their mutual friend Mark Gertler, and had written to Brett (10 Jun. 1919), 'Gossip — tittletattle, Nina Hamnett & Gertler *spreading the news* — all that fills me with horror' (*CLKM* II. 328). Her reminiscences, *Laughing Torso*, was published in 1932.

To Dorothy Brett, [3 May 1922]

[Victoria Palace Hotel | Rue Blaise Desgoffe | Rue de Rennes]
My dear Lamb

If I sound cold and horrid – unloving – sometimes, forgive me. I try to help it but I don't succeed very well. What I ought to say is "I am writing about Bolshevism and so on for two reasons. (1) Because it is interesting in a superficial way but (2) because I want to tide over a difficult moment."[1] (2) is the most important thing. Its rather like the nonsense people talk in doctors' waiting rooms. You know? Not being able to keep quiet or to show what I feel I hand you the copy of Punch or whatever it is . . . Forgive me, my little Brettushka. And do understand once and for always its not for lack of love.

I am so thankful you are in your house. I long to see it. Is it *very* nice? Are you really snug? Are you *firm* with your servant about feeding you properly? Heaven bless your hearth! I wish I could come this very day with my gift for the new house and sit & talk to you. Its rather an important day for me. I am beginning my long serial half of which has to be finished in a month from now! And I have also signed away all the rest of my book to be ready sans faute by the end of the summer. The serial is very exciting. Its 24.000 words, a short novel in fact. I want it to end with a simply scrumptious wedding – rose pink tulle frocks for the bridesmaids, favours on the horses heads, that marvellous moment at the church when everyone is waiting – the servants in a pew to themselves. *The cook's hat.* But all all divinely beautiful if I can do it[2] – gay, but with that feeling that "beauty vanishes beauty passes. Though rare, rare it be . . . "[3] Goodbye little artist. Its still cold here and my old reaction has started in the other lung now. Basta!

Tig

MS Newberry. *LKM* II. 210.

---

[1] See letter to Brett (29 Apr.).   [2] Nothing of this story survives.
[3] Walter de la Mare, 'An Epitaph', *The Listeners and Other Poems* (1912), a favourite poem of KM's.

To Eric Pinker, 3 May 1922.

Victoria Palace Hotel | 6–8 Rue Blaise Desgoffe | Rue de Rennes | Paris
3 V 1922

Dear Mr Pinker,

Very many thanks for your letter. About *In a German Pension.*[1] I think it would be very unwise to republish it. Not only because its a most inferior book (which it is) but I have, with my last book, begun to persuade the reviewers that I don't like ugliness for ugliness sake. The intelligenzsia might be kind enough to forgive youthful extravagance of expression and youthful disgust. But I don't want to write for them. And I really cant say to every ordinary reader "Please excuse these horrid stories. I was only 20 at the time!"

But perhaps these reasons have too much sentiment in them. As a business proposition it would I am sure be bad. It would, quite rightly provoke all those critics who have been good enough to let byegones be byegones in judging the Garden Party. It is true, in a German

To Alice Jones, 3 May 1922

[Victoria Palace Hotel, Rue Blaise Desgoffe, Rue de Rennes]
Paris
3.V.1922

Dear Mrs Jones,

Will you please pardon me and ask Hugh to for not having answered your letter and thanked him for the lovely postcard before! I have had influenza and am still in the stage of getting over it. The weather here has been glacial and so damp that everybody has caught cold. I am so glad to hear from your letter to JMM today that Hugh is better. It seems *too* dreadful that he should have had such a bad time. Poor little chap! You must be very proud of his courage but still one would rather little children didn't have to be brave. I do hope this will be the very last of his battles, and I wish I were in London so that I could show you in a more neighbourly way how much I wish him well.

Yours very sincerely
Katherine Middleton Murry.

MS Texas.

To Hugh Jones,[1] *5 May 1922*

[Victoria Palace Hotel, Rue Blaise Desgoffe, Rue de Rennes]
May 5, 1922

My dear little Hugh,

First I must beg your pardon for not having thanked you for that lovely postcard you painted for me. But I wanted to run out and buy you a little present to pop in the letter and I have not been able to yet, for I have been ill, too. But I won't forget. The very first time I go out I will drive to a shop that sells presents.

How very nicely you painted that bee-hive. I have always wanted to live in a bee hive, so long as the bees were not there. With a little window and a chimney it would make a dear little house. I once read a story about a little girl who lived in one with her Grandma, and her Grandma's name was old Mrs. Gooseberry. What a funny name!

Mr. Murry thinks you write very well. He liked the "R" best. He said it looked as if it was going for a walk. Which letter do you like making best? "Q" is nice because of its curly tail.

I have pinned the postcard on the wall so that everybody can see it. I hope you are nearly well again.

With much love from
"Mrs. Murry"

MS Lacking. *LKM* II. 210–11.

---

[1] The son of Alice Jones.

To Ida Baker, [5 May 1922]

[Victoria Palace Hotel, Rue Blaise Desgoffe, Rue de Rennes]

Dear Ida,

You will send me the *bills* in good time, won't you? So that all can be settled up there.

With regard to Jacks possessions. Will you please pack his breeks, his cricket shirts, all socks or stockings, his summer underclothes, and in fact anything he may need this summer – in his large suitcase & bring it with you? Is that possible? Fur rug & striped tick blanket & so on must go into another box. Blue serge suit please *throw away*. He'd like his white trousers please. And will you bring his camera?

M. says there are people in every station who deliver bags, if you don't want to come straight here. I should think you'd better come here for the day. But I don't know your plan. I could see you at *eleven* & suggest you stay to lunch & tea. I think we ought to write a kind of official letter to Mrs M. too. Send me her address – will you? You seem quite dotty about money. Unless you have learned to make it at the Regina.[1] Ill send you £10 for yourself there & we'll talk it over when you come. People still use money, you know. You can't pay your way with biscuits.

Poor little Wing. He must be terribly conceited by now. Ether too? I see him bandaged to the eyebrows.[2]

Yes I am terribly terribly busy. Its worse every day. And the letters. Oh – these letters. They stream in & have to be answered. I ousted my flu finally with ½ bottle of champagne. I felt really awful [the] first few days & then one day ordered champagne for lunch & it did the trick. Its worth knowing. Its not an extravagance. It saves hundreds of bipalatonoids[3] & their kind.

This [is] a note written on the arm of a chair with the room not done, & Jack[4] looking for something in old copies of The Times.

Heaven help us all!

K.M.

MS BL.

---

[1] A hotel where Ida had worked.

[2] The cat was operated on for an infected wound.

[3] Bipalatinoids, iron pills KM had taken for some years.

[4] In a letter Murry sent to Ida Baker the next day, he concluded, 'It seems that the Treatment has been on the whole a great success. Certainly Tig's general condition is immensely improved' (MS BL).

To Walter J. de la Mare,[1] 6 May 1922

Victoria Palace Hotel | 6–8 Rue Blaise Desgoffe | Rue de Rennes
Paris.

6

v

1922

My dear W.J.D.

I have been trying to arrive at this moment ever since your letter came about J.M.Ms book. But the cares of my dilapitated little house take up nearly all my time. Last month I really began to breathe again, as they say, but in stalked the influenza and he is a persistent fellow; he's not gone yet. This is very annoying. But please do not hate me for it...

I did not expect you to write to me about my Garden Party. But I wanted you to have a copy. A strange thing – the night of the day when I last wrote to you, just before I fell asleep I *saw*, in the air, the envelope of my letter to you about Miss M. I had addressed it 14 Annesley Road.[2] But it seems to me impossible you should not know how much I loved Miss M.[3] She is part of my world. I wish you were here; I wish we could talk about her for a *long time* – no less than walk through whole chapters. But these are bold words.

Your Fanny seems to me so much the one and only Fanny that I feel I must apologise for using her name in vain in The Nation.[4] Florence[5] (whom I feel understands Fanny best) I expected to challenge me to a duel. Speaking of Florence, there *is* a Florence Dela Mare in this hotel. We keep no end of an admiring eye on her. Sometimes she is late for lunch and we pine. Then she comes down to dinner in a frock to take the breath. We met her first in the lift - flew up in the air with her. And J.M.M. said 'Florence De la Mare' and I said 'of course'. But she is incognito and will not recognise us.

MS Bodleian.

---

[1] Walter de la Mare (1873–1956), poet, short-story writer, novelist. KM had long been an admirer of his poetry, and felt warmly towards him as a friend. He had written to her on 29 Apr.

[2] She had confused his address, which was 14 Thornsett Rd, Anerley, South London.

[3] In de la Mare's novel, *Memoirs of a Midget* (1921), 'Miss M.' is the midget-narrator, infatuated as a young woman with the charming but finally ruthless Fanny Bowater. The novel concludes with Miss M's being displayed in a circus, and going insane.

[4] Fanny is the young wife in KM's story 'Honeymoon', *Nation and the Athenaeum* (29 Apr. 1922).

[5] Florence was De La Mare's eldest child.

To Alice Jones, 7 May 1922

Victoria Palace Hotel | Rue Blaise DesGoffe | Rue de Rennes
7.V.1922

Dear Mrs Jones,

I wonder if you would be so kind as to send to Constable for a copy of my book & post it to

Mrs Anne Estelle Rice Drey
80 Church Street
Kensington

with the enclosed page. I should be so grateful. And could you send me a copy of the May *Storyteller* published by Cassells.[1] If you are too busy of course I shall understand.
I am so glad to hear your better news.

Yours very sincerely
Katherine Middleton Murry.

MS Texas.

---

[1] 'A Cup of Tea', *Story-Teller* (May 1922), the last story published in her lifetime.

To Eric Pinker, 7 May 1922

Victoria Palace Hotel | 6–8 Rue Blaise Desgoffe | Rue de Rennes | Paris
7 V 1922

Dear Mr Pinker

I thank you for your cheque for £43.9.5 which I received yesterday.

Yours sincerely
Katherine Mansfield

MS Newberry.

To Dorothy Brett, [8 May 1922]

[Victoria Palace Hotel, Rue Blaise Desgoffe, Rue de Rennes]
Monday and Hot as Blazes!

Dearest Brett

Do you mean the true original Eva?[1] I always felt she was a wonderful creature! I feel inclined to steal her immediately. No, only in jest. But what amazing luck! I do hope she looks after you really well.

Do you regret Thurlow Road? One always regrets that skin. One always leaves something precious like a little hoard of treasure buried somewhere and back one goes to it like a ghost, seeking and tapping. How I feel that about Isola Bella! But next Winter M.and I are going to spend in the South! Oh God, what a joy! Brett, as soon as I have the money the little house will be bought in the woods above Bandol. But now I have flown off, darling and I meant to say I feel this house of yours is going to be a happy one. Don't you? Haven't you taken it to your heart?

I am going to get up today & attack solid food again. It sounds a joke but my last five days Ive had a fearful tummy upset – like poisoning – with pains & high fever. Isn't it extraordinary! I suppose these are the final rages of the devils The weather has been perfect & Ive been in my horrid old bed, useless as ever. But I think its on the wane again.

But the warmth! The sun! The air – so soft. The bells so gentle! It is impossible not to feel happy and thankful for Life – beautiful Life.

Dearest, I wouldn't if I were you make rules about not showing your work for so and so long. Let us talk it all out when you come over. The great thing is to go on quietly, steadily, *your own way*. Thats the secret. I think myself you have worked too much without someone near you to discuss what you are doing as you go along – to think it out, talk it over and so on. You have not had enough attention. Some people need a tremendous great deal in order to develop their own powers. Its as though you were a kind of plant, my lamb, that needs a 'frame' as well as the sun, for a bit. You need cherishing. You need the feeling that you are carried in the breast of another. I don't need that. There is something hard in me which even refuses it absolutely where work is concerned. But I know, quite simply I can give that to another. I can help others – for some reason (Im not 'proud' of it you know, any more than a water diviner is proud of his queer flair). There it just is. I wish you could make use of it.

About coming over. That is for you to say. We shall be here until the end of this month, and really all times are the same, now. But do I catch just the faintest hesitation – about leaving your house and so on just as you have got in? If its there darling lets put off meeting again until later. Please tell me bang out. Oh, before I forget. If you have not bought that linen please don't buy it. It suddenly horrifies me – the idea of anyone buying me all that awful white linen. How gruesome! How terrible! If you have bought it – Ill pay gladly – and ask you to keep it. But *dont* buy it for me! There would be a coffin worm in its folds. This is just a note written as usual on the flat of my back. Can you read such awful writing.

Love – love – a special summer line of love.

Tig

The Mountain passes through Paris on the 10th on her way to London. I am going to ask her to take a parcel to you. It will consist of among other things 3 frocks of mine (I love exchanging things like this!) which I thought you might like to have for gardening in. So simple to throw off & on & when finished throw over the wall. They are quite *good* as people say. There is no snag. If you hate them or feel insulted give em away to the next lady who wants to sell you a fern.

MS Newberry.

[1] A servant Brett was upset to lose a little later.

To Ida Baker, [10 May 1922][1]

[Victoria Palace Hotel, Rue Blaise Desgoffe, Rue de Rennes]
Confidential.
Dear Ida

As far as I can tell this treatment has been (I hesitate to use this big word) completely successful. I hardly ever cough. I have gained 8 pounds. I have no rheumatism whatever. My lungs have not been re-examined yet nor has the sputum. Ill let you know about these things. But so far – it seems I am getting quite well. My voice has changed back. I take no medecines. The only thing that remains is that my heart is tired and weak. That means I get breathless and cannot walk yet except at a snail's pace with many halts. But I have no palpitation or anything like that. And of course now that I don't cough or have fever my heart will gradually recover. Manoukhin says I ought to be able to walk for an hour in June, even. I put confidential to this letter because I don't feel its fair to tell anyone who may ask you until I have the *facts* like X ray & analysis. Should anyone ask – just say I am infinitely better & that Ive gained 8 lbs. I mean Hudson or Woodifield.

Jack told you – didn't he – we are coming to the Angleterre.[2] If you have time would you run down & SEE a couple of rooms? It would be very nice if you could as you are so near. I look forward beyond words to the early summer there for working. Any other place would take up too much time. We can settle in there in a day and start off. Both of us are behindhand. And its harder & harder to work here. The weather is really divine. I spent yesterday in the Bois at a marvellous place with the Schiffs. I think I should begin to dance if I stayed here long. You can't imagine how beautifully these women dance in the open under flowering chestnut trees to a delicious band. All the very height of luxury. I do like luxury – just for a dip in and out of. Especially in Paris because its made into such an Art. Money buys such really delightful things. And then all is managed so perfectly. One has tea out of doors but its so exquisite. One's cup & saucer gleams & the lemon is a new born lemon and nobody *fusses*. Thats the chief point of money. One can buy that complete freedom from *fuss*. But what nonsense I am writing. I must get up & go have my wool washed. The shutters are $\frac{1}{2}$ shut & through them gleams a red azalea that Jack bought at Poitiers. It looked a poor thing then but it has turned into a superb creature in this blessed oh how blessed heat and light!

Ida – can you take a parcel for me?? If not you & I will tie up one here & you'll nip out to the post with it. I must get rid of these old skins. Short of digging a hole in the carpet I cant with Jack about. Jack has accepted more or less a lecture tour in England this autumn. I go to Bandol when my time is up here – to the Beau Rivage.[3] I hope to get a maid before I leave here. But I haven't done anything about it yet. Someone I must have. But really as long as the sun shines nothing is urgent. It is as hot as San Remo.[4] I have slashed the sleeves off my blue charmeuse. Sleeves are intolerable. At 10.30 last night I paddled in the bath. But they still feed me on purée de lentilles and soissons. I had strawbug tartlets with the Schiffs yesterday. Can you make *them*? Forgive a very silly letter.

Ever
K.M.

My deep sympathies for Wingie. Ether too! Is he better? I think you'd better call your Tea room *The Black Cat*. Why don't you send the Bills?

MS BL. *MLM*, 193–4.

[1] A draft for this letter survives.

Dear Ida

    Just a line to say – Jack and I both have so much work to do this summer that we have decided when we leave here (end of this month) to go to the Hotel d'Angleterre, Randogne. Does that make you open your eyes! But in the summer June and July that place was so lovely & I know it. It would only take a day to settle and a look at the mountains before one could work. All other arrangements are too difficult – Germany & so on. We have not, literally, the time to discover a new place and take our bearings. Then we shall be near Elizabeth, too. The winter we are going to spend in Bandol at the Beau Rivage. I am going to get a maid now at once. I can't do without one. I simply have not the time to attend to everything and I can't bear as you know 'untidiness'. I shall advertise in the Daily Mail. Jack may be going to lecture in England this autumn too, so I should like to have a really trustworthy person to post letters and so on and be with me. By the way it may interest you Jack is really *very* successful now. His reputation is at least double what it was. He has a new job with The Times too which is being enormously successful. Don't speak of our plans, by chance, will you?

    There is a really superb professional pianist here. He plays nearly all day & one writes *to* his music.

Au revoir
K.M.

MS ATL. *KMN*, 293.

[2] The Hotel d'Angleterre in Randogne, a small village below Montana.

[3] Where KM and Murry had stayed in late 1915.

[4] KM was at San Remo, on the Italian Riviera, from early Sept. 1919–Jan. 1920.

To Elizabeth, Countess Russell, [c.10 May 1922][1]

[Victoria Palace Hotel, Rue Blaise Desgoffe, Rue de Rennes]

... I have been thinking of you ever since the first gleam of this perfect weather. I cannot tell what happiness it was to get your letter. These last few days, in the Bois and in the Luxembourg Gardens, you have been in my mind continually. You are the only being I have wanted to tell that I am out of prison. Even now, it's so like a dream that I hardly dare to write it for fear of waking up ... I've hardly any cough, I've gained pounds and pounds, and the only thing that remains is a tired heart which will of course recover now that it doesn't get such a persistent shaking ... I feel cured. I go out alone and nobody looks at me. I sit in the Luxembourg Gardens *hidden* and it's quite easy to pretend one is walking slowly just because one chooses to ... I sit inside my extraordinarily quiet body and think 'Have the Furies really left? Is it possible they are not coming back ... '

Will you feel we are haunting you in your glades and groves when you know we are going to the Hotel Angleterre in June? John and I both have so much work to do that we don't feel we can look for a new place or make holiday. And both of us long for that air, those mountains and the peace of it. I hope you won't mind us, Dearest Elizabeth. We won't intrude. But it would be heavenly to come to the Chalet in August. . . . .

I wonder if you will like *Ulysses*.[2] It might have been a wonderful book. But although there are pearls the size and blackness of the swine makes it hard to gather them. I shrink from Joyce's mind. He makes me remember all I choose to forget, and he seems to consider as important things that have no existence in a work of art. I really feel a fierce moralist about it but try to hide that feeling as it is 'unworthy'. I read the *Odyssey* afterwards. How exquisite it is − like a fresh water river flowing into a brimming sea. . . .

MS lacking. *De Charms*, 236.

---

[1] This, and the following letter, are possibly transcripts from the same original which does not survive, with different paragraphs included or omitted, and variants even in the one paragraph they have in common.

[2] Elizabeth had asked KM in a letter on 7 May 1922, 'Do you think I shall be able to appreciate Ulysses?' (TC Huntington).

To Elizabeth, Countess Russell, [c.10 May 1922]

[Victoria Palace Hotel, Rue Blaise Desgoffe, Rue de Rennes]
My dear Elizabeth,

How glad I was to hear from you! I had been thinking of you – feeling how you must love this weather. It is simply so perfect that I seem to spend the day in telling myself how exquisite it is. What else can one do? And one's self never grows impatient, which is such a relief, but agrees enthusiastically *every* time... And then it's so adorable of you to ask me how I am – to care about knowing. If you knew how I appreciate that! As far as I can see this treatment has been wonderfully successful. I have hardly any cough, I've gained pounds and pounds, and the only thing that remains is a tired heart. Which will of course recover now that it does not get such a never-ending shaking. I can't say that I am cured for certain until after the second series, but I feel cured, Elizabeth, quite absolutely different! Of course I can only crawl like a snail, but a [ ] snail – a rejoicing one. In fact it is so marvellous that it's still a dream...

Will you feel we are haunting you in your glades and groves when I say we are going to the Hotel d'Angleterre in June. We both have so much work to do that we don't dare to look for a new place or to make holiday. But I long for that air, those mountains, the shining peace of June. There is no place more beautiful! Don't mind us! We won't intrude! But it would be heavenly to come to the Chalet in August.

John is thinking of going to England in the autumn to give some lectures; we want to spend the winter in the South of France. I have never seen Paris look so lovely as it does just now. I've been watching this new dancing, and sitting in the haunts of the rich and great with the Schiffs. It has been great fun. But then the little silvery poet Paul Valery swooped down on us yesterday and began to talk so marvellously about the joy of writing and of being alive at just this moment that I felt I could never look at the Schiffs cream again.

TC Huntington.

To Ida Baker, [11 May 1922]

[Victoria Palace Hotel, Rue Blaise Desgoffe, Rue de Rennes]
Thursday
My dear Ida

I hasten to reply to your letter. Jack is writing Mrs M. *today* and asking her to reply to you *direct*. Ida, I don't see how you can leave until you get that reply! You were up there, I thought, to settle up the "leaving all in order". You can't leave it half done, surely? Why this rush now with Susie

de P. So like you! Shes the one bright star. But how maddening! I do beg
you to stay there & see all is arranged. We shall tell Mrs M. about Ernestine
going in once a week. I have already wired about the boxes. Of course it
would be folly to have lids at that price if the others are strong. I beg you –
its so utterly absurd! – now that you have been up there for nearly 3 months
to see to settling up the house not to rush off before its done. I send you a cheque
for £10 for yourself. If you want more, tell me. That is for your own
personal expenditure. Send us the bills for the boxes. But I have faithfully
believed I could leave this matter of the chalet to you. If you are going to let
me down – wire at once. It is absolutely distracting. *You must go through the*
inventory with Mrs M's representative & get him to sign that all is in order and that the
house is in order. I have no reply whatever, otherwise, to what Mrs M may
say.

   Yes, I think your idea of a Swiss hotel is the best. But there is another
thing. If the cat is ill would not the doctoress put it out of pain painlessly?
Its terrible cruelty to carry about a sick cat. I am absolutely certain Jack's
mother wouldn't take it. But I can't judge at this distance. This letter is
scribbled in great haste. I wish to Heaven you did not so throw one into
confusion. Now you must run after Susie de P! And all else is nothing
to you. "Youll manage somehow" about the house & leave Ernestine to go
through the inventory. That you really *cant* do. What a relief when the
whole business is over and there are no more waving strands like this.
It would kill me to live like you.

   You do understand, do you? This £10 is for your journey and your
personal expenses. Its no good my writing any more. I can only repeat that
I do think in this matter Susie de P. ought to consider you. Surely she knew
why you were at the chalet? Extraordinary!

K.M.

Why muddle? Why rush? Why fuss? Why kill yourself? Its your own fault.
I didn't ask you to go at 60 miles an hour. But I see plainly you're the
willing slave of the new 'person'. It really is humiliating.

MS BL.

To Violet Schiff, [11 May 1922]

   Victoria Palace Hotel | Rue Blaise Desgoffe | Rue de Rennes | Paris
Dearest Violet

   I shall love to come to lunch on Sunday as you suggest. It was delightful
to see you and Sydney on Tuesday. I shall bring the Dial on Sunday with
the 'slashing' attack on Murry[1] – queer world!

Yours with so much love
Katherine.

MS BL.

[1] Ezra Pound, in 'Paris Letter', *Dial* (Apr. 1922, 401–5), attacked British reviewers generally, and Murry in particular for his article 'Gustave Flaubert' in the *Dial* (Dec. 1921). His opening paragraph declared 'Mr Murry's article . . . lacked only one thing: an editorial note to the effect that the article was given in order that the reader might understand for himself, at first hand, with the bacilli of the disease under his own eye and microscope, why nothing, absolutely and utterly nothing, is to be expected from England.'

To Ida Baker, [13 May 1922]

[Victoria Palace Hotel, Rue Blaise Desgoffe, Rue de Rennes]
Dear Ida

Thank you for your letter. Here is the cheque. Does it matter its 10/- short? Not my fault. Tell me if that will do for you.

Yours
K.M.

All right about the box.

MS BL.

To Dorothy Brett, [13 May 1922]

[Victoria Palace Hotel, Rue Blaise Desgoffes, Rue de Rennes]
Dearest Brett,

I can't write a long letter as I would like to for I am infernally busy with work. But read inbetween the lines, dearest, & forgive me. About your coming. This hotel is absolutely full up. Not even a room for ½ an hour! And they don't know when there will be one. So you'll go to your Big Men?[1] Paris looks absolutely marvellous just now – it has never been more beautiful and so light, so airy-fairy. I hope you'll come. If you do – would you bring me 2 tablets Cuticura soap?[2] The only soap for the complexshun! Here it is so dear that one can't afford to wash one's face at all. You know the stuff done up in a horrid black & yellow packet, gooseberry green soap. But it is pure as a lily.

I went to the clinic for the last time yesterday. Manoukhin says I am not yet 'out of the wood'. My right lung is still a bad one. After 2 months of repose I have to go back for 12 more séances. However . . . I am infinitely better – as long as the sun shines. Why does the sun ever go in? Ask this question one of your Thursdays & tell me what your philosophers answer!

Dont be sad, my dear! Your house has tired you. Moving is dreadful. One moves everything – one's whole being is taken up & shaken & put down again with a hammer & nails. A little holiday will make you feel different. And try not to mind your people. How tremendously you do mind them! Too much, dearest Brettushka, far too much. For if you can't change them all your unhappy thoughts of them do no good & they exhaust you like all useless thinking does. I know what its like. But try & shake them off. Its because you find it a bit hard to work just now that you feel as you do – isn't it? When I cant get on I want to (and I find my self doing it) almost torture myself.

Oh, I wish you could hear this man playing the piano, practising below me. But so beautifully! He is listening to every tone, working quietly and carefully & now and again giving himself a treat by breaking off his exercises & bursting into 'something rich and strange'.

Read something very nice! Be happy! Find something lovely in your garden. I wish I were with you to give you a small hug. Take care of yourself. I feel so tenderly towards you! If only you knew. If only you would feel yourself loved. Don't care about the old boat. Its only for an hour or two.

When you come lets go really into the question of your deafness, too. Don't think I ignore it. I think of it often and often. I feel sure that there is a way out – not with X-rays though. Have I ever told you Ive been deaf in my right ear for nearly 2 years now with noises in my head always going on – sometimes less and sometimes more. What a warrior!

And now Im starting the dentist on Monday. Pray Heaven he'll leave me a tooth to stand on.

Goodbye for now. This is, as you see just a scratch.

Yours ever
Tig

MS Newberry.

<hr>

[1] See p. 118, n. 1.
[2] Proprietory name for an antibacterial soap.

To Violet Schiff, [14 May 1922]

[Victoria Palace Hotel, Rue Blaise Desgoffe, Rue de Rennes]
Sunday.

Dearest Violet

I am so very sorry – I cannot lunch with you and Sydney today. I waited until this morning in the hope that my lung would be better, but its no go, and I daren't walk about. I am dreadfully disappointed; Ive been looking forward to seeing you both all the week. And what makes it more aggravating is that its only a recurrence of the réaction due to the treatment that has given me a touch of inflammation. It will be all over in a day or two . . . And here's the sun; its going to be fine. I see you and Sydney in my mind's eye and Im not with you. Cursèd fate!

Please forgive

Your most loving
Katherine.

MS BL.

To Ida Baker, [18 May 1922]

[Victoria Palace Hotel, Rue Blaise Desgoffe, Rue de Rennes]

Dear Ida

You are waiting to hear from me about the various arrangements, are you? I will try & reply. But if I leave anything unsaid you must just use your discretion. I am *so* busy.

Yes, leave E. the revolver[1] – *un*loaded! No, we don't want the fur rug. It would be a good thing to have the *rug case* up there at the hotel. Yes, please leave the iron there. The address for the boxes is Pope's Furniture.

I think that is all. How soon are you coming? Have you heard from Mrs M? We heard this from her yesterday. It doesn't sound v. satisfactory. I mean I am afraid she is taking her time.

So sorry to write at such haste. Many thanks for your letter. Jack who is reading off of this cant understand a word. I suppose you can't either. Stand on your head & try it through a looking glass . . . I think that is all. I can't think.

Goodbye for now. The little house must be v. spick & span. I expect it will be horrid to leave it.

Yours ever
K.M.

MS BL.

[1] For some time, KM had kept a revolver close to her when she was alone. As she had written to Ottoline Morrell, late May 1921, 'On my bed at night there is a copy of Shakespeare, a copy of Chaucer, an automatic pistol & a black muslin fan. This is my whole little world' (*CLKM* IV. 244–5).

To S. S. Koteliansky, [25 May 1922]

[Victoria Palace Hotel, Rue Blaise Desgoffe, Rue de Rennes]

Dear Koteliansky

I feel you ought to know this. I met Bunin last Tuesday evening. He seemed very surprised that he had received nothing for this story in The Dial[1] and that he had not been consulted in anyway about the English translation of his stories. He realised that there is no law by which a Russian author can claim any sum of money for the translation rights of his stories. But it was evident that he felt, in the existing circumstances, when he receives no money at all from Russia and finds it terribly difficult to live at all, he was entitled to a share of whatever profits there may be. I don't know. Perhaps you have a scheme by which he may benefit later. But if that is the case would you write to him and explain? I think it would relieve him greatly.[2] You see they do not know you and poverty has made them resentful. Zinaida Hippius (whom I detest) chipped in with the fact that you had received 500 dollars for the American acting rights of her play[3] and that you had told her she was not entitled to a penny. But it is

Bunin who matters. He is a very decent man – awfully decent, and both he and Manoukhin believe Hippius' story.

You understand why I write this?

Yours ever
Katherine.

MS BL.

[1] See p. 14, n.1.

[2] Koteliansky told Ruth Elvish Mantz, the author with J. Middleton Murry of *The Life of Katherine Mansfield* (1933), that he was angered by this letter, feeling that KM had no right to act as an intermediary, and that he, or he and Lawrence, were the ones to settle directly any business matters with Bunin and Hippius (Mantz, *Garsington Gate*, unpublished TS, Texas, 455).

[3] Koteliansky had translated Hippius's play, *The Green Ring* (1920).

To Ottoline Morrell, 26 May 1922[1]

Victoria Palace Hotel | Rue Blaise Desgoffe | Rue de Rennes

26
v
1922

Dearest Ottoline,

I feel as though I have lived for years – for a whole life time – in this hotel. The weeks pass and I am always hoping for that uninterrupted *free* time when I may sit down and write to you. I hate writing to you in a hurry. I always want not to be haunted by the idea of Time. But perhaps that is to ask too much. It was just the same when I was with you.

MS BL.

[1] This fragment and the following letter were unposted.

To Ottoline Morrell, [26 May 1922]

[Victoria Palace Hotel, Rue Blaise Desgoffe, Rue de Rennes]

I feel as though I have become embedded in this hotel. The weeks pass and we do less and less, and seem to have no time for anything. Up and down in the lift, along the corridors, in and out of the restaurant – it's a whole, complete life. One has a name for everybody; one is furious if someone has taken 'our table', and the little gritty breakfast trays whisk in and out unnoticed, and it seems quite natural to carry about that heavy key with the stamped brass disk 134, and Murry is 135.

Oh, dear – I have so much to tell you, so much I would like to write about. Your last enchanting letter has remained too long unanswered. I wish you could *feel* the joy such letters give me. When I have finished reading one of your letters, I go on thinking, wishing, talking it over, almost listening to it. . . . Do feel, do know how much I appreciate them – so much more than I can say!

I must reply about *Ulysses*. I have been wondering what people say are saying in England. It took me about a fortnight to wade through, but on the whole I'm dead *against* it. I suppose it was worth doing if everything is worth doing . . . but that is certainly not what I want from literature. Of course, there are amazingly fine things in it, but I prefer to go without them than to pay that price. Not because I am shocked (though I am fearfully shocked, but that's 'personal': I suppose it's unfair to judge the book by that) but because I simply don't believe.

MS lacking. *Scrapbook*, 211–12.

To Ida Baker, [27 May 1922]

[Victoria Palace Hotel, Rue Blaise Desgoffe, Rue de Rennes]

Saturday

My dear Ida

I was so infinitely relieved to get your wire & to know you had arrived safely. It was kind of you to send it. My heart was wrung at the last moment of parting from you, as you must have known.[1] I could not believe it. It seemed solemn and wrong. But dont lets call it or consider it a *parting*. We shall make some arrangement sometime that will make it possible for us to be together. Aren't you certain of that? I am. Dont let S. de P. tire you. Don't send me back any money. Spend your money! If you knew what that little account book made me feel. I could have howled for misery like a dog. And then they snatched £5 from you & left you hard up! It is too bad.

I don't seem to have said anything to you at all. But the heat was overpowering and my tooth added to it. Perhaps it doesn't matter so very much. But oh! how I hate to see you travelling. I feel your fatigue and I know you will hurry and wont eat enough and your hat will hurt and so on for ever. When I am rich, my dear Ida, I shall buy you a house & ask you to keep a wing & a chicken wing & a Wingley for me in it. In the meantime I wish you could stay with Mrs Scriven[2] and eat Easter custards or play with Dolly's[3] babies.

It is nice to know the poor little cat is out of its basket. Awful to love that cat as one does. I suppose you imagine I don't care a bean for him because I keep on talking of having him destroyed. To *say* that and see his little paws dodging in and out of the wool basket, & see him sitting in the scales or returning from his walk with paw uplifted stopping now and then . . . In fact I shall one day write a cat story which will be *heart breaking*! In the meantime I do hope he will not die & that you will give him an occasional sardine tail . . .

Its less fearfully hot here. There is a breeze. It has been terrifically hot until tonight (Saturday.) I went to the Louvre this afternoon & looked at

Greek sculpture – wonderfully beautiful. The difference between the Greek and the Roman stuff is extraordinary; the Greek lives, breathes, floats; it is like life imprisoned – except that imprisonment sounds like unhappiness and there is a kind of radiant peace in the best of it. Scraps of the Parthenon frieze – figures greeting, and holding fruits and flowers and so on are simply divine. I never realised what drapery was until today. I had a good stare at the Venus de Milo with all the other starers. And she is lovely as ever – the balance is most marvellous. Its intensely fascinating to see the development of that perfection – to trace it from heads that are flat as flatirons with just one dab for a nose – then to the period of tree worship when all the bodies are very round and solid like the trunks of trees, then through the Egyptian influence when they begin to have stiff and terrible wings, and at last that perfect flowering flower. It makes one in love with the human body to wander about there – all the lovely creases in the belly and the roundness of knees and the beauty of thighs. The Louvre is a superb place; one could spend months there.

We hope to leave here next Friday evening. Next week will be a rush. We have so many engagements, lunches, dinners and I must go to that dentist every day. I feel we are only just leaving Paris in time; one would be swept away. And these little social affairs take up such an amount of the day – preparing for them, seeing to ones gloves & brushing ones coat and skirt and so on and cleaning shoes. It takes me hours to get ready. But I shall speed up later. Already we are putting off engagements until the autumn . . . I sound rather smug and as tho I liked it all, don't I? No, its not that. As one is here its the only thing to do. Serious work is out of the question in a city. One simply *can't* feel free enough. So one accepts distractions; thats all.

Its half past eleven. Jack is still 'dining out'; I suppose he's gone to a café. As usual, as I lie here I have got *very hungry*. Oh for a cup of tea and something to eat! Its just the hour for it. And theres a jug full of old fashioned moss rosebuds on my table smelling of years and years ago (I bought them from a little street boy last night).

Well, this is the awful kind of a letter you get from me. I can only make the pen move; it wont really run, or show off its action. Not that I am in the least tired. Only my hand is. How is everybody? Tell me! I had better end this letter quickly for the old feeling is coming back – an ache, a longing – a feeling that I can't be satisfied unless I know you are *near*. Not on my account; not because I need you – but because in my horrid odious intolerable way I love you and am yours ever

K.M.

MS BL. *MLM*, 195–7.

---

[1] Ida saw KM in Paris on her way to London.
[2] Ida's aunt in Lewes, where at last a permanent home was found for Wingley.
[3] Her friend Dolly Sutton, who lived in Chiswick.

To Arnold Gibbons,[1] 27 May 1922[2]

On and after June 1st | Hotel Angleterre | Montana-sur-Sierre
Valais. Suisse
27.V.1922

Dear Arnold Gibbons,

In Arthur-or-Richard's last letter he told me you had had the idea of letting me see some of your work sometime. Is that right? I'd feel most awfully happy and honoured if you would show me some of your stories. Its harder to know which is the greater pleasure – writing stories or reading other people's. And can I talk them over when I've read them? The address at the top will find me until August. I won't ask you to send them to Paris, one can attend much better in Switzerland.

I hope you and the person I like to think of as my young brother are enjoying this weather.

Until I hear from you I'll look forward to those stories.

Yours very sincerely
Katherine Mansfield.

MS ATL.

[1] Arnold O. Gibbons (b. 1901) had been at Emanuel School, London, with Richard Murry, who noted how his friend sometimes accompanied him when he visited KM at 2 Portland Villas, East Heath Road, Hampstead, where the Murrys lived from late Aug. 1918 to Sept. 1919. Gibbons 'tried his hand at writing. K. was kind enough to look at his efforts. He later became an electrical engineer like his father, and finally an expert on and designer of lighting for the theatre.' (TS ATL).

[2] A draft of this letter survives:

On and after June 1st | Hotel Angleterre | Montana-sur-Sierre |Valais. Suisse

27.V.1922

Dear Arnold Gibbons,

In a recent letter from Arthur-or-Richard I read you had had the idea of letting me see some of your work sometime. Do you still feel inclined to do so? I can't tell you how awfully pleased I'd be if a parcel (the bigger the better) did find its way to Switzerland.

MS ATL.

To Richard Murry, 28 May 1922

Address on and after June 1st: Hotel Angleterre | Montana-sur-Sierre
Valais. Suisse

Paree, Sunday.

Riccardo mio

I have just written as you suggest to Arnoldo. I do hope he will send me some of his work. Id very much like to see it. It is most awfully decent of him to have had the idea – don't you think? I remember that story The Student of his very well. I begin to believe you are as much a little ray of sunshine as I am. Beams appear in your last two letters. It is a relief to think your horrid old chilblains have gone and that you are looking your beautiful self again. But seriously – isn't it almost frightening the difference fine weather can make? I wish Einstein[1] could find some way of shooting a giant safety-pin at the sun and keeping it there. It has been tremendously hot in Paris. Like an oven. Jack and I gave up writing altogether. We were overcome and could do nothing but fan ourselves, he with a volume of Anthony Trollope[2] (very cool) and me with my black penny paper one. The strawberries and cherries came out in swarms – very big cherries and little wild strawbugs. Finally we found a spot in the Louvre among the sculpture which was cool as a grotto. Jack had an idea of making himself a neat toga, taking the Nation for a parchment roll and standing becalmed upon a Roman pedestal until the weather changed. There are glorious things in that first room in the Louvre – Greek statues, portions of the Parthenon Frieze, a head of Alexander, wonderful draped female figures. Greek drapery is very strange. One looks at it – the lines seem to be dead straight, and yet there is movement – a kind of suppleness and though there is no suggestion of the body beneath one is conscious of it as a living, breathing thing. How on earth is that done? And they seemed to have been able to draw a line with a chisel as if it were a pencil – one line and there is an arm or a nose – perfect. The Romans are deaders compared to them. We had a long stare at the Venus de Milo, too. One can't get away from the fact – she is marvellously beautiful. All the little people in straw hats buzz softly round her. Such a comfort to see something they know. "Our Maud has ever such a fine photograph of her over the piano." But 'she' doesn't care.

About Rubens.[3] I never can forget his paintings in Antwerp. They seemed to me far more brilliant than the London ones – I mean impressive. He must have enjoyed himself no end adoing of them. But I confess I like his small paintings best. One gets really too much for ones money in the big ones. There's rather a fat woman wading in a stream in the National Gallery[4] – quite a small one. Its very good, isn't it?

I shall have no time to look at pictures here till we get back from Switzerland. Its terrible how Jack and I seem to get engaged. We are pursued by dinners and lunches and telephone bells and dentists. Oh, Richard, do you FEAR the dentist? He reduces me to a real worm. Once I am established in that long green plush chair with my heels higher almost than my head all else fades. What a fiendish business it is! One day I shall write a story that you will have to tie up your face to read. I shall call it *Killing the Nerve.*

Since I last wrote to you a great deal seems to have happened. But that is the effect of living in a city. I long to get away and to work. We are spending June and July at a hotel about 750 feet below Montana. It is a very simple place and isolated, standing in one of those forest clearings. There are big grassy slopes almost like lawns between the clumps of trees and by the time we get there the flowers will all be out as they were last year. Paris is a fine city but one cant get hold of any big piece of work here; the day splits up into pieces and people play the piano below ones window or sing even if one sits with the door locked and the outside world put away.

There is just a vague idear that Jack may go to England this autumn for a few weeks. I hope he does. We both intend to come over next spring whatever happens and rescue our furniture and make one final tremenjous effort to catch a little house in the country.

Forgive this letter – all in bits, all scattered – Ill write a different one when I get to Switzerland. Richard, I wish – but no – things can wait. In the meantime we never see a painting without thinking of you, talking of you. In fact its hard to tell you how much of our life we share with you, the far away one.

Wingley, our small enchanted brother, passed through Paris last week on his way to England with Ida B. who is going to keep him until we can offer him a real home. It wrung my heart to see the poor little chap sitting in his bastick.

With love, dear Richard, a special summer line of love.

Katherine.

MS R. Murry, *LKM* II. 211–12.

[1] Albert Einstein (1879–1955) was awarded the Nobel Prize for physics in 1921, for his work on light quanta.
    [2] Anthony Trollope (1815–82), prolific novelist and travel writer.
    [3] Peter Paul Rubens (1577–1640), Flemish baroque painter whose work KM had seen in Antwerp in Apr. 1909.
    [4] KM seems to be thinking of *Woman Bathing*, a painting not by Rubens but by Rembrandt van Ryn (1606–69).

To S. S. Koteliansky, [29 May 1922]

Victoria Palace Hotel | Rue Blaise Desgoffe | Rue de Rennes
Dear Koteliansky

You cannot have believed for one moment that I was taken in by the Hippius tale. Whoever spoke to me unfavourably about you would speak in vain. But that you know, of course; it is absurd to write it. My only reason for telling you of the affair was that I considered you had a right to know. Such things should not be said behind your back. I am going to see Manoukhin today and I shall tell him the facts of the shameful, revolting story. It is hard to understand how anyone can be taken in by her who has seen her. I have never felt a more complete physical repulsion for anyone. Everything about her is false – her cheeks, glowing softly with rouge. Even her breath – soft and sweet. She is a bad woman, and it is simply infernal that she should worry you. In one evening I saw enough of her to write a whole book about. And little Dmitri M. who listens to every word, leaning forward with a hand to his ear like a shady little chemist leaning over his counter – They will live for ever, though. Nothing could kill Hippius. If there were a wreck at sea she and Dmitri would be in the first boat. In fact she thrives on disaster. That evening she attacked me. I *could not* get rid of her. She followed me; sat by me always gently laughing, and I felt her power of hatred was supra-normal – like the hate felt by a hunchback. I shall never forget her. This week I shall see Bunin if possible and write to you. I don't want to see any of them ever again. To be with them is exactly like being with women who excite themselves by talking about internal complaints. Just as it is indecent to talk about illness or to describe one's symptoms (and it is an *unpardonable* thing to do) so it seems indecent to hear them talking of "les cadavres", and Gorki's cutlets. I hope that does not sound heartless. Manoukhin is absolutely different; Tchekhov would have liked him very much. I wonder if [?Bien Stock]¹ was the young man, a kind of spy who sat behind Hippius and never spoke a word, but listened. He had a head like this ⬡. Hippius gave him a cigarette during the evening; I think it was his ⬡ month's wages.

Away with them! What is worst of all is that they should have made it necessary for you to write this long letter.

I am leaving Paris on Saturday for the Hotel Angleterre, Montana-sur-Sierre (Valais) Suisse, where I shall be for the next two months. It will be a relief to get away from this city. Paris is beautiful to look at but it is nothing. It has nothing to give. If one is rich one can buy things. But who really wants the things that money can buy? There is not enough *feeling* to cover a threepenny bit. To live in Paris one must have one's soul removed exactly as the dentist takes the nerve out of a tooth; then it would not matter.

Midday is striking. It is so hot, fine, still. I wish we were spending the afternoon together somewhere far away. As I write, now, this moment, I feel so near you.

I am

Yours ever
Katherine.

MS BL. Dickinson, 93–4.

---

¹ Unidentified.

To Ida Baker, [c. 30 May 1922]

[Victoria Palace Hotel, Rue Blaise Desgoffe, Rue de Rennes]
Dear Ida

Just to say we leave here on Friday for Switzerland. I was so glad to hear of your safe return & to know that you had spent two peaceful days – would they were twenty! I am anxious to know whether you get into touch with Miss Franklin[1] again. She always sounded a delightful woman – different *in kind* to the others. Do let me know as much as you can of what happens. Dont for goodness sake take thought when you write to me. Why should you, my dear? I am not as horrid as you think. Ill write from la bas. Its so terribly hot here – as hot as ever & my dentist is really a terrible trial. That, and engagements & packing & so on have taken up all my energy for the moment. But I'll send you a *real* letter from Switzerland. Dont send me any more money. You ought not to have sent this. Though I won't deny it was most terribly useful as Ive had to pay out rather a lot. But *spend the £20* without a qualm.

Ever your loving
K.M.

MS BL.

[1] As Ida explains, she and KM met Miss Franklin in Baugy, near Montreux, where they had stopped in early May 1921, after leaving Menton. 'She was a delightful, sincere woman on holiday from India, where she was working at a mission hospital' (*MLM*, 165). She had pressed Ida, who knew India from her childhood, to return with her and work at the mission. Presumably KM is hinting that this might still be possible.

To S. S. Koteliansky, 31 May [1922]

[Victoria Palace Hotel, Rue Blaise Desgoffe, Rue de Rennes]
May 31st

Dear dear Koteliansky

I am writing to you in the hall of the hotel; the doors are open and a warm, light wind blows through. It is nine o'clock but the evening seems just to be beginning. People pass walking slowly and talking in low tones.

I went to Manoukhin. I found him alone at the clinic. It was nice. But he simply would not hear the Hippius story. He understood only "trop bien" as he said. He was disgusted with her. And he *begged* me – but in such a very simple awfully nice way to write to you and to tell you how extremely sorry he would be to think you did not know how he regretted all the trouble you had had with the Hippius. "Please, please write! Please do this for me!" he said over and over again. Please say to Koteliansky "je comprends, je comprends absolument." I said I would. Manoukhin is really a good man. It is pleasant to be with him. He thinks of coming to Switzerland during the summer with Bunin. I hope they come. *But* I am afraid that on the top of every mountain there would be Hippius and Dmitri always on the skyline.

Do you imagine I shall forget you in Switzerland, my dear precious friend? ... When I come back here in August, after my next 10 séances I have decided to come to London for a week to see my doctor there & let him examine my lungs and so on for an "advertisement" for Manoukhin. It is the least I can do. Brett says I may have a room in her little house for this week. Let us meet then! But what I would like most of all would be if you would ask me to come to Acacia Road[1] to that top room that used to be mine. To sit there and talk a little and smoke. How happy I should be!

Its getting dark. How I love to watch the dark coming. Even a city is beautiful then. But I must get away from all this and *work*. I have a terrible amount to do. Do you dislike my work? I wonder very often. I wanted to send you The Garden Party and yet I felt it would seem arrogant of me. For there is so little in it which is worth reading. When I write a book as well as I possibly can I should send you a copy.

However – it is foolishness to talk about my "work". One must simply go on quietly and hope to do better.

It has been strange to see Brett. There is something very real and true in her. Her secret self is too deeply buried, though. I wish I could make her happier. I feel she has been ignored, passed by. No one has ever *cherished* her. This is sad.

Goodnight.

I press your hands

Katherine.

Why are you not here?

MS BL. Dickinson, 94–5.

[1] Koteliansky lived at 5 Acacia Road, St John's Wood, which KM and Murry rented from June to mid-Oct. 1915. It held a special place in KM's affections, for it was here that her brother Leslie spent his final leave before going to France.

III
SWITZERLAND – SIERRE
JUNE–AUGUST 1922

By the end of her first course of X-ray treatments, KM had put on weight, and felt well enough to intend returning for further sessions in the autumn. Summer back in the mountains at first seemed idyllic, until the usual 'Furies', as she called them, regrouped. She contracted pleurisy, and begged Ida Baker to return from London to take care of her. Then she and Murry found it was impossible to share the same hotel. He seemed unable to take on board how ill in fact she was, and as she frankly admitted, 'It's hellish to live with a femme malade' (to Elizabeth Russell, 5 June). But more divisive was KM's growing interest in ideas that Murry found alien, although there is little hint in her letters of how this conflict was played out. Her revived friendship with her old mentor A. R. Orage ('you taught me to write, you taught me to think,' as she wrote to him 21 February 1921, *CLKM* IV, 177) was taking her in directions that would lead to Gurdjieff and Fontainebleau, although that too would not be apparent in her correspondence for several months.

The day before KM, Murry and Ida Baker set off for London in mid-August, she made her will. 'My heart has been behaving in such a curious fashion I can't imagine it means nothing' (to Murry, 7 August, in a letter to be read after her death).

To Ida Baker, [4 June 1922]

Hotel d'Angleterre | [Montana-sur-Sierre | Valais] | Switzerland

Sunday.

My dear Ida,

I am at last on the balcony overlooking the same mountains. Its hot with a small wind: grasshoppers are playing their tambourines & the church bells of old Montana are ringing. How we got here I shall never know! Every single thing went wrong. The laundry didn't come back in time. We were off late. Brett was laden with large parcels which we could not pack & which she promised to store for us – until when? And only when we got to the Gare de Lyons we remembered it was Whitsun. *No* porters. People wheeling their own luggage. Swarms & thousands of people. Fifteen thousand young gymnasts de Provence arriving & pouring through one.

Poor Jack who had my money gave away a 500 note instead of a 50. And at last arrived at the Couchettes we found ordinary 1st class carriage with 3 persons a side. No washing arrangements – nothing. It was the cursed Fête de Narcisse at Montreux yesterday so conducted parties crammed the train. What a night! And the grime! At Lausanne we both looked like negroes. Then came a further rush for the Sierre train (registered luggage tickets lost) & finally two hours late we arrived at the Belle Vue, starving, as we had no food with us & there was no food on the train. But that enchanted hotel was more exquisite than ever. The people so kind and gentle, the wavy branches outside the windows, a smell of roses and lime blossom. After a very powerful wash and an immaculate lunch – why do the glasses & spoons shine so? – I lay down & went to sleep & Jack went out. The next thing was: "La voiture est là Madame." Heavens! Nothing was packed. Jack had not come back. The bill was not paid and so on. I am quite out of the habit of these rushes. Finally we found Jack at the post office & just got to the station in time. Then at Randogne there was no room for our luggage in the cart. So we went off without it. (Last bulletin de bagage lost Jack simply *prostrate*) and we'd scarcely left the station when it began to pour with rain. Sheets, spouts of cold mountain rain. My mole coat & skirt was like a mole skin. We got soaked and the road which hasn't been remade yet after the winter was exactly like the bed of a river. But the comble was to get here & see these small pokey little rooms waiting us. We took the ground floors three as you said they were so BIG and so NICE. Good God! Whatever made you tell such bangers. They are small single rooms & really they looked quite dreadful. Also the woman told us she had *no* servants. She & her sister were alone to do everything. I thought at first we'd have to drive off again. But that was impossible. So I decided to accept it as a kind of picnic. "The kind of place R.L. Stevenson might have stayed at"[1] or "some little hotel in Russia". Jack looked much happier then. But there wasn't even an armchair or a glass in my room. No washtable in his. I made the old woman get us these things. She is amiable & kind and poor soul – very frightened. And before supper the luggage arrived; we unpacked and my room looked much better. We were just settling down when I found Jack had left the dear little square clock in the train. I was devoted to that clock – & he found he had lost his only fountain pen!

However, wild horses wont drag me away from here for the next two months. I think we shall be able to get decent food. At any rate they have excellent eggs & good butter milk & their own vegetables. I felt inclined to cry when I saw how hard they had tried to impress us last night at supper with their cooking – even to a poor little boiled custard that floated airy fairy with little white threads in it.

But at last it *is* peaceful. This balcony is perfect. And the air – after Paris – the peace, the outlook instead of that grimy wall. Cities are too detestable. I should never write anything if I lived in them. I feel base, and distracted. And all those dreadful parties. Oh how odious they are. How I hate the word '*chic*'. C'est plus chic, moins chic, pas chic, très chic. French women haven't another note to sing on. And the heat! It was frightful. And the stale food. I had to give up my dentist at last until a more propitious moment. I couldn't stand it.

Well, thats enough of Paris. I shant mention it again. Write to me when you get this. All my underclothes are in rags. Shall I ever have time to mend them. All the tops of my knickers are frayed & the seams of my 'tops' are burst & my nightgowns are unsewn. What a fate! But it really doesn't matter when one looks at the sky & the grass shaking in the light.

What are you doing? What are your plans? How is Wing? How is 'everybody'?

Yours ever
K.M.

Ms BL. *MLM*, 198–9.

¹ KM has in mind Robert Louis Stevenson's *Travels with a Donkey in the Cevennes* (1879).

To Dorothy Brett, [5 June 1922]

Hotel d'Angleterre | Montana-Sur-Sierre | Valais | Suisse.
My dearest Lamb,

I must write to you before I begin work. I think of you so often and at this moment sitting on the balcony in THE sweater, which isn't a jot too warm but is perfect – so snug and soft – I feel as though my song of praise must reach you wherever you are.

Aren't last moments of any kind awful? Those last feverish ones at the hotel – how detestable they were.¹ And I kept thinking afterwards that perhaps, darling, you felt I shouted at you in the hall. I hope to Heaven you didn't. It is on my mind. I wasn't as careful as I should have been. Forgive me! And throw away those odious great parcels if they worry you. You can't think – you can't imagine how you helped me. How can I repay you? But Ill try and find out a way some day.

We had an awful journey. The station was crammed with a seething mob. No porters – people carrying their own luggage. No couchettes after all – only a packed 1st class carriage, coated in grime. It was Whitsun of course – Ive never taken Whitsun seriously before but now I know better. Poor dear M. left things in the rack, gave a 500 note instead of a 50, lost the registered luggage tickets…When we reached Sierre and that lovely clean hotel, smelling of roses and lime blossom we both fell fast asleep on a garden bench while waiting for lunch. Then at Randogne, after shinning up a hill to reach the little cart, a big black cloud saw us far off, *tore* across and we'd scarcely started when down came the cold mountain rain. Big drops that clashed on one like pennies. It poured in sheets and torrents. We hadn't even a rug. The road which has only just been dug out & is like a river bed became a river, and for the most of the time we seemed to drive on two wheels. But it was heavenly, it didn't matter. It was so marvellously fresh and cool after Paris. A huge dog plunged after our cart & leapt into all the streams – a dog as big as – a big sofa. Its name was Lulu. When we arrived, sleek as cats with the wet, a little old grey woman ran out to meet us. There wasn't another soul to be seen. All was empty, chill and strange. She took us into two very bare plain rooms, smelling of pitch pine with big bunches of wild flowers on the tables, with no mirrors, little washbasins like tea basins, no armchairs, no nuffin. And she explained she had no servant even. There was only herself & her old sister who would look after us. I had such fever by this time that it all seemed like a dream. When the old 'un had gone Jack looked very *sad*. Oh, how I pitied him! I saw he had the awful foreboding that we must move on again. But I had the feeling that perhaps we had been living too soft lately. It was perhaps time to shed all those hot water taps and horrid false luxuries. So I said it reminded me of the kind of place Tchekhov would stay at in the country in Russia! This comforted M. so much that the very walls seemed to expand. And after we had *un*packed and eaten eggs from the hen not the shop M. got into a pair of old canvas shoes & a cricket shirt.

The air is so wonderful. Its not really hot here except in the sun. Theres just a faint breeze – a freshet that blows from across the valley. Its all silky and spring like. The grasshoppers ring their little tambourines all day and all night too. The view is so marvellous that you must see it to believe it. And behind this hotel, dearest, there are immense lawns dotted with trees; its like a huge natural park. We sat there yesterday watching the herds – a few bright sheep, an old woman with her goat, a young girl far away with some black cows. When the beasts were being driven home at milking time they began to *play*. I have never seen a more beautiful sight. They are so joyful to be out again & in the green fields that great cows lowed softly for delight and skipped and jumped and tilted at each other and little sheep flew along like rocking horses and danced and gambolled. The slender girls with mushroom white handkerchiefs on their heads ran after them. But they caught the infection and began to laugh and sing, too. It was like the beginning of the world again.

Brett, cities are cursed places. When I have my little house in the South Ill never go near them & I shall *lure* you away. I long for you to be here next month. The hotel will still be empty. But thats nice. It is so still. As one crosses the hall it echoes. The old woman has very kind eyes. She is simple and gentle. She keeps promising me that I will get better here, and she is determined to make me drink all kinds of teas made of fresh strawberry leaves and hay and pine needles. I suppose I shall drink them – bless her heart! I feel a bit better today but the pain is still there and Ive got collywobbles and a temperature still. But it will all pass.

How are you? Where are you? Write to me. You won't mind the mountains here at all. Really its not high and its all so marvellously *level*. And the stillness! The peace! To sit in the grass & feel little creepy things running up ones sleeve again – Oh what bliss!

Goodbye for now, my precious little artist. Has anyone ever told you what beautiful eyelids you have. You ought to have been told often and often for they are very very lovely. Take care of yourself. Are you happy?

I am

Your very loving
Tig

MS Newberry. *LKM* II. 213–14.

---

[1] Brett visited Paris the week before KM left for Switzerland.

To Eric Pinker, 5 June 1922

Hotel d'Angleterre | Montana-sur-Sierre | Valais | Suisse

5 VI 1922

Dear Mr Pinker

Will you kindly note my change of address. I shall be here until the end of August.

I beg to acknowledge your cheque for £16.19.4. Very many thanks.

Yours sincerely
Katherine Mansfield.

MS Newberry.

To Elizabeth, Countess Russell, [5 June 1922]

Hotel d'Angleterre | Montana-sur-Sierre | (Valais) | Suisse.

Monday.

Dearest Elizabeth

I have been waiting until we got here before I answered your last letter. Rather a disappointing thing has happened. I suppose my enthusiasm was too much for the Furies. At any rate I wish now I had waited before praising so loudly. For they have turned about their chariots and are here in full force again. It was 'silly' to be so happy and to say so much about it;

I feel ashamed of my last letter. But I felt every word of it at the time and more – much more. However, perhaps the truth is some people live in cages and some are free. One had better accept one's cage and say no more about it. I *can* – I *will*. And I do think its simply unpardonable to bore one's friends with 'I can't get out'. Your precious sympathy, most dear Elizabeth I shall never forget. It made that glimpse of the open air twice as marvellous. But here I am with dry pleurisy, coughing away, and so on and so on. Please don't think I feel tragic or despairing. I don't. Ainsi soit-il. What one cannot understand one must accept.

My only trouble is John. He ought to divorce me, marry a really gay young healthy creature, have children and ask me to be godmother. He needs a wife beyond everything. I shall never be a wife and I feel such a fraud when he still believes that one day I shall turn into one. Poor John! Its hellish to live with a femme malade. But its also awfully hard to say to him 'you know darling I shall never be any good'.

But enough of this. I want to tell you what a perfect glimpse we had of the Chalet Soleil[1] as we bumped here in the cold mountain rain. It was raining but the sun shone too, and all your lovely house is hidden in white blossom. Only *heavenly* blue shutters showed through. The little 'working' chalet is in an absolute nest of green. It looked awfully fairy; one felt there ought to have been a star on top of the slender chimney. But from the very first glimpse of your own road everything breathed of you. It was like enchantment.

We are alone in this big, very airy, silent hotel. The two ancient dames look after us and pursue me with 'tisanes'. They are very anxious for me to try a poultice of mashed potatoes on my chest pour changer avec une feuille de moutarde. But so far I have managed to wave the pommes de terre away. Its peaceful beyond words after that odious, grilling Paris. John goes out for walks and comes back with marvellous flowers. He says there are whole fields of wood violets still, and carpets of anemones. We are both working but I feel dull and stupid as though I have been living on a diet of chimney pots. I never want to see a city again.

We hope to stay here until the end of August. I am too much bother to have in a house, my dearest cousin. It would have been wonderful, but as it is I feel I should be a nuisance and Im frightened you would 'turn' against me. Fancy meeting me on the stairs, very short of puff, or seeing me always about. One can never get invalids out of one's eye – its the very worst of them. But it would be lovely if John might spend a few days with you . . . It will be such a joy to see you! I do look forward to that.

With much, much love

Yours ever
Katherine.

MS BL. *De Charms* 238–9.

[1] Elizabeth's home in Randogne, within walking distance of the Hotel d'Angleterre.

To Ida Baker, [7 June 1922]

[Hotel d'Angleterre, Montana-sur-Sierre, Valais]

This is short hand & the result of *weeks* of thinking.

Ida

If you are not finally fixed up for the summer – listen to me.[1] Its no go. I am almost as ill as ever I was, in every way. I want you if you can come to me. But *like this*. We should have to deceive Jack. J. can *never* realise what I have to do. He helps me all he can but he can't help me really & the result is I spend all my energy – every bit – in keeping going. I have none left for work. All my work is behind hand & I *cant do it*. I simply stare at the sky. I am too tired even to think. What makes me tired? Getting up, seeing about everything, arranging everything, sparing him, and so on. That journey nearly killed me literally. He had no *idea* I suffered at all, and could not understand why I looked 'so awful' & why everybody seemed to think I was terribly ill. Jack can *never* understand. That is obvious. Therefore if I can possibly possibly ask you to help me we should have to do it like this. It would have to come entirely from you. Ill draft a letter & send it on the chance. If you agree, write it to me.[2] Its not wrong to do this. It is right. I have been wanting to for a long time. I feel I cannot live without you. But of course we'll have to try & live differently. Dear Ida, I can't promise – or rather I can only promise. If you cannot 'honourably' accept what I say – let it be. I must make the suggestion; I must make a try for it.

Yours ever
K.M.

Forgive me for saying all these things *bang out*. Theres no other way. I shall understand of course if its out of the question and if you think my letter – my 'draft' – horrid throw it away. The truth is I cant really work unless I know you are *there*. I havent got the strength. But Ill manage some sort of compromise if we can't arrange this. This is a black moment because Ive got pleurisy badly & it always affects my spirits.

MS BL. *MLM*, 200–1.

---

[1] Ida had arranged to set up a tea-room with her friend Susie de Perrot, but at once abandoned this plan to return to KM.

[2] The letter KM 'drafted', and which immediately was sent back as though from Ida.

Dear Katherine,

Ive been thinking over what you said to me about a maid, and Id like to suggest something. So far I have not found anything that *just* suits me. Would you be inclined to take me on in a really professional al capacity this time – lets call it companion-secretary. I do feel I could help you more than anyone else if we managed to keep things on a proper footing. For instance would you pay me £6 a month – I don't think I could do with less – and keep me? You see I am being quite frank.

I want to leave sentiment quite out of it. This is what you would call a practical proposition. And I only suggest it until you have finally settled down – wherever you do settle down. Afterwards we could see. Surely we could each have a life apart and yet be of use to each other. Cant we ignore what was so unsatisfactory in the past and start afresh. Pretend you haven't known me & try me as a companion-secretary? Give me a six months trial even. You can always say you don't think it works & there will be no harm done. Let me know as soon as you can – will you? I have thought this over a long time.

Yours ever.

Ida.

MS BL. *MLM*, 201–2.

To Ida Baker, [11 June 1922]

[Montana]

BETTER THANKS

Telegram BL.

Hon. Dorothy Brett, [11 June 1922]

[Hotel d'Angleterre, Montana-sur-Sierre, Valais]

Sunday

Dearest Brett

Summer has deserted us, too. Its cold and we are up [in] the clouds all day. Huge, white woolly fellows lie in the valley. There is nothing to be seen from the windows but a thick, soft whiteness. Its beautiful in its way. The sound of water is beautiful flowing through it and the shake of the cows bells.

Yes, I know Utrillo's[1] work from reproductions; M. has seen it. Its very sensitive and delicate. Id like to see some originals. What a horrible fate that he should be mad. Tragedy treads on the heels of those young French painters. Look at young Modigliani[2] – he had only just begun to find himself when he committed suicide. I think its partly that café life; its a curse as well as a blessing. I sat opposite a youthful poet in the filthy atmosphere of the L'Univers[3] and he was hawking and spitting the whole evening. Finally after a glance at his mouchoir he said "Encore du sang. Il me faut 24 mouchoirs par jour. C'est le desespoir de ma femme!" Another young poet Jean Pillerin[4] (awfully good) died (but not during the evening!) making much the same kind of joke. Talking about 'illness', my dear, I feel rather grim when I read of your wish to bustle me and make me run! Did it really seem to you people were always telling me to sit down? To me that was the fiercest running and the most tremendous bustling and I couldn't keep it up for any length of time. In fact as soon as I got here I wrote to the Mountain and asked her to come back and look after things as otherwise I'd never be able to get any work done. All my energy went in 'bustling'. So she's coming back to me in a strictly professional capacity to look after us both. M. needs someone very badly too, and I can't face the thought of a stranger. No, Im afraid its not only a question of weak muscles; I wish it were! You ask Manoukhin. Don't lets discuss my health.

We heard from Philip yesterday to say the Browns are still in the Manorette[5] and three people are promised it *if* they ever get out. In the event of those three people partaking of the same dish and dying he would be delighted to rent it to us. But it doesn't sound very hopeful. M. wrote saying we would put in central heating and good bathrooms etc. as a *bait.* But I fear it will never be ours. I think Philip was very relieved to have Toronto[6] back. The chickens had been leading him a dance, one felt.

Elizabeth has such a character staying with her. I wonder if you happen to know her – Lady Mary Mallett[7] – one time private secretary to the Dear Queen. She is the spit of all those people – large hat with lace veil caught on her shoulder with a diamond brooch, figure, gloves, shoes, rolled umbrella and *hair.* M. has had tremendous conversations about the D.Q's dislike of seeing anyone without her cap and so on. But I can't get off the subject of Venice with her. She will describe Venice to me and *all* its beauties. When she says the word beauties she shuts her eyes. She is painting a series of water colours of wild flowers in her spare time. I think Elizabeth is suffering tortures at having her so very much on the spot, though.

I must get up and start work. There's a huge beetle creeping over my floor, so cautiously, so intently. He has thought it all out. One gets fond of insects here; they seem to be in their place and its pleasant to know they are there. M. was saying the other night how necessary *snakes* are in creation. Without snakes there would be a tremendous gap, a poverty. Snakes complete the picture. Why? I wonder. I feel it, too. I read an account of unpacking large deadly poisonous vipers at the Zoo the other day. They were lifted out of their boxes with large wooden tongs. Can't you see those tongs? Like giant asparagus tongs & think of one's feelings if they suddenly crossed like sugar tongs too. Brrr!

What are you reading out of Sylvia Beach's library?[8] I am glad you have changed your opinion of her. Im sure she is kind and very decent. She knows Paris inside and out like a sleeve, I think.

I do hope you haven't sent me that frock. What wickedness! I must – I must get up. My story is waiting and my young people are going off for a picnic. Write again dearest when you are inclined. I feel you have become quite a Parisian. I hope G. is nice and even Mme D.

With so much love

Yours ever
Tig.

[1] Maurice Utrillo (1883–1955), French painter known mainly for his Parisian street scenes, in a style derived from the Impressionists. His life at this time was troubled by drug and alcohol addiction.

[2] Amadeo Modigliani (1884–1920), Italian painter whom KM had met through Beatrice Hastings early in 1915. KM is mistaken about his death, which was caused by tuberculosis.

[3] The Café de L'Univers, on the corner of rue Sainte-Honore and rue de Rohan, had been a favourite with KM and Murry when they spent time in Paris before the First World War. It was here they recently and accidently had met Francis Carco, her lover in 1915, who recorded 'Le regard de Katherine m'effara et j'eus d'abord une certain peine à le soutenir, tellement la fièvre lui donnait une ardeur pathétique' (*Bohème d'artiste*, 1940, 259).

[4] Jean Pellerin (1885–1920), whose poems were influenced by Le Groupe Fantaisiste, with their ironic tone and emphasis on modern life.

[5] JMM had approached Philip Morrell, the husband of Lady Ottoline Morrell, about renting a cottage at Garsington Manor.

[6] Frank 'Toronto' Prewitt (1893–1963), a Canadian, part Sioux Indian, whose *Poems* were published by the Hogarth Press (1921).

[7] Marie Mallet (1862–1934), whose letters from Court 1887–1901 were published as *Life with Queen Victoria*, ed. Victor Mallet (1968).

[8] The American Sylvia Beach (1887–1962), who with her lover Adrienne Monnier established the Paris bookshop, Shakespeare and Company, in 1917. The bookshop published James Joyce's *Ulysses* in 1922.

To Ida Baker, [12 June 1922]

[Hotel d'Angleterre, Montana-sur-Sierre, Valais]

My dear Ida

I sent you a wire yesterday c/o Dolly in case you were with her and en train to fix up any negotiations. I wish I knew how firmly you and Susie were united. I deserve that you should have just found the ideal spot & that you answer me in immense haste with one eye on your first baking. But I am a little bit tired of getting my deserts & so I shall hope still that my plan is possible. Its not bad here. The place is too high for me. But then I always knew that. There was nothing else to be done, however. Make a strange journey & arrive at a strange place alone with Jack was out of the question. But I can not move about at all so far, and my heart thuds in my ear just as it did and bangs twice as fast all day. It is hateful to again have to give up baths, to again have to dress sitting down & sipping water and so on . . . But what the devil can one do? If you were here we would go to Lake Maggiore. There's no point in writing, however, until I get an answer to my letter. Re Wing. Don't you think he had better be doctored? He fights *too* much. Im glad you have bought one or two 'bits of things'. No, I don't want anything in that line.

Yours ever
K.M.

MS BL.

To Ida Baker, [14 June 1922]

[Hotel d'Angleterre, Montana-sur-Sierre, Valais]

Dear Ida,

Your 'letter' came and had precisely the effect it was intended to have.[1] Thank you. I believed in it myself as I read it. It sounded so real. I have had your telegrams. I understand about Susie. Do as you think best. Dont tire yourself by rushing. I don't think the little lady needs too much consideration, though, after the very casual way she has treated you. Miss Franklin is the person I like & your Mrs Scriven. They both sound delightful women.

About plans . . . Do you want any money? I will send you a cheque for £7 to buy yourself any odd clothes you may need. I mean – stockings and so on. England is the only place for them, and to pay for your journey. I don't know what it costs. About the *cat*. Where can you leave him? Do you know of anywhere? Would Mrs S. have him if he was doctored? That wld mean hed be a quiet cat & not a fighter. Its impossible to have him here. For my plans are so vague.

At the moment, too, I cant write letters. I haven't the time. Im late now for the Sphere & its a difficult job to keep all these things going. I write to nobody. Please forgive this, understand it & don't get anxious & dont telegraph unless you have to! I have such a horror of telegrams that ask me how I am!! I always want to reply *dead*. Its the only reply. What, in Heaven's name, can one answer? And then this poor silly old girl spelling it out over the telephone – Barkeer. Bettre zee lettre – "c'est bien, c'est bien, c'est anglais – ça? Ah – voilà." And so on, while I sit smiling & the unseen me fells her to the earth.

And listen to the old Adam in me for a moment will you, my dear? *Dont* take advantage of me because I have begged you to come & say I can't do without you. I havent turned into a grateful angel. Im at heart a distraught creature with *no time* for anything for the moment. When this work is done Ill be better. But try & believe & keep on believing without signs from me that I do love you & want you for my wife. And come as soon as you *reasonably* can. Let me know when you arrive & Ill send the cart to the station. Elizabeth has come. I am glad for it frees me from the worry of Jack, a little. I am a bit better physically but the labour of getting up, tidying, brushing clothes, carrying cushions & so on is so great that mentally I confess I feel absolutely exhausted! But it must be got through somehow. Theres no help for it & I am bound to deliver the goods by the end of this month.

Yours ever
K.M.

Poor Roma W. [Webster] is getting worse & worse, she says. She is spending what she calls a 'last spring' in Italy. Thank Heavens her surroundings sound just what she would wish & she is being really well looked after. This is a cursed disease.

[*Across top*:]

No, perhaps its best if you let me know what money you want. I still find it rather hard to understand how you can so cheerfully lend my hardly earned pennies to anyone who asks. *You* have a right to them & youre welcome. But thats not at all the same.

MS BL. *MLM*, 202–3.

---

[1] The letter to 'deceive' Murry, which KM had drafted and sent to her on 7 June.

To Dorothy Brett, [14 June 1922]

[Hotel d'Angleterre, Montana-sur-Sierre, Valais]

My dearest Brett

You sent me such a lovely letter. I wanted to answer it at once. But I am working at such pressure. It sounds absurd. But it is really difficult to *find time* for letters, even. First, about your health. Do you feel better? Is the pain in your lung? Is there anyone who would paint you with *iodine* – in French *tincture d'iode*. Or if not won't you buy a packet of *Thermogène*[1] and clamp it on the spot & keep it there until the pain is gone. Do, look after yourself. Eat! Rest! Don't carry your paint box. I shall be thankful when you are here in really good air with the old girls looking after you and feeding you properly. And remember to put on warm clothes for the journey here – woolies. Its fresh in the mountains; its sometimes cold. You can always shed them in the train & then wind yourself up when you reach Sierre.

Now about the journey. The night train is best. The one we took from the Gare de Lyon – 9-something. You have to change at Lausanne next morning at about 9. But I looked on your account for Cook's men[2] & I saw two in full view. Even without them the change is perfectly simple & there is no rush. Plenty of time. At Sierre M. will meet you. I hope to be there, too. Then there is only a gentle ride ½ way up the mountains and then there is a cup of tea. This place is so flat, so full of lawns and so on that one feels as though one was on the level, or one's eye does. I wish my heart would believe my eye but it wont. But don't forget about the coolness, darling. I have a galumptious pair of cornflower blue woolen stockings I shall give you on arrival – Lawrence would swoon at sight of them.[3] I am hoping they will keep your little toes in a gentil glow...

Paris feels remote at last. The pianos have died down. The lift no longer goes up & down in ones head. That cursed restaurant has faded. Little creepy things have crept back and clover and the sky and a feeling as though one would in a moment give thanks to the Lord. The cherries are just beginning to *flash* into ripeness. There are still masses of flowers. But why do the peasants work so hard. It wrings ones heart to see them! The women can just stagger under gigantic loads and they are all bent, all hardened, like trees by a cruel wind.

What will you paint here – I wonder? Herd girls, goats, trees? That is interesting about the white of Paris houses. What I love, too, is white with just a tinge of pink as one sees in the South – or just a tinge of yellow. Do you like to pat houses? Pat their walls? I used to go outside my little Isola Bella & pat it as if it was a cat. I hope you find your little boy again. I hope you never see that horrid Richborough[4] again. Vile man! How dare he say such things. I am v. sorry to hear about Eva.[5] Of course *I* suspect J. [J. W. N. Sullivan] and Mrs D. [Dobrée] for frightening her. Servants are simple creatures; they don't like surprises. They expect to be looked after (alas) and the best of them are stern moralists. If you want to live just as you like you must teach the servant to understand that – train her into strange ways & she'll accept them. But not otherwise. They feel they have a right to expect a certain conduct from the people they serve. I am sure of that. And Sullivan turning up out of the blue must have scared your Eva. Was he drunk or was it Gertler? I must say I find that hard to forgive in *your* house with *you* away. How can people be so shamelessly insensitive. Speaking of people reminds me of your brilliant remark about Toronto – vain without vanity. I am sure that is absolutely right!

What is Waterlow saying about your Thursdays. He is a bit of a mischief maker. It is because of his Marge.[6] I feel he is absolutely under her thumb and her mental plumbing is so very awful. I expect you will get all the latest gossip from G. I do *not* like those London people, dearest. Koteliansky is the only company I really want to see, ever again. There is something – a kind of superciliousness & silly suspicion mixed in the others which makes me turn from them. They are no worse than other city people. But that is not saying much is it? The truth is I don't want to *discuss* literature or art, as they do. I want to get on with it, and in leisure hours, live and love and *enjoy* the people I am with. Play, in fact. Play is a very necessary part of life.

I must post this unsatisfactory letter. Its written as usual on my knee & so my writing has no backbone but is all wobbly like the handwriting of a fish. Forgive it. I still cough like billy-oh, and am short of puff and so on. The old story, in fact, just as it was when I was here before. But it don't signify, Miss Dombey.[7]

This all rushes along. But it's the surface. Underneath there is something steady, deep, and yours – my love for you. I too, feel we are only at the beginning. But already I have *such* memories of you to think over – moments, glances, words spoken and left unsaid. Feel I am with you. You are dear to me. I look forward – to a real friendship. But a close, tender friendship, no less. We shall have a marvellous time, darling. Don't you feel that, too?

With love, my precious little artist

Yours
Tig

MS Newberry.

[1] A medicated cotton wool.

[2] Agents for the travel firm, Thomas Cook & Son.

[3] Perhaps a reference to the fact that in D. H. Lawrence's *Women in Love* (1920), the character Gudrun, based in part on KM, has a penchant for coloured stockings.

[4] Not identified.

[5] The much-valued servant who had just left Brett.

[6] Sydney Waterlow had married Helen Margery Eckhard in 1913. The marriage was not a happy one.

[7] KM's memory of the bashful and inarticulate Mr Toots, who repeats 'It's of no consequence' at moments when he wishes to say something important, in Charles Dickens's *Dombey and Son* (1847–8).

To William Gerhardi, 14 June 1922

Hotel d'Angleterre | Montana-sur-Sierre | (Valais) | Suisse

14.vi.1922

My dear Mr Gerhardi,

Your handwriting on the envelope made me feel a guilty thing; I hardly dared open the letter. And when I did there wasn't a single reproach in it. That was *very* kind of you – very generous.

The truth is I have been on the pen point of writing to you for weeks and weeks but always Paris – horrid Paris – snatched my pen away. And during the latter part of the time I spent nearly every afternoon in a tight, bony dentist's chair while a dreadfully callous American gentleman with an electric light on his forehead explored the root canals or angled with devilish patience for the lurking nerves. Sometimes, at black moments, I think that when I die I shall go to the DENTISTS...

I am glad you did not come to Paris after all; we should not have been able to talk. Its too distracting. It is like your "twelve complete teas ices and all" all the time. One is either eating them or watching other people eat them, or seeing them swept away or hearing the jingle of their approach, or waiting for them, or paying for them, or trying to get out of them (hardest of all). Here, its ever so much better. If, on your walk today you pass one of those signs with a blameless hand pointing to the Hotel d'Angleterre, please follow. The cherries are just ripe; they are cutting the hay. But there are English delights, too. Our *speciality* is the forest à deux pas, threaded with little green paths and hoarse quick little streams. If it happens to be sunset, too, I could show you something very strange. Behind this hotel there is a big, natural lawn – a wide stretch of green turf. When the herds that are being driven home in the evening come to it they go wild with delight. Staid, black cows begin to dance, to leap, to cut capers. Quiet, refined little sheep who look as though buttercups would not melt in their mouths suddenly begin to jump, to spin round, to bound off like rocking-horses. The goats are complete Russian Ballet dancers; they are almost too brilliant. But the cows are the most surprising and the most naive. You will admit that cows don't look like born dancers – do they? And yet my cows are light as feathers, bubbling over with fun. Please tell dear little Miss Helsingfors[1] that its quite true they *do* jump over the moon. I have seen them do it – or very nearly. Ah, Mr Gerhardi, I love the country! To lie on the grass again and smell the clover! Even to feel a little ant creep up one's sleeve was a kind of comfort... after one had shaken it down again...

I have been thinking about your book today. I see it is announced in the Nation. I do feel little Cobden-Sanderson is the right man for a first novel. He has not too many people; hes very keen; and he advertises well. Also he has a very good reputation and people are curious about his books. They look out for them. I am very anxious to see a copy and you may be sure I shall tell my friends not to miss it. What are you writing now? Have you begun another novel? Is it possible to write at Oxford. You always sound so gay – and I feel the little telegraph boy you mention in your letter was the last of a long line of little telegraph boys. And shall you go to Garsington, I wonder? I don't mind Lady Ottoline's dresses. If you know her you accept them; you wouldn't have them different. They are all part of her. But they do offend your sense of the *très chic*, I feel... It is a pity. Julian, the daughter, is very attractive. And she's so fresh, so unspoilt, young in a way your Nina[2] is young.

I am in the middle of a very long story written in the same style – horrible expression! – as The Daughters of the Late Colonel. I enjoy writing it so much that even after I am asleep – I go on. The scene is the South of France in early Spring. There is a real love story in it, too, and rain, buds, frogs, a thunderstorm, pink spotted chinese dragons. There is no happiness greater than this leading a *double life*.[3] But its mysterious, too. How is it possible to be here in this remote, deserted hotel and at the same time to be leaning out of the window of the Villa Martin listening to the rain thrumming so gently on the leaves and smelling the night-scented stocks with Milly?[4] (I shall be awfully disappointed if you don't like Milly.)

Have you read Bunin's stories. They are published in English by the Hogarth Press. The Gentleman from San Fransisco is good, but I dont care much for the others. He tries too hard. He's too determined you shall not miss the cucumbers and the dyed whiskers. And the last story called *Son* I can't for the life of me understand.[5] I met Bunin in Paris and because he had known Tchekhov I wanted to talk of him. But alas! Bunin said "Tchekhov? Ah – Ah – oui, j'ai connu Tchekhov. Mais il y a longtemps, longtemps." And then a pause. And then, graciously, "Il a écrit des belles choses." And that was the end of Tchekhov. "Vous avez lu mon dernier..."

I shall be here until the end of August. After that I go back to Paris for two months and then I want to go to Italy to a little place called Arco near the Lake of Garda for the winter.

When you are in the mood please write to me and tell me what you are writing. I am sorry you did not like The Fly and glad you told me. I *hated* writing it. Yes I remember the story about the little boy and the buzzing insects. His father came home from the town and found him sitting up to the table cutting Kings & Queens out of a pack of playing cards. I can always see him.[6]

Here comes my ancient landlady with a cup of tea made from iceland moss and hay flowers. She is determined to make a new man of me – good old soul – and equally convinced that nothing but herb tea will do it. My inside must be in a state of the most profound astonishment.

Goodbye for now. All success – every good wish for your book. And don't be grateful to me, please; Ive done nothing.

> Yours ever
> Katherine Mansfield.

MS ATL. *LKM* II, 216–19.

[1] Not identified.

[2] The young girl in *Futility* with whom the author is in love.

[3] A thought which had persisted with KM since she wrote as a schoolgirl, 'Would you not like to try *all* sorts of lives – one is so very small – but that is the satisfaction of writing – one can impersonate so many people' (to Sylvia Payne, 24 Apr. 1906, *CLKM* I. 19).

[4] The young girl in the abandoned, or partly destroyed, 'The Doves' Nest', first published in *The Doves' Nest and Other Stories*.

[5] A story in which an older woman, after a single adulterous occasion with a nineteen-year-old man, compels her lover to shoot her, believing he will follow her death with his suicide. Instead, he goes temporarily insane and fires shots into the street.

[6] This story is untraced.

To Ida Baker, [16 June 1922]

> [Hotel d'Angleterre, Montana-sur-Sierre, Valais]
> Friday.

Dear Ida,

After your detailed letters I quite understand the situation as between you and Susie. I hope you will not be too distressed at the thought you 'cannot' help her. Was she quite within her moral rights (legal rights don't count) in fixing up a place without you having seen it? That seems to me a trifle queer as between partners but then I don't know.

I hope you will be able to come to me fairly soon. I need someone very much for many reasons.

But whatever happens please don't think of bringing Wing. It would be absolutely impossible. I shall not stay here for any length of time; I shall be in Paris in the autumn (I expect) and then I rather think of going to Italy instead of the S. of France for the winter. Jack goes over to England at the end of August for the autumn – perhaps until the spring. But the cat *we* cant have. Imagine my temper if you had that poor creature in a train. I should get out of the train. Besides no decent hotel will take a cat & the cruelty is really abominable to drag about a helpless animal. Wing would be happy with anyone who gave him food and a warm corner. If you can't find anyone what about your writing to Jeanne? The trouble is she has her beloved dog Kuri. But is it impossible to keep a cat & a dog? Her address is Woodhay, Lyndhurst, Hants. I shall write to Koteliansky today. But I fear the Farbmans,[1] with whom he lives would not feed Wing well. They'd give him old bits of shoe leather or anything that was to [be] thrown away. Still, perhaps thats a libel. Yes, I am sure it is.

I send you back £1 note. Would you buy me a pot of face cream – a *food* for the skin – you know what this climate does. With the rest buy your Mrs S. a little something for herself from of course yourself. I expect you won't feel you have the money for presents. Do this, please.

Yours
K.M.

I hope Henley is not too dreadful. It always sounded to me a very very 'Swiss' idea. Dont you think it rather a mistake to take so many peoples advice – to listen to so many people AND to discuss your private affairs with everybody? I mean why must the whole of Montana have known what you intended to do – servants and all? That seems to me very dreadful. If ever you discuss my future plans, Miss, I shall deny them absolutely and at once. But please dont do it. Refrain from telling all & sundry what WE intend to do. I cant bear it! To hear Ernestine discussing you and your 'thee raom' & her fear it would be trop cher! . . . I know you long for intimacy with people but intimacy isn't giving them the right to interfere. These are only my personal views, of course. I don't mean them to sound arbitrary. Im afraid they do – Im sorry.

MS BL.

---

[1] Michael Farbmann, Russian journalist and political journalist, and his wife Sophie were Koteliansky's landlords at 5 Acacia Road.

To S. S. Koteliansky, [17 June 1922]

Hotel d'Angleterre | Randogne-sur-Sierre | (Valais) Suisse.

Koteliansky

Would you care for a cat? I have a cat who is at present in England and I cannot have him with me. It is too cruel to make cats travel. He is a beautiful animal, except for a scratch on his nose, one ear badly bitten and a small hole in his head. From the back view however he is lovely for he has a superb tail. In all his ways he can be trusted to behave like a gentleman. He is extremely independent and, of course, understands everything that is said to him. Perhaps Mademoisel Guita would like him?

But this is not urgent. At present he is with Ida Baker. She would hand him over to anyone in a basket. But I dont *want* you to have him. I mean I am not for one moment asking you to have him. Of course not. Simply, it occurred to me that you might find it a not unpleasant idea ... I must confess he will not catch mice. But mice do not know that and so the sight of him keeps them away. He has a fair knowledge of French.

It is very nice here, remote, peaceful, but not remote enough. It is difficult to manage one's external life as one would wish. I have been working towards one thing for years now. But it is still on the horizon. Because I cannot yet attain to it without "misunderstanding" it cant be mine yet. But it comes nearer – much nearer. But I do not like to talk 'prudently'. In fact it is detestable.

To change the subject. I saw something awfully nice the day after I got here. Behind this hotel there is a big stretch of turf before one comes to the forest. And in the late afternoon as the herds were driven home when they came to this turf they went wild with delight. Staid, black cows began to dance and leap and cut capers, lowing softly. Meek, refined-looking little sheep who looked as though buttercups would not melt in their mouths could not resist it; they began to jump, to spin round, to bound forward like rocking horses. As for the goats they were extremely brilliant dancers of the highest order – the Russian Ballet was nothing compared to them. But best of all were the cows. Cows do not *look* very good dancers, do they? Mine were as light as feathers and really gay, joyful. It made one laugh to see them. But it was so beautiful too. It was like the first chapter in Genesis over again. "Fourfooted creatures created He them."[1] One wanted to weep as well.

Goodbye my precious friend

Katherine.

MS BL. Dickinson, 95–6.

[1] KM's memory of Genesis 1: 24–5.

To Ida Baker, [20 June 1922]

[Hotel d'Angleterre, Montana-sur-Sierre, Valais]

In reply to your Friday letter. Don't wait for me. Come when you are free.[1] Do you want money for the journey? Please wire if you do. I am only too anxious for you to be here. But please accept this as final. As soon as you can leave and come out here I shall be happy to see you. Your room is taken. It is indeed now that I am so greatly in need of someone. But of course you must realise that. I have told you so often how desperately pressed for time I am & how hard it is to look after things as well. But I have said as much in every letter to you; I can't say more.

K.M.

Postcard BL.

---

[1] Ida left England at once to join KM. As Ida recollected, she 'tried to make things easier for them. I lived quite separately in a different part of the large, empty hotel . . . and I went to their "flat" when I could do things for Katherine or massage Jack's ankle' (*MLM*, 203).

To Harold Beauchamp, [21 June 1922]

[Montana]

WELCOME TO ENGLAND LOVE FROM KASS AND JACK

Telegram TC ATL.

To Harold Beauchamp, [21 June 1922]

Hotel d'Angleterre | Montant-sur-Sierre | (Valais) | Suisse.

My dearest Father,

I cannot tell you how much you are in my thoughts to-day. I keep picturing your arrival at Southampton, your meeting the girls, and the arrival in chief at Wood Hay! How I wish I were with you all. I cannot imagine a more happy little reunion. Welcome once more to England, darling. I hope with all my heart that your stay will be a very happy one.

We were so delighted to hear from you at San Francisco. Since then much seems to have happened. I will try and give you my news in brief. The treatment I underwent in Paris was successful on the whole – not quite as miraculous as depicted by the doctor. But that was to be expected. Just as I was feeling the benefits of it, however, (this sounds so like my dear Aunt Ag) the heat wave descended on Paris and laid me low with an attack of pleurisy. It was rather a fierce attack while it lasted. But we got away from that gridiron of a city at the earliest possible moment and migrated here – to a very simple hotel about 700 feet below Montana proper. Here, as my Papa might say, we seemed to fall on our feet. For the hotel is kept by two excellent elderly sisters, who look after me splendidly. I am well round the corner again, pulling up the hill in fact at a great rate and able to get out and stay out all day under the pines. We intend to stay here until the end of August. Then, before my second course of treatment in Paris, I had the idea of coming over to England for a week or ten days to see you (Jack is going to spend this Autumn in England). But, of course, dearest, these plans are subject to yours. I could strike camp here at an earlier date and meet you wherever you proposed. I feel very strongly it would be a mistake for you and the girls to come here. Of course, you may have no thought of doing so, but I write this just "in case". Montana is depressing for those who are not ill. There are too many signs of illness; too many sanatoria. And there is no escaping them. It is different in the Winter. Then there is a "floating population", which arrives for the sports and the whole place changes its appearance. But Summer is the time for les malades to show themselves; one is rather conscious of them here.

While I am on this doleful and none too cheery subject, darling, may I be allowed a personal detail. I am myself no longer actively consumptive, i.e. no longer infectious in any way. My present condition is merely the result of $4\frac{1}{2}$ years severe illness, but active disease there is absolutely none. The Paris doctors assure me that after the second course of treatment the healing process will be very advanced. Indeed, they go so far as to say I shall be as good a man as I ever was. But experience teaches me to put a large pinch of salt on the tail of these fly-away words. I wanted to tell you this to put your mind at rest, however, as I know what one feels about such matters.

I long to see you. You will tell me how you would like us to arrange it. Would England be the more satisfactory rendez-vous? There is a through train from here to Calais. And by the end of July, even, I shall not think anything of the journey. Perhaps Chaddie will tell you I have attached Ida B. to me as a kind of body-guard. It's not possible to get on without some one and "she is faithful, she is kind", as no one else could be.

Jack and I are very busy working. I am hard at a short novel which is to appear serially in the Sphere this Autumn. I am rather behind-hand and am making up for lost time in these favourable circumstances. After that, I am bound by contract to hand over a new book this (late) Autumn. Thank God for work, say I!

We were very interested to read in the New Zealand papers the news of your retirement from the Bank. I cannot imagine how they will get on without you; I feel that your reports were the cornerstone of the entire business.[1]

Well, dearest, I will end this egotistical letter. It comes to you with much love and the deepest truest gratitude for your last letter to me. If only

I could be with the three of you in spirit as you walk round the garden at Wood Hay. There is nothing to equal an English Garden, and I am sure the girls have done wonders.

Jack is writing himself in the course of a day or two. He begs to be remembered.

With much, much love to you from me, dearest,

I am,

Ever your devoted and grateful child,

Kass.

Please excuse the jagged outline of this paper. It refuses to be torn from the parent block. K.

TC ATL. Cited Alpers 1980, 361.

---

[1] Among many other business interests, Harold Beauchamp was a director of the Bank of New Zealand 1898–1936. He had just retired as chairman after filling that position for fifteen years. His annual reports he sent on for his daughter to peruse.

To Dorothy Brett, [22 June 1922]

[Montana-sur-Sierre | Valais]

In the Forest.

Dearest

All the same you will be met by one of us, so be sure to let us know the exact day.

Im sitting writing to you in a glade under a pine tree. There are quantities of little squat yellow bushes of a kind of broom everywhere that give a sweet scent & are the humming homes of bees. M. & I have been here all day. Now he is climbing up to Montana to buy a large bottle of castor oil! Its sad to feel so completely a creature of air as one does in this forest and yet to find ones insides have ordered a general strike. Such is our awful condition. Its divinely lovely out here, and warm again, with just a light breeze swinging in the trees. A little blue sky with puffs of white cloud over the mountains.

You know darling I must say I think that 'set' in London including Mrs D. [Dobrée] and Co is simply detestable. They seem to be always on the lookout for unpleasantness. *I* shouldn't feel savage personally (though I understand it is your nature so to do). I should simply retire with a door between us. They are pleased when you do lash out. They feel they have drawn blood – the horrid creatures. Mrs D. sounds a perfect pig of the largest kind and Carrington ought to have pulled her nose.[1] But its such a waste of time – waste of life – waste of energy. One might as well live in the bosom of a large family as among those people: there's no difference that I can see.

Im awfully keen to see your new paintings. Last evening as I sat on a stump watching the herds pass I felt you may take furiously to cows & paint nothing but cows on green lawns with long shadows like triangles from this shaped tree 🌲 and end with a very grave cow complex. I have one. Up till now I have always more than resisted the charm of cows but now its swep' over me all of a heap, Miss. Insects, too, even though my legs are both bitten off at the knee by large and solemn flies. Do you mind turning brown, too? Or peeling? I had better warn you. These things are bound to happen. And I am *hatefully* unsociable. Don't forget that. Its on the cards you may turn frightfully against me here and brain me with your Toby.[2] You see every day I work till 12.30 and again from 4.30 until supper – every blessed day Sundays included. Can you bear that? In the mornings we may even meet as I go abroad & sit under the trees. But I shall regard you as invisible & you will haughtily cut me. In this way, when we *are* free we feel free & not guilty. We can play & look at beetles in peace. I must get the ancient sisters to simplify their ideas of picnics, though. Today they brought M. boiled beef & trimmings in a saucepan. Its awful to open such a vessel under the very Eye of ones Maker. I like eggs, butter, bread and milk at picnics. But M. disagrees. He regards such tastes as female flippancy.

Oh my story wont go fast enough. Its got stuck. I must have it finished and done with in 10 days time. Never shall I commit myself again to a stated time. Its hellish.

Your Port Said hat is all faded. What will you say? Its an absolute lamb of a hat for out of doors – perfect. That stuffy tea cosy I bought on my way back from the dentist will stay on the shelf until I get back to civilisation. But don't be afraid. You shall have it back the day you come. If I sent you the dibs could you bring me a woolly jacket a kind of cardigan, the simple sort – as simple as possible with buttons down the front, you know – in hyacinth or blue bell or crocus or pastel blue? If you can't do it – say the word. You will always say the word wont you darling? And if you think I am a callous creature to ask you – say that, too. Its so much more restful. I am thankful you are feeling better. This place will do you a great deal of good, I hope. One eats the air in slices with big bits of sun spread on them. I do hope Gertler is nice. I feel sorry for poor little Carrington and for Partridge, too. Take care of yourself. Be happy.

With much much love, my little artist

Ever your

Tig

MS Newberry. *LKM* II. 219–20

[1] Dora Carrington (1893–1932), whom KM had been close to in 1916, married Ralph Partridge, Cambridge graduate and soldier, in 1921, and both lived with Lytton Strachey in a complicated emotional triangle. KM would have heard from Brett the intricate events when Carrington's husband discovered that his best friend, the painter Gerald Brennan, was in love with her, and that Vivienne Dobrée's recent pursuit of Partridge was in part to assist Brennan's access to Carrington.

[2] Brett's ear-trumpet.

To Arnold Gibbons, 24 June 1922

Hotel d'Angleterre | Montana Village | (Valais) | Suisse.

24.VI.1922

Dear Mr Arnold Gibbons,

I feel I have kept your stories a long time. Forgive me if it seems too long. The days pass so quickly here and although I have been on the pen-point of writing to you several times it is only now that Ive got down to it.

Very many thanks for your letter & for letting me see the five stories. I'd like immensely to talk about them a little. But you'll take what I say as workshop talk, will you? – As from one writer to another. Otherwise one feels embarrassed.

I think the idea in all the five stories is awfully good. And you start each story at just the right moment and finish it at the right moment, too. Each is a whole, complete in itself. But I don't feel any of them quite come off. Why? Its as though you used more words than were necessary. There's a kind of diffuseness of expression which isn't natural to the English way of thinking. I imagine your great admiration for Tchekhov has liberated you but you have absorbed more of him than you are aware of and he's got in the way of your individual expression for the time being. Its very queer; passages read like a translation! Its as though you were in his shadow and the result is you are a little bit blurred, a bit vague. Your real inmost self (forgive the big words but one does mean them) doesn't seem to be speaking except occasionally. Its almost as though you were hiding and hadn't the – shall I call it courage? – of your own fine sensitiveness. When you do get free of Tchekhov *plus* all you have learnt from him you ought to write awfully good stories. 'Pleasure' gives me an idea of how good. There you seem to me very nearly in your own stride. It is convincing. One believes in that little cat and its meat for breakfast; one sees your old chap wiping the glass case with his handkerchief; & one sees his audience turn & then turn back to him. I think this story is much the best of the five.

To return to your Russianization for a moment. It seems to me that when Russians think they go through a different process from what we do. As far as one can gather they arrive at feeling by a process of . . . spiritual recapitulation. I don't think we do. What I imagine is we have less words but they are more vital; we *need* less. So though one can accept this recapitulating process from Russian writers it sounds strange to me coming from your pen. For instance, in Going Home you get in five lines: "enthusiasm, doubtful, mistrust, acute terror, anxious, joy, sadness, pain, final dissolution, filth and degradation." *Or* (p.2) "the unhappiness, the misery and cruelty, all the squalor & abnormal spiritual anguish." Again, last page but one of *The Sister* "futility, monotony, suffocated, pettiness, sordidness, vulgar minuteness." When one writes like that in English its as though the *nerve* of the feeling were gone. Do you know what I mean?

I realise its all very well to say these things – but how are we going to convey these overtones, half tones, quarter tones, these hesitations, doubts, beginnings, if we go at them *directly*? It is most devilishly difficult, but I do believe that there is a way of doing it and thats by trying to get as near to the *exact truth* as possible. It's the truth we are after, no less (which, by the way, makes it so exciting).

To come to a few details. In *Going Home* would the wife say 'old dog's body'? That sounds to me like a woman in a public bar talking. Its almost too strange. In *Emptiness* – I am not sure that a v. young baby can bite its mother's breast so as to cause cancer. If it did, if the breast were removed surely she would never suckle it still. Cancer is a recurring thing. And at any rate the *idea* is frightful – it overweights the whole story. Its a whole most terrible story, itself. And (this is so grim that really I hardly dare) how are you going to prevent the same baby – no, I leave that to my horrid imagination.

Has this letter offended you, I wonder? I hope it hasn't. If you ever feel inclined to talk about this short story writing at any time Id be most sincerely glad to hear from you.

Again thanking you for showing me these

Yours ever
[Katherine Mansfield]

John Middleton Murry sends his regards & remembrances.

MS ATL. *LKM* II. 220–2.

To Dorothy Brett, *[25 June 1922]*

Hotel d'Angleterre | Montana Village
Sunday

My dearest Brett,

I have put this address at the top but the other is just as good. Don't pay any attention to it. Of course it doesn't matter a straw about the 29th. I shall be so glad when you are here in the country[1] even though the weather is *im*perfect – to be very polite to it. Its warm & then its chill. Not so much windy as draughty. But where is perfect weather? Palm Beach, California, they say. But if I arrived there'd be a snowstorm. The Mountain arrived yesterday. The relief to have her is *so* great that Ill never never say another word of impatience. I don't deserve such a wife. All is in order already. M. and I sigh & turn up our eyes. M. in fact, to pay her a little compliment has wrenched the ligaments of his foot & can't walk. HE is tied to a chaise longue! Isn't it awful bad luck! But what marvellously *good* luck that the Mountain was here & produced bandages and vinegar and all that was needful. The Ancient Sisters of course, hovered over him too and made him cover his foot in a poultice of *parsley* last night. He went to bed looking like a young leg of lamb.

I wish you had been here this afternoon. They brought us in branches of cherries, all dark & glistening among the long slender leaves. I should like to have given them to my little artist.

Has Cooks told you the day & hour of your arrival? Be sure to let me know, won't you! Perhaps a wire would be safest. For we have to order the cart in advance. Now as M. can only hop and I can't fly it will be the Mountain who will meet you at Sierre. Lean hard on her! Shes an awfully good person for those occasions and so gentle and capable. The country is looking marvellous. They are just beginning to cut the hay. You will have your choice of about 30 bedrooms but I shall have one prepared next door to Ida so you can knock on her wall if you want anything. There's such good honey here – dark like dark amber. I have a camera (rhymes with amber) & I intend to take ravishing photographs of you under the trees and among the calves. We really must make a little book of photographs to remember ourselves by.

Be careful of yourself on the journey. Its no good. Anxious about you I always shall be when you are en voyage. Thank God theres no sea & I must say Swiss railways are the nicest I know. I mean the porters are fearfully nice – a band of brothers. But I shan't really be happy until I *see* you.

Yours ever and ever with tender love
Tig.

MS Newberry. *LKM* II. 216.

---

[1] Brett arrived to stay with KM early in July. But before she arrived, KM decided that the altitude of the Hotel d'Angleterre strained her heart and, being weakened also by the pleurisy she had caught on her journey from Paris, she decided to descend to the Chateau Belle Vue hotel in Sierre, while JMM went to stay at Elizabeth's chalet in Randogne. Also, as Ida put it, 'All was not well between Katherine and Jack' (*MLM*, 204). KM's increasing scepticism of conventional medical treatment, and the possibility that 'spiritual' values might serve her better, was another strain between them.

To Michael Sadleir, [? June 1922]

Hotel d'Angleterre | Montana Village (Valais)

Dear Michael Sadleir,

Would you tell Knopf 'no'. I seem to be haunted by that miserable German Pension. Its bones are always shaking at me from another quarter. *Such* bad bones, too.[1]

May I say how much I enjoyed your delightful book. I wish, rather, there had been a longer essay on Mrs Gaskell.[2] But that's greed – one wants a long essay on everybody.

Jack & I owe our 'discovery' of Trollope to you.[3] We had always avoided him for some reason. Which was shameful.

Yours ever
K.M.

MS Targ.

[1] Yet again, KM turned down the offer for a new edition of *In a German Pension*, this time with her New York publisher Knopf.
[2] *Excursions in Victorian Bibliography* (1922). More a scholarly than a critical work, it included essays on several writers, but only an extensive bibliography of the novelist Mrs Gaskell (Elizabeth Cleghorn Gaskell, 1810–65).
[3] JMM would review Sadleir's new edition of Anthony Trollope, *An Autobiography*, in the *Nation and the Athenaeum* (28 Apr. 1923).

To Elizabeth, Countess Russell, [? June–July 1922[1]]

Dearest Cousin,

I seem to have snapped up the caramels without so much as a word. And it was sweet of you to bring them to me!

I am sending a Bouquet by John. You *do* know, you *do* believe with how much love I send them? Really and truly it is just what I said today . . . I get frightened of a cloud sometimes because I can't believe in such blessed good fortune.

Your devoted
Katherine.

MS BL.

[1] Elizabeth's diary (TC Huntington) records several visits to KM during June and July. It is not possible to fix a date to the visit mentioned here.

To S. S. Koteliansky, [4 July 1922]

Hotel Chateau Belle Vue | Sierre (Valais)
Tuesday.

Dear Koteliansky

I want to write to you before I begin work. I have been thinking of you ever since I woke up, thinking how much I should like to talk to you. Today for instance is such an opportunity. Brett is staying here for a week or so but she has gone up the mountains for the day. And I am the only guest left in this big, empty, dim hotel. It is awfully nice here, my dearest friend. It is full summer. The grasshoppers ring ring their tiny tambourines, and down below the gardener is raking the paths. Swallows are flying; two men with scythes over their shoulders are wading through the field opposite, lifting their knees as though they walked through a river. But above all it is *solitary*.

I have been feeling lately a horrible sense of indifference; a very bad feeling. Neither hot nor cold; *lukewarm*, as the psalmist says.[1] It is better to be dead than to feel like that; in fact it is a kind of death. And one is ashamed as a corpse would be ashamed to be unburied. I thought I would never write again. But now that I have come here and am living alone all seems so full of meaning again, and one longs only to be allowed to understand.

Have you read Lawrence's new book?[2] I should like to very much. He is the only writer living whom I really profoundly care for. It seems to me whatever he writes, no matter how much one may 'disagree' is important. And after all even what one objects to is a *sign of life* in him. He is a living man. There has been published lately an extremely bad collection of short stories – Georgian short stories. And 'The Shadow in the Rose Garden'[3] by Lawrence is among them. This story is perhaps one of the weakest he ever wrote. But it is so utterly different from all the rest that one reads it with joy. When he mentions gooseberries these are real red, ripe gooseberries that the gardener is rolling on a tray. When he bites into an apple it is a sharp, sweet, fresh apple from the growing tree. Why has one this longing that people shall be rooted in life. Nearly all people swing in with the tide and out with the tide again like heavy sea weed. And they seem to take a kind of pride in denying Life. But why? I cannot understand.

But writing letters is unsatisfactory. If you were here we would talk or be silent – it would not matter which. We shall meet one day, perhaps soon, perhaps some years must pass first. Who shall say. To know you are there is enough. This is not really contradictory.

Goodbye for now.

Katherine.

MS BL. *LKM* II. 223–4.

[1]   Not from the Psalms but from Revelations, 3:16, 'So then because thou art lukewarm, and neither cold nor hot, I will spue thee out of my mouth.'
[2]   *Aaron's Rod* (1922).
[3]   'The Shadow in the Rose Garden', first collected in *The Prussian Officer*, (1914), was included in *Georgian Stories*, ed. Arthur Waugh (1922). KM's story 'Pictures' was also in the anthology.

To J. M. Murry, [5 July 1922]

[Hotel Chateau Belle Vue, Sierre]

Dearest,

With one eye on the future – if you can possibly manage to write a short note to my Da it would I think be a good idea. He has seen a doctor who finds him "in fairly decent shape" – so you'd only have to say you were glad to hear that the Doctor reported favourably & hoped he'd be well in England ... This is extremely boring. My pen won't write any more of it. If I didn't so wish for a chimley stack I'd never suggest it.

Was yesterday nice, I wonder? Brett is very very chastening. God has sent her to me as a Trial. I shall fail. It serves him right. There are the most darling swallows here – little forked tails & wings like gold fins. And someone calls drowsily from a window "Fraülein *Wir*kel?" Then the soft sound of the gardener raking the paths ... Summer.

A bientot

Tig.

Many thanks for the papers. I hate the N. & A. worse than ever. I despige it. The Lit. Sup. was bad too. There seems to be a positive blight on English writing. Really really *nothing* to say. Their review of Garnett made me realise again how first chop your criticism is.[1]

Postcard ATL. *LJMM*, 656–7.

[1]   Under 'Tracts for the Time', *TLS* (29 June 1922), a pedestrian review of Edward Garnett, *Friday Nights, Literary Criticisms and Appreciations*. JMM reviewed the same book, *Nation and the Athenaeum* (22 July 1922).

To Harold Beauchamp, 9 July 1922

Hotel Chateau Belle Vue | Sierre | (Valais)

9 July 1922

My dearest Father,

I was greatly delighted and relieved to hear that your doctor reported favourably on your health. Thank you for letting me know so soon. I am sorry that my letter re Sorapure came too late. But should you ever feel inclined to consult another opinion I hope you will give him a trial. Cousin Sinner[1] thought extremely high of him. And that is rare in doctors in that quarter of London.[2] He is a Big Wig without the manners of one. Very much like dear little Frank Payne[3] in that, whose appearance always reminded me of the man in Cole's Book Arcade Annual (do you remember it?) of whom it was said that "the birds of the air made a nest in his hair".[4]

What awfully bad luck you have had as regards weather! One can, at a pinch, put up with the English winter in the winter time, but in July it is a most horrid infliction. So disappointing for the girls too, and their garden. I do feel for them after the way they had looked forward to showing it to you in all its perfection.

I found mountain conditions plus cold, mist and rain too much for me once more. And shifted to this small town, which is in the valley. Here I shall stay until I return to Paris. Jack has, however, remained up aloft and only comes down for week-ends. This is an excellent really first rate hotel – the pleasantest I have ever known. It is simple but extremely comfortable and the food is almost too good to be true. Sierre is only 1700 feet high, which makes a great difference to my heart, too. If one had no work to do it would be a dull little place, for apart from the hotel there is nothing much to be said for it. But another great point in its favour is there is a farm attached, where the faithful old Swiss gardeners allow me to explore. This is all complete with cows, turkeys, poultry and a big rambling orchard that smells already of apples. The damson trees are the first I remember seeing since those at Karori. After all, a country life is hard to beat. It has more solid joys than any other that I can imagine. I thank heaven and my papa that I was not born a town child.

I was much interested in the photograph of yourself taken with Andrew and John. It is not good enough of you, really. But it is a delightful record of your visit. John's likeness to Vera at that age is remarkable. He looks a very taking little chap – very sensitive. I should think Andrew was like Mack. They are both "getting big boys now, Eliza". Vera must be very proud of them.

Yes, indeed, I too wish that I were taking a trip home with you. It would be a marvellous experience. The very look of a "steamer trunk" rouses the old war horse in me. I feel inclined to paw the ground and smell the briny. But perhaps in ten years time, if I manage to keep above ground, I may be able to think seriously of such a treat.

Dearest, would it be all the same to you if I fixed our rendezvous in Paris for August 23rd? If that is agreeable to you, I shall regard it as a definite arrangement, and shall be there, D.V.,[5] by the Wednesday morning, August 23rd. If, on the other hand, you prefer the former date, of course I shall keep to that. You may rely upon me not to make another change, or to suggest another. But the latter date would give me another week to finish up my work here – always supposing it suits you equally well.

This morning I received two reviews from America, where my book was published recently by Knopf of New York. They may amuse you. So I send them along. I am glad the Americans appear to be taking to it.

I have just finished a story with a canary for the hero, and almost feel I have lived in a cage and pecked a piece of chick weed myself. What a bother!

Well, darling, I must bring this letter to a close and write Marie a line for her birthday. I do hope you are having sunshine and fair winds at last!

With my fondest love,

Ever your devoted child,

Kass

TC ATL. *LKM* II. 224–5.

[1] Her father's first cousin, Sir Sydney Beauchamp (1861–1921), who was knighted after his acting as physician to the British delegation at the Treaty of Versailles.

[2] Sorapure's rooms were in Harley Street.

[3] Joseph Frank Payne (1840–1910), a distinguished physician and medical historian, Emeritus Harveian Librarian at the Royal College of Physicians. His mother was the sister of KM's maternal grandfather, and his daughter Sylvia, KM's closest friend during her years at Queen's College, London.

[4] Cole's Book Arcade opened in Melbourne in 1882, and subsequently published numerous annuals and comic collections for children. KM is running together two memories from *Cole's Funny Picture Book* (1883, 26, 83). The first is the line 'All the birds of the air,' from a version of 'Cock Robin'; the second from the limerick:

> This nice looking man with a beard
> Remarked, 'It's just as I feared:
> Four larks and a hen, two owls and a wren,
> Have all built their nests in my beard.'

[5] 'Deo voluntate', Latin for 'God willing'.

To William Gerhardi, 10 July 1922

Hotel Chateau Belle Vue | Sierre | (Valais)

10. vii. 1922

My dear Mr Gerhardi,

Many many thanks for your book.[1] I am delighted to have it, and I think it looks awfully nice. Ive read it again from beginning to end. How good it is! (Here, as you don't believe in such a thing as modesty you will say "Yes isn't it.") But I can only agree. Don't change, Mr Gerhardi. Go on writing like that. I mean with that freshness and warmth and suppleness, with that warm emotional tone and not that dreadful glaze of 'intellectuality' which is like a curse upon so many English writers... And there's another thing. You sound so free in your writing. Perhaps that is as important as anything. I don't know why so many of our poor authors should be in chains, but there it is – a dreadful clanking sounds through their books, and they never can run away, never take a leap, never risk anything . . . In fact its high time we took up our pens and struck a blow for freedom. To begin with – what about Walpole?[2] He is a ripe, fat victim. I agree with every word you say about him, his smugness is unbearable, his "Oh my Friends let us have Adventures" is simply the worst possible pretence. You see the truth is he hasn't a word to say. It *is* a tremendous adventure to him if the dog gets into the kitchen & licks a saucepan. Perhaps it is the Biggest Adventure of all to breathe 'Good Night, dear Lady' as the Daughter of the County hands him his solid silver bedroom candlestick. All is show, all is made up, all is rooted in vanity. I am ashamed of going to the same school with him – but there you are. And he's Top Boy with over £7000 a year and America bowing to the earth to him . . . Its very painful.

But after this long parenthesis let me come back to 'Futility' one moment. Shall I tell you what I think you may have to guard against? You have a very keen, very delightful sense of humour. Just on one or two occasions (par exemple when you took Nina into a corner & slapped her hand to the amusement of the others[3]) I think you give it too full a rein. I wonder if you feel what I mean? To me, that remark trembles towards – – a kind of smartness – a something too easy to be worth doing. I hope one day, we shall have a talk about this book. Let me once more wish it & you every possible success.

Now for your photograph. Its so kind of you to have sent it to me. I am very happy to have it. When I possess a room with a mantelpiece again on the mantelpiece you will stand. Judging by it you look as though you were very musical. Are you?

I am extremely interested to hear of your book on Tchekhov. Its just the moment for a book on Tchekhov[4]. I have read, these last weeks, *Friday Nights* by Edward Garnett which contains a long essay on him. But little is said & what is said doesn't much matter. For instance, Garnett seems greatly impressed by the importance of T's scientific training as a doctor, not the *in*direct importance (I could understand that) but the *di*rect. He quotes as a proof The Party & T's letter in which he says "the ladies say I am quite right in all my symptoms when I describe the confinement."[5] But in spite of T's letter that story didn't need a doctor to write it. There's not a thing any sensitive writer could not have discovered without a medical degree. The truth of that "importance" is far more subtle. People on the whole understand Tchekhov very little. They persist in looking at him from a certain angle & he's a man that won't stand that kind of gaze. One must get round him – see him, feel him as a whole. By the way isn't Tolstoi's little essay on The Darling a small masterpiece of stupidity.[6]

– – And when you say you don't think T. was really modest. Isn't it perhaps that he *always* felt, very sincerely, that he could have done so much more than he did. He was tormented by Time, and by his desire to live as well as to write. 'Life is given us but once.' Yet, when he was not working he had a feeling of guilt; he felt he ought to be. And I think he very often had that feeling a singer has who has sung once & would give almost anything for the chance to sing the same song over again – *Now* he could sing it . . . But the chance doesn't return. I suppose all writers, little and big, feel this but T. more than most. But I must not write about him; I could go on and on and on . . .

Yes, the title of your novel is lovely, and from the practical standpoint excellent. I see so many pretty little hands stretched towards the library shelf . . . 'About Love'.[7] I don't see how *any* body could avoid buying a copy. But très serieusement, I am so glad you are at work on it. Do you intend to 'adopt a literary career' as they say? Or do you have to make literature your mistress. I hope Bolton is not a permanent address if you dislike it so.[8] I was there 17 years ago. I remember eating a cake with pink icing while a dark intense lady told me of her love for Hadyn Coffyn[9] & that she had 13 photographs of him in silver frames in her bedroom. I was very impressed, but perhaps it wasn't a typical incident. I meant to tell you of the lovely place where I am staying but this letter is too long. The flowers are wonderful just now. Don't you love these real summer flowers? You should see the dahlias here, big spiky fellows, with buds like wax, and round white ones and real saffron yellow. The women are working in the vines. Its hot and fine with a light valley wind.

Goodbye. I am so glad we are friends.

Yours ever
Katherine Mansfield.

MS ATL. *LKM* II, 225–7.

[1] *Futility* had just been published.

[2] KM twice reviewed Hugh Walpole (1884–1941) indifferently, and wrote to him defensively in response to his challenging her review of his novel *The Captives*, *Athenaeum* (15 Oct. 1920; see *LKMM* IV. 86–7).

[3] A minor incident in Part III, Chapter IX. Nina is the elusive Russian girl with whom the narrator of the largely autobiographical fiction is in love. The absurdist novel, with its theme of constant and pointless optimism, is based on Gerhardi's experiences with the British Military Mission to Siberia during the Bolshevik Revolution.

[4] Gerhardi was then writing the first full-length study of the Russian writer in English, *Anton Chekov: A Critical Study* (1923).

[5] 'Tchehov and His Art', *Friday Nights, Literary Criticisms and Appreciations*, 54. KM is referring to a letter Garnett quotes to A. S. Suvorin (15 Nov. 1888).

[6] Chekov published 'The Darling' in 1898; Tolstoy his essay on it in 1906.

[7] Gerhardi abandoned this, his second novel being *The Polyglots* (1925).

[8] Financially hard up, Gerhardi was living with his parents in Bolton.

[9] Hadyn Coffin, popular actor and singer.

To Arnold Gibbons, 13 July 1922

Hotel Chateau Belle Vue | Sierre | Valais | Switzerland.
13.VII.1922

Dear Mr Gibbons,

I am appalled that I expressed myself so clumsily as to make it possible for you to use the word 'plagiarism'. I beg you to forgive me; it was far from my meaning. It was *absorbed* I meant. Perhaps you will agree that we all, as writers, to a certain extent, absorb each other when we love. (I am presuming that you love Tchekhov.) Anatole France would say we eat each other,[1] but perhaps nourish is the better word. For instance Tchekhov's talent was nourished by Tolstoi's Death of Ivan Ilyitch.[2] It is very possible he never would have written as he did if he had not read that story. There is a deep division between the work he did before he read it & after... All I felt about your stories was that you had not yet made the 'gift' you had received from Tchekhov your own. You had not yet, finally, made free with it & turned it to your own account. My dear colleague, I reproach myself for not having made this plainer.

Id like, if I may, to discuss the other points in your letter. Let me see if I understand you. You mean you can only 'care' for such things as the little cat, the old man, the note of a bird, in the period of reaction against your belief in Pain & a life of sacrifice & yourself. But as your belief is all-important to you that period of reaction means little. Am I right? Therefore the last of the five stories was the only one you really cared about for there you express your very self... I mean, you are writing with real conviction. Do you know what I feel? To do this successfully you will have to do it more *in*directly. You will have to leave the student out. Now there is a moment in that story where you succeed. Its where the little girl's throat works – she weeps. She wants the apple & is afraid she is not going to have it. (Always remembering this is just my personal feeling.) Your student argues, explains too much. He ought perhaps to have said not a single word.

But I hope you will go on writing. The important thing is to write, to find yourself in losing yourself. (There is no truth profounder. I do not know myself whether – this world being what it is – pain is not absolutely necessary. I do not see how we are to come by knowledge & Love except through pain. That sounds too definite expressed so baldly. If one were talking one would make reservations... Believe in pain I must.

Yours ever
Katherine Mansfield.

I shall always be glad to hear from you.

MS ATL. *LKM* II. 228–9.

[1] Anatole France (1844–1924), French novelist, poet, critic, and editor. A biting ironist, elegant stylist, and socialist, he was awarded the Nobel Prize for Literature in 1921. His deep scepticism of social behaviour led to his frequently remarking on the human propensity to devour each other.
[2] Published 1886.

To Richard Murry, [16 July 1922]

Hotel Chateau Belle Vue | Sierre (Valais)

Sunday

Caro Riccardo

I keep on thinking about you. I am tired of having no news from you & now Jack has come down here for the weekend & he has not heard.

Send me even a p.c. – will you? I don't want to ask you for news about things unless you are in the mood to talk about them,[1] but a sight of my dear little brother's handwriting would be most awfully welcome.

Jack, as you know, will be in England for August–September...?

With so much love, Richard dear.

Yours ever
Katherine.

I enclose a little photo taken in the garden. Do you like it. Brother & sister of the painter, R.M., you observe.

MS R. Murry. *Adam* 370–5, 27.

[1] Richard was waiting to hear of a scholarship to the Slade School of Art.

To S. S. Koteliansky, 17 July 1922

Chateau Belle Vue | Sierre (Valais) | Suisse

17.VII.1922

Dear precious Koteliansky,

After all, I shall not have the money to come to England for a week this autumn. I must be in Paris on August 20th and then for about 10 days I must attend to my Father who is coming to see me there on his way back to New Zealand. After that, I shall be alone for the autumn, and for 10–12 weeks I must go to the clinique once a week. But I tell you all these tedious details simply because, in spite of my Spartan feelings in my last letter, I wonder again if there is any possibility of your coming across during that time. I do – I *long* to see you and for us to talk. Do not think I am trying to interfere or to make demands. It is not that at all. But it would be so nice, so awfully nice to look forward to such happiness. I want to talk to you for hours about – Aaron's Rod, for instance. Have you read it?

There are certain things in this new book of L's that I do not like. But they are not important or really part of it. They are trivial, encrusted, they cling to it as snails cling to the underside of a leaf. But apart from them there is the leaf, is the tree, firmly planted, deep thrusting, outspread, growing grandly, alive in every twig. It is a living book; it is warm, it breathes. And it is written by a living man with *conviction*. Oh, Koteliansky, what a relief it is to turn away from these little predigested books written by authors who have nothing to say. It is like walking by the sea at high tide eating a crust of bread and looking over the water. I am so sick of all this modern seeking which ends in seeking. *Seek* by all means, but the text goes on "that ye shall find".[1] And although of course there can be no ultimate finding, there is a kind of finding by the way which is enough, is sufficient. But these seekers in the looking glass, these half-female, frightened writers-of-today – you know, darling, they remind me of the green-fly in roses – they are a kind of blight.

I do not want to be hard. I hope to God I am not unsympathetic. But it seems to me there comes a time in life when one must realise one is grownup – a man. And when it is no longer decent to go on probing and probing. Life is so short. The world is rich. There are so many adventures possible. Why do we not gather our strength together and LIVE. It all comes to much the same thing. In youth most of us are, for various reasons, slaves.[2] And then, when we are able to throw off our chains, we prefer to keep them. Freedom is dangerous, is frightening.

If only I can be a good enough writer to strike a blow for freedom! It is the one axe I want to grind. Be free – and you can afford to give yourself to life! Even to believe in life.

I do not go all the way with Lawrence. His ideas of sex mean nothing to me.[3] But I feel nearer L. than anyone else. All these last months I have thought as he does about many things. Does this sound nonsense to you? Laugh at me if you like or scold me. But remember what a disadvantage it is having to write such things. If we were talking one could say it all in a few words. It is so hard not to dress ones ideas up in their Sunday clothes and make them look all stiff and shining in a letter. My ideas look awful in their best dresses.

(Now I have made myself a glass of tea. Every time I drop a piece of lemon into a glass of tea I say 'Koteliansky'. Perhaps it is a kind of grace.) I went for such a lovely drive today behind a very intelligent horse who listened to every word the driver and I said and heartily agreed. One could tell from his ears that he was even extremely interested in the conversation. They are thinning the vines for the last time before harvest. One can almost smell the grapes. And in the orchards apples are reddening; it is going to be a wonderful year for pears. But one could write about the drive for as many pages as there are in Ulysses.

It is late. I must go to bed. Now the train going to Italy has flashed past. Now it is silent again except for the old toad who goes *ka*-ka − *ka*-ka − laying down the law.

Goodnight.

Your
Katherine.

MS BL. Cited Dickinson, 96.

[1] Luke 11:10.

[2] KM may have had in mind a letter she translated with Koteliansky, published in the *Athenaeum*, (25 Jul. 1921), in which Chekov wrote to A. S. Souverin, 7 Jan. 1889, outlining a story of a young man who 'squeezes the slave out of himself' (*CLKM* IV. 312).

[3] As KM wrote to Beatrice Campbell from Higher Tregerthen, Zennor, 4 May 1916, when she and Murry lived next door to the Lawrences, 'I shall *never* see sex in trees, sex in the running brooks, sex in stones & sex in everything. The number of things that are really phallic from fountain pen fillers onwards!' (*CLKM* I. 261).

To Eric Pinker, [c. 24 July 1922]

Hotel Chateau Belle Vue | Sierre Valais | Switzerland

Dear Mr Pinker,

Your letter about Mr Gerhardi only reached me today. I should be delighted if I might be the means of putting you in touch with him. His address is *40 Bradford Street, Bolton*. Please mention my name, if you care to do so, in writing to him. I thought Futility a very remarkable first novel & highly *promising* considering the youthfulness of the author. Much better in fact than a great many 'assured successes'.

I am finishing my twelve stories for Shorter.[1] They have turned into a kind of short novel. I hope to send you the typescript in a fortnights time. Perhaps some American magazine would not consider it too long.

In the matter of that short story <At the> Her First Ball for the American Anthology,[2] I am quite willing to let them reprint it.

Many thanks for disposing of *The Fly*[3] for me in America.

Yours very sincerely
Katherine Mansfield.

MS Newberry.

[1] Again, KM is suggesting that she has done far more on these stories than was the case.

[2] Not listed in Kirkpatrick.

[3] 'The Fly' was reprinted in *Century Magazine*, New York (Sept. 1922).

To William Gerhardi, [c. 24 July 1922]

Hotel Belle Vue | Montana-sur-Sierre | (Valais) | Suisse

Dear Mr Gerhardi,

I had a letter from Mr. Pinker, my agent, today, asking me if I would put him in touch with you. I hastened to send him your address & to say he might mention my name. If you have not already got an agent I'd most cordially recomment Mr Pinker to you.

What a good notice of Futility in the Lit. Sup![1] I hope you're having splendid reviews.

Yours ever
Katherine Mansfield

MS ATL.

[1] The unsigned, highly favourable review in the *TLS* (20 July 1922), described *Futility* as 'a story which Tchehov omitted to tell... [Gerhardi's] performance is, without exaggeration, astonishing'.

To William Gerhardi, [late July 1922]

[Hotel Chateau Belle Vue, Sierre]

Dear Mr Gerhardi,

I have written to you, since this letter,[1] to the same wrong address. It was a business letter with regard to my agent Mr Pinker. Have you received it?

Yours sincerely
Katherine Mansfield

MS ATL.

[1] Gerhardi notes that KM's letter of 10 July, 'erroneously addressed to Yorkshire instead of Lancashire, was returned to her by the P.O. at Sierre. She sent it me a second time, with this slip' (ATL).

To Harold Beauchamp, 28 July 1922

Hotel Chateau Belle Vue | Sierre | (Valais)

28 July 1922

Dearest Father,

The days seem to whisk away here so fast that I don't think the farmer's wife would be in time to chop off their tails.[1] I spend a large part of them tapping out my new *long* story or *short* novel on my little Corona. But I have been thinking of you so much, dearest, and hoping that your climatic and physical conditions are both more settled. I heard from Chad that you had been to see my good Doctor. I hoped he satisfied you and that you did not think I had over-praised him. It would be very nice to know from you what you thought of him.

Since I last wrote we have had every variety of weather from Winter to Spring. To-day, for instance, began with a cold downpour, gradually changed until it was a damp tropical morning, and now its a sharp Autumn evening. Its very difficult to adjust one's attire to these lightning changes. The only safe recipe is to start with flannel next to the skin, and build up or cast off from that. What a frightful bother! But judging from the reports in the Times, England has turned over a summer leaf again. Long may it remain fair.

I hope you have enjoyed your time in London and that you have not found it too tiring. I suppose dear little Rally[2] is just the same. And have you listened to Lou's[3] rattle. She seems to run up conversation as if with a sewing machine. I have never met any one so incessant. I get quite dazed after a time, and don't even try to pipe above the sound. But her courage and good humour are amazing.

There is a remarkable old talker here at present – an American, aged eighty eight – with his wife and daughter. The daughter looks about sixty five. According to the ancient gentleman, they have been on the wing ever since he retired at the age of seventy five, and they intend remaining on the wing for another fifteen years or so! He is full of fire still, dresses every night for dinner, plays bridge, and loves to start a gossip with "In the year 1865". Its very interesting listening to his memories of early Noo York and of American life generally 'way back. I think he mistook me for a young person home for the holidays. For he introduced himself with the words "Boys seem skeerce here. May be you wouldn't mind if I tried to entertain you a li'll". When he said boys, I thought at first he must be alluding to farm labourers, but then memories of American novels "put me right", as they say.

Jack is still in his lofty perch among the mountains. At the week-ends, whenever the weather is wet, we play billiards. There is a splendid table here and we are both very keen. Its a fascinating game. I remember learning to hold a cue at Sir Joseph Ward's[4], and I can see now Rubi Seddon's[5] super-refinement as if she expected each ball to be stamped with a coronet before she would deign to hit it. Jack is extremely keen on all games. I often think of what an enthusiast he would become on board ship.

Dear little "Elizabeth" has been spending the afternoon with me. She is on the eve of a very large house party at her chalet

TC ATL. *LKM* II. 231–2.

[1] As she did in the nursery rhyme, 'Three Blind Mice'.
[2] KM's cousin and Elizabeth's brother, the rather ineffectual Ralph Beauchamp.
[3] Another Beauchamp relative.

[4] Sir Joseph Ward, Liberal Prime Minister of New Zealand 1906–12, and again 1928–30, whose daughter Eileen was a teenage friends of KM's.

[5] Rubi, the wife of Richard Seddon, another Liberal Prime Minister of New Zealand, 1893–1906. Both the Ward and Seddon families were close friends of the Beauchamps.

To Edmund Blunden,[1] *[c.30 July 1922]*

[Hotel Chateau Belle Vue, Sierre]

It is awfully kind of you to have sent me a copy of your lovely poem, *Old Homes*.[2] Many, many thanks. I like especially the verse beginning:

Thence, too, when high wind through the black clouds pouring – One walks straight into your chill, pale, wet world as one reads.... I love the sound of water in poetry.

How are you, I wonder, and where are you spending the summer? It's the moment here when all the dahlias are out, every little child is eating a green apple, the vines have been cut down for the last time and the grapes are as big as marbles. In fact, this whole valley is one great ripening orchard. Heavens! how beautiful apple trees are! But you know these things a great deal better than I do.

If H.M.T. [Tomlinson] is near by – give him my love, will you?

MS Lacking. *LKM* II. 232.

[1] Edmund Blunden (1896–1974), poet and scholar, who had worked under Murry on the *Athenaeum*. His war experiences and war poems were published as *Undertones of War* (1928).

[2] His long poem in rhyming couplets celebrated memories of childhood and village life. The section KM commends describes the impressions made by a storm, with its premonitions of 'the world's end and final Arbiter'. Blunden placed the poem at the beginning of his collection, *English Poems* (1930).

To J. M. Murry, [31 July 1922]

[Hotel Chateau Belle Vue, Sierre]

D.B.

I was quite wrong about Arco. L.M. had 'made a little muddle' about the A.Ms and p.ms. The truth is you start from here at about 11 o'clock one morning & you are in Arco the next evening at about 8.30. That is if you spend the night in Milano. It you don't you change at midnight & so on & so on. If you would still like to go I will find out everything very exact.[1] I sent your toospeg cream after you today. What an awful man on this p.c.[2] Why? After that I say no more Betsy.

Postcard ATL. *LJMM*, 657–8.

[1] The postcard was sent to Murry at the Chalet Soleil, where he was still staying with Elizabeth. KM is sending him times for his proposed trip to Italy, a plan which was abandoned.

² The picture is of La Rue Garibaldi, Castellar, Alpes Maritimes, with two men speaking together in the mid-distance. One is a clean-shaven workman, the other a middle-aged bearded man in a suit.

To J. M. Murry, [late July 1922]

[Hotel Chateau Belle Vue, Sierre]

D.B.

We could not phone you last thing, when this letter came, because of the Festa. Will you decide what you would like to do & phone Ida here. She will then get through to Zurich.

I am glad its nice where you are. We had a quite wonderful time here in the garden before the rain fell. (Huge great drops like $\frac{1}{2}$d buns.) But the garden was lighted by lanterns & a faraway band played & there were Bengal lights, golden rain, rockets. Marvellous! There was a special dinner, too, with a whole great salmon lying on a bed of roses with little crayfish adoring.

I am *v* glad the ladies are nice. Isn't it pleasant to sit in friendly tumpany again?

Yes, Somerset Maugham lays it on too thick. Its too downright good a *story* – don't you think? Too oily! And there is not enough rain in it.[1] The rain keeps stopping. The whole story ought to have been soaked through & through – or steamed with the after the rain feeling. And it isn't & doesn't.

What about Northanger Abbey?[2] Is it possible? And the New Statesman?

I like you awfully

Y.W.

MS ATL.

[1] Somerset Maugham's short story, 'Rain', in *Trembling of a Leaf* (1921).
[2] Jane Austen, *Northanger Abbey* (1818).

To Elizabeth, Countess Russell, [31 July 1922]

Hotel Chateau Belle Vue | Sierre

Monday.

My dear Elizabeth

It would be too marvellous if we might be men and brothers for once, and I am more grateful than I can say.[1] I will pay it back the moment my book is paid for. But that will not be before the late autumn ... May I keep it as long as that? Of course, if in the meantime my Papa shakes a money bag at me – But it is far more likely to be a broomstick. Thank you from my heart, dearest Cousin!

It is on my conscience that I was odious about poor Brett the other afternoon. I am so sorry for her, really. But to talk to her is exactly like talking to someone for an hour for two hours over the telephone. There she is, at one end of the line, waiting & listening. One ought to feel nothing but pity and I am ashamed of my impatience.

Its such a divine night. Are you in the garden, I wonder? I think to watch the moon rise is one of the most *mysterious* pleasures in Life.

Lovingly yours
Katherine.

MS BL. Alpers 1980, 364.

---

[1] Elizabeth's diary recorded 'tea and talk' with KM on 28 July (TC Huntington, 31). The conversation must have touched on KM's fear that she would not have the £75 necessary for her second round of treatment with Manoukhin, as well as the travelling expenses to visit London, for Elizabeth wrote to her on 30 July 'Do let me lend you £100! . . . I know if you had just finished a book as I have and got paid and I was hard up I'd *certainly* ask you to give me a hand for the moment. Men do these things so simply and never give it another thought. Is it *really* so impossible for us to be brothers?' (Alpers 1980, 363–4).

To S. S. Koteliansky, [2 August 1922]

[Hotel Chateau Belle Vue, Sierre]

My dear Koteliansky,

I hope you are better. If you need a doctor *Sorapure* is a good man – intelligent and quiet. He does not discuss Lloyd George[1] with one, either. This is a great relief. All the other English doctors that I know have just finished reading The Daily Mail by the time they reach me. It is a pity that Lawrence is driven so far. I am sure Western Australia will not help.[2] The desire to travel is a great, real temptation. But does it do any good? It seems to me to correspond to the feelings of a sick man who thinks always 'if only I can get away from here I shall be better.' However – there is nothing to be done. One must go through with it. No one can stop that sick man, either, from moving on and on. His craving is stronger than he. But Lawrence, I am sure, will get well.

Perhaps you will be seeing Brett in a few days? She goes back to England tomorrow. I feel awfully inclined to Campbell[3] about her for a little. But it would take a whole book to say all that one feels. She is a terrible proof of the influence ones childhood has upon one. And there has been nothing stronger in her life to counteract that influence. I do not think she will ever be an adult being. She is weak; she is a vine; she longs to cling. She cannot nourish herself from the earth; she must feed on the sap of another. How can these natures ever be happy? By happy I mean at peace with themselves? She is seeking someone who will make her forget that early neglect, that bullying and contempt. But the person who would satisfy her would have to dedicate himself to curing all the results of her unhappiness – her distrust, for instance, her suspicions, her fears. He would have to take every single picture and paint it with her, just as a singer, by singing with his pupil can make that weak voice strong & confident... But even then, she would not be *cured*.

I believe one can cure nobody, one can change nobody fundamentally. The born slave cannot become a free man. He can only become free-er. I have refused to believe that for years, and yet I am certain it is true – it is even a law of life. But it is equally true that hidden in the slave there are the makings of the free man. And these makings are very nice in Brett, very sensitive and generous. I love her for them. They make me want to help her as much as I can.

I am content. I prefer to leave our meeting to chance. To know you are there is enough. If I knew I was going to die I should even ask you definitely to come and see me. For I should hate to die without one long, uninterrupted talk with *you*. But short of it – it does not greatly matter.

I press your hands

Katherine.

MS BL. *LKM* II. 234–5; Dickinson, 96.

[1] Lloyd George (1863–1945), Welsh Liberal politician who dominated the coalition cabinet during the First World War, and was elected post-War Prime Minister, a position he was to lose in Oct. 1922.

[2] KM presumably heard from Koteliansky that Lawrence had arrived in Freemantle on 4 May, and stayed in Western Australia for the next fortnight. He was now living at Wyewurk, Thirroul, in New South Wales.

[3] 'To Campbell', or 'Campbelling', was an expression going back to KM's meeting in 1912 with the Irish barrister, Gordon Campbell, and his wife Beatrice Campbell. The phrase meant to talk thoroughly over some matter of special interest.

To Elizabeth, Countess Russell, [3 August 1922]

Hotel Chateau Belle Vue

Thursday

Dear Elizabeth

Many many thanks once more.

I am so sorry to hear of your misfortunes.... My story isn't a bit wonderful; I wish to God it were. But I'm panting for new scenes, new blood – everything brand new! In fact, you've lent that £100 to a fearfully desperate character.[1]

Ever, dear Elizabeth,

Yours lovingly,
Katherine.

MS BL. Alpers 1980, 364.

[1] Elizabeth had sent a cheque on 2 Aug., with a note saying she had lost her cook, and was unwell. She had also written that 'John says you have written a wonderful story' (Alpers 1980, 394). KM's last completed story was 'The Canary', written early in July.

To J. M. Murry, [early August 1922]

[Hotel Chateau Belle Vue, Sierre]

Early Edition.

D.B.

I think Amos Barton is awful[1] & there is nothing to say for it. In the first place poor George Eliot's Hymn to the Cream Jug[2] makes me feel quite quesy (no wonder she harps on biliousness & begins her description of a feast 'should one *not* be bilious there is no pleasanter sight'[3] etc.). In the second place the idea of lovely, gentle, fastidious, Madonna-like Mrs Barton having 8 children in 9 years by that pockmarked poor 'mongrel' (her own words) with the blackened stumps for teeth is simply disgusting! If I thought the poor little pamphlet was designed to put in a word in favour of Birth Control I could bear it. But far from it. Each chubby chubby with a red little fist & TEN BLACK NAILS (how is that for charm?) rouses a kind of female cannibalism in G.E. She gloats over the fat of babies.

I have always heard Amos Barton was one of her best stories. You know its very very bad that we haven't sincerer critics. Having spread my peacock tail to that extent I had better depart. *Not* before saying what a truly frightful need England hath of thee.[4]

Yours ever & ever
Wig.

Later Edition. D.B. darling, I have just got your Lawrence review & note. You didn't send the Pope, love ... But Ill get L.M. to ask for the two receipts and will print the address in a fair white linen hand. About your review[5] – I think you are absolutely right in every word of it – every word. I think you occasionally use more *words* of praise than are necessary, it sounds too effusive & will raise suspicion. Shall I tone it down a bit on my typewriter or send as it is? I'll phone you & ask. Gerhardi comes off with a nice little pat. But can't be helped. Oh, I *long* for a paper this morning!! I have been "making up" a paper ever since I read your review. I *shall* start one, too, jolly soon. For three years only. But what years! Dont you think it might be a good idea if this week you came on Sunday instead of Saturday? Give us a longer week. That is if you are at all pressé or inclined to the notion. (No! See below). Otherwise you wont mind will you dear, if I do a bit of work on Saturday while you are in the garden. H'm yes. After my spartan suggestion has been written *I take it back.* I say instead what I have said about working . . . & *hope* Ill be able to look out of [the] window & see your summer feltie below. Yes, indeed, come Saturday unless you don't want to, or think that the female will is determined to drag you here. Its not, my dear darling.

Once the Dove's Nest is finished I shall leave here. But it will take a fortnight, not a week. Its too expensive. I *must* draw in my horns for the next six months, somehow. Blow!

My watch is still a li'll golden angel. And what a big brown angel that chest is! With two little windows at the sides & a chimney at the top we could almost live in it – open the lid softly for the milkman & the wild strawberry man.

Ever your
Wig.

MS ATL. *LKM*, 232–4.

---

[1] KM lists details from *The Sad Fortunes of the Rev. Amos Barton*, the first of George Eliot's short novels in *Scenes from Clerical Life* (1857). The story moves through mild satire on the parish life of an unattractive and impecunious curate, towards a sentimental account of his wife's exhaustion and death.

[2] Early in Chapter I there is an extended account of 'the dulcet strength, the animating blandness of tea, when sufficiently blended with real farmhouse cream'.

[3] A general statement on dining well in Chapter VI.

[4]
Milton! thou shoudst be living at this hour:
England hath need of thee: she is a fen
Of stagnant waters . . . (William Wordsworth, 'England, 1802').

[5] JMM had sent her a copy of 'Two Remarkable Novels', his extended discussion of D. H. Lawrence's *Aaron's Rod*, and a brief note on William Gerhardi's *Futility*. The review would appear in the *Nation and the Athenaeum* (12 Aug. 1922).

To J. M. Murry, 7 August 1922

[Hotel Chateau Belle Vue
Sierre]
7.VIII.1922

Dearest Bogey

I have been on the point of writing this letter for days.[1] My heart has been behaving in such a curious fashion that I cant imagine it means nothing. So, as I should hate to leave you unprepared, I'll just try & jot down what comes into my mind. All my manuscripts I leave entirely to you to do what you like with. Go through them one day, dear love, and destroy all you do not use. Please destroy all letters you do not wish to keep & all papers. You know my love of tidiness. Have a clean sweep, Bogey, and leave all fair – will you?

Books are yours of course, & so are my personal possessions. L.M. had better distribute my clothes. Give your Mother my fur coat, will you? Chaddie & Jeanne must choose what they want & I suppose Vera would like something. My small pearl ring – the 'daisy' one I should like to wear. The other, give to Richard's love when you know her – if you approve of the idea.

I seem, after all, to have nothing to leave and nobody to leave things to. Dela Mare I should like to remember and Richard. But you will give a book or some small thing to whoever wishes . . . Monies, of course, are all yours. In fact, my dearest dear, I leave everything to you – to the secret you whose lips I kissed this morning. In spite of everything – how happy we have been! I feel no other lovers have walked the earth together more joyfully – in spite of all.

Farewell, my precious love.

I am for ever and ever

Your
WIG.

MS ATL. Lea, 95.

[1] This letter was not immediately sent to Murry, but left for him at her bank in London, where he received it after her death. Her official will she made on 14 Aug., which read: 'All manuscripts notebooks papers letters I leave to John Murry likewise I should like him to publish as little as possible and to tear up and burn as much as possible. He will understand that I desire to leave as few traces of my camping ground as possible. To Ida Constance Baker I leave my gold watch and chain and my clothes for her to dispose of as she shall think fit with the exception of my Spanish shawl which I leave to my friend Anne Estelle Drey & my fur coat which I leave to my mother in law Mrs Murry. I leave to Richard Murry my large pearl ring. To my cousin Countess Russell I leave my copy of Shakespeare. All my books I leave to my husband John M Murry desiring that he shall send one book each to Walter de la Mare H. M. Tomlinson Doctor Sorapure Alfred Richard Orage Sydney & Violet Schiff J. D. Fergusson Gordon Campbell and D. H. Lawrence. To my sister C.M.Perkins I leave my writing case. To my sister Jeanne Beauchamp I leave my piece of greenstone. To my father Harold Beauchamp I leave the brass pig and my bible. To my sister Vera Mackintosh Bell I leave my Italian toilet boxes. My carved walking stick I leave to S. Koteliansky. All the remainder of my property I leave to my husband the said John Middleton Murry' (PC ATL).

To Dorothy Brett, [7 August 1922]

[Hotel Chateau Belle Vue]
Sierre
Monday

Dearest

If you don't hear from me until Wednesday week – don't mind! I can only reply to your letter by silence, & by clasping your hand. The reason is that my plans are all in the air and I am horribly tired & I must somehow finish this story. So I must retire into my shell, & be silent until Wednesday week. Then I shall send you a budget. But wait for me till then!

All is just the same in every way. I can only do this because I know and trust you and I believe you know & trust me. Im a fearfully imperfect friend, at present. But once I get out of my silly prison I will be nicer in every way – please God. In the meantime, tho' I don't write I think about you and am as *ever*

Your

Tig

Later Your second letter has just come about Paris.[1] But blow Paris for the moment. Don't think, my dear little precious artist, that because I am dumb until Wednesday week that I am changed a jot. For I am NOT! I loved your letter. Fancy old Sullivan in his cap with Sylvia[2] . . . They made such a funny drawing as you described them! I laughed as we laughed here together. Many many thanks for the hotel. Its too dear though. Its only for the Rich Bugs not for the Poor ones. But wait! I may have a small surprise for you on Wednesday week.

What a bad man Murry is to put that tombstone in your parcel, and how just like him! Its surprising he did not ask you to take the oak chest back with you filled with books. He is having a very good time. The big lady sings something beautiful, Miss – Russian & French songs & they are very gay.

Goodbye for now

Tig.

MS Newberry.

---

[1] Sent when Brett was on her way back to London, after her stay with KM.
[2] See p. 323, n.1.

To Violet Schiff, 9 August 1922

Hotel Chateau Belle Vue | Sierre | Valais

9.VIII.1922

Dearest Violet,

Forgive me for not answering your dear letter sooner. I wanted to & I could not. Do you know the mood when one really *cant* write a letter? It sounds absurd, but if anyone will understand it – you will . . .

I am constantly thinking of you and Sydney. I wonder when we shall meet again? I only stayed a week or two in the mountains, then I telegraphed Jones to join me and we came down here where we've been ever since. Its a relief to have Jones again. I have almost made her swear never to leave me even if I drive her away. I have been working here after a fashion but Ive had trouble with my heart & again I can't walk & Ive fever – die alter geschichte which doesn't bleib immer treu to anyone. However, there it is. Perhaps one ought to learn to accept it as one's destiny and not fight against it. Who knows? Its hard to decide.

The author of Futility is only known to me through letters. I call him in my mind my little undergraduate. He wrote to me, from Oxford last summer, and later sent me the MSS of his novel. I helped him with it a little & suggested a publisher. Since then we have kept in touch. He sounds a very delightful, impulsive, young man. Full of enthusiasm. But what I like him for is I think he has real feeling. His letters breathe. Perhaps you will meet him one day. Curiously enough, I have often felt you would. I hope success will not spoil him.

Have you read Aarons Rod – Lawrence's latest book? There seems to me something very fine in it – so vigorous – so full of growth. I had a long miserable disgusted look at Rebecca Wests Judge.[1] Ugh! How dreadful! I felt horribly ashamed of it.

Yes, wasn't the Times shameful about Proust.[2] The coarseness of the mind that could write so! But never has English criticism been at such a low ebb as at this moment. Nobody has anything to say. As for the Nation it is as dead as mutton.

A storm rages while I write this dull letter. It sounds so splendid, I wish I were out in it.

Murry has spent the summer in the mountains. At present he is with Elizabeth – the real one, of course. He looks forward, I know, to seeing you next month. I go to Paris in about a fortnight. But my plans are very vague. I *hope* to spend the winter in Italy. Murry sent me Sydney's letter about his novel. I envied him such a letter with all my heart. Goodbye, dearest Violet. The time I spent with you & Sydney in Paris is so vivid. I love to think of it. With much love to you both.

Ever yours
K.M.

MS BL. *Adam* 300, 117–18.

[1] Rebecca West's novel *The Judge* had just been published.
[2] Under 'Foie Gras', the *TLS* (3 Aug. 1922), carried an unappreciative review of *À la Recherche du Temps Perdu*, Tome V, *Sodome et Gomorrhe* II, hoping for Proust 'to come to the end of his long story'.

To Harold Beauchamp, 10 August 1922

Hotel Chateau Belle Vue | Sierre | (Valais) | Switzerland.
10 August 1922

My dearest Father,

I have delayed answering your letter – which I was most happy to receive – because I felt there was a possibility that I might be forced, for reasons of health only, to make a little change in my plans. I hoped this would not be necessary, but it is. To "come straight to the horses" – my heart has been playing up so badly this last week that I realise it is imperative for me to see Doctor Sorapure before I go on with my Paris treatment. As I am due to begin this Paris treatment on September 1st, I have decided that my best plan is to come straight to London next Tuesday, arriving Wednesday, 16th. Until I have had an opinion on the present condition of my heart I am really a thoroughly unsatisfactory companion. I could neither go about with you and the dear girls, nor add to your enjoyment in any way. And to sit with me in the bedroom of a foreign hotel would be extremely small beer indeed! And I could not forgive myself if my disquieting symptoms became aggravated in Paris and caused you uneasiness. You know what a heart is like! I hope this trouble is something that can be corrected easily. I feel sure it is. But until I know just what it is there is always the feeling I may be doing the very thing that will send me on my last journey before my work is anything like finished here below! That's what I have been feeling all this week.

I should not dream of worrying you with all this, my dearest, if it wasn't that we had arranged to meet in Paris, and that I have upset your plans. Do believe me it costs me a great deal to have to do so. Nothing short of necessity would induce me to.

I shall go straight to my good friend, Miss Brett, on arrival. My address, therefore, will be:-

C/- Hon. Dorothy Brett,
  6, Pond Street,
    HAMPSTEAD.

I shall try and see Sorapure on Thursday. If you are in London, would you telephone me, or let me know where I may write or telephone you. If you are at Wood Hay, perhaps it would be best if I write you a report of proceedings after my interview with Sorapure. Please don't be cross with me for being such a bothersome child. I feel it with my whole heart, even though it's a "sickly" one. In any case, darling, I will communicate with you on arrival, and we can, I hope, arrange to meet then. Will the girls forgive me, too?

With my fondest love,

Ever your devoted child
Kass

TC ATL. *LKM* II. 235.

To Vera McIntosh Bell, 10 August 1922

Hotel Chateau Belle Vue | Sierre (Valais)

10.VIII.1922

My dearest V.

Forgive me, if you can, for delaying so long in answering your card & the photograph of my little neffys & the Cook Book for Ida. You see I put them in order of precedence but I was delighted to receive the first two, especially, and more especially, the second. Andrew & John have grown into such big boys now Eliza that there is no recognising them at all. John is the image of you, isn't he. Do you remember a photograph of yourself taken with Guy Tonks?[1] If John only had curls he would be you as a child over again. Andrew looks extremely like Mack. Is he? The expression even seems to me to be his Father's. They are darling little boys & you must be tremendously proud of them. I wish I could think I might see them sometime in the near future. Id so like to hear them and watch them, don't you know? Jack was very interested in the photograph, too. Supposing I was critical...Is Andrew in a school uniform? Is that why he wears a linen collar? With that kind of suit English children of his age and 'station' wear cricket shirts with soft turn-down collars. But I feel rather like Grandma B. [Beauchamp] commenting on what is no doubt a Canadian fashion. Don't be cross with me, darling!

The Cook Book is at present an inspiration only to Ida, but a very real one. Jack & I hung over it, too, and wondered if those were the 'plats' one ate at Almonte. The moment I have a kitchen again and a meek maid Ida is determined to reproduce the coloured illustrations exactly and dazzle us and our friends. How very well these books are got up in Canada and America. They are written for an entirely different class of woman to the English ones. I mean they presuppose brains. English cookbooks always seem to be written for basement readers, only.

I am hoping to see Papa next week. I had intended to meet him and the sisters in Paris but now I find I shall have to go direct to London from here and see my dear faithful doctor. My heart has been playing up very badly. But no more of that. I hate writing about illness. The point is I shall see Papa & the girls in England. I so look forward to that. I am afraid Papa's visit has been flooded with rain. What a dreadful summer England has had! Its very unfortunate especially as he has not been well. I put him on to my doctor & I think he feels more comfortable, now. After London I go to Paris for the autumn & we hope to spend the winter at a little place called Arco on the Lagodi Garda. It sounds lovely – very sheltered – and famous for oranges and lemons. But plans are as usual, rather en l'air. Its no fun, my dear, to be chased over the globe. And what must it be like for poor Jack who longs for nothing so much as to settle, unpack, and bury his luggage under an oak tree for ever! He hates travelling and is a very unhappy traveller. He sheds his possessions like leaves, poor darling. But on we fare. I hope it will end one day.

I have spent the summer down here at work on a kind of short novel. Jack has been up the mountain side chez Elizabeth. I cannot breathe so high, I can only gasp. So they come down to me from time to time instead. He has been very happy with her, and I have loved it here. Sierre is such a fascinating small valley town, full of orchards & vineyards & funny little mountains that skip like young sheep. This hotel has a farm attached to it, too, and one can wander at will among the beasts and birds. I love farms – do you? Sometimes I wish Jack was a farmer & I was a farmers wife & wore a big apron & cut bread and butter for the children. There must be very solid joys in that.

By the way this has been a marvellous year for dahlias. Do they grow well in Canada? We have saffron yellow, big spiked red ones, white ones and a little round bright orange kind – most lovely. As for the antirrhynms they are superb. I think I ought to have called them snap-dragons though. I'm sure that spelling is wrong. And do you grow zinnias? I wish I could see your garden. Dear little Jeanne seems to be a very fierce, successful gardener. We all as a family seem to inherit the tastes of our First Parents.

Do you have much time for reading and what do you read, I wonder? I thought the Canadian novel, Marie Chapdelaine,[2] was very charming. But there are precious few new books one can like. One always falls back on the old ones. Ive just remembered I have two copies of a novel on Russian themes which might amuse you. I think it has great youthful charm. The writer has, in fact just left Oxford. I suppose you would scorn to read German. Goethe's conversations with Eckermann is a wonderful book – full of riches. Have Andrew and John a library? But I am asking you too many questions and its so tiresome to have to answer them in a letter.

This dreadful handwriting is because I'm lying down, and my hand is tired with typing. Can you make it out? I hope so. Ida would I am sure send her love if she were by. She is very excited at the prospect of England and buns again. I mean to really feast on my friends, or on all those who are within reach. Such joy after a long exile.

Well dearest sister, the dressing gong has boomed up and down the corridors. I must preparer descendre. Give my remembrances to Mack. My love to the little boys, and accept much for yourself.

From your own sister
K.

My *permanent* address is:
C/o The Nation & The Athenaeum
10 Adelphi Terrace
London W.C.2.

MS ATL.

---

[1] A childhood acquaintance in Wellington.
[2] Louis Heman, *Marie Chapdeleine* (1914), a French Canadian classic of harsh pioneering life.

To Elizabeth, Countess Russell, [c.10 August 1922]

[Hotel Chateau Belle Vue, Sierre]

Dearest Elizabeth

I want so much to give you a little present before I leave here...And I have been casting about and Ive nothing except this brand new little jac-quette which is the colour of zinnias and reminds me of them. Would you like it? May it hang behind your door or where such things hang in well regulated bedrooms.

Our little tour is my dream. I hope it won't always remain a dream.

And if I was frightfully dull at lunch the other day – don't judge me by that, dearest! Ive been out of company for so long that I feel beyond words...shy.

With my devoted love
Katherine.

MS BL. *De Charms*, 244.

To Dorothy Brett, [10 August 1922]

[Hotel Chateau Belle Vue, Sierre]

CAN YOU HAVE ME WEDNESDAY

Telegram Newberry.

To Dorothy Brett, [10 August 1922]

[Hotel Chateau Belle Vue, Sierre]

Dearest

I wired you today. This is just to say how glad I shall be if you can put me up on Wednesday. I have been horribly ill since you left; I must see Sorapure with as little delay as possible. Please don't tell anyone I am coming not even Koteliansky. And could you possibly, if you have the time, find out by any means an address for Ida? Any boarding house or hotel in Belsize Park?[1] Id be most fearfully grateful. Dont make preparations for me – will you? What would be *perfect* would be to feel you just let me in without giving me a moment's thought. You know what I mean? Everything will be nice, darling. Theres only one thing. If you can put me into a bedroom rather than the sitting-room...No, I take that back. Thats nonsense. If you knew how those orange flowery curtains are waving in my mind at this moment! Will you *really* be at your door on Wednesday? Or is it a fairy tale?

Ever your loving
Tig.

MS Newberry. *LKM* II. 237.

---

[1] Close to Brett's house in Hampstead. Ida would stay with a friend in Chiswick.

To Dorothy Brett, [11 August 1922]

[Hotel Chateau Belle Vue, Sierre]

My dear darling Lamb,

How did your telegram arrive so soon? ? ? ? Miss a turn. I sent mine at about 3 p.m. & yours was here at 7 p.m. This is a mystery. I can't arrive before Thursday afternoon. No sleeper (Pay 1d) before then. Your clouds like Feather Boas are perfeck! This (yours) is such a very nice letter that its a good thing we shall meet so soon. I feel inclined to come by the perambulator & have done with it. You are quite right about Richard. Its splendid to know you can do that for him. Keep him to his paying up regular. That is so right, too.

Why do things need so many nails. Why cant one use safety pins? They are so much quicker & they are so Madly Secure. Once you have clasped yourself to a safety pin human flesh & blood cant separate you. (Let us go & see Charlie Chaplin[1] when I come. Shall we? On the Fillums, of course, I mean). This place is flaming with Gladioli, too. As for the dahlias they are rampant everywhere. The pears which we had for lunch are iron pears, with little copper plums & a zinc greengage or two.

Ida, smelling the luggage from afar, is in her element. She is hung with tickets already and almost whistles & shunts when she brings me my tisane. I am moving already myself, the writing table is gliding by & I feel inclined to wave to people in the garden.

If my Papa rings you up on Wednesday will you please say I am coming Thursday?

Poor Ottoline. I feel almost like a cannibal, using this bag. I feel it was torn fresh from her side. God forbid you should make a pincushion of the pieces left over.

Elizabeth came yesterday with one of the Ladies Fair. I must say she had ravishing deep deep grey eyes. She seemed, too, divinely happy. She is happy. She has a perfect love, a man. They have loved each other for eight years & it is still as radiant, as exquisite as ever.[2] I must say it *is* nice to gaze at people who are in love. Murry has taken up golf. Ive always wondered when this would happen . . .

Thats all for now, little artist.

Thursday

Tig.

MS Newberry. *LKM* II. 235–6.

[1] Charlie Chaplin had long been a favourite of KM's. His most recent films were *The Kid* and *The Idle Class* (1921); *Nice and Friendly* and *Pay Day* were made in 1922.

[2] KM is perhaps deliberately clouding the facts for her cousin's sake. Soon after the war, Elizabeth had met the twenty-four-year-old Alexander Stuart Frere-Reeves, who was then at Cambridge after serving in Egypt, Gallipoli, and France. He became Elizabeth's lover, but her affair with a man thirty years her junior was nowhere as 'radiant' as the letter claims. KM did not much like 'Frere', nor did he care for her.

To Alfred Knopf, 11 August 1922

C/o The Nation & The Athenaeum | 10 Adelphi Terrace
London W.C.2

11
viii
1922

Dear Mr Knopf

I wonder if you would be good enough to send me a copy of the Garden Party. I should very much like to see it in its American Dress. It would be nice to know whether it has been successful at all. I have seen three or four reviews which were fairly favourable, & one from the New York World by a man who hated me so much that I felt quite friendly.[1]

With my kind regards to Mrs Knopf & yourself.

Yours v. sincerely
Katherine Mansfield

PC Texas.

¹ Some confusion here, as no review appeared in the *World* between publication in late May and the date of this letter.

To Richard Murry, 14 August 1922.

[Hotel Chateau Belle Vue, Sierre]
August 14th 1922

My dear Richard,

I did a thing today which it has been in my mind to do for a long time. I made a will, signed it & got it duly witnessed. In it, I left you my large pearl ring. My idea in leaving it to you was that you should give it – if you care to – to your woman whoever she may be. I hope you won't think this ghoulish. But Jack gave me the ring and I feel it would be nice to keep it in the family.

This doesn't mean, of course, that I am not as large as life and twice as natural. But just in case I was 'taken sudden' Id like you to know why the ring is yours.

With love, Richard dear

Yours ever
Katherine.

I shall be in London on Thursday staying with Brett. Will there be any chance of seeing you?

MS R. Murry. *LKM* II. 236.

To Harold Beauchamp, 15 August 1922

[Hotel Chateau Belle Vue]
Sierre | SWITZERLAND.
15 August 1922.

Dearest Father,

I shall not arrive in London before Thursday evening, as I cannot get a sleeper before then. It is like mid-Autumn here, cloudy and cold. I do hope you are having very different weather in England. A little real August heat would be very comforting.

I so look forward to hearing from you that my change of plans has not too greatly inconvenienced you.

With fondest love,
Kass

TC ATL.

IV
ENGLAND — LONDON
AUGUST–SEPTEMBER 1922

When KM arrived in London at the beginning of August, she told friends she would return to Paris in October, and complete her treatment with Manoukhin. There had even been earlier talk of then going to northern Italy, or perhaps Germany. While in London there was the immediate satisfaction of the pleasant room she took at Dorothey Brett's in Hampstead, the warm and healing meetings with her father who was visiting England, and the chance to see the small number of friends who mattered to her, especially Koteliansky, with whom she began work on new translations from Russian. Beyond these reunions, and only hinted at in her letters, was the move towards the momentous decision that would mean a further rift between herself and the bewildered Murry, and remain a puzzle to many who knew her. At Orage's prompting, she went to meet P. D. Ouspensky (1878–1947), a Russian writer and philosopher who brought together science and mysticism, and listened to his lecture on the teachings of his friend George Gurdjieff, who recently had established his Institute for the Harmonious Development of Man at Fontainebleau-Avon, a short distance from Paris. She met other friends of Orage's – some of them old acquaintances of her own – who shared his interest in what, for KM, offered the chance of a last ditch stand for simplicity and sincerity, and a haven from the kind of intellectual pessimism that, however much she loved Murry, she thought so defined him. Most of those who knew her believed she would complete her medical treatment when she returned to Paris, yet again with Ida Baker in attendance.

To Harold Beauchamp, [18 August 1922]

[Knightsbridge]
SEEN SORAPURE QUITE SATISFACTORY WRITING LOVE
MURRY.

Telegram TC ATL.

To Harold Beauchamp, 18 August 1922

6 Pond Street | Hampstead. N.W.3.

Friday.

My dearest Father,

Upon my arrival here yesterday, I was more than glad to receive your dear letter. Many, many thanks for it. I still feel guilty at having so disarranged your plans. My only consolation is that travelling on the Continent, at this moment, is very poor fun. Even when one has reserved seats on all the trains and so on the immense crowds intrude. First class carriages are full of third class passengers, and the boat absolutely swarmed with ladies and babies all in an advanced state of mal de mer!

However, travelling never tires me as it does most people. I even enjoy it, discomforts and all. And we arrived here to find all kinds of thoughtful preparations, down to the good old fashioned Bath Bun[1] with sugar on the top – an old favourite of mine. It made me feel I was anchored in England again.

I saw Doctor Sorapure this morning and went over the battlefield with him. As far as one could say from a first view, it was not at all unsatisfactory. He says my heart is not diseased in any way. He believes its condition is due to my left lung, and its tied up with the lung in some way for the present. It's all rather complicated. But the result of the interview was that there is nothing to be feared from its behaviour. I mean its tricks are more playful than fierce. And the more exercise I take in the way of walking and moving about the better. It may stretch it. Sounds rather rum, doesn't it. But the point is, darling, Jack and I can meet you any where in London, any time. This house is rather hard to find. Its a queer nice little place, but on the Bohemian side i.e. I would trust its teas only – not its lunches or dinners. I am not in the least an invalid in my appearance or my ways and require no special consideration. If the girls would put us up for a night, would you like to see us at Wood Hay – you see I propose this sans fasons as one of the family. But except for another appointment with Sorapure on Monday afternoon, I am free as yet. And free I shall endeavour to remain until I hear from you.

Sorapure thought I looked amazingly better, of course. Everybody does. One feels a great fraud to have a well built outside and such an annoying interior.

What appalling weather it has been for you, dearest. The country looked an absolute swamp from the train yesterday. And I had a fire in my bedroom last night. This is the famous August!

With fondest love, dearest Father. Its so delightful to feel you are so near and we are all to meet so soon.

> Ever your devoted child
> Kass.

TC ATL. *LKM* II. 237–8.

¹ A currant bun topped with icing or sugar, named after the city where it was first made.

To Harold Beauchamp, [19 August 1922]

[Mayfair]
SUGGEST STEWARTS LUNCH ONE O'CLOCK OR POND STREET TEA AT FIVE

LOVE.

> KASS.

Telegram TC ATL.

To William Gerhardi, [c.20 August 1922]

> 6 Pond Street | Hampstead N.W.

Dear Mr Gerhardi,

I am in London for a few weeks. Is there any chance of seeing you? I should so much like to meet the author of so successful a godchild. I hear golden opinions of 'Futility' from everyone.

Did you get my letter about Pinker? If you do not reply to this one I shall begin to believe I have offended you. I hope not.

> Yours very sincerely
> Katherine Mansfield.

The telephone number is Hampstead 2140.

MS ATL.

To Dorothy Brett, [c.20 August 1922]

> [6 Pond Street, Hampstead]

Wicked Little B.,

I observe you have been to Heals. Who has bought glasses? Who came in with a Huge Great Parcil?

But this is to say I found you had been a Faery in my room and made it all warm and put a book on the pillow. Thank you darling. I am in a fever to see your studio and to sit tight in my scribbling basket.

Love,
Tig.

MS Newberry.

To Richard Murry, [c.20 August 1922]

6 Pond Street | Hampstead

Dear Richard,

If you do come up from Brighton it will be my 'shout'. Then when you are richangreat you can take me *to* Brighton to pay back.

If it won't disturb your holiday too much it would be a very great pleasure to see you. Jack is here, too. We came over together.

Supposing we wait for you here on Friday. Then we can go off & have lunch together. But I think it would be more satisfactory to meet & have a smoke & talk here first. Its less disturbing than public grottos.

I have just seen Charlie in The Kid. How old fashioned that must sound to you – as though Id seen my first airyplane. He is a marvellous artist. Its a pity he is tied to the public, even the little he is. I mean its a pity he considers them at all.

Until we meet

Ever
Katherine.

If Friday doesn't suit you suggest a day that does & I'll keep it free.

MS R. Murry.

To Ottoline Morrell, [20 August 1922]

[6 Pond Street, Hampstead]

Dearest Ottoline,

Its too horrid. Lunch is impossible for me tomorrow. I have a farewell engagement with my Papa that I cant escape, or be free from in the early afternoon. If only Belsize Park were nearer Oxford Square I'd love to ask if I might see you here tomorrow morning for 11 o'clock tea. But these distances are so great! I am so very very sorry to miss you. More than I can say.

Ever
Katherine,

Postcard Texas.

To Violet Schiff, 21 August 1922

6 Pond Street | Hampstead N.W.3
21.VIII.1922

Dearest Violet,

I am so hoping I may see you and Sydney shortly. Do you return to town soon? I came over from Switzerland last week & have decided to stay here for the next 2 – 3 months to continue my course of treatment here instead of in Paris. (My doctor knows a London man who understands the Manoukhine treatment & will charge me only half what I paid before.) I am looking for a small furnished flat. How awfully nice it will be if there are real chances of real talks with you & dear Sydney this autumn! How are you both? My warm love to you!

Its strange to be here again. London is empty, cool, rather shadowy – extraordinarily unlike Paris. I feel sentimental about it. Only the people Ive seen so far seem fatigué fatigué beyond words! One feels that they have come to an agreement not to grow any more, to stay *just so* – all clipped and pruned and tight. As for taking risks, making mistakes, changing their opinions, being in the wrong, committing themselves, losing themselves, being *human beings* in fact – no, a thousand times! "Let us sit down and have a nice chat about minor eighteenth century poetry" – I never want to sit down & have that chat as long as I live.

But it doesn't matter. They can't alter the fact that Life is wonderful. Its wonderful enough to sit here writing to you, dear precious friends, & to lean back & think about you. The past lets nothing be. Even our meetings in Paris are changed almost beyond recognition. One sees them, linked together now, and one realises the immense importance of the *hero* of them (whom I never saw & never shall see.)[1]

But I could write to you for ever today. And instead Im going out to lunch with Massingham père. Could one possibly shake him up – lean across the table & say quietly ... what?

With much love to you both

Ever
Katherine.

MS BL. *LKM* II. 238–9.

[1] References to the concerns and method of Marcel Proust's *À la Recherché du Temps Perdu*, whose final volume, *Le Temps Retrouvé*, would be translated by Sydney Schiff, as Stephen Hudson, after the death in 1930 of C. K. Scott-Moncrieff, translator of the rest of the work.

To Harold Beauchamp, 22 August 1922

6 Pond Street | Hampstead N.W.3
22.VIII.1922

Dearest Father

Just a note to say how very very happy I was to see you yesterday and how much I enjoyed our lunch and talk! I only hope you *feel* as young as you look and that your bout of ill health is a thing of the past. The girls looked so well and charming, too. Wee Jeannie though looks almost too young to have a real live husband.[1] She ought to be married in a daisy chain with the Wedding Service read from a Seed Catalogue, as it used to be when we were children.

It is a sad pity that New Zealand is so far, dearest Papa. How nice if we could all foregather more often. By this same post I am sending you a copy of my book. With fondest love

Ever your devoted child
Kass.

MS ATL. *LKM* II. 239.

---

[1] KM's youngest sister Jeanne would marry later in the year.

To Sydney Waterlow,[1] 22 August 1922

6 Pond Street | Hampstead N.W.3
22.VIII.1922

My dear Sydney,

I understood you agreed to lunch with me tomorrow though how when or where I hadn't a notion. I don't think you would care about dining here – Brett is having one of her Thursdays, I gather. Supposing we meet then? Even if I don't come downstairs & sit among die Propheten perhaps you would come up & have a little chat.

Its awfully, strangely nice being in London again.

Yours ever
Katherine.

MS ATL.

---

[1] Sydney Waterlow (1878–1944), related to KM through his mother Charlotte Beauchamp, sister of Elizabeth Russell. Educated at Eton and Cambridge, he was later knighted for diplomatic services.

To Harold Beauchamp, 23 August 1922

6 Pond Street | Hampstead. N.W.3.

23 August 1922

Dearest Father,

Many, many thanks for the excellent photograph of yourself, which I received this afternoon. It could not be a better likeness, in my opinion, and I am so happy to have it. People talk so easily of a speaking likeness, but this really is one. I think it is by far the best photograph you have had taken. I shall try and "return the compliment" in a small way by having some taken at Swains[1] next week. They have asked me to sit to them more than once, but I have put it off so far. As you know from experience, dearest, I do not "take" like my Papa.

Jack is quite delighted with your portrait, too, and thinks it could not be better.

Please excuse a hasty note. I wanted to acknowledge so welcome a gift immediately.

With so much love,

Ever your devoted child

Kass

Will you please thank the girls for the lovely flowers. They are much appreciated. Such a lovely country box full of small surprises!

TC ATL.

---

[1] John Swain and Son, photo-engravers in The Strand.

To Elizabeth, Countess Russell, [23 August 1922]

6 Pond Street | Hampstead N.W.3

My dear Elizabeth

Its so strange to be writing to you from London! I feel half here, half in one of those green chairs in the Belle Vue garden, overlooking the valley. Yet events seem to have moved at lightning speed since I saw you and your lovely crocus, columbine, hyacinth, lilac hat – early Italian wild violet hat, too.

John's little grand tour died at Sierre while he was telling me the name of his hotel in Verona. "Why shouldn't I come to London with you? (Pause) Dash it all I will come. (Pause) Ill toss for it. Heads London tails Italy. (Pause) Its tails. That settles it. I go to London tomorrow." But his journey is only postponed. I have decided to stay here for the next three months. There is a man who understands the Manoukhin treatment and is willing to take me. So I shant have to go back to odious Paris and hotel dusters. I have 'taken' Brett's first floor; and John has arranged to live in a small flat next door.[1] Brett has swept away her other lodgers, who must regard me as the cuckoo in the sparrow's nest. But its fun to think of three months in London and oh, such a relief to be *private*, not to be a number. John's small flat is extremely romantic but so high that I shall never be able to go to tea. He will dine here in the evenings. It seems to me a much better arrangement than setting up house together.

We have seen my Papa. He will live for hundreds of years, growing redder and firmer and fatter for ever. As to his "fund of humorous stories" it doesn't bear thinking about. I felt I must creep under the table during lunch. I said to my sisters while we powdered our noses together "Dont you find his stories a little tiring". And they cried (they always say the same) "Oh but the old dear does so enjoy telling them and he really is most amusing!" The only reply was to cross oneself.

I saw Sydney last night who delivered a formal apology for the way he has spoken and written about John. But he regards me with a very mistrustful eye. He expects to find a pin in every crumb one offers; this is not very exhilarating. Bother these solemn, intellectual, superior old mind-probers. I wish I had warm hearted simple friends who had never heard of Einstein.

Much, much love, my dearest Cousin

Ever
Katherine.

MS BL. *De Charms*, 244.

[1] Murry was renting a room next door to Brett's from the artist, Boris Anrep.

To S. S. Koteliansky, [23 August 1922]

[6 Pond Street, Hampstead]

Dear Koteliansky

I have been sitting in the empty house, thinking, since you left, chiefly about Murry and Lawrence's review. I do not see that he was to blame. How could he, being himself, act otherwise? The first book he hated and said so. (The manner of saying it was wrong.) The second book he immensely admired and said so. He praised it because he thought it was a good powerful book. I dont see what personal motive or interest he could have had in such a change of front.[1] On the contrary. Surely he risked being called a turn coat...

You know I am deeply sorry for Murry; he is like a man under a curse. That is not melodrama. That is why I am determined to remain his friend and to make him free of his own will. Special cases need special methods. There is no general treatment for all.

But, dear precious friend, I must not speak against him to you. I feel we both know too much for that to be necessary. It is better to be silent about him. In these last months away from all his associates here I think he has got much more like he used to be. I can't help wishing, for the sake of the people you know in common, that you could just accept him – knowing him as you do.

Now that I am no longer in a false position with Murry, now that I am, in the true sense of the word 'free' I look at him differently.[2] His situation is very serious. But who am I to say anyone is beyond hope – to withdraw my hand if there is even the smallest chance of helping them.

Will you think this all very wrong – I wonder?

Yours ever
Katherine.

MS BL. Lea, 50; Dickinson, 97.

[1] Koteliansky must have spoken to KM about 'the change of front' between JMM's strong dislike of *The Lost Girl*, which he reviewed under 'The Decay of Mr D. H. Lawrence,' *Athenaeum* (17 Dec. 1920), and his enthusiasm for *Aaron's Rod*, *Nation and the Athenaeum* (12 Aug. 1922).

[2] This is the first direct admission of a serious rift between herself and Murry. Yet, as so often, fact may be touched up a little for the sake of her correspondent.

To Violet Schiff, 24 August 1922

6 Pond Street | Hampstead N.W.3
24.VIII.1922

Dearest Violet,

Many many thanks for your letter. Will you forgive me if I do not accept your invitation to come and stay with you and Sydney? The truth is I am such a bad visitor (as one is a bad sailor) that I have made it a rule nowadays never to stay with anyone unless it is absolutely necessary. I hope this does not sound too extravagant and ungracious. I could give you literally hundreds of reasons for it. I look forward immensely to seeing you both in town next month. Isn't the country rather chill? The country is so terribly airy.

Murry is staying at this address for a week or two. He then moves into a small flat next door for the autumn. I have 'taken' Brett's first floor for the next three months and hope to be settled soon. At present all is in the air, and I can't work or even think of work. It will be very nice to have my own possessions and to be out of hotels for a time, without being en ménage. I *haven't* the domestic virtues.

I see Elliots new magazine[1] is advertised to appear shortly. It looks very full of rich plums. I always speak so grudgingly of Elliot to you. Yet I think Prufrock by far and away the most interesting and the best modern poem.[2] It stays in ones memory as a work of art – so different in that to Ulysses. The further I am away from it the less I think of it. As to reading it again, or even opening that great tome – never! What I feel about Ulysses is that its appearance sometime was inevitable. Things have been heading that way for years. It ought to be regarded as a portentous warning. But there is little chance of that, I fear.

Are you well? I feel so much better these last few days. My doctor, who is an angel, seems to be curing my heart with dark brown sugar!

With much love to you both, dearest Violet

Ever yours
Katherine.

MS BL. *LKM* II. 239–40.

[1] T. S. Eliot's new journal, *Criterion*.
[2] 'The Love Song of J. Alfred Prufrock', in *Prufrock and Other Observations* (1917). Clive Bell, in *Old Friends* (1956, 122), records that KM read the poem aloud at Garsington in June 1917. She also wrote parodies of other poems in the same volume.

To Ottoline Morrell, 25 August 1922

6 Pond Street | Hampstead
25.VIII.1922

Dearest Ottoline,

I have been waiting to write to you until my plans were more settled. Everything has been so much in the air these last few weeks. But now that Im staying in London for three months I *do* so hope I shall be able to see you and really talk.

I haven't written lately for the very same reason – the old reason – that Ive only had external things to say – things that don't matter. All my other life has been spent in wondering why I felt as I did and whether my heart would go on or stop and why I couldn't get upstairs ... You know how horribly absorbing these thoughts are! People who don't realise them cannot imagine their power; they darken the sun. And though I 'keep it up' and 'pretend' to others I feel I cannot with you. I suppose the truth is I take advantage of the fact that you understand and will not imagine it is because I am indifferent that I don't write. Far far otherwise!

But since I have seen Sorapure I feel marvellously better – nearly well for the moment. I have gained pounds and pounds – too many pounds! And I do simply long to see you, dearest Ottoline. Shall you be in London at any time?

Its impossible to tell you how sorry I am that you have been ill again.

Forgive this illegible note to be put into Murry's pocket.

I will write a real letter this weekend.

With so much love

Yours ever
Katherine.

MS Stanford.

To William Gerhardi, 26 August 1922

6 Pond Street | Hampstead NW3

26.viii.1922

No, dear Mr Gerhardi,

I don't *always* feel I have offended you – I only felt it once when the pause was so long. But now its hard to write to you when I know you are laughing at my poor little 'y's and 'g's and 'd's. They feel so awkward; they refuse to skip any more. The little 'g' especially is shy, with his tail in his mouth like an embarrassed whiting.[1]

I am very very sorry you are ill. I hope you will soon be better. I shall send you a little packet of tea on Monday. Please have a special little pot made and drink it with un peu de citron – if you like citron. It tastes so good when one is in bed – this tea, I mean. It always makes me feel even a little bit drunk – well, perhaps drunk is not quite the word. But the idea, even, of *the short story* after a cup or two seems almost too good to be true, and I pledge it in a third cup as one pledges ones love – –

I have decided to stay in London for three months. Then I go to Italy to the Lago di Garda. Perhaps we shall meet before then. I have taken a minute flat at this address and by the end of next week I shall be working again. I have a book to finish and I *want* to write a play this autumn ... Its very nice to be in London again, rather like coming back to one's dear wife. But I wish the intelligentsia were not *quite* so solemn, quite so determined to sustain a serious conversation only. They make one feel like that poor foreigner arraigned before Mr Podsnap on the hearthrug in 'Our Mutual Friend'.[2] I shall never, while Life lasts, be able to take Life for granted in the superb way they do.

Are you able to work? I am glad Middleton Murry's short notice pleased you.[3] I hope the Evening News man has done you proud,[4] too. And someone wrote to me and wondered if you would come to lunch one Sunday. But who am I to say.

Your letter has not come back from Sierre yet. I am very much ashamed of my geography.[5]

With many good wishes

Yours ever
Katherine Mansfield.

MS ATL. *LKM* II. 240–1.

---

[1] Gerhardi had teased her on her handwriting.

[2] KM is conflating two incidents on the same occasion in Chapter XI of Charles Dickens's *Our Mutual Friend* (1864–5). A 'poor foreigner' is certainly confronted by Mr Podsnap, but it is another 'meek man' who is arraigned on the hearthrug shortly after.

[3] Murry's note in the *Nation and the Athenaeum*, see p. 234, n.5.

[4] Gerhardi was not to know that the longer favourable unsigned review of *Futility*, 'A Remarkable First Novel', *Evening News* (23 Aug. 1922), was also by JMM.

[5] That is, her wrongly addressing an earlier letter.

To Harold Beauchamp, [28 August 1922]

6 Pond Street | Hampstead N.W.3
Monday.

Dearest Father,

I cannot understand why you have not received my book. I gave it to Ida to post days ago. As far as I can make out, she seems to sit on the books and parcels I give her rather like old Amina (of Pelorus Sounds fame)[1] used to sit on the peaches to ripen 'em.

I meant to draw your attention, if I may, to one little sketch, "The Voyage", which I wrote with dear little Grandma Beauchamp in mind. It is not in any way a likeness of her, but there are, it seems to me, traces of a resemblance.

Here we are tasting a good old fashioned London fog: it's very nearly dark (11.30 a.m.) I am thankful to be in Hampstead and not down in London proper.

I wonder where little Jeanne will settle down finally? I suppose intensive bulb and mushroom growing or any *novel* form of farming of that kind, to be practised in England, would be too tame for her. I feel there is more money to be made out of new ideas on a small scale nowadays (especially when followed up by some one with little J's brains) than in large and more risky schemes. Poultry, according to Ida, is fascinating, especially if blended with the illusive runner duck. But I expect nothing smaller than a full-sized gee-gee will satisfy her. I am all for concentrating on brains rather than physique if brains are the strong point. But its no business of mine, as the little dear would no doubt tell me, gently.

Jack and I have a very busy week ahead, seeing people who are very kind but rather embarrassing. I'd rather not talk about what I have done until the achievement is of more reasonable size. It's like making conversation about a new-born baby, and "a very little one" at that.

What fun your motor jaunts must be *when* it doesn't rain. It is a splendid way of really getting to know the lay of the land.

Much love, darling Father,

Ever your devoted child,
Kass

TC ATL.

[1] A Maori 'character' KM remembers from her childhood holidays with her father's relatives at the top of the South Island.

To Anne Drey, 28 August 1922.

6 Pond Street | Hampstead N.W.3
28 VIII 1922

Anne darling,

I am going to ask you to put off our T Party until you return from Dieppe. All is too unsettled, too ugly here. By the time you are back I shall be in my own rooms with my own cups and saucers and able to receive David as he ought to be received – the lamb! If he came here on Wednesday my head would be knocked off at once and pricking with a needle would be too good for me. Its not a *bit* nice *or* private. But at the end of this week I am moving into my own rooms and Ill be settled soon after. I shall just simply love to see David and his Mummy then.

I can't tell you what a joy it was to see you yesterday, dear and très très belle amie. How I loved looking at you again! And hearing you. And seeing your home – everything. I so look forward to our meeting after this autumn. I do hope we may. Jack Murry sends his love. Hes just had a new suit made & is standing in front of me.

J.M.:	"Are the trousers full enough?
K.M.:	Quite full enough!
J.M.:	You're sure?
K.M.:	Certain!
J.M.:	They're not too full?
K.M.:	Not in the least!
J.M.:	You're sure?
K.M.:	Certain!"

I must run and get a Bible and swear on it. "Those trousers are PERFECT!!" Men are funny – aren't they? But very nice, too. All my love darling. I hope your holiday is a great success.

Ever your devouée.
Katherine

MS ATL. *LKM* II. 241.

To Ottoline Morrell, [28 August 1922]

6 Pond Street | Hampstead N.W.3.

Monday

Dearest Ottoline,

I would simply love to meet you at Taylor's[1] whenever you ask me to come. Or if you would rather I met you anywhere else – I shall be there. I can't walk yet – absurd as it sounds – only a few puffing paces – a most humiliating & pug-like performance. But once I get my legs back or rather once my heart is stronger I shall not be dependent on Taxis. I live in them since I have come to London. I have got Fat. Wyndham Lewis I hear is also fat, May Sinclair[2] has waxed enormous, Anne Rice can't be supported by her ankles alone. I try to comfort myself with many examples. But I don't really care – its awful how little one cares. Anything – rather than illness – rather than the Sofa, and that awful dependence on others!

I wish you were better. I feel a heartless wretch to run on so glibly... But never never shall I forget for an instant what it means.

I rather look forward to these three months in London, once I have got out of my boxes and into a real corner of my own. I dream of brand-new friends – not the dreadfully solemn 'intensive' ones – not the mind probers. But young ones who aren't ashamed to be interested. Dear little Gerhardi who wrote Futility is one – he *sounds* awfully nice. And theres another I met in Switzerland – so attractive! I don't think I care *very* much for the real intelligentsia, Ottoline dearest. And they seem to be so uneasy, so determined not to be caught out! Who wants to catch them?

I *wish* you would come to Italy for part of next winter. Do you know the Lago di Garda? They say it is so lovely. And the journey is nothing.

It will be such a real *joy* to see you again.

With love

Ever your affectionate
Katherine.

MS Newberry. *LKM* II. 243.

---

[1] Untraced.

[2] May Sinclair (1863–1946), feminist, philosopher, and prolific novelist. KM had twice reviewed her fiction in the *Athenaeum*, each time with strong reservations: *Mary Oliver: A Life* (20 June 1919), and *The Romantic* (22 Oct. 1920).

To Sydney Schiff, [28 August 1922]

6 Pond Street | Hampstead N.W.3

Monday

My dear Sydney,

Your letter made me feel angry with myself & very ungracious at having refused your so kind invitation. Please forgive me! I look forward more than I can say to seeing you and Violet in London. By the time you come I hope to be *settled* in my new rooms (they are at this address). I already dream of *no end* of a talk before my fire.

I shall never be able to say a word to the intelligentsia, Sydney. They are too lofty, too far removed. No, that is unfair. Its simply that they are not in the least interested. Nor do they appear to know what one is driving at when one groans at the present state of English writing. As I see it the whole stream of English literature is trickling out in little innumerable marsh trickles. There is no gathering together, no force, no impetus, absolutely no passion! Why this is I don't know. But one feels a deathly cautiousness in everyone – a determination not to be caught out. Who wants to catch them out or give them away? I can't for the life of me see the need of this acute suspicion and narrowness. Perhaps the only thing to do is to ignore it all and go on with one's own job. But I confess that seems to me a poor conclusion to come to. If I, as a member of the orchestra think I am playing right, try my utmost to play right, I don't want to go on in the teeth of so many others – not playing at all or playing as I believe falsely. It is a problem. Let us talk it all over.

About Lawrence. Yes, I agree there is much triviality, much that is neither here nor there. And a great waste of energy that ought to be well spent. But I did feel there was growth in Aaron's Rod – there was no desire to please or placate the public. I did feel that Lorenzo was profoundly moved. Because of this perhaps I forgive him too much his faults.

Its vile weather here – real fog. I am alone in the house – 10.30 p.m. Murry & Brett are both at parties. Footsteps pass and repass. That is a marvellous sound – and the low voices – talking on – dying away. It takes me back years, to the agony of *waiting* for one's love . . . I am lunching with Orage[1] on Wednesday. What happiness! Goodnight dear friend. I press your hand.

Katherine.

MS BL. *Selected*, 268–9.

[1] KM had known A. R. Orage (1873–1934) since he published her Bavarian stories in the *New Age* in 1910, and took her up as a protégée. After they fell out for several years when she joined forces with JMM and *Rhythm*, she again wrote for the paper in 1917. Meeting with Orage would now awaken her interest in ideas that led to Fontainebleau. He recalled his conversations with her in the last months of her life in 'Talks with Katherine Mansfield', *Century Magazine* (Nov. 1924).

To Harold Beauchamp, 29 August 1922

6 Pond Street | Hampstead, N.W.3.
29 August 1922

Dearest Father,

Very many thanks for your letter. It is dear of you to ask me to tea so soon after your arrival in London, but would any other afternoon next week suit you equally well? On Tuesday evening we have a long-standing engagement to dine with the Literary Editor of the Times.[1] Business and pleasure combined, don't you know. And just at present I don't feel up to afternoon and dinner engagements on the same day. Do not trouble to reply to this dearest. If one of the girls would 'phone me here on Tuesday, we might, if agreeable to you, fix up something then. I think I'll dine alone this time and keep our pow-wow "en famille". We shall be delighted to lunch with you at Bath's Hotel[2] on Thursday, September 4, at one o'clock. I have made a note of the date.

Another dull *March* morning. I heard from Elizabeth, who is basking in radiance from dawn to dark. But I have noticed people take rather a delight in gloating over the kind of weather one is *not* enjoying here! Its a pity we cannot all settle in Florida and found a little Sunshine Colony.

With very much love, in which Jack joins me,

Ever your devoted child,
Kass

TC ATL.

[1] Bruce Richmond (1871–1964), who edited the *Times Literary Supplement* from its foundation in 1902 until 1938.
[2] Bath Hotel, 35 The Strand.

To S. S. Koteliansky, [30 August 1922]

[6 Pond Street, Hampstead]

Koteliansky,

I am so unsettled this week that I would rather we did not meet until next week when I shall be able to ask you to my *new flat*. Will you come then? I will telephone you on Monday and ask you what day will suit you. But at the moment practical details like gas rings and teapots dot my path. I don't want to talk to you about them or to hear them knocking at the door when you are there. Added to this I am arranging a splendid scheme by which Murry shares a country house with a man called Locke Ellis,[1] who will live with him for ever and ever, I hope. This is a truly magnificent idea. I shall have to go there later on with Ida Baker to wind up the works and start the toy going. But then I do not think it will ever run down again.

It will be a relief when these rooms here are finished and we can meet. Will you come in the evenings then? It is the time I like best of all.

The other evening when Brett went to Acacia Road and I was in this house by myself I thought so much of you. It was very quiet here – still – and I had a fire. I felt it would have been so nice to talk or not to talk, then.

I press your hands.

Katherine.

MS BL. Dickinson, 98.

[1] Vivian Locke-Ellis, a minor poet whose restored seventeenth-century mansion at Selsfield, East Grinstead, KM and Murry had visited some years before. He now invited JMM to share his house. His first book of verse was published in India in 1903, soon after his leaving Cambridge. After his *Lyrical Poems* (1908), his next and final book was *Collected Lyrical Poems* (1946).

To Harold Beauchamp, 1 September 1922

6 Pond Street | Hampstead, N.W.3

1 September 1922.

Dearest Father,

I am so sorry to have made that foolish mistake about the date – writing 4 for 14. It was right in my mind and wrong on paper. I shall be delighted to take tea with you at Bath's Hotel next Monday afternoon at 4 o'clock, thank you, darling.

This afternoon Jack and I are going down to East Grinstead for the week-end to "see a man about a house". It sounds a very nice one and in the pink of condition. His idea is that we shall share it with him. But I will not enter into detail here. If anything comes of it, I shall be able to tell you on Monday.

How extremely unfortunate that poor Renshaw[1] should be afflicted so seriously with malaria! More especially that he should be in for a bad bout of attacks just now. It is a complaint I know very little about. I wonder if it responds to inoculation? I know Ida's father,[2] who specialised in these matters, used to say it was a thirteen years' infection but unless one became reinfected it disappeared. But there's no great consolation to be derived from that. I can imagine poor little Jeanne's distress.

Yes, isn't the weather past praying for. There has not been one out and out fine summer day since we came back.

With fondest love, Father dear,

Ever your devoted child,

Kass

TC ATL.

[1] Her sister Jeanne was engaged to Charles Renshaw, formerly a captain with the Persian Rifles.

[2] Ida Baker's father, Colonel Oswald Baker, had served as an army doctor in Burma. A morose and demanding man, he was the model for the father in 'The Daughters of the Late Colonel', as Ida herself and her sister May were for the two timid daughters.

To Ottoline Morrell, [3 September 1922]

6 Pond Street | Hampstead N.W.3

Sunday

Dearest Ottoline,

I simply haven't known what to answer for it has been as difficult for me to reach 11 Oxford Square as for you to come to horrid Hampstead. Apart from seeing Father last week, I *had* to rest. I've been deadly tired. Its a bore. I cannot walk more than a few yards yet and 'getting about' is a great difficulty. How fantastic is seems! The second time you asked me I had an appointment with my X ray man and it took *hours* of what they are pleased to call overhauling. I am to start the new series of this treatment this week.

Variations on an ancient theme. I seem to write to you of nothing else. And I feel you must think me perfectly horrid!

Yet the fact is I *long* to see you and if [you] can still bear the thought of me I will come any time you propose (except Tuesday afternoon). I ought to have answered your letter immediately! Why didn't I? I felt I COULD not refuse again.

Do let me come if you can! I hate to appear so odious. But my beastly half-health gets in the way of all I want most to do.

I wish I knew how you are. If we *did* meet I feel I should like to talk for ever.

Yours (in spite of my badness) ever devotedly.

Katherine.

MS Texas.

To J. M. Murry, [early September 1922]

[6 Pond Street, Hampstead]

Wages	1. 5. 0
Laundry	11. 3
Milk	6. 9
Grocer	1.12.11$\frac{1}{2}$
Mrs S.	2.16. 9
2 wks.Express	1. 5. 6$\frac{1}{2}$

(milk butter eggs for one week, chiefly eggs & butter for second week)

Bread	6. 5$\frac{1}{2}$
	£8. 8.10$\frac{1}{2}$

Dearest Bogey

These are the bills which I have paid for the last week. They seem to be prodigious. I have examined each and I can't find a single extravagance. I think living in England is a great deal dearer than one imagines. What your share is passes my comprehension. I feel inclined to leave it at any contribution however small will be gratefully received by your very obliged

Wig.

Of course we had Sullivan for 2 dinners and 2 breakfasts, Richard for 2 dinners and L.E. for one. Also your egg & milk special diet accounts for a trifle with the Express.

MS ATL.

To S. S. Koteliansky, [6 September 1922]

[6 Pond Street, Hampstead]

My dear Koteliansky

I could not ring you up. I was too tired. I had been out seeing the X ray specialist & having my lungs photographed and so on and so on ... Please forgive me.

Will you come here on Friday afternoon or evening – whichever suits you best? I have not been alone till now.. Workmen have been in the house, noises of hammering, ringing of bells and so on. But by Friday all will be over.

I *long* to see you.

Katherine.

MS BL. Dickinson, 98.

To Dorothy Brett, [c.9 September 1922]

[6 Pond Street, Hampstead]

Darling little B.

Here's your apricot cover. I have put an old ribbing in its place... It doesn't look bad.

Will you come to tea in my room tonight & have a long-and-cosy chat after? There seem to be masses of things to say – but I don't want to say them in a rush. And if you are safely pinned into a chair I shall know you are resting.

You are frightfully clever to have made those rooms. But you know that. You are also frightfully nice.

Minnie is very sad still & she won't let me have no marmalade things being as they are. She will do anything rather than go,[1] however. Well, it will all settle itself. I don't think its anything to worry about a pin. (Hullo: marmalade has just come.)

Ever & ever
Tig.

Its a lovely day!!

MS Newberry.

---

[1] The servant KM employed. A notebook has the entry for 9 Sept., 'Gave Minnie notice' (*KMN*, 327).

To Andrew Bell,[1] *11 September 1922*

6 Pond Street | Hampstead N.W.3
XI.IX.1922

Dear little Andrew

You are growing up so very fast that I had better be quick and call you little before it is too late. Many many thanks for your letter. I can hardly believe the tiny person I said goodbye to in London is able to write with such grownup handwriting.

Do you really think about me? That is awfully nice of you. I hope we would be friends if we lived near each other. You see I don't know a bit the kind of life a little Canadian boy leads or the things he learns at school – or out of school. I wonder if you know a lot about birds. Some of the nicest men I know are fearfully keen on birds and can tell you marvellous things about them. If you would like me to send you a book on birds send me a card to let me know and you shall have it. Or are you interested in plants – wild flowers, as well? I was staying at a house this weekend[2] where all the guests have made a habit of bringing roots and bulbs and cuttings from wherever they have been and planting them in the garden. So you come across a little Spanish flower, or a little rock plant from Cornwall, or a lovely little tuft of grasses from France, or a Swiss daisy. Don't you think its a good idea? The little boy who lives in the house is eight years old and he is a great naturalist. He has stocked a pond with fishes he has caught himself and knows all about them – carp, and dace and tench. I wonder if you have those kinds in Canada?

Aunt Chaddie and Aunt Jeanne are coming to tea with me this afternoon. I expect I shall hear all the news about the wedding then. If Aunt Jeanne goes to live in New Zealand I shall be living in Italy, I expect and Aunt Chaddie in England. You will have to make a tour when you are grownup and come and visit us all.

Does John ever write letters? Granpapa has told me about him, too. I am quite up to date in the news of what happened on his visit.

With much love to both my dear little nephews. I shall keep my first letter from you for a 'remembrance'.

Ever your affectionate
Aunt Katherine.

MS Bell.

[1] Andrew Bell (1912–77), her sister Vera's elder son.
[2] Vivian Lock-Ellis's home at Selsfield.

To J. M. Murry, [19 September 1922]

[6 Pond Street, Hampstead]

My dear Bogey,

There seems to me little doubt that the wave of mysticism prophesied by Dunning[1] is upon us. Don't read these words other than calmly! But after yesterday to read that little leader in the Times[2] this morning was quite a shock. We had a most interesting after-lunch talk at Beresford's.[3] Orage gave a short exposition of his ideas and we asked him questions and made objections. It seemed strange to be talking of these dark matters (with passionate interest) in a big sunny room with trees waving and London 1922 outside the windows. Ask Sullivan about it when you see him in the country. He liked Orage and he found a very great similarity between his ideas and Dunnings. In fact the more we talked the more apparent were the resemblances. This pleased me for I felt you would accept what Dunning believed and like that you and I would find ourselves interested equally in these things.

I came back & found Richard here. He had tea with me and we had a most *terrific* talk. Nice is not the word for your little brother. Richard does believe it is possible to 'imagine' an artist a much more complete being than he has been up till now – not that exactly. But more *conscious of his purpose.* But if I try to reproduce his youthful conversation I shall antagonise you. For I can't put in all the asides and all the implications. Sullivan came back for supper & he & I talked of all these ideas afterwards. It was, as he said, a "simply stunning evening". I do hope you see Sullivan for a longish time and that you see Dunning, too. Is this interference. Its hard not to interfere to the extent of wishing you found life as wonderful as it seems to me. Even the least idea – the fringe of the idea – of 'waking up' discovers a new world. And the mystery is that 'all' of us in our unlikeness and individual ways do seem to me to be moving towards the very same goal. Dear dear Bogey. I hope I don't sound like Mrs Jellaby.[4]

Give my dear love to Selsfield – to the stairs especially and the chimney room and oh, dear, the late light coming in at the small window by the fireplace – *all* the garden! I love Selsfield.

I had a card from Lawrence today – just the one word 'Ricordi'.[5] How like him. I was glad to get it though. Schiff continues his espistolary bombardment. I refuse to reply any more. He is a silly old man.[6]

Do you want anything sent? Anything bought? Command me. Ill command Ida. Its a warm still day with a huge spider looking in at my windypane. Spider weather.

Greet Locke-Ellis for me – Accept my love.

Yours
Wig.

MS ATL. *LJMM*, 662–3.

[1] JMM's friend Millar Dunning was deeply interested in Eastern religions and the practise of yoga. An undated notebook entry from 1920 suggests his influence even then on KM and JMM. 'After the talk with Dunning there *is* a change.... I believe that D. has the secret of my recovery and of J's awakening' (*KMN* II. 194).
[2] Under 'De Minimis' in *The Times* (19 Sept. 1922), a short essay moved from why tropical diseases make life difficult for Europeans, to the fact that for modern mankind 'the solid world of matter disintegrates before his astonished eyes' into the bewildering findings of modern science. Our own lives reflect an 'endless series of minute but intense acts'. KM seemingly took this to reinforce her growing conviction that life was to be radically reassessed in a fresh response to experience.
[3] J. D. Beresford (1873–1947), science-fiction writer, novelist, dramatist and journalist. Their shared interest in Gurdjieff was presumably enough to allow congenial meetings after KM's scathing dismissal of his novel *An Imperfect Mother*, *Athenaeum* (9 Apr. 1920), for its 'essential emptiness'.
[4] In Charles Dickens's *Bleak House* (1852–3), the philanthropic Mrs Jellaby loses sight of reality to the extent of starving her own children as she tirelessly works for the African missions.
[5] En route from Sydney to San Francisco, Lawrence on 15 Aug. called in for one day at Wellington, where he posted a card to KM.
[6] The disagreeable lunch with Wyndham Lewis and the Schiffs (see next letter) effectively finished KM's warm feeling for her old friends.

To Violet Schiff, [19 September 1922]

6 Pond Street | Hampstead N.W.3
Tuesday

Dearest Violet,

I am so sorry my letter distressed you.[1] But what was 'your doing', my dear? There is nothing to undo as far as I am concerned. I felt Sydney would have been – much more than bored. I wanted to spare him. And I felt, too, reluctant to speak of important things just now...that Id nothing 'useful' to say. Don't you think one has these moments in life?

'No', you are saying 'this won't do, Katherine. Why, if all this is true, didn't you on Sunday...' But the fact is I did not realise until Sunday – until after Sunday my need for reflection.

Dont, if you can help it, think me *too* horrid. Indeed I am with all my heart

Devotedly yours
Katherine.

MS BL.

¹ The letter, which has not survived, was sent on Sunday evening, 17 Sept., after a lunch with the Schiffs that KM described as '*Odious*', *KMN* II. 328. Another guest was Wyndham Lewis, who as the Schiffs well knew deeply disliked KM and resented her current success. Alpers speculates that she spoke unguardedly of her growing interest in Gurdjieff, and Lewis attacked her for her credulity. Whatever the facts, JMM wrote to Violet Schiff as late as 21 Dec. 1948, saying 'He positively outraged her, and she felt that Sydney and you did not protect her, as she thought you should have done.' When Violet received the letter KM wrote her after the lunch, she sent it on to Lewis who replied, 'I don't see how … you could have foreseen this rather comic dénouement of my meeting with the famous New Zealand Mag-story writer, in the grip of the Levantine shark' (see Alpers 1980, 371–2).

To Sylvia Lynd,¹ [19 September 1922]

6 Pond Street | Hampstead N.W.3

Tuesday

My dear Sylvia,

Its the most miserable news to know you are in bed again and that again such bad sorrowful things have been happening to you … What can one say. I had so hoped and believed that your lean years were over. May they be over now!

Id love to come and see you. But stairs are unclimbable by me. I am better but I can't walk more than a few yards. I can walk about a house and give a very good imitation of a perfectly well and strong person in a restaurant or from the door across the pavement to the taxi. But thats all. My heart still wont recover. I think I shall be in England 2–3 months, as there is a man here who can give me the X ray treatment Ive been having in Paris. After that I shall go to Italy. But all is vague. Im seeing the specialist today. I may have to go back to Paris almost immediately. What it is to be in doctors hands!

If I stay I do hope we shall be able to meet later on perhaps. Let us arrange some easy place for both of us then. It would be most awfully nice to have a talk. Im living in two crooked little rooms here in a little crooked house. Its a relief to be away from hotels after five months in Paris in a hotel bedroom overlooking a brick wall. John is going to live for a time in Sussex with Locke-Ellis (do you know him?) at a place called Selsfield – a very lovely house on a hill top. Shall you be going back to Steyning in October?

Ill never be able to knock any spots off this city, my dear. It frightens me. When Im with people I feel rather like an unfortunate without a racquet standing on the tennis court while a smashing game is being played by the other three. Its a rather awful and rather silly feeling.

Don't forget how much Id love to see you! Or how sorry I am for everything.

Lovingly yours.
Katherine M.

Postcard ATL. *LKM* II. 244.

¹ Sylvia Lynd (1888–1952), a popular novelist and story writer whom KM came to know when she submitted poems to the *Athenaeum*. Her husband was the literary journalist Robert Lynd.

To J. M. Murry, [23 September 1922]

[6 Pond Street, Hampstead]
Saturday

Dearest Bogey

Im so glad to hear from you. Our goodbye reminded *me* of the goodbye of a brother and sister who weren't each others favourites . . . But it didn't matter, a little bit.

L.M. has been to Popes.[1] Ill tell her about Turner's Hill in case she cares to telephone.

I don't think I can come to S. until my treatment here is over. I regret, very much, missing autumn that I love so. But at the same time I am happy in London just now. Not because of people but because of 'ideas'. At last I begin to understand the meaning of 'Seek and ye shall find'.[2] It sounds simple enough, but one seems to do anything *but* seek . . . However, that sounds a little too airnest for a letter.

Darling, Im too shy to write proposing myself to Will Rothenstein. If you care to send him a card saying I am agreeable I'd be pleased to be in a book.[3] But wouldn't that be the best way to do it? Richard came yesterday and did a drawing. It was extremely well done. He's been to the Aeolian Hall and chosen rolls for the pianola.[4] So this little house sighs like a shell with Beethoven.

Ah, Bogey, I had such a sad letter today from Roma Webster. Goodbye Arco. She is afraid there will be no Arco for her. And goodbye Paris and the Manoukhin treatment. It cannot be for her. "Every day I am getting worse". Brave noble little soul shining behind those dark lighted eyes! She has wanted so much, she has had so little! She wants so terribly just to be allowed to warm herself, to have a place at the fire. But she's not allowed. She's shut out. She must drive on into the dark. Why? Why cant I go to Rome? I should like to start for Rome today just to kiss her hands and lay my head on her pillow.

It is so terrible to be alone. Outside my window there are leaves falling. Here, in two days, it is autumn. Not late autumn but bright gold everywhere. Are the sunflowers out at the bottom of the vegetable garden? There are quantities of small Japanese sunflowers, too, aren't there? Its a mystery, Bogey, why the earth is so lovely.

God bless you

Wig.

Later. Richard has just been in again to finish his drawing. Then we went downstairs and he played. But what am I telling you? Nothing! Yet much much happened. Don't you think its queer how we have to talk 'little language',[5] to make one word clothe, feed, and start in life one small thought.

MS ATL. *LKM* II. 244–5.

The Hammersmith firm of furniture and luggage removers.
Matthew 7:7–8.
The painter William Rothenstein (1872–1945) was a war artist and head of the War Propaganda Bureau, before becoming principal of the Royal College of Art in 1920. His recent pencil portrait of JMM would appear the next year in *Contemporary Portraits*, but the suggestion that KM make herself available for the same collection came to nothing.
The Aeolian Hall in New Bond Street, which as well as its concert hall contained a musical library and shop.
The phrase used by Jonathan Swift (1667–1745) of the baby-talk in his correspondence with Esther Johnson, as in 'Why, madam, I can tell you he has been dead this fortnight. Faith, I could hardly forbear our little language about a nasty dead chancellor' (25 Nov. 1710), *Journal to Stella*, ed. J. K. Moorhead (1924, 61).

To J. M. Murry, [26 September 1922]

[6 Pond Street, Hampstead]
Tuesday

Dearest Bogey

I am still so sorry about your neck.[1] Is it better. I told Sorapure this morning who said no tonic will do you as much good as a régime of *milk* & *oranges*. Not alone. Not together. But in this order.

Every morning drink a large glass of milk & $\frac{1}{2}$ an hour after eat an orange. Every afternoon – do the same. The lime salts are what you need, & they are helped to disperse by the citric acid. $\frac{1}{2}$ an hour after you have drunk that milk, it reposes, a solid curd, in your stomach. Along comes the orange juice & a most important meeting with very valuable consequences takes place...Will you do this? Its about 200 per cent stronger than Sanatogen.[2]

The weather is absolutely grey here, every day not a spot of blue sky. In fact the sky is like a big enamel pail. People don't seem to mind, though. I don't think they even notice.

Did I tell you Im having my first treatment tomorrow? I hope I shall get off with 8.

Ask for anything you want done, or sent. And tell me about your health, won't you? Did you see the perfectly lovely sketch of Johnnie Keats in Sundays Observer?[3]

Ever, darling
Wig.

MS ATL. *LJMM*, 660.

[1] JMM was suffering from boils. [2] Proprietary name for a tonic wine.
[3] Under 'A New Portrait of Keats', the *Observer* (24 Sept. 1922), reproduced the pencil sketch of John Keats made by his friend Charles Armitage Brown in 1820.

To J. M. Murry, [27 September 1922]

[6 Pond Street, Hampstead]

Dearest Bogey

I have changed my plans and am going to Paris on Monday for the treatment – i.e. for 8–10 weeks. I am not a little bit satisfied with the purely experimental manner of it here, and as I realise more than ever these last foggy days how dreadful it would be to go back or not to go forward I would endure any hotel – any Paris surroundings for the sake of Manoukhin himself. I'm sure you'll understand. You see Webster is simply a radiologist.[1] He doesn't examine one, or weigh one or watch the case as they did at the clinic. Everything was different. It's quite natural – he knows nothing. He is experimenting. And I don't feel I'm in the mood for experiments.

If I leave on Monday I'll get another treatment next Wednesday at 3 Rue Lyautey.[2]

I shall leave my rooms here just as they are. If Brett cares to let them furnished she may. I shall be only too pleased. But no harm will come to them. And in the spring when I am at Selsfield it will be nice to have them. (That's not sincere. Ugh! How I hate London and all its bricks! Perhaps I shan't then, though.) But there it is. It couldn't be helped. I suppose I was too quick. At any rate no harm has been done yet. I shall have to count on making money in Paris. I have over £80 in the bank. Money does not worry me. I'll go to the Victoria Palace for the first week or so and Ida has a famous list of hotels. She will find another and a better one I hope, then – somewhere more *cosy*. It's a little pity you can't take these rooms and let your flat. They are so fearfully nice & self-contained, with hot baths, attendance, food, telephone, and so on. Brett is a very good creature, too. This won't alter anything, will it? It only means that instead of being in London I shall be in Paris. I really have a very great belief in Manoukhin. So have you, I know. Do you care to come up for Sunday night, say? There is no need to. Phone me if you don't, dear Bogey and write me anything you would like done before I go. I'm seeing Orage Saturday or Sunday evening but otherwise I am free. I don't expect you to come, and don't even recommend the suggestion. It's so unsettling just as you are I hope beginning to settle down. I think Id better say – its fairer – that I am engaged on Saturday from 8 to 10.30 and on Sunday from 8 to 10.30 – even though the engagement is only provisional. All the rest of the time I am free.

Ever
Wig.

MS ATL. *LJMM*, 663–4.

---

[1] Dr Douglas Webster.
[2] KM already had in mind that she would go the Gurdjieff Institute, and used the excuse of resuming her treatment with Manoukhin to get back to Paris.

To Harold Beauchamp, 27 September 1922

6 Pond Street | Hampstead, N.W.3

27 September 1922

My dearest Father,

Yesterday, with a box of late flowers from Wood Hay, came a letter from you written to the girls, and posted, I think, at Marseilles. I was so very interested to hear of your news, and, oh, how I envied you the sun and fine warm weather as I looked out of my window at the cold, murky regular wintry day! Once I get through with this treatment, I shall certainly fold my tent like that famous Arab.[1] England has so many charms – friends, for instance, and the real charm of being in a country where one's own tongue is spoken. But the climate spoils everything. It is a perfectly infernal climate. I have such a cold that at this moment I feel more strongly than ever on the subject. But, literally, since you left we have had in London *one* fairly fine day with a piece of blue in the sky. I shall be glad when little Wilfred is settled in the sunshine of Otaki[2] or thereabouts. I am sure she is not suited to the raging elements.

Chad's letter, which accompanied yours sounded very cheerful and busy. Fancy a dance at the Trinders![3] Quite an occasion.

I wondered whether Captain A., Charles' friend, had an eye on Chad. That's the worst of matchmaking. Once it is started one sees an interesting meaning in every simple statement. But I so much dislike people who do that, that I shall curb my imagination.

Dearest, what very bad luck that your indigestion should have returned. Also that your hand should be giving you gyp. I hope you give that hand and finger sun treatment on the way out – keep it exposed to the sun. I am sure there is nothing more powerful. Perhaps, I do sincerely hope, your indigestion will disappear as you are more rested.

Poor Jack's neck is giving him a very bad time. The boil developed into a carbuncle, and now another has declared itself at the very back of the neck. Sorapure seems to think he is in for a series. In the meantime, Jack, with his neck swathed in a large silk handkerchief, looks like a depressed burglar. They are very painful things, though.

Last Sunday Charlotte [Chaddie Waterlow] came to tea with me. She looked so like Granny,[4] white kid gloves, faint violet perfume and all. She is going on to Switzerland to "fetch Elizabeth home" in a week or so. Those two are most devoted sisters. Charlotte, in fact, is quite fierce in her loyalty. I cannot quite imagine what Charlotte does with her life. She sees very little of her family. She seems to have no interests, if one excepts an exquisite small house. And just as Granny clung to Bertha, so she clings to her maid, Mary. But her life has been rather a broken one, I fancy.

I see that Hutchinson has sold 140,000 copies of "This Freedom". Very comfortable for him. I read it out of curiosity. But it seemed to me no end of a wallow.

If the Mother's knee is absolutely essential, how did it happen that Anne, who was brought up on it, came to grief and committed suicide? No one could have had a more unlimited range of it than she had. Indeed, she was pure knee according to the book. What a bother! Also, I go so tired of that perfect man saying "Mice and Mumps" that I had no sympathy left for him. Its easy to understand his popularity, though.[5] I shouldn't mind a little of it if I could get it by honourable means!

I am racing on with my next book, which I have promised the publishers to deliver at the end of October. I think I shall call it "The Dove's Nest". I'm rather tempted to call it "The New Baby". That seems to be a selling title. But perhaps it is not quite serious enough.

Well, darling, I must go off to Cavendish Square to have a dose of X rays. The man here seems to know his job, but he had not the Paris specialists' experience. I wish I could have gone through with the original inventor. Even now, if things do not go well, I am tempted to borrow £100 and go off to Paris with Ida. It seems so like spoiling the ship for a $\frac{1}{2}$d of tar (a rather expensive $\frac{1}{2}$d though).

I have sent my little baby book[6] back to Princess Louise[7] this week. I believe the books are bound exquisitely in leather with gilt edges. I should like to see it complete.

Dearest, I do look forward to hearing from you. You will send me a copy of the newspaper with your interview in it? I shall be deeply interested. It was "simply lovely" to see you again. I really do mean to try and come to New Zealand in the near future. The trip would be such pleasure, and how I should like to walk into the office and ask for Mr. Beauchamp!

With much, very much love, darling Father,

Ever your devoted child,

Kass

TC ATL.

[1]   And the night shall be filled with music,
        And the cares, that infest the day,
      Shall fold their tents, like the Arabs,
          And as silently steal away. (Henry Wadsworth Longfellow, 'The Day is Done', 1844.)

[2]   Wilfred, a family nickname for Jeanne. Otaki was a small settlement on the western coast north of Wellington.
[3]   KM's maternal aunt Belle – the aunt Beryl of her stories – had married Harry Trinder, a wealthy English stockbroker.
[4]   Harold's mother, Mary Beauchamp, died in 1917. There is an affectionate portrait of her in KM's story 'The Voyage'.
[5]   *This Freedom*, by A. S. M. Hutchinson, regarded as an attack on feminism, was an immediate and popular success when published in 1922.

⁶ A number of miniature handwritten books by celebrated contemporary writers were commissioned by the architect Sir Edward Lutyens for the library of the exquisitely elaborate dolls' house – a replica of rooms in Windsor Castle on a scale of 1 to 12 – he constructed for Queen Mary. KM's contribution is not listed in the current holdings of the library.
⁷ Princess Louise, Duchess of Argyll (1845–1939), daughter of Queen Victoria.

To Sylvia Lynd, 29 September 1922

6 Pond Street | Hampstead N.W.3
29.IX.1922

My dear Sylvia Lynd,

How glad I should have been to have seen you next week. But I am being swep' away again to Paris next Monday, to go on with my X ray treatment. Why do I always have to write to you about complaints! It is a horrid fate. But there it is. The bad weather here these last few days (its fine, of course, since I bought my ticket) has brought my cough back again, stronger than ever for its small holiday. And my Paris doctor threatens me with a complete return to the sofa if I don't go through with his course. I thought I could manage to have the same thing done here. But it's not the same, and its frightening to play with these blue rays.

So there are my steamer trunk and hatbox on the carpet, eyeing each other, walking round each other, ready to begin the fight all over again. And I shant see you or talk to you or give you tea or hear about anything. Im so very very sorry!

Are you really better? Its good news to know you are able to come as far as Hampstead. I have been staying in a tiny little house here, behind a fan of trees, with one of those green convolvulus London Gardens behind it. Its been beyond words a rest to be in a *private* house again with a private staircase and no restaurant, nobody in buttons, no strange foreign gentleman staring at your letters in the letter rack. Oh, how I hate Hotels! They are like permanent railway stations without trains.

There's the dinnerbell. I must go down into the hold and eat. I have [been] doing the house keeping here. It was very home like to hear the sole domestic say "I know a Party, m'm, as is a nice 'and with mouse oles. Having them in the kitchen something dreadful!" So unlike pert Susanne and jolie Yvonne.¹

Fare well. We *shall* meet some day? I shall go on looking forward. Keep well dear Sylvia Lynd. Even if you dont write to me for another year I am

Yours ever with love
Katherine.

PC ATL. *LKM* II. 245–6.

¹ Typical names for French servants.

To Harold Beauchamp, 30 September 1922

6 Pond Street | Hampstead N.W.3.

30
ix
1922

Dearest Father,

Just a note to inform you that for the first time, I think, I have drawn my *next* months allowance in advance. I hope you will not mind. My reason was this. I went off to have my first treatment by the London man here and it was, to put it mildly, not *at all* satisfactory. It seemed to me all the appliances were different and the whole thing was of so experimental a nature that it made one feel very uneasy. Ever since I have not been well. Unpleasant internal symptoms manifested themselves at once. And the long and the short of it is that feeling rather "skeered" I have decided to return to Paris at once and to go through with it there, on the spot by the true original pa X rayer who did me so much good before. It seems such folly and more to spoil the ship for a ha'porth of tar, even though the ha'porth is an expensive one. So the faithful Ida and I shall go straight off on Monday, look for a cheaper hotel than last time and there I shall remain until I am pronounced cured and then I shall wing my way to the South while the winter lasts. What an upheaval! But you know the very unpleasant feeling it is to be experimented on, for that is what the London treatment came to. The radiologist was most kind and anxious to do his best but there it was – he didn't know the exact spot even, it seemed to me, and I'm sure he started wandering blue rays in my liver. A great bother!

My faithful Cane steamer trunk and hat box, good as ever after all these years are on the carpet again, eyeing each other, almost walking round each other, all ready for the fray.

But to return to my New Zealand bank moutons.[1] As my funds were rather low, darling, I sent a cheque and a note to Mr Mills asking him if he would oblige me with the money. He thereupon telephoned me from the Bank and said he would be delighted.

I must say I don't look forward to hotel life again. Mais que voulez-vous? Anything to get quite well again and to be an independent human being who doesn't need any special attention.

This is not a letter. I will write fully from Paris.

With fondest love, dearest Father,

Ever your devoted child
Kass

MS Cains.

---

[1] A play on the French expression 'Revenons à nos moutons', to return to the subject.

To Anne Drey, 30 September 1922

6 Pond Street | Hampstead NW3

30 IX 1922

Darling Anne,

Here are the books. So many thanks for them. I think some of the stories in A Hasty Bunch are quite extraordinarily good.[1] All of them have interested me immensely. There is something so fresh and unspoilt about the writer, even when he is a little bit self conscious – in the youthful way, you know. But he has got real original talent and I think he'll do awfully good work. He's much more interesting than these sham young super cultured creatures. I hope he gets on with his job. I feel Id like to help him if I could in some way. But I expect hed scorn that idea.

Do you know, cherie, Im off back to France on Monday. I want to go on with that treatment there rather than here and for many many reasons I – enfin – well, there is something in England that just pushes me off the nest. Its no good. I shall never 'settle' here. But Brett is keeping my two little rooms here for flying visits. Its nice to have them.

I am going to try your Hotel Jacob. I hope they will have rooms. Of course, ever since I took my ticket the sun has come out and theres a kind of blue tinge in the sky, quite a piece of it. But if I tore my ticket up it would be snowing at tea time.

I shall never forget my LUNCH with you. I wish I had been nicer to that precious child. Wish I wasn't frightened of nannies. He is a lovely radiant small being, Anne, and I can imagine faintly your pride and joy in him.

Please give my love to Drey. To you, dear darling woman, my warm love as ever. Its been a joy seeing you – May we meet again before too long.

I am ever your devouée

Katherine

MS ATL. *LKM* II. 246–7.

[1] Robert McAlmon, *A Hasty Bunch* (1922).

To S. S. Koteliansky, [? September 1922]

[6 Pond Street, Hampstead]

Dear Koteliansky,[1]

Where you query children may I suggest 'little ones', 'small people', 'youngsters' (not tender enough, I feel). 'Small people' is nicest. But does he say that?

I have received the 2nd part of The Possessed and your note.

(1) Leporine ideas – jumpy ideas is very good, I think. *Hare leaps.*
(2) Let us then, keep <omin.>[2]

Criticise my translation unsparingly as you would the work of a business enemy. Then I feel 'free'. I will get on with the plan of The Possessed this next week. For 'biliousness', Gravensky's complaint, I think 'summer sickness' is best.[3] There are some uncomfortable words and phrases, but one must give them. I see that.

Yours,
K.M.

(I was not fair to dear 'Dosty' – Your Collaborator.)

MS BL.

---

[1] There is a puzzle regarding this letter. KM is offering suggestions in the second paragraph for the originally suppressed chapter in Dostoevsky's *The Possessed* (1871). Yet this section of the novel was published as *Stavrogin's Confession and the Plan of the Life of a Great Sinner*, trans. S. S. Koteliansky and Virginia Woolf, by the Hogarth Press in 1922. Presumably Kot had in mind a new translation of the entire novel, as he did not think highly of Constance Garnett's version of *The Possessed* when it appeared in 1914. An eighty-one-page typescript of Koteliansky's, *The Creative History of 'The Devils' (The Possessed;* 1922), is held in Texas. Koteliansky acknowledged KM's help with this fragment; see Kirkpatrick, 85.

[2] Russian, 'Amen'.

[3] Summer sickness, or Gravensky's complaint, suffered by Stepan Trofimovich Verkhovensky, father of Peter Verkhovensky, the leader of the 'devils' who create havoc in the provincial town where the novel is set.

To S. S. Koteliansky, [? September 1922]

[6 Pond Street, Hampstead]

Dear Koteliansky

I enclose the first half of D's letters[1] which I have gone through three times. I think they are 'smooth'. It would be a good idea, wouldn't it, to get it published in England as well.

I will send the plan of The Possessed as soon as possible. It is hard. I have read it far more often than twice.

Business plans don't tire me at all. I read them with my business side. I, too, hope the book will be published soon. The letters really are awfully interesting.

Yours ever,
Katherine.

MS BL.

---

[1] See p. 292, n.1, for KM's collaboration with Koteliansky on translating Dostoevsky's letters.

V

FRANCE – PARIS AND FONTAINEBLEAU-AVON OCTOBER 1922–JANUARY 1923

Gurdjieff's 'teachings' were not what drew KM, so much as the kind of life his Institute allowed her to attempt. Ouspensky's lectures had appealed both to those who responded to intricate theoretical argument, laced with versions of Eastern mysticism, and those who more pragmatically sought some way out from the depression and shallowness that seemed the legacy of the First World War. What attracted her to Fontainebleu was the possibility of a place at last where she might experience physical harmony, attempt self-knowledge, share communal values, and achieve the balance, as Gurdjieff would say, of one's emotional, mental and physical 'centres'. The emphasis was on truthfulness to oneself and with others, and to fitting oneself to the natural world, to its enduring cycles and realities. It seemed a simple – even naïve – regimen to accept. It was tough and uncomfortable as well as richly fulfilling. There is no doubt, from these last letters, that it provided her with what sufficed.

To J. M. Murry, [3 October 1922]

Select Hotel | Place de la Sorbonne | Paris
Tuesday 11.30 a m

Dearest Bogey

After great grief and pain we have at last found a hotel. Ida has gone off for the bagage registré and Im in one of those gaps, looking before and after, in a room thats not ready with luggage half unpacked – you know? Its not bad, though – rather nice, in fact. My room is so pleasant after *all* the rooms I saw yesterday night! I even went back to the Victor-Pal and had a glimpse of the 'uncles' still there and the Mlle at the Bureau – toujours la meme camisole. Happily, it, too was full. It was a glorious soft brilliant night – very warm – only man was vile ... This hotel is the one I stayed at during the war.[1] My room is on the 6ieme rather small and low but very possible. Shabby, but it gets the sun. Outside the window there's the Sorbonne roofs with tall grave signors in marble peignoirs holding up a finger. Also a coy, rather silly looking eagle poised over a plaque called Géologie.

I think youd find a change in Paris even since we were here. The lower orders are much more disagreeable – downright horrid, in fact. One has to fight with them for everything, even the right of sitting in their taxis. There's a queer feeling that the war has come back. Even waiting in the Victoria Palace last night I noticed an immense advance in de-civilisation in the faces. I don't think its just fancy.

Yesterday at Calais reminded me so of our first voyage to France together.[2] It was so hot and the train didn't go. Outside the windows old women held up baskets of pears. The sun was positively fiery.

Oh, I meant to suggest to you to ask for Yeats Memoirs to review.[3] I think they are coming out this autumn. I believe you would find them very interesting. Hes not a 'sympathetic' person, as far as I know, but hes one of those men who reflect their time. Such men have a fascination for me. Haven't they for you?

I wish we lived nearer to each other. I should like to talk more to you. But there is time. When this jungle of circumstances is cleared a little we shall be freer to enjoy each other. It is not the moment, now. Tell me what you can about yourself. Not even you could wish for your happiness more than I do. Don't forget that dragons are only guardians of treasures and one fights them for what they keep – not for themselves.[4]

Goodbye darling Bogey. I hope to see Manoukhin tomorrow. I'll tell you what he says.

Ever yours lovingly
Wig.

MS ATL. *LJMM*, 664–5.

[1] KM and Ida were at the Select Hotel from 21 Mar.–11 Apr. 1918, while the city was under German bombardment, and they were not permitted to travel on to London.

[2] When they had gone to Paris together for Christmas 1912.

[3] Murry did not review W. B. Yeats's *The Trembling of the Veil* (1922).

[4] The reality of KM's mood, beyond the apparent candour of this letter, she confided that evening to her notebook:

'What feeling? Very little. . . . I have been a perfect torment to Ida who is pale with dark eyes. I suspect my reactions so much that I hardly dare say what I think of the room and so on. Do I know? Not really. Not more than she. I have thought of M. today. We are no longer together. Am I in the right way, though? No. Not yet. Only looking on – telling others. I am not in body and soul. I feel a bit of a sham . . . And so I am. One of the K.M. is so sorry. But of course she is. She has to die. *Don't* feed her' (*KMN* II. 328).

To Dorothy Brett, 3 October 1922

Select Hotel | Place de la Sorbonne | Paris.

3 X 1922

Dearest

I can see your eyes laughing at the name of my hotel. What a name! One can only breathe it. Never mind. If you knew how glad I am to be in it after our chase round Paris last night. But thats not the beginning of my letter. The beginning is you at the station and my not being able to talk to you from the carriage. I hate seeings off at stations. And the fact you'd had to run up & down all those fiendish stairs was in the back of my mind all the time . . . Did you go back and rest. How can I say take care of yourself & feel that you do it? . . . Id like to think of you curled up in the Colossus with a li'l black boy handing you paint brushes and cream. Oh – Brett! I have not really left your little house – Its there, just round the corner. And I feel your French blood[1] will whiff you to France at any moment. But first do your series of Portraits & Ill finish my book. Then we can take a small holiday.

You know how dear you are to me. I remember every single thing. And the Beethoven means the same to me, too.

We had a divine crossing. Very still silvery sea with gulls moving on the waves like the lights in a pearl. It was fiery hot in Calais – whoof! It was blazing. And there were old women with pears to sell wherever you looked or didn't look. Voici mes jolies poires! Yellowy green with leaves among them. Old hands holding up the satiny baskets. So beautiful. English ladies buying them and trying to eat them *through* their veils. So awful. The way to Paris was lovely too. All the country just brushed over with light gold – and white oxen ploughing and a man riding a horse into a big dark pond. Paris too, very warm and shadowy with wide spaces and lamps a kind of glow-worm red – not yellow at all. Then began the chase. It ended in a perfectly FEARFUL room that looked like the scene of a long line of murders. The water in the pipes sobbed and gurgled and sighed all night & in the morning it sounded as though people broke open the shutters with hatchets.

Then I remembered this hotel where I stayed during the bombardment. Still here. Still the same. I have a funny room on the 6th floor that looks over the roofs of the Sorbonne. Large grave gentlemen in marble bath gowns are dotted on the roof. Some hold up a finger; some are only wise. A coy rather silly looking eagle is just opposite perched on a plaque called Geologie. I like this view *fearfully*. Every hour a small rather subdued regretful little bell chimes. This is not at all a chic large hotel like the Victoria Palace. Its quiet. One goes out for food which is much the best arrangement. Its very cheap, too. Gone are my sumptuous days of suites and salles de bain. I always hated them & now I don't need them, thank God.

I rang up Manoukhin just now. He, Madame & the Secretary all talked on the phone at once. Russian, French and English. I felt I had known them all my life and the idea of meeting tomorrow is such a joy. What dear people! I shall not write to the Carpet[2] until tomorrow. I wish you could walk into my funny little room for tea. You will at Christmas, perhaps...

Make Mrs S. take care of you. Tell me how your household affairs go. See that she gives you good food, for she can cook really well if she is made to.

Its perfect weather, so far – still and warm. Everywhere there are grapes to sell, small purple ones and yellow ones, with apples as red as wine. I think for some reason Paris is nearer ones spiritual home than London. Why? But it feels nearer.

Goodbye dearest. I am thinking of you. Tell me all you can. It was happiness – really happiness when one looks back. We *did* have moments. We *shall* have more of them.

Ever your loving
Tig.

MS Newberry. *LKM* II. 247–8.

[1] Brett's mother was Sylvain Van de Weyer, the daughter of the Belgian minister to London; her paternal grandmother was from Alsace.
[2] A reference to Gurdjieff, famous for his collection of Eastern carpets.

To Richard Murry, 3 October 1922

Select Hotel | Place de la Sorbonne | Paris
3.X.1922

Darling Richard,

Goodbye for just now. I have come back to Paris to go on with that treatment. I found the London man knew nothing of it really, & it seemed very silly not to go on with it and get quite well. One additional reason, one more little tilt to the scales was the idea of you and me going to dances together. What fun we should have.

You know how I have loved seeing you and talking to you again. The fact is you get nicer and nicer and I don't think you will ever stop. It has been a very real pleasure, too, to see your work. I shall think of you often. I shant expect to be written to. But a card now and then... when you are in the mood.

How marvellous the first movement of the Hammerklavier is![1] I shall try and hear some music this autumn in Paris. And Ill try and see some pictures too.

Richard I am so sorry I haven't seen your Mother this time. You see, thinking I was going to be in London for so long I put it off until I was a little more able to get down to Wandsworth.[2] Will she understand and forgive me?

I hope all goes well with you, my dear no longer little brother. Even if dragons come along don't forget that ten to one (the best dragons at any rate) they are guardians of treasure.

Its summer still in Paris. Really hot. Everywhere there are grapes for sale – withered old women holding out big satiny baskets of little yellow and purple ones. Theres a man below making a very good song of the fact he wants to mend umbrellas.

Yours ever
Katherine.

MS R. Murry. *Adam* 370–5, 36.

¹ Beethoven's Piano Sonata no. 29, op. 106, 1818.
² Where Richard's parents lived in Coplestone Road.

To J. M. Murry, [4 October 1922]

[Select Hotel, Place de la Sorbonne]
Wednesday.

Dearest Bogey

I don t *feel* influenced by Youspensky or Dunning. I merely feel Ive heard ideas like my ideas but bigger ones, far more definite ones. And that there really is Hope – real Hope – not half-Hope...As for Tchekhov being damned – why should he be? Cant you rope Tchekhov in? I can. Hes much nearer to me than he used to be.

Its nice to hear of Richard sawing off his table legs and being moved by the greengrocer. Why is it greengrocers have such a passion for bedding people out?...In my high little room for 10 francs a day with flowers in a glass and a quilted sateen bedcover I don't feel far from Richard, either. Oh, its so awfully nice to have passed private suites and marble tops and private bathrooms by! Gone! Gone for ever. I found a little restaurant last night where one dines ever so sumptuous for 6–7 francs, and the grapes are tied with red satin bows, and someone gives the cat a stewed prune and someone else cries "le chat a mangé une compote de pruneaux!"

True, one is no longer *of* people. But was one ever. This, looking on, understanding what one can is better...

Ive just come from the clinic. Manoukhin is far and away nicer. Donats beard is cut in a very chic way. Poor Madame who opens the door has had a terrible grippe and still her fringe is not curled. She said she thought she was filait de mauvais coton. But Manoukhin is an old friend, you know. Language doesn't matter. One talks as Natasha in War & Peace says "just so" and its quite enough. He and Donat promise me complete and absolute health by Christmas. My heart is much better. Everything is better. The sparks, the dark room, the clock, the cigarettes, Donats halting step all were so familiar one didnt know how to greet them with enough love! Dear! What wonderful people there are in this world. There is no denying *that*, Bogey.

Is it really warm in England. Here one wears thin stockings again and my window is wide open day & night. Today is especially lovely – the air just moves on fanning wings – the sky is like a pigeon's breast.

Im sending you some copies of Manoukhins and Donats pamphlets.[1] Do you feel inclined to send them to – Sorapure, say, and Massingham or anyone you know. I told him you would do this for him.

Goodbye, dearest. I hope you see Elizabeth and shes nice (haunted by the word nice)

Wig.

I wish I could send you some of our brown bread. You know the kind. Its better than ever. I have a little food cupboard with 'snacks' in it. Youd like it. Green and black figs are a 1d a 100 or thereabout.

Hippius & Dmitri and the Bunins live in a HUGE chateau – all together. Dmitri rides out on a dragon while Hippius watches from a tower. She puts pins in Bunin's bread but he doesn't notice *yet*. Manoukhine has moved into a pension de famille. 'Il le faut.' He seems much happier. Donats mysterious daughter whizzed her père away dans un auto for the summer. I think they went *over* the Mediterranean, as well as by it.

MS ATL. *LKM* II. 249–50.

---

[1] Manoukhin published in 1922 a booklet *Le traitement de la tuberculose par la leucocytolyse consécutive a la l'rradiation de la rate*, referring the reader to Donat's 'conclusions flatteuses' in an article in the weekly journal *Le Progrès Médical*, 1 April 1922. There Donat claimed an extremely high success rate for the treatment, which even in desperate cases could bring about 'de veritables résurrections'.

To S. S. Koteliansky, [4 October 1922]

Select Hotel | Rue de la Sorbonne | Paris

My dear Koteliansky,

Has the weather changed in London too? Here it is simply beautiful – clear, warm, still, so warm one can sit at the open window late at night, smoking a *good* cigarette. It is late summer, not autumn at all.

I saw Manoukhine today. It was real happiness to meet even though we cant talk, hardly. It doesn't seem to matter. One talks as Natasha would say 'just so'. And thats enough. I don't think he has any more patients but he seems much happier. As I knew would happen Hippius came flying to him with my 'insulting' letter – showed it to everybody! Manoukhine sees her no more. She is living in an immense CHATEAU (can't you see Dmitri going for rides on a dragon?) And the Bunins share the ménage. Im sorry for that. Manoukhine knew all about the money from America. "Comme elle est mauvaise, très très mauvaise." I think he is a bit disappointed though, he has not heard from Mr Farbman. He wondered if later you and I would do some translation for him. I said for my part 'yes' & that I would write to you. It is not just yet. I hope we can help him. He is a most awfully nice man, in every way. It was like coming home to go back there. The same voices, the same dark room, the sparks, the table, Doctor Donats halting step, Doctor Manoukhine's cigarettes. Even the servant was an old friend. It was impossible to love everything too much.

Paris is better this time. I have a little room on the 6th floor overlooking the roofs of the Sorbonne. Stern marble gentlemen in marble peignoirs wander over the roofs and point a finger at one. There is also rather a silly, coy looking eagle. My room has sloping roofs like an attic. It is very simple and clean. One can work here. A little thoughtful, regretful sounding bell chimes from the Sorbonne tower – a highly romantic bell.

Do you like green and black figs, Koteliansky? Here they are so cheap, about 1d a thousand.

I shall send the MS on Friday – as much as I have done.[1] Now that I do not go over it with you first I feel the changes look very drastic in ink. But you will understand.

Its a queer thing that in spite of the fact that to judge by the faces de-civilisation is going on far more rapidly here than in England – in spite of that there is a 'feeling' in France which makes everything far more vivid. The English channel is such a big carving knife.

I press your hands

Katherine.

I had to pay 7 francs for my cigarettes & because I said it seemed a lot I was just not clapped into prison.

MS BL. Dickinson, 98–9.

---

[1] The Dostoevsky letters she was working on with Koteliansky.

To J. M. Murry, [6 October 1922]

[Select Hotel, Place de la Sorbonne]

Friday.

Dearest Bogey

How very strange about your soldier! I wish I had seen him. Petone! The Gear Co![1] And fancy you remembering about those rugs. The way you told me the story reminded me of Lawrence, somehow. It was quite different.

I saw the soldier so plainly, heard his voice, saw the deserted street on early closing day, saw his clothes, the sack, "old boy . . ." It was strangely complete.

By the way I wonder why things that happen in the rain seem always more wonderful. Do you feel that? There's such a freshness about them, something so unexpected and vivid. I could go on thinking of that for hours.

I heard from Jeanne this morning. She is marrying her young man on October 10th (before he sails) & wondered if you'd go to the wedding. Just in case you should have the faintest feeling I'd like you to go (you know these queer feelings) this is to say I havent.

Its the most lovely morning. There's just a light sailing breeze & the sun is really hot. Thinking of London is like thinking of living in a chimney. Are there really masses and masses of books? I do hope you don't forget to send me that Tchekhov. I look forward to it *very* much! Can one get hold of Tolstoi's diaries.[2] Is there a cheap English edition that is not too cut and trimmed? I wish you'd let me know.

I enclose a letter from Gerhardi. He is passing through rather an awkward age it seems, cutting his teeth, poor young man, to the accompaniment of many a coral rattle. But if he's any good he'll come through.

Im so glad your neck is better & that your lecture is finished. Have you ever been to Newcastle? Its on Tyne isn't it. Sounds so mysterious. I was wondering if next time you went to the Dunnings you took a bottle of barley sugar to those young heroes. I feel things like barley sugar are apt to be a little scarce in that household, & however wonderful your Da may be – to have a pull, take it out & look at it & put it back again – does mean something. I am sure Michael[3] especially would agree. Then youll be for ever after the barley sugar man – which is a nice name.

Your
Wig.

MS ATL. *LKM* II. 250.

[1] Harold Beauchamp had long been a director of the Gear Meat Company in Petone, a settlement a few miles north of Wellington, at the far end of the harbour.
[2] The three volume *The Diaries of Leo Tolstoy*, trans. C. J. Hogarth and A. Sirnia, 1917.
[3] One of Dunning's sons.

To J. M. Murry, 8 October 1922

Select Hotel | Place de la Sorbonne | Paris
8.X.1922

My darling Boge,

Do not bother to write to me when you are not in the mood. I quite understand and don't expect too many letters.

Yes this is where I stayed pendant la guerre. Its the quietest hotel
I ever was in. I don't think tourists come at all. There are funny rules
about not doing ones washing or fetching in ones cuisine from dehors
which suggests a not rich an' grand clientèle. What is nice too is one can
get a tray in the evening if one doesn't want to go out. Fearfully good what
I imagine is provincial cooking – all in big bowls, piping hot, brought
up by the garçon who is a v. nice fellow in a red veskit & white apron &
a little grey cloth *cap* (!) I think some English traveller left it in a cupboard
about 1879. The salt & pepper stand, by the way is a little glass motorcar.
Salt is driver & Pepper esquire is master in the back seat – the dark fiery one
of the two, so different to plain old Salt . . . What a good fellow he is,
though!

Yesterday the wind was nor'north by north by east by due east by due
east north east. If you know a colder one it was there, too. I had to thaw a
1 franc piece to get the change out of it. (That is a joke for your Sunday
paper only!)

Of course I should like to read your lecture.[1] I ve just read you on
Bozzy.[2] You awe me very much by your familiarity with simply all those
people. Youve always such a vast choice of sticks in the hallstand for when
you want to go walking, and even a vaster choice of umberellas – while I go
all unprotected & exposed with only a fearful sense of the heavens low-
ering.

Lawrence has reached Mexico and feels ever so lively.[3] Father has
reached Port Said. He quoted a whole poem by Enid Bagnold to say so.
"I am a sailor sailing in summer seas".[4] All the same a marvellous wash of
blue crept up the page as I read his letter, which had nothing to do with E.B.

By the way do you read letters at Selsfield? Do you ever read letters? You
never do. You only skate over them. 'Heres a letter', and down you sit, clap
on your skates, do a dreamy kind of twirl over the pages and thats all. Or is
that libelling you?

Mercy! Theres a most beautiful magpie on *my* roof. Are magpies still
wild? Ah me, how little one knows.

I must go out to lunch. Goodbye my darling Bogey. I hope to send you
some MSS to type this next week. Give my love to L.E. Tell him of this
hotel in case he comes to Paris. I think he'd like it. My room is on the
6ieme. Didn't I tell you? I feel *sure* I did.

I know that Water Music.[5] It is lovely – so very watery – reminds me too
in bits of Spencer's Swans.[6]

Ever
Wig.

MS ATL. *LKM* II. 251.

---

[1] 'On the Nature of Poetry', a lecture published in the *TLS* (12 Oct. 1922).

² 'Was Boswell a Fool?', a review of *Young Boswell*, by Chauncey Brewster Tinker, *Nation and the Athenaeum* (7 Oct. 1922).
  ³ KM would have heard from Koteliansky that Lawrence arrived in Taos, New Mexico, on 11 Sept.
  ⁴ 'I was a sailor sailing on sweet seas,' the opening line of 'The Sailing Ships' by Enid Bagnold, *The Sailing Ships* (1918).
  ⁵ George Frederick Handel's 'Water Music Suite' (1717).
  ⁶ See Edmund Spenser, 'Prothalamion' (1596, ll. 37–64).

To Dorothy Brett, [9 October 1922]

Select Hotel | [Place de la Sorbonne]

Dearest

I wish you would see what it is that gives you headaches. An aspirin bottle is not any real good. Why don't you go to Sorapure? It makes such a terrible difference to feel well if you have to fight a winter climate. I am sure Sorapure could help me [you]. Perhaps the reason is however, you have been 'listening' so much more lately & its been a new strain to get used to. That may be an explanation. I hope Mrs S. carries up your meals when you don't feel like going *down*. Don't forget beaten eggs in milk if you don't want solids.

I am so glad you are going to start on Milne¹ immediately. I feel you will have a whole gallery of *les jeunes* ready by the Spring for a Show of Portraits. Its yourself you ought to paint in a turban; a creamy pinky silvery one, can't you see it?

Dont be cross with me if I am dull just now. My cough is so much worse that I *am* a cough – a living walking or lying-down cough. Why I am allowed to stay in this hotel I can't imagine. But there it is. I must have terribly kind neighbours. As soon as it gets better I shall present a bouquet to the left door and to the right. "From a grateful Patient." Its only the X-rays doing their worst before they do their better. But its a nuisance. Such a queer effect on the boulevards here: the trees are out for a second spring – frail small leaves like you see in April. Lyrics in middle age – love song by old chestnuts over 50. All the same ones heart aches to see them. There is something tragic in spring.

If you knew how vivid the little house is – but vivid beyond words. Not only for itself. It exists apart from all – it is a *whole* in life. I think of you ... One has such terribly soft tender feelings. But to work – to work. One must take just those feelings and work *with* them. Life is a mystery – we can never get over that. Is it a series of deaths and series of killings? It is that too. But who shall say where death ends and resurrection begins. Thats what one must do. Give to the idea of *resurrection* the power that death would like to have. Be born again and born again faster than we die ...

Tell me, my dove, why do you "warn" me. What musn't I be "too sure" of? You mystify me. Do you think I am too sure of Love? But if Love is there one must treat it as though one were sure of it – how else? If its not there Id rather be sure of that, too. Or do you mean something else?

It has turned as cold as ice – and colder. The sun shines but it is soleil glacé. Its due north and due east all mixed up in the same frozen bag. If it wasn't for the blue up above one would cry.

Dont let our next meeting be in Paris. Its no *fun* meeting in hotels & sitting on beds & eating in nasty old restaurants. Lets wait a little longer & meet in the south in a warm, still place where I can put a cricket at your third ear so you can hear its song.

Ever, my dearest dear

Your loving

Tig

MS Newberry. *LKM* II. 252–3.

---

[1] Herbert Milne, classical scholar and assistant keeper in the Department of Manuscripts at the British Museum, a close friend of JMM.

To S. S. Koteliansky, 9 October 1922

Select Hotel | Place de la Sorbonne | Paris

9 X 1922

My dear Koteliansky

I have finished the Letters; here they are. They are, the more one looks into them, a remarkable revelation of what goes on *behind the scenes*. Except for 'Kiss the foal' & "buy the children sweets; even doctors prescribe sweets for children",[1] there is hardly one single statement that isn't pure matter-of-fact. The whole affair is like the plot of a short story or small novel by himself; he reacts to everything exactly as he would react to a *written* thing. Theres no expansion, no evidence of a LIVING man, a REAL man. The glimpse one has of his relationship with Anya is somehow petty and stuffy, essentially a double bed relationship.[2] And then "Turgenev read so badly"; they say *he* (D.) read so superbly.[3] Oh dear, oh dear, it would take an Anna Grigorevna to be proud of such letters.

Yet this was a noble, suffering, striving soul, a real hero among men – wasn't he? I mean from his books . . . The one who writes the letters is the house porter of the other. I suppose one ought not to expect to find the master at his own front door as well as in his study. But I find it hard to reconcile myself to that. I do not think these deep divisions in people are necessary or vital. Perhaps it is cowardice in me.

It is very queer that the Rem. have not sold. Perhaps it is because Andrejev is very little known over here.[4] The Gorky on Tolstoi book would have fetched a big price anywhere because people would want to know what he said about *Tolstoi*.[5] I may be wrong but I think that in England Gorki *qua* Gorki is not "popular" (with editors of course I mean.)

Letters from Brett are of course as thick as migratory swallows. But she will soon get over this particular feeling. Many things in me she does not like. For instance, that I treat her explanations 'lightly', that when she is going to cry I say "what a pity you are going to cry. It is so tiring." She wants romance, she wants above all *yearning*. For unattached women love is that. It is unlimited, heavy, soft yearning. It is seaweed, under the water forever, pushing out against nothing, waving, flowing, terribly heavy, terribly *strong*, but weed.

Write to me about the letters, darling Koteliansky dear.

Katherine.

MS BL. *LKM* II. 251–2.

[1] As she had done several times in the past, KM helped to put Koteliansky's translations into good English. Kirkpatrick notes, p. 85, Koteliansky's manuscript has KM's corrections, but there was no acknowledgement of her contribution in *Dostoevsky: Letters and Reminiscences*, translated by S. S. Koteliansky and J. Middleton Murry (1923). The two quoted phrases are from letters to Dostoevsky's wife (8 June and 2–3 June 1880).

[2] There are frequent frank declarations of love in Dostoevsky's letters to his wife, Anna Grigorevna.

[3] Ivan Sergeyevich Turgenev (1818–83), novelist and short-story writer. He and other eminent Russian authors gave readings to celebrate the unveiling of a memorial in Moscow for the poet Alexander Pushkin (1799–1837). Dostoevsky's account of these events details his own success, and his rivals' failings.

[4] During her recent stay in England, KM and Koteliansky had worked on Maxim Gorky's *Reminiscences of Leonid Andreyev*, trans. Katherine Mansfield and S. S. Koteliansky, published first in New York (1928), then in London (1931), but at this time they were unable to find a publisher. Andreyev (1871–1919), prolific short-story writer, novelist and playwright, was the foremost Russian writer between the 1905 and 1917 revolutions. As an anti-Bolshevik, his last years were spent in Finland.

[5] Maxim Gorky, *Reminiscences of Leo Nicolayevitch Tolstoi*, trans. S. S. Koteliansky and Leonard Woolf (1920).

To William Gerhardi, [c.10 October 1922]

Select Hotel | Place de la Sorbonne | Paris.

What a name.
You must only
breathe it.

Dear Mr Gerhardi,

Im very shaken today after a small minor revolution in the night. I put a vacuum flask full of boiling tea on the table by my bed last night and at about 2 oclock in the morning there was a most TERRIFIC explosion. It blew up everything. People ran from far an [*sic*] near. Gendarmes broke through the shutters with hatchets, firemen dropped through trap doors. Or very nearly. At any rate the noise was deafening and when I switched on the light there was my fiaschino outwardly calm still but tinkling internally in a terribly ominous way and a thin sad trickle oozed along the table.

I have nobody to tell this to today. So I hope your eyes roll. I hope you appreciate how fearful it might have been had it burst *out*wardly and not *in*wardly.

Bon jour, Mr Gerhardi. I am so sorry we have not met in England. But after all I had to come abroad again and I shall spend the next 3 months in Paris instead of London. Perhaps we shall not meet until you are very old. Perhaps your favourite grandson will wheel you to my hotel then (Im doomed to hotels) and instead of laughing, as we should now, a faint, light airy chuckle will pass from bath chair to bath chair – – –

I don't awfully like the name of your new book,[1] but I am *sure* the booksellers will. But then I don't very much like the idea of so called somersaults in the first person. But I am *certain* the public will.

I wonder for how long you have put aside your novel About Love. Please tell me when you take it up again. No, I didn't see the English review.[2] Was the lady Princess Bibesco? A most dreadful young person – very very emotional. Its raining. I must rescue my dear little John Milton from the window sill.

Rescued...

I have written to John Middleton Murry whose address is Selsfield House, East Grinstead, Sussex. I am sure he will be only too delighted. I wish you'd send a copy of your book[3] to him. He would be immensely interested.

People went on asking me about Mr Gerhardi. His past, his present, his future, his favourite jam, did he prefer brown bread for a change sometimes. I answered everything.

I hope to have rather a better book out in the spring. Im glad you are staying with Cobden Sanderson.

Goodbye. Are you quite well again? The weather is simply heavenly here.

Katherine Mansfield.

MS ATL. *LKM* II. 248–9.

[1] Gerhardi notes 'The book was abandoned', as was the other novel KM mentions, 'About Love'.
[2] In a letter of 2 Oct., he railed vigorously against the short story 'A Roman Dream' by Nadejda Stancioff, *English Review* (Oct. 1922, 373–6). Stancioff was Russia's first woman diplomat, recently appointed to Washington.
[3] His book on Chekov.

To J. M. Murry, [11 October 1922]

[Select Hotel, Place de la Sorbonne]

Wednesday.

Dearest Bogey

I have a letter and a card of yours to answer. How horrid your Father is – really horrid![1] I am so sorry for your Mother. Do you think your policy of keeping silent for her sake is a good one? I quite see quarrelling would be no use but I *do* feel a few *chosen words*, so that he can't preen himself upon having 'had the best of it', would be worth while. Give him something solid to think over. J.M.M. (quite quietly): "You know Dad youre a horrid bully. Nobody loves you." I am afraid hell live for ever, too. Why should he die? All his life is there coiled up, unused, in a horrid way *saved*. He is a very odd character. I feel you left your Mother, thinking of her with real, tender love, seeing her at Selsfield even, helping her out of the car. Or am I wrong?

That lecture must have been a queer little aside – wasn't it? A sort of short loop line.

It has got very cold here. I feel it. I am adjusting myself to it and it makes me rather dull – distrait, you know. I have had to leave my dear little grenier au 6ieme for something less lofty more expensive but warmer. However, its a very nice room 'et vous avez un beau pendule' as the garçon said. *He* thoroughly approves of the change. All the same, you say 'tell me all about yourself'. Ill have a try. Here goes.

A new way of being is not an easy thing to *live*. Thinking about it preparing to meet the difficulties and so on is one thing, meeting those difficulties another. I have to die to so much; I have to make such *big* changes. I feel the only thing to do is to get the dying over – to court it, almost (Fearfully hard, that) and then all hands to the business of being reborn again. What do I mean exactly? Let me give you an instance. Looking back, my boat is almost swamped sometimes by seas of sentiment. 'Ah what I have missed. How sweet it was, how dear how warm, how simple, how precious.' And I think of the garden at the Isola Bella and the furry bees and the house wall so warm. But then I remember what we really felt there. The blanks, the silences, the anguish of continual misunderstanding. Were we positive, eager, real – alive? No, we were not. We were a nothingness shot with gleams of what might be. But no more. Well, I have to face everything as far as I can & see where I stand – what *remains*.

For with all my soul I do long for a real life, for truth, and for real strength. Its simply incredible, watching KM, to see how little causes a panic. Shes a perfect corker at toppling over.

I envy you Selsfield. How I should like to be there now, this morning. How beautiful it is – how gracious. I am so glad you are there, my darling Bogey. I feel it *is* the house of your dreams – isn't it? Do you have flowers on your writing table? Or only pipes in pots and feathers! *You wont forget the Tchekhov will you?* Id *like* the Lit. Sup. with your review if it wasnt too much of a bore to send it.[2]

Ever your
Wig.

MS ATL. *LKM* II. 253–4.

[1] John Murry, driven to rise above the poverty of his youth, was hardworking but dour, and now, at eighty-seven, a difficult civil servant pensioner.

[2] Murry reviewed Chekov's *Love, and Other Stories*, translated by Constance Garnett, *TLS* (19 Oct. 1922).

To J. M. Murry, 13 October 1922

S. H. [Select Hotel, Place de la Sorbonne]
13.X.1922

Dont mind if I don't talk about health – will you . . . Its a *useless* subject.
My dearest Bogey dear

That was a massive 1st instalment from Newcassel. What an observer you are become. But I don't think the North is at all simpatico – do you? Those big bones make one feel like a small Jonah in a very large cold whale.

Its a divinely beautiful day – so was yesterday. I hope you are having the same weather at Selsfield. The sky is as blue as the sky can be. I shall go to the Luxembourg Gardens this afternoon and count dahlia and baby heads. The Paris gardens are simply a glorious sight with flowers – masses of beloved Japonica, enough Japonica at last. I *shall* have a garden one day and work in it, too. Plant, weed, tie up, throw over the wall. And the peony border really will be staggering. Oh, how I love flowers! I think of them with such longing. I go through them, one after another, remembering them from their first moments with love – oh with rapture as if they were babies! No its what other women feel for babies – perhaps. Oh Earth! Lovely unforgettable Earth. Yesterday I saw the leaves falling, so gently, so softly, raining down from little slender trees golden against the blue. Perhaps Autumn is loveliest. Lo! it is autumn. What is the magic of that? It is magic to me.

At that very minute in came your letter with the rose – and the aspen tree, the two little birds the ring from the anvil and the far away rooster. You never gave me such a perfect birthday present before. A divine one. I love you for it. Beautiful Selsfield sounds. I hope you *do* care for

DeLaMare – warmly. I feel that he is different to the others, but he too is hidden. We are all hidden, looking out at each other; I mean even those of us who want not to hide. But I understand perfectly what you say of friendship. With you it is love or nothing, and that you are in love with Elizabeth when she loves you. A relationship which isn't what you call a *warm* one is nothing to me, either. Feel I must. But then darling, oughtn't you to express your feeling & risk losing those people who think you 'ridiculous' or who don't understand it? That's hard to decide. For instance, I feel you & Locke-Ellis only touch the fringe of what your relationship might be if you both were 'free' with each other. But perhaps Im quite wrong. Yes, I care for Lawrence. I have thought of writing to him and trying to arrange a meeting after I leave Paris – suggesting that I join them until the spring. Richard, too, I think of with love. That reminds me. Won't you ask Milne[1] down for a weekend? But he is so shy perhaps he would refuse. Do you know what I think he is? A Dreamer. A real one. He chooses to dream.

I am going to Fontainebleau next week to see Gurdjieff.[2] I will tell you about it. Why am I going? From all I hear he is the only man who understands there is no division between the body and the spirit, who believes how they are related. You remember how I have always said doctors only treat *half*. And you have replied 'Its up to you to do the rest'? It is. Thats true. But first I must learn how. I believe Gurdjieff can teach me. What other people say doesn't matter – other people matter not at all.

But you matter to me – more and more. Id like to say I believe as never before in the possibility of real living relationship between us – a *true* one. Again, my love, I thank you for the rose.

Ever
Wig.

MS ATL. *LKM* II. 254–5.

---

[1] H. J Milne. See p. 291, n.1.

[2] KM's first mention in her letters of George Gurdjieff (1872–1949), a widely travelled Armenian Greek who established his Institute for the Harmonious Development of Man in Moscow in 1914. He left Russia in 1921 with P. D. Ouspensky, whom KM met and heard lecture in London. He was now reviving his Institute at La Prieuré, a former Carmelite monastery near Fontainbleau.

KM already had discussed Gurdjieff and Ouspensky with JMM, and was prepared for his opposition. As he wrote looking back from 1936, it was this deep disagreement that led to their separation before she returned to Paris. 'Had I been older and wiser, maybe I should have been more tolerant. . . . But at that time I felt that the only thing that remained to me – my own integrity – was at stake. It is not that I felt superior to Ouspensky's disciples: still less did I feel superior to Katherine. But . . . I could scarcely bear to discuss the doctrines of Ouspensky with Katherine. The gulf between us was painful to us both; and living under the same roof became a kind of torture' (Lee, 90–1).

When JMM received this letter telling him of her decision, he wrote back, 14 Oct., 'Your letter has disturbed me very much. Your going to Gurdjieff's institute may be everything you think: I'm sure you know and I don't. But to give up Manoukhin, as you evidently are doing, though you don't say so, seems to me criminal. I really mean wrong, utterly wrong' (Murry, 365).

To J. M. Murry, 14 October 1922

S.H. [Select Hotel, Place de la Sorbonne]

14 X 1922

My darling Bogey

Your sweet telegram[1] and letter are here. Thank you my angel. I do think Selsfield sounds perfect but its no good my coming there while I am a creeping worm. When I can fly I will come if you will have me. So very deeply gladly. I am more than happy to know you are there. Most blessed house! How it lives in my memory. Fancy the blackberries ripe. There are some, aren't there? Along the fence on the way to the Hen Houses, I seem to remember. Michaelmas daisies remind me of a solitary bush in Acacia Road. Do you remember? I like them. They have such very delicate arrowy petals.

I send back Elizabeths letter. If that is grist you have a very superior mill indeed. Why do you mind punching holes in me? If you punch holes in her?[2] I do think *she* writes the most 'fascinating' letters. If I were a man I should fall in love every time I had one. What qualities she has – and tenderness, real tenderness, hasn't she? I feel it, or perhaps I want to feel it.

About doing operations on yourself. I know just what you mean. Its as though one were the sport of circumstance – one *is*, indeed. Now happy – now unhappy, now fearful, now confident, just as the pendulum swings. You see one can control nothing if one isn't conscious of a purpose – its like a journey without a goal. There is nothing that makes you ignore some things, accept others, order others, submit to others. For there is no reason why A should be more important than B. So there one is – involved beyond words – feeling the next minute I may be bowled over or struck all of a heap. I *know* nothing.

This is to me a very terrible state of affairs. Because its the cause of all the unhappiness (the secret profound unhappiness) in my life. But I mean to escape and to try to live differently. It isn't easy. But is the other state easy? And I do believe with all my being that if one *can* break through the circle one finds "my burden is light".[3]

I have met two awfully nice men here. One is Mr Pinder[4] – did I tell you about him? The other is a Doctor Young.[5] He came up from Fontainebleau today to meet Orage who arrives tonight. And on his way to the station he spent a couple of hours with me, talking about Gurdjieff and the institute. If I were to write it all to you it sounds fabulous and other worldly. I shall wait until Ive *seen* it. I still hope to go on Monday & Ill take a toothbrush and peigne and come back on Wednesday morning, only.

Ive had such a queer birthday. Ida bought me a brin of mimosa. And I had my poem and the telegrams. Wasn't it awfully nice of L.E. and

DeLaMare to send one. Its been sunny, too. But all the same Id rather not think about my birthday.

Oh, the little Tchekhov book has come. Do you think I might have the Lit. Sup. with your article in it? I see no papers here at all. Thats not a complaint, though. For Paris flaps with papers as you know. I havent seen a single newspaper since leaving London. There! Does that shock you?

My *darling* Bogey

I am your
Wig.

MS ATL. *LKM* II. 255.

[1] A telegram for KM's birthday from Murry and his friends at Selsfield.

[2] Murry noted *LJMM* 672, 'I had a letter file which required this operation.'

[3] 'For my yoke is easy, and my burden is light' (Matthew 11:30).

[4] Major Frank Pinder, formerly a British Intelligence officer, had been a Gurdjieff follower for some years. He had escaped from Rostov in 1920, after being condemned to death by the Bolsheviks.

[5] James Carruthers Young (d. 1950). He later discarded his belief in Gurdjieff, but recorded his experience at the Institute in 'Experiment at Fontainbleau – a Personal Reminiscence', *New Adelphi* (Sept. 1927).

To J. M. Murry, [15 October 1922]

[Select Hotel, Place de la Sorbonne]
Sunday

I have opened my letter darling to add something. Its this. Darling Bogey in your spare time, however little that is, get nearer the growing earth than that wheelbarrow and spade. *Grow things.* Plant. Dig up. Garden. I feel with all the force of my being that 'happiness' is in these things. If its only cabbages let it be cabbages rather than chess. Sweep leaves. Make fires. Do anything to work with your hands in contact with the earth.

You see chess only feeds your already over developed intellectual centre. And that regular spade-and-barrow becomes a habit too soon, and is likely only to feed your moving centre – to exercise your machine. Does that sound awful rot to you?

Why don't you get some animals? Im not joking. Two hours a day would be enough for them. Birds, rabbits, a goat – *anything* and live through it or them! I know you will say you haven't the time. But you'll find your work is a 100 times easier if you come to it refreshed, renewed, rich, happy. Does this sound like preaching. Dont let it. I am trying to tell you what I feel deep down is your way of escape. It is to really throw yourself into life, not desperately but with the love you even don't feel yet. People wont do. We know too well that unless one has a background of reality in oneself people can't endure in us. When we have a table spread we can afford to open our door to guests, but not before. But enough of this. I am afraid of boring you.

Did you ask L.E. about tulips? Has he got anemones in the garden? *You* ought to see to them; they are your flowers. Why don't you write to Suttons[1] and ask their advice.

Oh, if you knew how I believe in Life being the only cure for Life.

Ever your own
Wig.

About being like Tchekhov and his letters. Dont forget he *died* at 43. That he spent – how much? – of his life chasing about in a desperate search after health. And if one reads 'intuitively' the last letters they are terrible. What is left of him. "The braid on German women's dresses – bad taste",[2] and all the rest is misery. Read the last! All hope is over for him. Letters are deceptive, at any rate. Its true he had occasional happy moments. But for the last 8 years he knew no *security* at all. We know he felt his stories were not half what they might be. It doesn't take much imagination to picture him on his death bed thinking "I have never had a real chance. Something has been all wrong . . . "

MS ATL. *LKM* II. 256; *LJMM*, 673–4.

---

[1] Sutton and Sons, a firm of garden suppliers in Reading.

[2] Chekhov wrote to his sister Marie from Berlin, 8 June 1904, 'Fearfully bad taste . . . I have not seen one beautiful woman, nor one who was not trimmed with some kind of absurd braid' (*Letters of Anton Tchekov to his Family and Friends*, trans. Constance Garnett, 1920).

To Dorothy Brett, [15 October 1922]

[Select Hotel, Place de la Sorbonne]

My dearest little Queen B.

I never had a lovelier letter from you. And it came on my birthday – wasn't that good fortune. Wasn't that like you – the billiard champion? I did love you for it! You have a real very rare gift for writing letters. And Oh how nice and long they are. Arrows, little side borders, little flower beds very tight packed with words along the edge – I follow them all and even dip into the Egyptian Maze though never to find my way in it!

Ah, my dear. Priceless exquisite treasures came floating out of your letter. I have gathered them all up. But that reminds me of the canary feathers. I am having a pair of wings made of them for delicate occasions. Did you ever feel anything so airy-fairy?

I sat in the Luxembourg Gardens today and thought of you. I am glad you were not with me for I felt like a chat malade, sitting in the sun, and not a friend of anybody's. But all was so ravishingly fall-of-the-year lovely[1] that I feel how you would have responded. The gardener was sweeping leaves from the bright grass. The flowers are still glorious, but still, as though suspended, as though hardly daring to breathe. Down, down, soft and light floated the leaves. They fall over babies and old people and the laughing young. The fat pigeons-out-of-the-Ark are no longer quite so fat. But they swing between the trees just as they did, swooping and tumbling as if trying to scare one. Heavens! What a lovely earth it is!

I am glad you are going to Scotland. I feel it may do you good to have a change. And it's nice to think of you fishing. Forgive me if I feel the fish show off just a tiny little bit when you come near, flash about, blow bubbles swim on their heads. But that's only my wickedness. For I feel you are very expert and grave really, and I should stand on the bank – *awed*! You see I've only fished with things like cottage loaves and a bent pin and a worm.

Tell me about Scotland. I do so hope it's going to be nice. I wonder if you will take your velour hat. It suits you marvellously. When I am rich you shall have velour hats by the dozing, and a Persian lamb jacket made like your jazz velvet coat, lined with pale yellow brocade. A pinky pigeon grey very soft pleated skirt to go with it, crocodile shoes, thick grey silk stockings. And inside the coat a straight tunic of silver jersey de soie. I confess I am quite ravished away by you in the Persian lamb coat. I have just been with you to a concert – you wearing it. Everybody turned round; the orchestra stopped; the flute fainted and was carried out. A dark gentleman stepped forward and presented you with the Order of the Sun and Moon; it was the Shah of Persia. But I must stop. Though I could go on for ever.

It's Sunday evening. 6.30. I am lying in bed writing to you. Just as before I get up at midi and have to go to bed at about half past five. But I feel far more ill this time than last time. I don't know what is the matter. I am sick all the time – and cold. But as I've never imagined cold before – an entirely new kind. One feels like wet stone. Piping hot water bottles, covers, grandma jaegers, nothing will stop it. Then it goes and one burns instead. And all this in a little bandbox of a room. Never mind. It will pass. Tomorrow I am going to see Gurdjieff. I feel certain he will help me. I feel equally certain that this particular horrid hour is passing, and I'll come out of it – please Heaven – a much nicer creature. Not a snail, love. Not a creeping worm, either. I shall come and make the *whole* of your garden before you can say 'Painting-brush'. You just wait!

I saw Ottoline on the green couch, telling you of the medium. What a picture it made. J.M. told me you'd had a Beethoven orgy. Does he seem well? And your cold? Is it gone. I do hope Mrs Saunders is being satisfactory still. My dear little rooms – I shall be in them in the spring, if I manage to escape and I really think I shall.

I have seen very few people since I came – only men connected with the Institute – a very nice Dr Young[2] and a quite remarkable other man – rather like the chief mate on a cargo steamer. A type I like. Work I can't at all for the present. Even reading is very difficult.

The weather is marvellous. Where it is not blue, it is gold. Oh, I must tell you. We took a taxi out to lunch today (there is no food here except supper trays) and who should be at the restaurant but (of course you guess) Mrs Dobrée. Très très très chic with such an extra passionate Sunday Paris mouth – and so terrifically at home! I must say I liked her for it. It was so young. She sat behind us. As we got out she saw me and I gave her a wretched cool nod. Not on purpose. But at that moment I was overcome with this confounded sickness and hardly knew what I was doing. But I hope she won't think me very horrid for it. I don't like doing such things.

I am glad you wrote about Ida. I understand perfectly. And I feel that any kind of confusion we may have felt about it is over for ever. It's only while Ida is my legs that she is so present. It's a false position, you see. I pretend I am doing things for myself and so on. In reality I am using Ida. And that makes her wrong (for she doesn't know where she 'is') and in fact it is so wrong all round that it's a marvel to me we *have* come through. When we meet again (when I am better) you will see the difference, darling.

And I want to say I trust you absolutely. I shall love you and trust you more and more. For these things always increase as one spends them; a divine kind of money. But I am still not sincere with you. In my heart I am far more desperate about my illness and about *Life* than I ever show you. I long to lead a different life in every way. I have no belief whatever in any kind of medical treatment. Perhaps I am telling you this to beg you to have faith in me – to believe that whatever I do it is because I can't do otherwise. That is to say (let me say it bang out) I may go into the Institute for 3 months. I don't know that I shall. But if I have more faith in it than in Manoukhin I certainly must. Keep this private, darling. I know you will. But don't speak to anybody about it.

Manoukhin isn't a magician. He has cured some people – a great many – and some he hasn't cured. He made me fatter – that is quite true. But otherwise? I'm exactly where I was before I started. I 'act' all the rest, because I am ashamed to do otherwise, looking as I do. But it's all a sham. It amounts to nothing. However – this is just speculation. But as I am thinking it I felt I ought to write it to you. See? It is not a serious proposition.

Don't let us meet until I am a bit better. I realise the importance of nearness, too. But we shall have it in the future and so far differently. Tell me about your work. Goodbye for now – dearest precious little artist.

Ever your
Tig

MS Newberry. *LKM*, 256–9.

¹ Again, KM's deeper mood can be gauged from a notebook entry the same day. 'Nietzsche's Birthday.
Sat in the Luxembourg Gardens. Cold, wretchedly unhappy. Horrid people at lunch, everything horrid from angfang bis zum ende' (*KMN* II. 329).

² Dr James Young had visited her at the Select Hotel to examine her, and confirm that she was able to visit Fontainebleau.

To J. M. Murry, [16 October 1922]

[Paris]

DEAR HOUSE DEAR FRIENDS ACCEPT MY LOVE
KATHERINE¹

Telegram ATL.

¹ In reply to the birthday telegram on 14 Oct.

To J. M. Murry, [16 October 1922]

[Select Hotel, Place de la Sorbonne]

Dearest Bogey

Here is a note from Jeanne that you may care to read. I received at the same time a card from Marie to you telling you where to go for the wedding.¹ It had been posted to me by mistake. So to prove *your* good faith I posted it back to her. Poor Marie! She writes she is heartbroken to be giving up her little Jeanne.

Thank you darling for the Times article.² It is extraordinarily interesting. I read it twice. The writing, apart from everything else, is so good and clear and not too persuasive. Do you know what I mean? I don't want any more books at present of any kind. I am sick and tired of books and thats a dreadful fact. They are to me like sanwiches out of the Hatter's bag.³ Ill get back to them, of course.

A queer thing. I have cramp in my thumb & can hardly hold the pen. That accounts for this writing. Ida & I are off to Fontainebleau this morning. I am taking my toothbrush & comb. Young phoned me yesterday that there is a lovely room all ready. Ill see Gurdjieff and come back tomorrow. Its not sunny today. What a terrible difference *sun* makes. It ought not to. One ought to have a little core of inner warmth that keeps burning and is only added to by the sun. One has I believe if one looks for it.

An extremely fat Nation has come with your review of Switzerland.⁴

So Marie Lloyd is dead – is she? Poor old H.M.T. He *is* a sentimentalist – isn't he? I mean his article on M.L. begs the question so utterly. What's the good of that? What's the good of turning a blind eye to half of her?⁵

It was a painful copy of the Nation, altogether. Massingham's Holiday Moods and his visit to the Old Vic. made one hang one's head.[6]

Did you ever see such squiggles as I am making? Forgive them darling. But for the sake of your reine claude[7] eyes I shall stop until my hand is a little rested.

I feel I shall have masses to tell you of my adventure today. Oh Bogey I am so glad W.J.D. [W.J. Dunning] was real. I felt he would be. If he gets that house it would be wonderful in the spring wouldn't it to have them all so near.

I must get up. The puffi train is, as usual, steaming up and down my room at the very idea of going away, even for half a day.

White lupin! Oh how lovely. I don't think much of Albert,[8] though. You ought to take him in hand. Why is Albert such a very queer name?

Ever, my darling Bogey

Your
Wig.[9]

MS ATL. *LJMM*, 674–5.

[1] Her sister Jeanne was married at St Margaret's, Westminster, on 17 Oct.

[2] JMM's unsigned essay, 'On the Nature of Poetry', *TLS* (12 Oct. 1922).

[3] KM is supposing what the Hatter *might* take from his hat, rather than anything he actually did, at 'A Mad Tea Party', Chapter 7, in Lewis Carroll's *Alice's Adventures in Wonderland* (1865).

[4] Review of Wilhelm Oechsli, *History of Switzerland*, trans. Eden and Cedar Paul, the *Nation and the Athenaeum* (14 Oct. 1922).

[5] Marie Lloyd (1870–1922), the popular music hall singer, died on 7 Oct. H. M. Tomlinson's unsigned 'Marie Lloyd' praised her extravagantly, passing over her difficult private life and three marriages.

[6] Under his pseudonym 'A Wayfarer', H. J. Massingham assembled in 'Holiday Moods' a collection of weak epigrams on morals, youth and politics, while under 'A hint to "The Old Vic" ' he deplored the quality of its *1 Henry IV*, asserting that to visit the theatre should be like going to church and entering 'a religious atmosphere'.

[7] Greengage.

[8] The gardener at Selsfield.

[9] KM wrote that day in her notebook: 'To be wildly enthusiastic, or deadly serious – both are wrong. Both pass. One must keep ever present a sense of humour. It depends entirely on yourself how much you see or hear or understand. But the sense of humour I have found true of every single occasion of my life. Now perhaps you understand what to be indifferent means. It's to learn not to mind, and not to show you mind' (*NKM* II. 329).

To S. S. Koteliansky, [19 October 1922]

[Le Prieuré, Fontainebleau, Avon]

My dear Koteliansky

I hope this letter will not surprise you too much. It has nothing to do with our business arrangements. Since I wrote I have gone through a kind of private revolution. It has been in the air for years with me. And now it has happened very very much is changed.

When we met in London and discussed 'ideas' I spoke as nearly as one can the deepest truth I knew to you. But even while I spoke it I felt a pretender – for my knowledge of this truth is negative, not positive as it were cold, and not warm with life. For instance all we have said of 'individuality' and of being strong and single, and of growing – I believe it. I try to act up to it. But the reality is far far different. Circumstances still hypnotise me. I am a divided being with a bias towards what I wish to be, but no more. And this it seems I cannot improve. No, I cannot. I have tried. If you knew how many notebooks there are of these trials, but they never succeed. So I am always conscious of this secret disruption in me – and at last (thank Heaven!) it has ended in a complete revolution and I mean to change my whole way of life entirely. I mean to learn to work in every possible way with my hands, looking after animals and doing all kinds of manual labour. I do not want to write any stories until I am a less terribly poor human being. It seems to me that in life as it is lived today the catastrophe is *imminent*; I feel this catastrophe in me. I want to be prepared for it, at least.

The world as I know it is no joy to me and I am useless in it. People are almost nonexistent. This world to me is a dream and the people in it are sleepers. I have known just instances of waking but that is all. I want to find a world in which these instances are united. Shall I succeed? I do not know. I scarcely care. What is important is to try & learn to live – really live, and in relation to everything – not isolated (this isolation is death to me).

Does this sound fabulous? I cannot help it. I have to let you know for you mean much to me. I know you will never listen to whatever foolish things other people may say about me. Those other helpless people going round in their little whirlpool do not matter a straw to me.

I will send you my address this week. In the meantime all is forwarded from the Select Hotel by Ida Baker, with whom I must part company for a time.
I press your hands, dear dear friend

Katherine.

All this sounds much too serious and dramatic. As a matter of fact there is absolutely no tragedy in it, of course.

MS BL. *LKM* II. 259–60.

To J. M. Murry, [21 October 1922]

Le Prieuré | Fontainebleau-Avon | Seine-et-Marne
My dear darling Bogey,

I have been through a little revolution since my last letter. I suddenly made up my mind (for it was sudden, at the last) to try and learn to live by what I believed in, no less, and not as in all my life up till now to live one way and think another. I don't mean superficially of course, but in the deepest sense Ive always been disunited. And this, which has been my 'secret sorrow' for years has become everything to me just now. I really cant go on pretending to be one person and being another any more, Boge. It is a living death. So I have decided to make a clean sweep of all that was 'superficial' in my past life and start again to see if I can get into that real living simple truthful *full* life I dream of. I have been through a horrible deadly time coming to this. You know the kind of time. It doesn't show much, outwardly, but one is simply chaos within!

So – my first Leap into the Dark was when I came here and decided to ask Mr Gurdjieff if he would let me stay for a time. 'Here', is a very beautiful old chateau in glorious grounds. It was a Carmelite monastery then one of Madame de Maintenons 'seats'.[1] Now it is modernised inside I mean chauffage centrale, electric light and so on. But its a most wonderful old place in an amazing lovely park. About 40 people, chiefly Russians, are here working, at every possible kind of thing. I mean, outdoor work, looking after animals, gardening, indoor work, music, dancing – it seems a bit of everything. Here the philosophy of the 'system' takes second place. Practice is first. You simply *have* to wake up instead of talking about it, in fact. You *have* to learn to do all the things you say you want to do.

I don't know whether Mr Gurdjieff will let me stay. I am 'under observation' for a fortnight first. But if he does Ill stay here for the time I should have been abroad, and get really cured – not half cured, not cured in my body only and all the rest still as ill as ever. I have a most lovely sumptuous room a kind of glorified Garsington for the fortnight. As for the food it is like a Gogol feast.[2] Cream, butter – But what nonsense to talk about the food. Still its very important, and I want you to know that one is terribly well looked after, in every way. There are three doctors here, real ones. But these too seem details. The chief thing is that this is my Selsfield for the time, the house of *my dreams*. If Mr Gurdjieff wont let me stay I shall go to the South, take a little villa and try and learn to live on my own, growing things and looking after rabbits and so on, getting into touch with *Life* again. No treatment on earth is any good to me, really. Its all pretence. Manoukhine did make me heavier and a little stronger. But that was all if I really face the facts. The miracle never came near happening. It couldn't, Boge. And as for my spirit – well, as a result of that life at the Victoria Palace I stopped being a writer. I have only written long or short scraps since '*The Fly*'. If I had gone on with my old life I never would have written again, for I was dying of poverty of life.

I wish, when one writes about things one didnt dramatise them so. I feel awfully happy about all this, and its all as simple as can be. Its just the same for us, darling, as though I had stayed on in Paris *except* that I hope I shall be well when you see me again, instead of knowing it would be a variation on the old theme.

Will you send me letters here for a fortnight? Ida will be at the Select Hotel for that time so if you prefer to send them there she'll post them on. At the end of that time Ill either stay on here or as I say, go off to some warm place where I can turn into a worker. But I hope it will be here.

Mr Gurdjieff is not in the least like what I expected. Hes what one wants to find him, really.[3] But I do feel *absolutely confident* he can put me on the right track in every way, bodily and t'other governor.

I havent talked money to Mr Gurdjieff yet. But in any case I shant write any stories for 3 months, and Ill not have a book ready before the spring. It doesn't matter. When we have discussed finances Ill tell you. The fact is Ive hardly talked with him at all. Hes terribly busy just now and he only speaks a few words of English – all is through an interpreter. I cant say how 'good' some of the people seem to me here – its just like another life.[4] I start Russian today, and my first jobs which are eat, walk in the garden, pick the flowers, and rest *much*. Thats a nice calm beginning, isn't it. But its the eat much which is the job when its Gurdjieff who serves the dish. I must stop this letter, dearest. Im awfully glad DeLaMare is a real person. I know just what you mean about Sullivan & Waterlow. It seems 'right', somehow, in a queer way.

I take back my words Betsy about your quarrying. It sounded very different when you told me about the sand.

Goodbye for now, darling Heart

Ever your own
Wig.

MS ATL. *LKM* II. 261; *LJMM*, 675–7.

[1] Françoise D'Aubigné, Marquise de Maintenon (1635–1719), tutored children of Louis XIV, became his mistress, and secretly married him after the death of Queen Marie Therese.

[2] There are numerous descriptions of food and feasts in the fiction of the Ukrainian-born Nikolai Gogol (1809–52). The reference is most likely to *Dead Souls* (1842), or the story *Old World Landowners* (1835), which was reputed to read like a menu.

[3] There is no record of how KM struck Gurdjieff, but his allowing her to stay was an act of kindness, knowing as he did from Dr Young her precarious health.

[4] While KM eagerly stayed on, Ida Baker, who had accompanied her to Fontainebleau, and intended to remain with her, left after two days. As Ida's diary recorded:

October 18th, Wednesday

Last evening spent in the salon before an enormous fire of great logs. 'Fire is condensed sunlight.' Music and tambourines – atmosphere intensely alive. Came to Paris for letters etc. for Katherine. Back for dinner. Dreadfully depressed and self-conscious. Spent evening upstairs alone. K. came up radiant, her eyes shining. She is staying for a fortnight under observation.

October 20th, Friday.

Came away for last time absolutely dazed. Decided in the train to go on the land or to Russia. I ought to bless and sing praises to life. I do in my reason, my heart refuses to join in.

(*MLM*, 214)

To Ida Baker, [c.22 October 1922]

Le Prieuré | Fontainebleau.Avon. | Seine et Marne.

Dear Ida,

This is the address. I have had no post so far. Perhaps its all got lost. Thank you for the things. The warm petticoats vest and scarf are a joy. It is cold here when one stops working.

Cold – but lovely.
I am glad your toothache is better.[1]
Thank you. *I am happy.*

KM

Whatever warm clothes the 1000 francs will buy *please send*. Especially a warm jacket for the evening of a big soft scarf.

Postcard BL. *MLM*, 215.

---

[1] Ida notes (*MLM*, 215), ' "Toothache": an emotional trouble, not physical.'

To J. M. Murry, [23 October 1922]

Le Prieuré | Fontainebleau-Avon | Seine-et-Marne

My darling Bogey

Ill tell you what this life is more like than anything; it is like Gulliver's Travels.[1] One has, all the time, the feeling of having been in a wreck & by the mercy of Providence, got ashore . . . somewhere. Simply everything is different. Not only languages but food, ways, people, music, methods, hours – *all*. Its a real new life.

At present this is my day. I get up at 7.30, light the fire (with kindling drying overnight) wash in ice cold water (Id quite forgotten how good water is to wash in & to drink) & go down to breakfast – which is coffee, butter, bread, gorgonzola cheese & quince jam & eggs. After breakfast, make my bed, do my room, rest, & then go into the garden till dinner which is 11 A.M. Which is a very large meal with things like beans minced with raw onions, vermicelli with icing sugar & butter, veal wrapped in lettuce leaves & cooked in cream. After dinner, in the garden again till 3 o'clock teatime. After tea, any light job that is going until dark. When all knock off work, wash, dress & make ready for dinner again at 7. After dinner most of the people gather in the salon round an enormous fire and there is music, tambourines, drums and piano, dancing & perhaps a display of all kinds of queer dance exercises. At ten we go to bed. Doctor Young, a real friend of mine, comes up and makes me up a good fire. In 'return' I am patching the knee of his trousers today.

But its all 'stranger' than that. For instance. I was looking for wood the other evening. All the boxes were empty. I found a door at the end of the passage, went through & down some stone steps. Presently steps came up & a woman appeared very simply dressed with her head bound in a <black> white handkerchief. She had her arms full of logs. I spoke in French, but she didn't understand. English – no good. But her glance was so lovely – laughing & gentle, absolutely unlike people as I have known people. Then I patted a log & she gave it to me & we went our ways . . .

At present the entire Institute is devoted to manual work, getting this place in order, out and inside. Its not, of course, work for the sake of work.

Every single thing one does has a purpose, is part of a 'system'. Some of the English 'arty' & theosophical people are very trying, too. But one can learn to use them, I am sure. Though Im not much good at it yet. On the other hand some of the advanced men and women are truly wonderful. I am still on my fortnight's probation, simply spending a fortnight here. Mr Gurdjieff hardly ever speaks a word to me. He must know me pretty well.

But even if he won't let me stay here I am finished for the time being with *old circumstances*. They have just not killed me, and thats all there is to be said for them. All the people I have known don't really matter to me. Only you matter – more and more, if that is possible, for now that I am not so 'identified' with you I can see the real tie that holds us.

Ida, of course was very tragic. She had got to the pitch of looking after me when she gave me a handkerchief without my asking for it. She *was* me. However, I am sure Ida will recover. There is something rock-like in her under all that passion for helplessness.

Jeanne's wedding made me feel sad, Bogey. I too dislike that man awfully. I think the fat purple fellow was MacGavin,[2] for some reason. Thank you for telling me about it. I must write to Marie in a day or two. Forgive this hasty writing. Do send Lit. Sups. They are so good for lighting fires. I wish you were here. Its such happiness. Ever my darling

Your
Wig Voyageuse.

MS ATL. *LKM* II. 261–2; *LJMM*, 677–8.

---

[1] Jonathan Swift, *Gulliver's Travels* (1726).   [2] A distant relative.

To Ida Baker, [24 October 1922]

[Le Prieuré, Fontainebleau-Avon]

D.I.

All the parcels arrived safely. Please send the cloth one. No, I dont want another petticoat or knickers. Don't send the book. Why should you? I don't want any books at present. Id like another sleeping jacket – a very warm one, and a *Tuteur* for teaching the 'cello[1] & a book of quite elementary exercises – for teaching. This is urgent.

I am staying here indefinitely. I feel better. But as a precaution I shall send my will to the Bank in case of accidents. I hope your toothache is quite cured. Write to me from time to time won't you? Jack seems to have toothache too. If you go back to England I hope you'll see him.

Ever
K.M.

Postcard BL. *MLM*, 215.

[1] As a young woman KM was a proficient cellist, and at one point before her return from Wellington to London in 1908 considered becoming a professional musician.

To J. M. Murry, [24 October 1922]

[Le Prieuré, Fontainebleau-Avon]

My darling Bogey,

I was so glad to get your second letter today. Don't feel we are silently and swiftly moving away from each other. Do you *really*? And what do you mean by us meeting 'on the other side'? Where, Boge? You are much more mysterious than I!

I have managed this badly for this reason. I've never let you know how much I have suffered in these five years. But that wasn't my fault. I could not. You could not receive it, either. And all I [am] doing now is trying to put into practice the 'ideas' I have had for so long of another and a *far more truthful* existence. I want to learn something that no books can teach me, and I want to try and escape from my terrible illness. What again you can't be expected to understand. You think I am like other people – I mean – *normal*. I'm not. I don't know which is the ill me or the well me. I am simply one pretence after another – only now I recognise it.

I believe Mr Gurdjieff is the only person who can help me. It is great happiness to be here. Some people are stranger than ever but the strangers I am at last feeling near and they are my own people at last. So I feel. Such beautiful understanding and sympathy I have never known in the outside world.

As for writing stories and being true to one's gift. I couldn't write them if I were not here, even. I am at the end of my source for the time. Life has brought me no *flow*. I want to write but differently far more steadily. I am writing this on the corner of the table against orders for the sun shines & I am supposed to be in the garden. Ill write again, my darling precious.

Ever your own
Wig.

MS ATL. *LKM* II. 262.

To J. M. Murry, [27 October 1922]

[Le Prieuré, Fontainebleau-Avon]

Darling Bogey

I was so glad to hear of your Sullivan excursion. But doesn't his chess obsession bore you dreadfully? It did me. But Beethoven[1] and the stars & the baby all sounded nice.

What are you going to do to the fruit trees? Please tell me. We have masses of quinces here. They are no joke when they fall exprès on your head. I do hope you are having this glorious weather. Day after day of perfect sunshine. Its like Switzerland. An *intense* blue sky, a chill in the air, a wonderful clarity so that you see people far away, all sharp cut and vivid.

I spend all the sunny time in the garden. Visit the carpenters, the trench diggers (we are digging for a Turkish Bath – not to discover one but to lay the pipes). The soil is very nice here, like sand with small whitey pinky pebbles in it. Then there are the sheep to inspect & the new pigs that have long golden hair very mystical pigs. A mass of cosmic rabbits & hens – and goats are on the way, likewise horses & mules to ride & drive. The Institute is not really started yet for another fortnight. A dancing hall is being built & the house is still being organised. But it has started really. If all this were to end in smoke tomorrow I should have had the very great wonderful adventure of my life. I have learnt more in a week here than in years of life la-bas. As to habits! My wretched sense of order for instance which rode me like a witch. It did not take long to cure that. Mr Gurdjieff likes me to go into the kitchen in the late afternoon & 'watch'. I have a chair in a corner. Its a large kitchen with 6 helpers. Madame Ostrovsky[2] the head, walks about like a queen exactly. She is extremely beautiful. She wears an old raincoat. Her chief helper, Nina, a big girl in a black apron – lovely, too – pounds things in mortars. The second cook chops at the table, bangs the saucepans, sings; another runs in and out with plates & pots, a man in the scullery cleans pots, the dog barks & lies on the floor worrying a hearth brush. A little girl comes in with a bouquet of leaves for Olga Ivanovna.[3] Mr Gurdjieff strides in, takes up a handful of shredded cabbage & eats it . . . There are at least 20 pots on the stove & its so full of life and humour and ease that one wouldn't be anywhere else. Its just the same all through – *ease* after *rigidity* expresses it more than anything I know. And yet I realise that as I write this its no use. An old personality is trying to get back to the outside & observe & its not true to the present facts at all. What I write seems so petty. In fact I cannot express myself in writing just now. The old mechanism isn't mine any longer & I can't control the new. I just have to talk this baby talk.

I would like you to see the dancing here. There again you see its not to be described. One person sees one thing; one another. I have never really cared for dancing before but *this* – seems to be the key to the new world within one. To think that later on I shall do it is great happiness. There may be a demonstration in Paris in a month or two. If so I wish you could see it. But would it just look like dancing? I wonder! Its so hard to tell.

Oh, about money. I don't need any, thank you Bogey. If I ever do need money I shall ask you first but at present I dont.

I wish you'd ask Ouspensky out to dinner when you are in London. His address is 28 Warwick Gardens. He is an extraordinarily sympathetic person.

There are masses of work going on in this garden – uprooting and digging and so on. I don't see why there isn't in yours. Or perhaps you are more forward. Won't you send Ida a card to Paris 'Select Hotel' and ask her to spend a weekend with you if she returns to England? I don't know her plans. Still got cramp in my thumb. Oh, I wish I could write to you from this self not the other.

Suppose you throw up every single job in England, realise your capital, & come over here to work for Gurdjieff. Burn every single boat for once! Do you like the idea? Thats why I thought you might care to see Ouspensky. Do you like that old mechanical life at the mercy of everything? And just living with one little tiny corner of yourself?[4]

You could learn the banjo here and if the worst came to the worst always make enough to keep you with playing it – or anything. But perhaps this sounds very wild talk. We are not really wild here, at all. Very serious, in fact.

My darling precious Bogey

Yours ever
Wig,

MS ATL. *LKM* II. 263; *LJMM*, 680–1.

[1] Their friend J. W. N. Sullivan, as well as being a trained scientist and a practising journalist, was a passionate scholar of Beethoven, and a few years later the author of *Beethoven: His Spiritual Development* (1927).

[2] Countess Julia Ostrowska, Gurdjieff's wife, was reputed to have been familiar with the Tsarina's court. She was the choreographer for the dances that were central to her husband's teaching, and to life at the Institute.

[3] Olga Ivanovna Lazovich Milanoff (1897–1985), daughter of the chief justice of Montenegro, in 1926 became the third wife of the American architect Frank Lloyd Wright. She recorded her memories of KM in 'The Last Days of Katherine Mansfield', *Bookman* (Mar. 1931).

[4] KM had long thought Murry stunted himself by being so purely an intellectual, and that this was the basis of his temperamental pessimism. As she had written while at Randogne, thinking of 'Jacques le Fataliste', 'I do not want to be a book *worm*. A worm burrows everlastingly. If its book is taken away from it the little blind head is raised, it wags, hovers, terribly uneasy, in a void until it begins to burrow again' (*KMN* II. 332).

To Ida Baker, [28 October 1922]

[Le Prieuré, Fontainebleau-Avon]

Dear Ida

Send the green skirt. But please dont write to me any more about clothes. I do not want any and I do not want to talk or think about them *at all*. I can't tell you about the other things either. Let me give you

Mr Ouspensky's address. It is *38 Warwick Gardens*. If you are in London why do you not write & ask if you may attend his lectures? I shall not write again just now. I do not want to hear about Miss Beach.[1]

K.M.

Postcard BL. *MLM*, 216.

---

[1] Ida was still at the Select Hotel in Paris. Presumably she passed on some story relating to Sylvia Beach.

To Dorothy Brett, [28 October 1922]

La Prieuré | Fontainebleau-Avon | Seine et Marne

Dearest Brett

I am so glad to get your letter saying you would quite understand if I were to join the Institute. I have joined it for a time. I thought of writing about it. But its useless. Its too much to explain in any letter and I have so little time to write. So will you think of me as 'en voyage'? Thats much the best idea and its the truest, too.

Ever
K.M.

You see I am taking you absolutely at your word.

Postcard Newberry.

To J. M. Murry, [28 October 1922]

[Le Prieuré, Fontainebleau-Avon]

Saturday.

Darling Bogey,

Forgive me if I don't write often just now. I am so glad you are happy.[1] I am happy, too. And our happiness does not depend on letters. I feel certain we shall move towards each other. But we shall do it in our several ways. If I write at present I 'falsify' my position and I don't in any way help yours. It's absurd to give you the news here. News there is none, that can be so expressed. As to the people I have known I know nothing of them and they are out of sight just now. If I am sincere I can only say we *live* here – every moment of the day seems full of life. And yet I feel I can't enter into it as I shall be able to; I am only on the fringe. But write about it I can't.

Dunning's phrase is $\frac{1}{2}$ good, I feel – no more. He always seem to me $\frac{1}{2}$ way in everything. He has insight but not direction. Can he really help?

There is always this danger of deceiving oneself. I feel it, too. I only begin to get rid of it by trying and trying to relax – to give way. Here one *learns* how to do it. Life never would have taught me.

But I am sure you will understand why it is so hard to write. We don't move in our letters. We say the same things over and over. As I tried to explain I'm in such a state of transition. I could not if I would get back to the old life and I can't deal with the new. But *anxiety* I never feel. Perhaps I shall; I cannot tell. But I am so busy and so many people are here – so much is happening.

Goodbye for now darling,

Wig.

Let us speak the new truth. What present relationship have we? None. We feel there is the possibility of one – that is deep down truth, don't you feel? But no more. It doesn't mean we are moving away, though! It's a thousand times more subtle.

MS ATL. *LKM* II. 263; *LJMM*, 681–2.

---

[1] When KM stayed on at Fontainebleau, Murry left Locke-Ellis's at Selsfield for a villa Millar Dunning found him near his own home at Ditchling, Surrey. Dunning was a practising yogi, and instructed Murry.

To Ida Baker, [28 October 1922]

[Le Prieuré, Fontainebleau-Avon]

D.I.

Everything has come. I am so grateful for the red scarf. It is just what I wanted. Here is the pattern. And can I have a pair of galoshes and a pair of garters. I love being here – I am perfectly looked after & I feel one of these people. My only fear is that I may have to go away for a few weeks later on (thats a little ambiguous. Of course Mr Gurdjieff would send me and so on.) I don't want to miss a day. The weather so far is perfect. But terribly cold. All the fountain basins were frozen this morning & we have not a flower left. The leaves fall all day & the grass smells good. We are making a Turkish Bath which will be very comforting. I don't do any 'work' just now except – well, its hard to explain.

I hope you are happy. Haven't you used that 1000 francs? Shall I send you another? Please ask me. And remember you can always get a job at Selsfield, doing chickens for Locke-Ellis.

Excuse my writing. Its on the corner of the table under rather awkward conditions.

Ever
K.M.

Alas! I gave my plaid skirt away. But I have the plain panne velvet.

MS BL. *MLM*, 216.

To Ida Baker, [30 October 1922]

[Le Prieuré, Fontainebleau-Avon]

Dear Ida,

So it goes on. I have *not* received the green skirt. I want it. I dislike very much the coral coat & can never wear it. It looks so vulgar. Please send no skirt. I dislike also v. much the jumper you bought for the tricot coat & skirt & if I am sincere the coat & skirt itself. I look like a skinned rabbit in it. Please stop buying & stop asking me questions about clothes!

K.M.

MS BL.

To J. M. Murry, [2 November 1922]

[Le Prieuré, Fontainebleau-Avon]

My own Bogey

Ever since my last letter to you I have been so enraged with myself. Its so like me. I am ashamed of it. But you who know me will perhaps understand. I always try to go too fast. I always think all can be changed & renewed in the twinkling of an eye. It is most fearfully hard for me, as it is for you, not to be 'intense'. And whenever I am intense (really this is so) I am a little bit false. Take my last letter & the one before. The tone was all wrong. As to my new truth – oh, darling, I am really ashamed of myself. Its so very wrong. Now I have to go back to the beginning & start again and again tell you that I have been 'over fanciful' and I seem to have tried to force the strangeness. Do you know what I mean. Let me try now to *face facts*. Of course it is true that Life here is quite different, but violent changes to ones individuality – of course they do not occur. I have come here for a 'cure'. I know I shall never grow strong anywhere else in the world except here. This *is* the place and here at last one is understood entirely, mentally & physically. I could never have regained my health by any other treatment and all my friends accepted me as a frail, half-creature who migrated towards sofas. Oh, my dearest Bogey, just wait and see how you and I will live one day – so happily – so splendidly. But in the meantime, love, please never take what I say for 'absolute'. I do not take what you say for 'final'. I try & see it as relative. Essentially, you and I are together. I love you & I feel you are my man. Its that I want to build on and realise and really live in one of these days. So I shall write at least twice a week & tell you any odd things that are happening. Will you tell me, too?

Last night, for instance, in the salon we learnt to make rugs from long pieces of corn. Very nice ones. Very easy to make, too. I have been in the carpenters shop all the morning. The small forge is alight, Mr Gudjieff is planing, a Mr Salzmann[1] is making wheels. Later on I shall learn carpentry. We are going to learn as many trades as possible, also all kinds of farm work. The cows are being bought today. Gurdjieff is going to build a high couch in the stable where I can sit & inhale their breath! I know later on I shall be put in charge of those cows. Everyone calls them already "Mrs Murrys cows".

This letter must be posted, love. Do please forgive my two silly ones. I learn terribly slowly, my precious Veen,[2] & I must not hurt you.

Ever your own
Wig.

I am making a cure of goats milk – 4 times a day!

MS ATL. *LKM* II. 264; *LJMM*, 682–3.

---

[1] Alexander de Salzmann, at various times a painter, inventor, Benedictine monk, dervish, and stage-designer, and an early follower of Gurdjieff.
[2] Yet another of KM's nicknames for Murry.

To Harold Beauchamp, 2 November 1922

Le Prieuré | Fontainebleau-Avon | France
ii 11 1922

Dearest Father,

I have been thinking of you so often this month as it is your birthday.[1] I hope you have a very fine day for it; I can hardly imagine a more enjoyable gift. It was most delightful to hear from you at Port Said and to know that your voyage, as far as climatic conditions were concerned, was so far successful. I only hope the blue sky and sea continued.

I have a minor misfortune to relate in connection with my second series of X-ray treatment. This time almost immediately my heart began to play up and after two applications I could hardly move at all. I felt extremely ill and disappointed, but it was out of the question to continue. But my black cloud showed what is apparently its silver lining quite soon. I got into touch with some other Russian (Russians seem to haunt me) doctors who claim to cure hearts of all kinds by means of a system of gentle exercises and movements. They are established at Fontainebleau where their method is put into practice. So down I came to *concentrate* (as old V. would say) on my heart for the next few months and then to see what I can do with my wings. Its very unlucky that I always have these chapters of accidents to recount but, you know, dearest, I feel they are in the picture for me for the moment.

I am as confident as ever I was that my lean years will be followed by fat ones. The one great thing, I believe, is to keep on trying. Not to give up and not to accept the life of an invalid. I am determined to regain my health, but it may take a little longer than I had hoped. All is very snug here, and I feel my general condition is a great deal better already. That is enough of me and *illness*.

I heard from Marie yesterday that she & little J and man intend to spend the winter in town. I am still sorry that little J. has married her Charles at this stage of the proceedings. It seemed to me an unwise move, as looked at from the outside. Jack, who was at the wedding, said she looked exactly like a child with tears of happiness in her eyes and that Charles looked very much the triumphant young man! Well he might, too, to have gained such a treasure. I find it difficult to feel for Charles as I should like to, but perhaps he will turn up trumps, and I am hardly the person to criticise such affairs of others.

This has been, so far, the most beautiful autumn. Today it was as clear and as dry as Switzerland. I am living here in a large chateau which has been taken and is being run by the Russians. The rooms are most lovely and to the picturesqueness is joined central heating and hot and cold water – most important at this season of the year. I am so longing to have your first letter from New Zealand. Was the Grange looking lovely?[2] What a joy to feel one is turned towards summer again . . . I receive the happiest letters from Jack who is as busy as usual. My 'busyness' is revealed in my hand writing which, bad at the best of times, is far worse owing to an attack of writers cramp. It is a most annoying complaint because it is so unimportant, and comes 'off and on' when one least expects it.

I heard from Doctor Sorapure last week. *Not* the letter I much care for, but an account for my London visits. I can't help feeling that doctors earn their money a great deal more easily than the rest of the world.

I wonder if you have seen Elizabeths new book?[3] I received it from her this week & read it immediately. My private opinion is it is very *tame* and even *tiresome*. I think she works her jokes about husbands and God far too hard. I am thoroughly bored by her comic husbands and equally bored by their wives. But perhaps I was not in the mood for that kind of thing. I shall find it very difficult to write to her about it.

I wonder if you happen to have come across a novel called "The Brimming Cup" by an American woman. The name of the writer is Dorothy Canfield.[4] It seemed to me a most charming book and extremely clever. I read Hutchinson's "This Freedom", too. It seemed to me the most fearful twaddle. But no doubt it has brought him in about £15,000. Very nice for him.

Well, darling, I must finish this letter & try & waggle my thumb into action again. One very pleasant thing here is that I have to speak Russian consistently and shall I hope, get as fluent in it as I am in French and German. After that I should like to rub up my Italian. Languages *fascinate* me.

Goodbye for now, my darling Father. I do hope your health is good, that all is well with you in every possible way. You are in my thoughts so often. I shall always wish we were nearer.

Ever your devoted child
Kass

MS Newberry.

[1] Her father was born on 15 Nov. 1858.
[2] Her father's handsome home in Wadestown, a hill suburb above Wellington city.
[3] *The Enchanted April* had just been published.
[4] Dorothy Canfield's *The Brimming Cup* was one of the best selling novels of 1921.

To Ida Baker, [2 November 1922]

[Le Prieuré, Fontainebleau-Avon]

Dear Ida

Forgive my harshness. Of course I have thought better of it & am ashamed. The galoshes & garters have come so has the black coat. Thank you v. much. The green skirt *never* came. I should indeed have liked it. Nor did the coat & skirt. I am all coats & no skirts – most awkward. What good soap! Thank you for it. Dont forget to let me know where you go after the hotel. These letters came for you. The weather is glorious here, too, like late spring. Still, I am so thankful for the galoshes. Do please tell me by return what I owe you.

Excuse this note. It is written in such haste. I do want one other thing. A perfectly plain chemise frock to wear without a petticoat to do exercises in the evening. You know the kind of thing. Cashmere would do – I mean a thin gabardine or anything like that – *dead* simple, though & preferably dark blue with as little lining as possible. But it mustnt show ones legs through. Shall I send you 500 francs?

Yours ever
K.M.

MS BL.

To Ida Baker, [6 November 1922]

[Le Prieuré, Fontainebleau-Avon]

Dear Ida

Here is 500 francs. How long will the Gay-Lussac address be yours? Let me know in time. Sometimes letters get delayed here for a day or two – very rarely, but just in case, I give you warning. I am so glad to have the green skirt. The black coat is like most of the other things much too small – two sizes too small, arms too short. And I *have* one black velvet jacket – why a black plush? I wish I could send it back to you. I so hate hard things that stand out, like plush. Will you tell me just what money you have? How much more than 1000 francs have you spent is what I want to know. The mouth pastilles you sent me are also useless. They do not dissolve in either hot or cold water. I TERRIBLY need a good mouth antiseptic, a good toothbrush, and some toothpicks. Also *water softener,* & an antiseptic like Condy.[1] I think & hope that will be the end of my needs. Of course I take back my words about the tops & knickers.

Yours ever
K.M.

MS BL.

---

[1] Condy's crystals, potassium permanganate used in a weak solution as an antiseptic.

To Ida Baker, [7 November 1922]

[Le Prieuré, Fontainebleau-Avon]

Dear Ida

I wrote to you at the Select Hotel & the letter was only posted on Saturday, I believe. I sent a cheque with it. Let me know if you have not received it.

The coat & skirt has come; it looks very nice & very useful. The coat is a little small for that kind of coat. I wish you could understand it is part of your "illness" (in the sense we are all of us ill) to believe I eat nothing and am the size of a pin.

I hope you like your farm.

Yours ever
K.M.

MS BL.

To J. M. Murry, [10 November 1922]

[Le Prieuré, Fontainebleau-Avon]

£5 note enclosed.

My darling Bogey

I had a letter from you today saying you had bought a pruning knife. I hope you succeed with the old trees. Here it is part of the 'work' to do a great many things, especially things which one does *not* like. I see the point of that. It's the same principle as facing people whom one shrinks from and so on. It is to develop a greater range in oneself. But what happens in practice is that no sooner do the people begin doing those things they don't like than the dislike changes. One feels it no longer. Its only that first step which is so terribly hard to take.

Are you having really divine weather? Its marvellous here – like late spring today, really *warm*. The leaves are still falling. The part belonging to this chateau is incredibly beautiful, and with our live stock roaming about it begins to look like a little piece of virgin creation.

I am fearfully busy. What do I do? Well, I learn Russian, which is a terrific job, have charge of the indoor carnations – no joke, & spend the rest of the day paying visits to places where people are working. Then every evening about 50 people meet in the salon and there is music and they are working at present at a tremendous ancient Assyrian Group Dance. I have no words with which to describe it. To see it seems to change ones whole being for the time.

Until I came here I did not realise with what a little bit of my mind, even, I lived. I was a little European with a liking for eastern carpets and music and for something that I vaguely called The East. But now I feel as though I am turned to that side far more than the other. The west seems so poor so scattered. I cannot believe knowledge or wisdom are there. I expect this is a phase. I tell it you because I said I would tell you my react-ions . . . In three weeks here I feel I have spent years in India, Arabia, Afghanistan, Persia. That is very odd, isn't it. And oh, how one wanted to voyage like this – how bound one felt. Only now I know!

There is another thing here. Friendship. The real thing that you and I have dreamed of. Here it exists between women & women & men & women & one feels it is unalterable, and living in a way it never can be anywhere else. I cant say I have friends yet. I am simply not fit for them. I don't know myself enough to be really trusted, and I am weak where these people are strong. But even the relationships I have are dear beyond any friendships I have known.

But I am giving the impression that we all live together in brotherly love & blissful happiness. Not at all. One suffers terribly. If you have been ill for 5 years you cant expect to be well in five weeks. If you have been ill for 20 years & according to Mr Gurdjieff we all of us have our 'illness' it takes very severe measures to put one right. But the point is there is hope. One can & does believe that one will escape from living in circles & will live a CONSCIOUS life. One can, through work, escape from falsity & be true to ones own self – not to what anyone else on earth thinks one is.

I wish you could meet some of the men here. You would like them very very much, especially a Mr Salzmann, who speaks very little. I must stop this letter. Is it a rigmarole?

I don't know what you mean darling by seeing me as an angel with a sword. I don't feel at all like one. There is another thing. You can't *really* be happy in my happiness. No one ever is. That phrase is only a kind of buffer – don't you think? Its like people living through their children. Well, they may do it. But its not life. Neither can I ever teach you how to live. How is it possible? You are you. I am I. We can only lead our own lives together.

But perhaps I am treating too seriously what you said.

Goodbye for now, my darling heart.

Ever your
Wig.

I enclose a £5 note. Will you pay Heals bill & keep the rest for any odd bills I may send you later. I know there are some. If you know anyone coming to Paris *do* give them 2 pairs of grey Milanese stockings (for size 5 shoes) to post on to me. I need them awfully. Merci en avance.

MS ATL. *LJMM*, 683–5.

To Ida Baker, [10 November 1922]

[Le Prieuré, Fontainebleau-Avon]

Dear Ida

I do not think Lisieux is a good idea.[1] It is too isolated. You need people & interchange of relationships to take you out of yourself. You will only get depressed and *dull* at the farm, I should think. That is my opinion. Would not the Palace at Montana be better? Or that V.A.D. place at Menton?[2] Or why not write to Jinnie F? [Fullerton] She might have an idea. I think it would be worse than folly to live a lonely life. Surely you know your need of people! Any kind of isolation is only possible for very great strong people.

Why are you so tragic? It does not help. It only hinders you. If you suffer, learn to understand your suffering but don't give way to it. The part of you that lived through me has to die – then *you* will be born. Get the dying over! But remember you will teach yourself nothing alone on a farm. You are not the type.

No, it makes no difference to me if you are in Paris or not . . . How I am? I am learning to live. But I have not 'disappeared'. Later I may go to Paris or London or Berlin or anywhere & we could meet and have a talk. I am far less disappeared than ever I was.

I meant the cheque to be 500. *Please cash it* and use it.

As for the clothes, later, I shall alter them myself.

But do you see that our relationship was absolutely wrong now? You were identified with me. I prevented you from living at all. Now you have to learn & its terribly hard.

Keep my keys, please. Write to me whenever you wish to.

Yours
K.M.

If you loved as you imagine you do how could you make such a moan because I was no longer helpless. Try & look at it like that.

MS BL. *MLM*, 217–18.

[1] Where Ida was considering taking work on a farm.
[2] See p. 125, n. 4.

To Ida Baker, [11 November 1922]

[Le Prieuré, Fontainebleau-Avon]

My dear Ida

I am hoping this may reach you before you leave Paris. A major-minor misfortune has happened to me. I have had stolen 3 weeks laundry including as you must know nearly all my underclothes. Pyjamas, crepe de chine nightgown, tricot de nuit, 3 pantalons, 3 'tops' (my best, of course), 3 stockings, wooly petticoat, knickers, 18 handkerchiefs & so on. If you are in Paris will you please go to the Galeries[1] or anywhere you think and fit me out again? Ill make a list of what I want. As regards the woolen petty & knickers they are best bought at the Magasin Jones, Avenue Victor Hugo *or* 24 Rue de Villejust where you buy cream woolen chemise & knickers at 20 francs the set. Quite plain, little closed shape knickers bound in cream silk. The other things I want are 3 tops (can you make them? Quite plain crepe or anything, bound with silk – *cream* I think for the colour of the tops.) 3 knickers (buy them. You can't make them. Quite plain again as I shall have to wash & iron them plus tard.) 1 tricot de nuit (cream if possible). 3 pairs woolen stockings (grey & not thick. There is no difference between thick & thin wool.) $1\frac{1}{2}$ dozen handkerchiefs – quite simple. 1 crepe nightgown. The others I have are too thin. The pyjamas I must let go. The nightgown I would prefer to be just a hole cut in the middle, the sides sewn up and a ribbon from the sides to tie at the waist at the back like I did my tops.

You know that red shawl you made me. Can you make me a cream one embroidered in cream?

Thats all. Its quite enough. Everything else has come. Send me the whole amount please & I will send a cheque by return. If you can't do these things, tell me and I will attack the shops. Its an awful curse to have had this loss but there you are and I am not alone in it. I shall never send another shred out of any kind.

I hope you are feeling better – The weather here is very good.

Yours ever
K.M.

MS BL. *MLM*, 218–19.

---

[1]   Galeries Lafayette, a large art nouveau-style department store on boulevard Haussmann.

To J. M. Murry, [12 November 1922]

[Le Prieuré, Fontainebleau-Avon]

Darling Bogey,

I have 2 letters of yours to answer. What a queer situation with regard to Sylvia Sullivan. Poor L.E.[1] That is what comes of trying to help people without *knowing* how to. It only aggravates their disorders. Don't you find Sylvia S. attractive at all? I feel there is a certain personality in you which would be greatly drawn to her. I am surprised that her relations with Sullivan are not good. He gave me to understand that Dunning had convinced him completely of – not only *her* need of him but of *his* of her. I am so sorry for you when you speak of your life as emerging from your study & disappearing into it again. Don't you *sicken* of shutting that door & sitting down to that table? One feels like a spider in an empty house. For whom this web. Why do I strain to spin and spin? Here, I confess, after only five weeks, there are things I *long* to write! Oh, how I long to! But I shall not for a long time. Nothing is ready. I must wait until la maison est *pleine*. I must say the dancing here has given me quite a different approach to writing. I mean some of the very ancient Oriental dance. There is one which takes about 7 minutes & it contains the whole life of woman – but everything! Nothing is left out. It taught me, it gave me more of woman's life than any book or poem. There was even room for Flaubert's Coeur Simple[2] in it & for Princess Marya[3] . . . mysterious. By the way I have had a great talk about Shakespeare here with a man called Salzmann, who is by 'profession' a painter. He knows & understands the plays far better than anyone I have met except you. He happens, too (this is by the way) to be a great friend of Olga Knippers.[4] His wife[5] is the chief dancer here – a very beautiful woman with a marvellous intelligence.

Dear Bogey I am not 'hypnotised'. But it does seem to me there are certain people here who are far beyond any I have met – of a quite different order. Some – most – of the English here don't even catch a glimpse of it. But I am sure. I remember I used to think – if there was one thing I could not bear in a community it would be the women. But now the women are nearer & far dearer than the men – of course I don't speak of Mr Gurdjieff. I couldn't say he was *near* or *dear* to me! He is the embodiment of the life here, but at a remote distance.

Since last I wrote to you I have changed my room. Now I am in another wing – another kind of existence altogether. Where all was so quiet outside the door all is noise & bustle. My other room was very rich & sumptuous. This is small & plain & very simple. When Olga Ivanovna & I had arranged it & she had hung her yellow dancing stockings to dry before the fire we sat together on the bed & felt like two quite poor young girls.... different beings, altogether. I like being here very much. I hope Mr Gurdjieff does not move us again too soon. But it is a favourite habit of his to set the whole house walking. Easy to see why when one saw the emotions it aroused.

About my stockings, darling. I heard from Ida today saying she goes to England tomorrow & would like to see you. She intends to return to France where she goes to work on some farm. Would you give the stockings to her? Ill ask her to write to you. I never think of Ida except when I get letters from her. Poor Ida! When I do I am sorry for her. I must finish this letter, darling. It is written on the arm of a chair, on a cushion on my bed, as I try to escape from the heat of my fire. Oh – I have so much to do this afternoon! Its terrible how the days pass. I had a bath this morning for the first time since leaving England! There's a nice confession. But its wonderful what can be done with a basin and a rough towel.

Have you read Elizabeths new novel? What do you think of it? Please tell me! How is your gardening getting on? Have you learnt to drive the car?

Goodbye my dear darling.

Ever your
Wig.

MS ATL. *LJMM*, 685–6.

[1] Sullivan married Sylvia Mannooch in 1917 and had two children, but the marriage was a difficult one (including Sylvia's recent affair with the diabolist and author, Aleister Crowley). She left Sullivan in 1921, and there were now complications with Vivian Locke-Ellis.

[2] *Un Coeur Simple*, the first of the stories in Gustave Flaubert's *Trois Contes* (1877), documents the dull self-sacrificing life of a devoted servant.

[3] Princess Marya, a romantic and forceful character in Leo Tolstoy's *War and Peace* (1865–72).

[4] Olga Knipper (1869–1959). One of the original members of the Moscow Arts Theatre, she took leading roles in Konstantin Stanislavsky's productions of Chekov's plays, and married the playwright in 1901.

[5] Jeanne de Salzmann, who remained an enthusiastic follower of Gurdjieff until his death in 1949, and at this time worked closely with him in choreographing therapeutic dance.

To Ida Baker, [13 November 1922]

[Le Prieuré, Fontainebleau-Avon]

Dear Ida

I have forgotten your Lewes address.[1] Please send it me. And tell me how long you will be in England, will you? I have asked Jack to give you some stockings to bring me. Id like another wrap, too, like my red one, but *cream* & another pair of slippers from Lewis[2] just like the ones I have. But Ill let you know, later. Jack seems v. well & v. happy. Do see him! I am so grateful for my toilet accessories. They are a comfort. The blue dress is about 2 miles too long. It trails. I shall have to take it up about ½ a yard for dancing.

DONT make me woollen tops please or woollen knickers. I don't need them. Id rather have a few thin crepe tops – I need *them* urgently, & some ribbons for head bands. Why did I ever throw away what I have thrown away!

Bon Voyage.

Yours ever
K.M.

MS BL.

[1] Where Ida would stay with her aunt.   [2] John Lewis, the Oxford Street department store.

To J. M. Murry, [19 November 1922]

[Le Prieuré, Fontainebleau-Avon]
Sunday 6.30

Darling Bogey

The affaire at Selsfield does so puzzle me. L-E is not at all the man we thought he was if he has made it or allowed it to be difficult for you to be there any longer. Why is it? Is Sylvia to be a permanency? What are the arrangements. I would like to know; they seem so strange.

I am thankful you have your little flat, darling. Rob mine to make yours snug. Take all you can or care to away. But do you keep warm enough? And what about food, I wonder? I have asked Ida to buy me a number of things while she is in England & to bring them over to Paris with her. Bogey, I have not got a cheque book for the moment. Would you send her a cheque for £10.0.0 on my behalf? Ill let you have it back in a week or two. But would you send it at once? As Ida is going to stay such a short while in England. Thank you, dearest.

It is intensely cold here. Quite as cold as Switzerland. But it does not matter in the same way. One has not the time to think about it. There is always something happening and people are a support. I spent the winter afternoon yesterday scraping carrots – masses of carrots – & half way through I suddenly thought of my bed in the corner of that room at the Chalet des Sapins...Oh how is it possible there is such a difference between that loneliness and isolation (just waiting for you to come in & you knowing I was waiting) and *this*. People were running in and out of the kitchen. Portions of the first pig we have killed were on the table and greatly admired. Coffee was roasting in the oven. Barker cluttered through with his milk pail. I must tell you, darling, my love of cows persists. We now have three. They are real beauties – immense – with short curly hair? fur? wool? between their horns. Geese, too, have been added to the establishment. They seem full of intelligence. I am becoming absorbed in animals, not to watch only but to know how to care for them & to know *about* them. Why does one live so far away from all these things? Bees we shall have later. I am determined to know about bees.

Your idea of buying some land & building a little house *does* seem to me a bit premature, darling. You know so little. You have never tried your hand at such things. Its not quite easy to change from an intellectual life like yours to a life of hard physical work. But your remark made me wish you did care for my 'ideas'. I mean by my 'ideas' my desire *to learn to work in the right way* and to live as a conscious human being. They are not more than that. There is certainly no other spot on this whole planet where one can be taught as one is taught here. But Life is not easy. We have great 'difficulties' – painful moments, and Mr Gurdjieff is there to do to us what we wish to do to ourselves and are afraid to do. Well, theoretically that is very wonderful, but practically it must mean suffering, because one cannot always understand.

Ouspensky came over last week. I had a short talk with him. He is a very fine man. I wish you would just see him – out of – lets call it curiosity.

I must get dressed for dinner. I badly need a good *washing*. Remarkable how clothes fall into their proper place here. We dress in the evening but during the day...the men look like brigands. Nobody cares, nobody dreams of criticising.

Oh, Bogey how I love this place! It is like a dream – or a miracle. What do the 'silly' people matter & there are silly people who come from London, see nothing & go away again. There *is* something marvellous here – if one can only attain it.

Goodbye for now, my dearest.

Ever your own
Wig.

I will write Elizabeth.

MS ATL. *LJMM*, 687–8.

To Ida Baker, [23 November 1922]

[Le Prieuré, Fontainebleau-Avon]

Dear Ida

I hasten to answer your letter. Please buy me NO dress of any kind and NO shoes. This is final! I cant risk the wrong things again & I prefer to go without. Please understand I am absolutely fixed in my mind about this. No dress, no shoes, no material for dress!

As from this week I have no more money so I can't buy any more clothes. I don't want them, either. The coats were in the Paris box, I am sure. Please pack that small silky blanket of mine as well, if possible, with the eiderdown.

Excuse a hasty note. I am busy and my pen is not good. I hope you like seeing Jack & that all goes well with you. Thank you for your letter with the snapshots of the cat.

When I say I have no money I do not mean I have not always money for you when you need it. I have. You have only to ask – so ask *please*.

Yours ever

K.M.

What a pity you and Jack could not start a small farm together. Why don't you suggest it if you like him enough.

MS BL. *MLM*, 219–20.

To J. M. Murry, [c.24 November 1922]

[Le Prieuré, Fontainebleau-Avon]

My darling Bogey

I have received your letter saying you will leave Selsfield & that L.E. and Sylvia are to join forces. It sounds a very bad arrangement to me – I mean for L.E. and Sylvia. They are nothing to each other as types – in fact they are so far apart as to be almost different kinds of beings. However – I don't suppose it matters.

I hope you & Sullivan do find a place together in the country somewhere near Dunning.[1] I am glad you feel Selsfield is too luxurious. It is very very lovely but it is not living. There is too much 'dinner is served, Sir' about it. Do you ever feel inclined to get into touch with Lawrence again? I wonder. I should like very much to know what he intends to do – how he intends to live, now his Wanderjahre are over.[2] He and E.M. Forster[3] are two men who *could* understand this place if they would. But I think Lawrence's pride would keep him back.[4] No one person here is more important than another. That may not sound much of a statement, but practically it is very much.

I shall be interested to hear of your meeting with Ida. That reminds me again of the stockings which arrived in perfect order. What an extraordinary brainwave to hide them in the Times. They are very lovely stockings, too, just the shade I like in the evening. Ones legs are like legs by moonlight.

It is intensely cold here – colder and colder. I have just been brought some small fat pine logs to mix with my boulets.[5] Boulets are unsatisfactory; they are too passive. I simply live in my fur coat. I gird it on like my heavenly armour and wear it ever night and day. After this winter the Arctic even will have no terrors for me. Happily the sun *does* shine as well and we are thoroughly well nourished. But I shall be glad when the year has turned.

Darling I must sit down to a Russian lesson. I wish you knew Russian. I have also been learning mental arithmetic beginning $2 \times 2 = 1$ $3 \times 3 = 12$ $4 \times 4 = 13$ $5 \times 5 = 28$ and so on at great speed to the accompaniment of music. Its not as easy as it looks especially when you start from the wrong end backwards. In fact at 34 I am beginning my education.

I can't write to E. about her book. I thought it so dreadfully tiresome and silly. It didn't seem to me like a fairy tale; I saw no fairies. In fact I saw nobody. And jokes about husbands, double beds, God and trousers don't amuse me, Im afraid. In fact it seemed to me a sad tinkle from an old musicbox.

Goodbye for now, my dearest Bogey

Ever your own
Wig.

MS ATL. *LKM* II. 264; *LJMM*, 688–9.

[1] JMM and Sullivan would move to Wayside Cottage, Ditchling, Sussex, which their friend Dunning found for them.
[2] In fact Lawrence was then in New Mexico, and would continue to travel out of England until his death in 1929.
[3] Edward Morgan Forster (1879–1970), novelist, short-story writer and essayist. Although KM did not know him well, and had reviewed his fiction indifferently, her opinion of him as a man was high.
[4] As would his loathing for Ouspensky's *Tertium Organum*. Lawrence's annotated copy in the Taos Public Library preserves his detestation.
[5] Coal nuts.

To J. M. Murry, [c.27 November 1922]

[Le Prieuré, Fontainebleau-Avon]

My darling Bogey

I understand affairs much better from your last letter. I am v. glad you are going to be near Dunning. Of course I do not feel that my way is 'the only way'. It is for me. But people have such hidden energy, such hidden strength that once they discover it in themselves why should they not do alone what we learn to do here? You were only joking, weren't you, when you said you might find Le Prieuré was your way, too. For one can only come here via Ouspensky, & *it is a serious step*. However, one can always go again if one finds it intolerable. That is true, too. But the strangeness of all that happens here has a meaning, and by strangeness I don't mean obvious strangeness – theres little of it – I mean spiritual.

Are you having really perfect weather (except for the cold). It is absolutely brilliantly sunny, a deep blue sky, dry air. Really its better than Switzerland. But I must get some wool lined overboots. My footgear is ridiculous when I am where I was yesterday – round about the pig sty. It is noteworthy that the pigs have of themselves divided their sty into two. One, the clean part, they keep clean & sleep in. This makes me look at pigs with a different eye. One must be impartial even about them, it seems. We have 2 more cows, about to calve in 3 weeks time. Very thrilling. Also our white goat is about to have a little kid. I want to see it very much. They are so charming.

You know I told you a Turkish Bath was being built. It is finished & working. It was made from a cave used for vegetables & of course all labour including the plumbing, the lighting & so on done by our people. Now one can have seven different kinds of baths in it & there is a little rest room hung with carpets which looks more like Bokhara than Avon. If you have seen this evolved it really is a miracle of ingenuity. Everything is designed by Mr Gurdjieff. Now all hands are busy building the theatre which is to be ready in 2 weeks. I have to start making costumes next week. All the things I have avoided in life seem to find me out here. I shall have to sew for hours on end just as I have to puzzle over these problems in mathematics that we get sometimes in the evening.

But I wish I could tell you of the people I live with. There is not only my friend Olga Ivanovna. There are the Hartmanns, husband & wife. He was – is – a musician she is a singer.[1] They live in one smallish room, awfully cramped I suppose. But to go & sit there with them in the evening before dinner is one of my greatest pleasures. Dear precious people! She is very quick, beautiful, warmhearted. No, its no good. I cant describe her. He is small & quite bald, with a little pointed beard & he generally wears a loose blouse spotted with whitewash, very full trousers, wooden boots. He is a 'common workman' all day. But it is the life between them; the feeling one has in their nearness. But so many people come forward as I write. They are all very different; but they are the people I have wanted to find – *real* people – not people I make up or invent. Tell me about your new plans when you can, my darling, will you? Was L.M. just the same? It is a horrible thing; I have almost forgotten her. And only 2 months ago it seemed I could not have lived without her care. Do Dunnings children have lessons? Why don't you offer to teach them something.

Its good to be in touch with children; one learns very much. Goodbye for now, my darling Bogey. I do feel we are nearer than we were. But there is so much, so very much one cannot write. One can only feel.

Ever your own
Wig.

MS ATL. *LKM* II. 265; *LJMM*, 689–90.

---

[1] Thomas de Hartmann (1886–1956), whose ballet *The Pink Flower* was performed at the Imperial Opera in 1907. He served as an army officer, and lived as a painter in Munich, before he and his wife Olga joined Gurdjieff in 1917. Later the two men collaborated closely in compositions for sacred dance. His memoir *Our Life with Mr Gurdjieff* was published in 1964. His wife Olga de Schumaker would be one of the witnesses named on KM's death certificate.

To J. M. Murry, [1 December 1922]

[Le Prieuré, Fontainebleau-Avon]
Friday: Piatnitse.

My darling Bogey

I seem to have snapped at that £10 like a dog with a bone, and I never even said merci in my last letter. I am most awfully grateful for it. I accept it with joy, though I *did* mean – yes, truly – to send it back to you. Did you see L.M. I wonder? Wayside Cottage reminded me of Rose Tree Cottage.[1] The name only. They are of the same type. I hope you are snug in it. I suppose you couldn't (or wouldnt care to) snare L.M. as working house-keeper & gardener. I dont see Sullivan as a great help in such matters. But perhaps I wrong him.

About Christmas. I want to be quite frank. For many reasons I would rather we did not meet till the spring. Hear my reasons before judging me for that, will you? For one the hotels at Fontainebleau are closed – the decent ones. You could not come to the Institute as a guest at present. Its not running smoothly enough. You would simply *hate* it. No, let me be very careful. I have not asked Mr Gurdjieff if you could come. He might say 'yes' but I can't [see] what on earth an outsider could do here just now. Its winter. One can't be out of doors. One can't just stay in one's room. Meals are at all hours. Sometimes lunch is at 4 p.m. & dinner at 10 p.m. And so on. But the chief *reason that matters* is this. Physically there is very little outward change in my condition so far. I am still breathless, I still cough, still walk upstairs slowly, still have to stop and so on. The difference is that here I make 'efforts' of a certain kind all day & live an entirely different life. But I have absolutely no life to *share* at present. You can't sit in the cow house with me at present or in the kitchen with seven or eight people. We are not ready for that yet. It would simply be a false position. Then when I first came here I had a most sumptuous luxurious room and so on. Now I rough it in a little, simple, but very warm room. But its tiny. We couldn't sit in it. Deeper still is the most sincere feeling I am capable of that I do not want to see you until I am better physically. I cannot see you until the old Wig has disappeared. Associations, recollections would be too much for me just now. I must get better alone. This will mean that we do not meet until the spring. If this sounds selfish it must sound selfish. I know it is not and I know it is necessary. If you do not understand it please tell me, darling.

I don't feel the cold as much as I have in other winters. Its often sunny, too & I have just bought for 23 francs very good *boots* lined with felt with felt uppers. But Ill say no more just now. I hope you will understand & not be hurt by my letter, dearest heart.

Ever your
Wig.

MS ATL. *LJMM*, 691–2.

<hr>

[1] KM had lived with JMM at Rose Tree Cottage, The Lee, near Great Missenden, a few miles from the Lawrences at Chesham, from late Oct. 1914 until she left for Paris in Mar. 1915.

To Ida Baker, [2 December 1922]

[Le Prieuré, Fontainebleau-Avon]

Dear Ida

In case this letter reaches you in time & you have the money, please buy me the warmest skirt and jumper & knitted coat you can find in a darkish colour – the coat a large size. Its against the cold.

Yours ever,
K.M.

MS BL.

To J. M. Murry, [6 December 1922]

[Le Prieuré, Fontainebleau-Avon]
Wednesday

My darling Bogey

Your Sunday letter arrived today. Until I have your answer to mine suggesting that we do not meet until the spring I will not refer to the subject again . . . I think that's best.

Your little house and way of life sounds so nice. I am very very glad that you feel Dunning is your friend. Do you have something of your Lawrence feeling for him?[1] I imagine it is a little bit the same. And Mrs Dunning[2] – you like her? And do you play with the little boys?

There are nine children here. They live in the childrens house and have a different mother every week to look after them. But I remember now I have told you all that before. Ill tell you instead about that couch Mr Gurdjieff has had built in the cowhouse. Its simply too lovely. There is a small steep staircase to a little railed off gallery above the cows. On the little gallery are divans covered with persian carpets (only two divans). But the whitewashed walls and ceiling have been decorated most exquisitely in what looks like a persian pattern of yellow, red and blue by Mr Salzmann. Flowers, little birds, butterflies, and a spreading tree with animals on the branches, even a hippopotamus. But Bogey all done with the most *real art* – a little masterpiece. And all so gay, so simple, reminding me of summer grasses and the kind of flowers that smell like milk. There I go every day to lie and later I am going to sleep there. Its very warm. One has the most happy feelings listening to the beasts & looking. I know that one day I shall write a long long story about it. At about 5.30 the door opens and Mr Ivanov comes in, lights the lantern and begins milking. I had quite forgotten the singing wiry silvery sound of milk falling into an empty pail & then heavier plonk–plonk! 'Mr' Ivanov is a very young man, he looks as though he had just finished his studies, rather shy, with a childlike beaming smile.

I don't know how you feel. But I still find it fearfully hard to cope with people I do not like or who are not sympathetic. With the others all goes well. But living here with all kinds I am simply appaled at my helplessness when I want to get rid of someone or to extricate myself from a conversation, even. But I *have* learnt how to do it, here. I have learnt that the only way is to court it, not to avoid it, to face it. Terribly difficult for me, in practice. But until I really do master this I cannot get anywhere. There always comes the moment when I am uncovered, so zu sagen, and the other man gets in his knockout blow.

Oh, darling, I am always meaning to ask you this. I came away this time without a single photograph of you. This is *intolerable*. I really must have one, Bogey. Not only because I want it fearfully for myself but people keep on asking me. And I am proud of you. I want to show them what you look like. Do please send me one for Xmas. This is very important.

Goodbye for now, my own Bogey. I am ever your loving

Wig.

MS ATL. *LKM* II. 265; *LJMM*, 692–3.

---

[1] Although their disputes were intense and sometimes bitter, the friendship between Lawrence and Murry was based on an initial deep attraction for each other.

[2] The friendship with Dunning was tested the next year, when his wife 'Bill' Dunning fell in love with Murry.

To J. M. Murry, [9 December 1922]

[Le Prieuré, Fontainebleau-Avon]

Saturday.

My darling Bogey

I have never had a letter from you that I so 'understood' as your last about your house & how you are living & the wages you gave to John & Nicholas.[1] I can't say what a joy it is to know you are there. It seems to me very mysterious how so many of us nowadays refuse to be cave dwellers any longer but in our several ways are trying to learn to escape. The old London life, whatever it was, but even the life we have led recently wherever we have been is no longer even *possible* to me. It is so far from me that it seems to exist in another world. This of course is a wrong feeling. For, after all, there are the seeds of what we long after in everybody and if one remembers that any surroundings are possible . . . at least.

What do you read? Has Dunning any unfamiliar books?[2] You have rather a horror of anything at all . . . Eastern – haven't you? I read Ouspensky's Tertium Organum[3] the other day. For some reason it didn't carry me away. I think it is extremely interesting but – perhaps I was not in the mood for books. I am not at present, though I know that in the future I shall want to write them more than anything else in the world. But different books. There is Mr Hartmann here with whom I have great talks nearly every evening about *how* and *why* and when. I confess present day literature simply nauseates me, excepting always Hardy and the other few whose names I cant remember . . . But the general trend of it seems to me quite without any value whatever.

Yesterday when I was in the stable Mr Salzmann came up. He had just returned from his work – sawing logs in the far wood. And we began to talk about poverty. He was talking of the absolute need for us today to be *poor again*, but poor in the real sense. To be poor in ideas, in imagination, in impulses, in wishes, to be simple, in fact. To get rid of the immense collection with which our minds are crammed and to get back to our real needs. But I shall not try to transcribe what he said. It sounds banal; it was not. I hope you will meet this man one day. He looks a very surly, angry and even fierce workman. He is haggard, drawn, old looking with grey hair cut in a fringe on his forehead. He dresses like a very shabby forester and carries a large knife in his belt. I like him almost as much as I like his wife. Together they seem to me as near an ideal couple as I could imagine.

Bogey are you having fine weather? Today is perfectly glorious. There was a heavy frost last night but its marvellously clear and fine. No, I don't want any money just now, thank you, darling heart. What nonsense to say those W.S. [War Savings] certificates are mine. Why? They are yours! And don't go building a 7 roomed house. 7 rooms for 2 people! I will write again in a day or two. Goodbye for now, dearest darling Bogey.

Ever your own
Wig.

Don't forget the photograph!

MS ATL. *LKM* II. 265–6; *LJMM*, 693–4.

[1] Dunning's sons.

[2] JMM replied to KM (17 Dec. 1922), 'As a matter of fact I have begun to read something Eastern, or rather something odder than Eastern,... And in a queer way I was *very much* impressed by it. Moreover I've promised Dunning that I will read an Indian book on, I think, Rama Yoga' (Murry, 366).

[3] P. D. Ouspensky, *Tertium Organum* (1912), whose title page reads in capitals, 'A key to the enigmas of the world, the mystery of space and time, shadows and reality, occultism and love. Animated nature. Voices of the stones. Mathematics of the infinite. The logic of ecstasy. Mystical theosophy cosmic consciousness. The new morality. Birth of the superman.'

To Viscountess Rothermere,[1] *10 December 1922*

[Le Prieuré, Fontainebleau-Avon]

10
Xii
1922

My dear Lady Rothermere.

I was so glad to hear from you, so sorry to know you are not coming to Fontainebleau until January. I have been hoping, for days, to hear of your arrival. We miss you here awfully.
[letter incomplete]

TC Texas.

[1] Mary Lillian Shere (d. 1937) married the press magnate Harold Sidney Harmsworth, 1st Viscount Rothermere, in 1897. Beautiful, unconventional and generous, she became for a time a pupil of Ouspensky, providing funds for Gurdjieff to purchase Le Prieuré, and was the financial backer for T. S. Eliot to found his quarterly, the *Criterion*, in 1922.

To Ida Baker, [12 December 1922]

[Le Prieuré, Fontainebleau-Avon]

My dear Ida

Many thanks for your two letters. The postman has told me this morning that my 6 colis are awaiting me at the post office. I'll send you a line when I have 'examined' them. I am sure they will be very nice. I will also send you a cheque for 300 francs for the coat & skirt in the course of a day or two. If that suits you. I hope you like your farm. Jean S.[1] is a very good youngish writer, I believe. You ought to try & get hold of his books in your library. Thank you for telling me about Jack. He sounds happy. I dont think I can talk 'fully' about my suggestion that you should join him in a farm. It seemed to me for many reasons a very good idea and I suppose I *had* deep reasons. But such explanations are futile. He wrote as though he liked the idea but you were not very keen, & mentioned the fact that beautiful hand weaving is done at Ditchling which might interest you to learn. I think it would be very well worth while for you to know Dunning. I am sure Dunning knows how to *live*. However, its as you please. And you may find Lisieux absorbing. I would be very glad if you would tell me your *financial position*. Will you? Quite frankly?

It is intensely cold here and very damp. Very rarely the house is heated. I have a fire in my little room though. I live now in the workers quarters & have the kind of bedroom Gertie Small might have. Bare boards, a scrubbed table for the jug & basin etc. At about 10.30 p.m. we start work in the salon & go to bed at about 1–2 a.m. The corridors are like whistling side streets to pass down – icy cold. My hands are ruined for the present with scraping carrots & peeling onions. I do quite a lot of that kind of kitchen work. But I shall be glad to exchange a very grubby washing up cloth for an apron or an overall. This life proves how terribly wrong & stupid all doctors are. I would have been dead 50 times in the opinion of all the medical men whom I have known. And when I remember last year & that bed in the corner week after week & those *trays*. Here there is no more fine food. You eat what you get & thats the end of it. At the same time I have wonderful what shall I call them? friends. When you leave Lisieux come to Fontainebleau for a few days. I will arrange to meet you there. Not before the late spring though.

Ill write to you again at Xmas – a long letter instead of a 'present'. For I haven't one for you. And tell me all you care to about your new life. I am sure I know a great deal more about cows than you do. I spend hours every single day with them.

Goodbye for now dear Ida.

Yours ever
K.M.

MS BL. *MLM*, 222–3.

[1] KM means Paul Schlumberger (1877–1968), novelist, journalist, and co-founder of the *Nouvelle Revue Française*. Ida Baker now worked on his mother's farm in Lisieux, Normandy.

To Ida Baker, [15 December 1922]

[Le Prieuré, Fontainebleau-Avon]

That, the ultimate remark in this letter was what I was driving at when I suggested you should join Jack. I felt then I'd be sure of you.

Dear Ida,

Forgive this paper. The parcels have arrived and are extremely satisfactory, thanks very much. Why are you still so awfully tragic? I feel you must be very ill physically. Tell me your *Physical health*. I am not dead though you persist in pretending I am. And of course I shall not be here all my life. 'Connected' with this work and these ideas, yes, but that is different. As soon as I am cured I shall leave here and set up a little place in the South and grow something. You can come and talk over the fence if you like and are not too mournful. Come and stay with me if you promise to smile now and again. *Dear* Ida! Thank you for the tops and for everything. As I have said I'll write again at Christmas and provided you are a happy nature I shall beg you to join forces with me when I leave here, if you care to, of course, in some kind of farm. So learn all you can for goodness sake.

With love, yours ever,
KM

MS BL. *MLM*, 223.

To Dorothy Brett, [15 December 1922]

[Le Prieuré, Fontainebleau-Avon]

Dearest Brett

Of course I listen; of course I am glad to hear. And do not think I don't appreciate the fact that you have gone on writing. I do – fully.

I wish I could write back. But for the moment there simply seems nothing to say and I know so little of what is happening. Your visit to Selsfield for instance you speak of as though I know about it. But I don't. And the Sullivan affair – scarcely at all. Its bound of course to come to a foolish end. Poor L.E! Thats where sentimentalism leads a man. She, of course will always look for the softer bed and the softer man and always hark back to Sullivan. She is an unpleasant little creature at this stage of her development. Why see her otherwise?

I am glad you are working. I don't at this moment feel near painting, though I had a long talk about it the other evening with a man who once had a collection of Gaugins[1] in Moscow. But his point was what is the use of painting unless one knows *the laws of art*. How can it have any compelling, real value if it is just dans le vague. You have to know not only the effect this painting has on you, but the principle underlying that effect. And so with music and so with literature. We play with the arts and produce something good by accident.

We have a great deal of music here, but its eastern not western. Quite another world. The dances too are often ancient Assyrian dances, or Arabian or Dervish Dances. I feel as though I have lived years in the East. There are between 50 and 60 of us here all occupied in different ways. One lives in the centre of such a various active world – no, not in the centre – one is part of it. It is very different from my life of the last few years.

I cannot today write of your last but one letter, dearest Brett. I rejoice for you.

Goodbye for now.

Ever your loving
Tig.

The tea is marvellously good. How did you know I was longing for some good tea of my own? It was one of your happiest flukes.

MS Newberry.

---

[1] Paul Gauguin (1848–1903). After associations with both Impressionism and Symbolism in France, he lived in poverty in Tahiti, achieving his unique fusion of European and Pacific influences.

To J. M. Murry, [?17–20 December 1922][1]

[Le Prieuré, Fontainebleau-Avon]

My darling Bogey

I am so delighted to hear of your ½ motorcar. I think it is a most excellent idea. What fun you and Sullivan will have with it. It is so pleasant to think of you two together and I like to know that Sullivan will now understand you from a real standpoint, after sharing your life & working with you in the real sense. Do you teach him to cook and to sew and to knit. The fairies in the keyholes must have a quiet laugh or two of a gentle kind. As to those four little wood gatherers[2] I love them. I hope your tooth is better. Just the same thing has happened to me. My biggest and brightest stopping has come out. But I shall have to hang on until the spring when I can get to Paris. So far all is well.

My fortunes have changed again. I have been moved back from my little bare servants bedroom on the general corridor to my beautiful sumptuous first room overlooking the lovely park. It seems almost incredible grandeur. I suppose – I feel I have learnt the lesson that other room had to teach me. I have learnt that I can rough it in a way you & I have never done, that I can stand any amount of noise, that I can put up with untidiness, disorder, queer smells, even, without losing my head or *really* suffering more than superficially. But how did Mr. Gurdjieff know how much I needed that experience? And another mystery is that last week when it was intensely cold I felt I had come to an end of all that room had to teach me. I was very depressed and longing beyond words for some real change and for beauty again. I almost decided to ask him to send me away until the weather got warmer. Then on Saturday afternoon when I was in the stable he came up to rest, too, and talked to me a little. First about cows and then about the monkey he has bought which is to be trained to clean the cows. Then he suddenly asked me how I was and said I looked better. "Now," he said "you have two doctors you must obey. Doctor Stable and Doctor New Milk. Not to think, not to write . . . Rest. Rest. Live in your body again." I think he meant get back into your body. He speaks very little English but when one is with him one seems to understand all that he suggests. The next thing I heard was that I was to come into here for the rest of the winter. Sometimes I wonder if we 'make up' Mr Gurdjieff's wonderful understanding. But one is always getting a fresh example of it. And he always acts at precisely the moment one needs it. That is what is so strange . . .

Dear Bogey darling I shall not have any Xmas present for you. But you know that £5 I sent you. How much did you spend. Would you buy a book each for Chaddie & Jeanne for me & keep the rest for yourself? Jeanne would like DeLaMares new poems Down-a-Down-Derry[3] I am sure (its 7/6, isn't it?) and Chaddie – hm – that is difficult! Some book that looks pretty and tastes sweet – some love poems. Is that too vague? And may I ask you to execute these commissions for me? I hope there will be something left over for you darling. Buy it with my love. I'll tell you what I want for a present. Your photograph. The proof of the drawing of course I should simply treasure,[4] but why should you send me that. Keep it. Of course if you could have it copied. There is a man here who is going to take a photograph of me one day. I have changed. I have no longer a fringe – very odd. We had a fire here the other night. A real one. Two beautiful rooms burnt out & a real fear the whole place would go. Cries of "Vode! Vode!" (water), people rushing past all black & snatching at jugs & basins, Mr Gurdjieff with a hammer knocking down the wall. The real thing, in fact.

What is the weather like with you. Its so soft & spring like here that actually primroses are out. So are the Christmas roses under the espalier pear trees. I *love* Christmas; I shall always feel it is a holy time. I wonder if dear old Hardy will write a poem this year.[5]

God bless you my darling precious

Ever your
Wig.

MS ATL. *LKM*, 266; *LJMM*, 694–6.

<hr>

[1] Murry gave both dates, 20 in *LKM*, 17 in *LJMM*.

[2] The Dunning children.

[3] Walter de la Mare, *Down-a-Down Derry, A Book of Fairy Poems* (1922). He bought Chaddie A. E. Housman's *Last Poems* (1922).

[4] The recent drawing of JMM by William Rothenstein, reproduced in Lea, facing p.14.

[5] JMM, while still editor of the *Athenaeum*, had published Thomas Hardy's 'At the Entering of the New Year' (31 Dec. 1920). Hardy did not publish a new poem as KM hoped. His only poem in the second half of 1922 was 'Ten Years Since', first published in *Human Shows* (1925).

To J. M. Murry, [23 December 1922]

[Le Prieuré, Fontainebleau-Avon]

Darling Bogey

Just a note to wish you a Happy Xmas. I am afraid it will not arrive in time for today is Saturday *not* Friday as I fondly imagined. But there! Put the blame on the poor Xmas postman. No, even to think of such an unfair thing wont do at all . . . A Happy Xmas, my dearest Bogey. I wonder very much how you who always say you hate Xmas so will spend it this year. Perhaps the Dunning children will make it seem real at last. Do tell me about them.

Here we are to have great doings. The Russian Christmas is not due for another fortnight so Mr Gurdjieff has decided the English shall have a real old fashioned English Xmas on their own. There are so few of them but that makes no difference to his ideas of hospitality. We are to invite all the Russians as our guests. And he has given us a sheep, a pig, two turkeys, a goose, two barrels of wine, whisky, gin, cognac etc, dessert of all kinds, an immense tree & carte blanche with which to decorate it. Tomorrow night we have our tree followed by the feast. We shall sit down to it about 60. Whoever gets the coin in the pudding is to be presented with our newborn calf – a perfect angel. Would that it were mine!

I do love to hear about your Dunnings. What a queer thing you should have found them just at this time. Not really queer for it does seem to me to be a truth that when one is in real need one finds someone to help. Are you and 'Bill' friends. I mean more friends than you and Frieda were, for instance, for you had no separate relationship with her really, did you.[1] I would like to know them both. Darling precious Bogey this is not a letter this time, only this note written on a table piled with paper chains, flowers, little bon bon cases, gold wire, gilded fir cones – you know the kind of thing.

I attended the obsequies of the pig this morning. I thought I had better go through with it for once & see for myself. One felt only horribly sad . . . and yesterday I watched Madame Ouspensky[2] pluck singe & draw our birds. In fact these have been 2 gory days, balanced by the fairy like tree. There is so much life here that one feels no more than one little cell in a beefsteak – say. It is a good feeling. God bless you darling.

Ever your
Wig.

MS ATL. *LJMM*, 696–7.

---

[1] JMM wrote on 17 Dec.: 'I sit in their kitchen-sitting room in the evenings, and we talk. I don't know how to describe it – it's so very simple. Sometimes it reminds me of the times when you & I used to sit with the Lawrences in their kitchen. But the differences are so tremendous that that is rather

misleading than otherwise. There's no *agitation*, it's all very calm and pure' (Murry, 366). (For KM's account of difficulties with the Lawrences at Zennor, Cornwall, from Apr. to Jun. 1916, see *CLKM* I. 259–68.)

[2] Sophie Grigorevna Ouspensky, 'an incisive, Junoesque matron, with dark, chestnut hair, imperious eyes, and a grownup daughter', as she was described at the time of her marriage to Ouspensky in 1916 (James Moore, *Gurdjieff and Mansfield*, 1980, 61).

To Ida Baker, [24 December 1922]

Le Prieuré. | [Fontainebleau-Avon]

Dear Ida

This is to wish you a happy Xmas. I meant to have something for you. For the moment I have nothing & can't get anything. I can't give people commissions nor get to Fontainebleau myself. So take whatever you please that I happen to have and that you think you would like. What about the green cardigan par exemple? Especially as you probably paid for it yourself. In the course of a week or two I shall send you the sleeping vests you bought me. I cant wear them. That kind of wool next to my skin brings me out in a rash . . . I presume of course, it doesn't you.

We are going to fêter le Noel in tremendous style here. Every sort of lavish generous hospitable thing has been done by Mr Gurdjieff. He wants a real old fashioned *English* Xmas – an extraordinary idea here! – & we shall sit down to table 60 persons to turkeys, geese, a whole sheep, a pig, puddings, heaven knows what in the way of dessert, & wines by the barrel. Theres to be a tree, too & Father Xmas. I am doing all I can for the little children so that they will be roped in for once. Ive just sent them over coloured paper & asked them to help to make flowers. Its pathetic the interest they are taking – –

Our pudding was made in a babys bath, stirred by everybody & Mr Gurdjieff put in a coin. Who gets the coin gets our darling new born calf for a present. The calf – 1 day old – was led into the salon to the beating of tambourines & to a special melody composed for it. It took it very quietly. But two minute baby pigs which were also brought in & allowed to play squealed & shrieked terribly. I have been v. interested in the calf. The cow didn't seem to mind the affair. She only lowed faintly & when a leg appeared Madame Ovstrovsky & Nina put a rope round it & pulled & presently a tall weak feeble creature emerged. The cows eyes as big as saucers reminded me of Charles.[1] I wish we gave our cows apples. Some of the names are Equivoqueveckwa, Baldaofim, Mitasha, Bridget. Our mule is Drabfeet.

My existence here is not meagre or miserable. Nothing is done by accident. I understand v. well why my room was changed & so on, and to live among so many people knowing something of them, sharing something, that is for me very great change & ca donne beaucoup.

I shall be glad though when the spring comes. Winter is a difficult time. You know you must not worry about me or say you do or don't. Its exactly as though you took a piece of my flesh and gnawed it. It helps neither you nor me. *Worry is a waste of energy*; it is therefore sin. And to see you waste energy destroys energy in me, so you sin in two ways. Thats surely easy to <say> see.

As to starting [?] gear why don't you begin taking photographs of your-self – take them all day. And look at them. Then begin to decide which are 'good' and which are 'bad' ones. Then try & sort the work bag in your mind before you begin to learn to think & direct your thought. Open your mind & really look into it. Perhaps you wont mind what you see. I mind.

I must end this letter. If youd like me for a friend as from this Xmas Id like to be your friend. But not too awfully serious, ma chère. The whole difficulty in life is to find the *way* between extremes – to preserve ones poise in fact to get a hold of the pendulum.

Jack said he would be delighted to have you whenever you felt like it. He sounds different in his letters, much simpler.

Yours ever
K.M.

MS BL. *MLM*, 224–5.

[1]   As Ida notes, 'The cat at Portland Villas, mother of Wingley and Athenaeum.'

To J. M. Murry, [26 December 1922]

[Le Prieuré, Fontainebleau-Avon]
Boxing Day

My darling Bogey

I think the drawing of you is quite extraordinarily good, and in a very subtle way. I had no idea Rothenstein was that kind of artist. People will say it makes you look old. That is true. But you have that look. I am sure c'est juste. I am more than glad to have it & I shall keep it v. carefully. Thank you, my dearest. The photograph I don't like so well for some reason. But photographs always pale before good drawings. Its not fair on them.

How is the old Adam revived in you, I wonder? What aspect has he? There is nothing to be done when he rages except to remember that its bound to be – it's the swing of the pendulum – ones only hope is when the bout is exhausted to get back to what you think you really care for aim for wish to live by as soon as possible. It's the intervals of exhaustion that seem to waste so much energy. You see, my love, the question is always '*Who am I*' and until that is discovered I don't see how one can really direct anything in ones self. '*Is there a Me.*' One must be certain of that before one has a real unshakeable leg to stand on. And I don't believe for one moment these questions can be settled by the head alone. It is this life of the *head*, this formative intellectual life at the expense of all the rest of us which has got us into this state. How can it get us out of it? I see no hope of escape except by learning to live in our emotional & instinctive being as well and to balance all three.

You see Bogey if I were allowed one single cry to God that cry would be *I want to be REAL.* Until I am that I don't see why I shouldn't be at the mercy of old Eve in her various manifestations for ever.

But this place has taught me so far how unreal I am. It has taken from me one thing after another (the things never were mine) until at this present moment all I know really really is that I am not annihilated and that I hope – more than hope – believe. It is hard to explain and I am always a bit afraid of boring you in letters.

I heard from Brett yesterday. She gave me a very horrid picture of the present Sullivan and his views on life and women. I don't know how much of it is even vaguely true but it corresponds to Sullivan the Exhibitionist. The pity of it is life is so short and we waste about 9/10 of it – simply throw it away. I always feel Sullivan refuses to face the fact of his wastefulness. And sometimes one feels he never will. All will pass like a dream, with mock comforts, mock consolations . . .

Our cowshed has become enriched with 2 goats and two love birds. The goats are very lovely as they lie in the straw or so delicately dance towards each other butting gently with their heads. When I was there yesterday Mr Gurdjieff came in and showed Lola and Nina who were milking the cows the way to milk a goat. He sat down on a stool seized the goat & swung its hind legs across his knees. So there the goat was on its two front legs, helpless. This is the way Arabs milk. He looked very like one. I had been talking before to a man here whose passion is astrology and he had just written the signs of the Zodiac on the whitewashed stable walls. Then we went up to the little gallery & drank koumiss.

Goodbye for now, my darling. I feel this letter is flat & dull. Forgive it. I am ever your own loving

Wig.

MS ATL. *LKM* II, 266–7; *LJMM*, 697–8.

To J. M. Murry, 31 December 1922

[Le Prieuré, Fontainebleau-Avon]
31 XII 1922

Darling Bogey

My fountain pen is mislaid, so as I am in a hurry to write please forgive this pencil.

Would you care to come here on January 8 or 9 to stay until 14–15? Mr Gurdjieff approves of my plan and says you will come as his guest. On the 13th our new theatre is to be opened. It will be a wonderful experience. But I wont say too much about it. Only on the chance that you do come Ill tell you what clothes to bring.

One sports suit with heavy shoes & stockings and a macintosh & a hat that doesn't matter. One 'neat' suit with your soft collar or whatever collar you wear & tie (you see you are my husband & I cant help wanting you to look – what shall I say?), slippers, and so on. That's all. If you have a cardigan of course bring it and a pair of flannel trousers in case you get soaking wet & want to change.

I am writing to ask Brett to go to Lewis' to get me a pair of shoes. Will you bring them. I may ask her to get me a jacket, too. But she will give you the parcel. Will you wire me your reply – just 'yes' or 'no' & the date if yes of your arrival.

There is a London train that reaches Paris at 4 something. You could then come on to Fontainebleau the same day. Otherwise its far better to stay the night in Paris as no cabs meet the late train. You get out of the train at *Avon* & take a cab here which costs 8 francs *with* tip. Ring the bell at the porters lodge and Ill open the gate.

I hope you will decide to come, my dearest. Let me know as soon as you can – won't you? I hope Tchekhov's wife will be here. I have gone back to my big lovely room, too, so we should have plenty of space to ourselves. We can also sit & drink kiftir in the cowshed.

I cant write of other things in this letter. I hope to hear from you soon.

Your ever loving
Wig.

MS ATL. *LKM* II, 268–9.

To Dorothy Brett, [31 December 1922]

[Le Prieuré, Fontainebleau-Avon]
Dearest Brett

What haven't I to thank you for! A letter, 2 photographs and the perfectly charming little Beaver Puff. They were all my Christmas presents from England (except for a drawing from J.M.M.). I am so glad to have the photographs. Have you sold the little landscape yet? Looking at it I went back to Sierre for a moment & sat in the carriage at the hotel door about to drive away down the sunny streets and out into the vineyards. It seems years and years ago, though the Beaver Puff is a great lamb and it feels incredibly soft – delicious.

Now for your letter. We are talking at cross purposes about Laws. Dear old Cezanne[1] didn't discover those shapes! They have meant what he said they meant for thousands & thousands of years. Also one cant start *laws* like hares nor can one light on them in 5 weeks. I mean something utterly different – far more difficult and profound. Laws are handed down to those who have *knowledge*. For all I know the *laws* of painting may have to do with the planetary movements; I don't know. But they are quite different to "inward spiritual beauty". However the subject is dreadfully unprofitable, and I shouldn't have started it. I wanted merely to hint at something, to suggest something – no more. I am too ignorant to talk.

Thank you for the two little heads of J.M.M., even though I don't like them. I think they are too soft, too rounded. He hasn't that full eye, that docile modelling of the lips and jaw. Did you see Rothensteins drawing of him. There was to my mind something *very* good in it. Real psychological penetration, immensely interesting. That is J.M.M. as I know him. I could not bear your J.M.M. Hes all dove and lamb – no serpent, no lion. Theres no *material* in him and J.M.M. has masses of material.

I have asked him to come over here for a week. If he does would you buy me a pair of shoes at Lewis? in Oxford Street – 'good old John Lewis'. I have drawn a line round the sole of one shoe to show you the size. It is made $\frac{1}{2}$ of velvet $\frac{1}{2}$ of cheap brocade with a long toe. I think they call it a 'Jester' shape. They have only the one kind. And is it possible to buy in London an indoor jacket – little coat – for the evening that is both gay and warm? Something rather sumptuous looking with a snip of cheap fur on it. Its to wear at a feast where everybody else will be in evening dress & for a skirt I shall wear that purple silk of mine with the tiny wreaths of roses on it – the 10 year old one. But only you could choose me such a jacket or know where they are to be found. Do get me one if you can will you, Brettushka? & give it to J.M.M. to bring. I would like it rather on the large size. I look so ugly in tight things. Ill send you a cheque by return for both.

The box that you threaten to send after the New Year is dreadfully intriguing. I shall *have* to send a box back by Murry.

This letter is as usual written in a tearing hurry. I am supposed to be at the new theatre that we are building. I must go. This morning I made breadcrumbs for 60 people – mountains of them.

A Happy New Year, dearest! I believe it will be one for you.

Ever your loving
Tig

MS Newberry.

---

[1] Paul Cézanne (1839–1906), who revolutionized the approach to form and volume in modern painting.

To Harold Beauchamp, 31 December 1922

Le Prieuré | Fontainebleau-Avon | Seine-et-Marne
31 XII 1922

My dearest Father

I am writing this letter when the old year is at his last gasp and in the very act of turning up his toes! May the New Year be full of happiness for you. I wish I could imagine we might meet in it but perhaps in the one after I shall be fortunate enough to turn towards home and to see you at the Grange. It is a dream I would love to realise.

Since I last wrote I have been leading a very tame semi-existence here. My heart, under this new treatment, which is one of graduated efforts and exercise, feels decidedly stronger, and my lungs in consequence feel quieter, too. Its a remarkable fact that since arriving here I have not had to spend one entire day in bed – an unprecedented record for me! I feel more and more confident that if I can give this treatment a fair trial – as I intend to do – and stay on for six months at least, I shall be infinitely stronger in every way. More I do not venture to say.

Did I tell you in my last letter that the people here have had built a little gallery in the cowshed with a very comfortable divan and cushions. And I lie there for several hours each day to inhale the smell of the cows. It is supposed to be a sovereign remedy for the lungs. I feel I must look a great pa-woman[1], perched up aloft. But the air is wonderfully light and sweet to breathe, and I enjoy the experience. I feel inclined to write a book called "The Cowiness of the Cow" as a result of observing them at such close quarters.

We had a very quiet Christmas here, as the Russian Christmas is not until January 6th. Their New Year is on January 13th. What a frightful bother! Christmas, in any case, is no fun away from ones own people. I seldom want to make merry with strangers, and that particular feast is only enjoyable because of its childish associations. I remember us all going to St Paul's[2] and Mother's enjoyment of "Hark the Herald Angels Sing."[3] And that makes me think of darling Leslie still a child, enjoying everything. Such memories do not make for gaiety.

I see by the papers I have received that my last book is nominated for the Vie Heureuse French Literary Prize[4] as the former one was. It has no chance of success, for the French never take short stories "seriously". However, it is a good advertisement and costs nothing.

Jack still sounds very happy and busy, dividing his time between the country and London, with a strong bias in favour of the country. I do wish the English climate were more temperate and that I could look forward to *settling down* there. But the idea of settling is to me what it seemed to be to grandpa Beauchamp. Only I am driven where he went willingly.

My new book will not be out before the spring. I am still a little undecided about the title. I feel the choice of titles ought to be studied as a separate art.

Chaddie and Jeanne write very happily. I have no idea of what Charles does all day, though. Of course Jeanne will make the best of it and find happiness, but I don't think it can be much fun living in a hotel in South Kensington.

Chaddie sent me a handkerchief for Christmas (her invariable present) and little Wilfred a morsel of ribbon that looked like her doll's sash. I still cannot imagine her a married woman.

Well dearest Father this letter is very fragmentary. I so look forward to hearing from you. I expect you found everything in apple pie order and I am sure you had a very warm welcome. How I envy you summer weather, though there is little to complain of in the winter so far. If I began asking you questions about Wellington ways there would be no end to it.

Forgive this handwriting, dearest Father. My constant plea! But as usual my letter case is balanced on my knee & at a rather groggy angle.

The New Year is already here. I must leave the fire and go to bed. God bless you darling Father. May we meet again at not too distant a date.

Ever your devoted child
Kass.

MS ATL. Cited Alpers 1980, 382; *Selected*, 283–5.

[1] See 131, n. 2.
[2] The Anglican cathedral in Wellington.
[3] The Christmas carol by Charles Wesley (1739).
[4] The Prix Femina–Vie Heureuse had been awarded on 13 Dec. to Jacques de Lacretelle's *Silbermann*.

To Elizabeth, Countess Russell, 31 December 1922

Le Prieuré | Fontainebleau-Avon | Seine-et-Marne

31
XII
1922.

Dearest Elizabeth,

Here is the £100 you lent me. I am sending it, as you see, at the last last moment while the old year is in the very act of turning up his toes.

I wish I could explain why I have not written to you for so long. It is not for lack of love. But such a black fit came on me in Paris when

I realised that X-ray treatment wasn't going to do any more than it had done beyond upsetting my heart still more that I gave up everything and decided to try a new life altogether. But this decision was immensely complicated with 'personal' reasons too. When I came to London from Switzerland I did (Sydney [Waterlow] was right so far) go through what books and undergraduates call a spiritual crisis, I suppose. For the first time in my life everything bored me. Everything and worse everybody seemed a compromise, and so flat, so dull, so mechanical. If I had been well I should have rushed off to darkest Africe or the Andes or the Ganges or wherever it is one rushes at those times, to try for a change of heart (one can't change one's heart in public) and to gain new impressions. For it seems to me we live on new impressions – really new ones.

But such grand flights being impossible I burned what boats I had and came here where I am living with about fifty to sixty people, mainly Russians. It is a fantastic existence, impossible to describe. One might be anywhere – in Bokhara or Tiflis or Afghanistan (except alas! for the climate!). But even the climate does not seem to matter so much when one is whirled along at such a rate. For we do most decidedly whirl. But I cannot tell you what a joy it is to me to be in contact with living people who are strange and quick and not ashamed to be themselves. It's a kind of supreme airing to be among them.

But what nonsense this all sounds. That is the worst of letters; they are fumbling things.

I haven't written a word since October and I don't mean to until the spring. I want much more material; I am tired of my little stories like birds bred in cages.[1]

But enough. Dear Elizabeth, I have not thanked you even for the Enchanted April. It is a delectable book; the only other person who could have written it is Mozart.

My [word missing], from the moment they arrived in Italy had a separate blissful existence of its own. How do you write like that? How? How?

Do you see John, I wonder? He sounds very happy and serene – Life is a mysterious affair!

Goodbye, my dearest Cousin. I shall never know anyone like you; I shall remember every little thing about you for ever.

Lovingly yours,
Katherine.

TC Huntington. *LKM* II. 267–8; *De Charms*, 251–2.

---

[1] An image from her last story, 'The Canary', written in July 1922.

To Charlotte Beauchamp Perkins and Jeanne Beauchamp Renshaw, 31 December 1922

Le Prieuré | Fontainebleau-Avon | Seine et Marne.

31
XII
1922

My dearest Marie & Jeanne

I am seizing the last moments of the old year to write to you, for I cannot let it depart without a letter from me. I have been such a very bad correspondent lately. I am only too painfully aware of it. But it was awfully difficult to write. There seemed nothing to say. Were I to attempt to describe my present surroundings and way of life it would all sound like a dream, and I have for the moment no interests outside it.

As you know I came here for a 'cure' but its not a 'cure' in any ordinary sense of the word. The cure consists in leading as full and as different a life as possible, in entering into as many new interests as possible, in taking up all kinds of new things of every sort and description. Purely medical treatment there is none, as we understand it, or not enough to mention.

We are about 50–60, mainly Russians established here in a colony, and leading a very particular kind of communal life.[1]

MS ATL.

[1] As JMM wrote to KM's sisters, 'This is the beginning of a letter I found among Katherine's papers' (ATL).

To Ida Baker, [Early January 1923]

Le Prieuré | Fontainebleau–Avon | Seine-et-Marne

My dear Ida

I have purposely not written to you before because I felt you wanted me to disappear . . . for a little. I was right, wasn't I? But you have been in my mind today. How are you? How are the cows? As you see I am sending you 100 francs. Play with it. I don't want it. Until your financial position improves its no good minding taking any small sums I can send you. And as I have lost my money complex you can take them quite freely.

Very much is happening here. We are in the throes of theatre building which ought to be ready by the New Year (Russian style) on January 13th. Its going to be a most marvellous place. Mr Gurdjieff has bought 63 carpets for it & the same number of fur rugs. The carpets which were displayed one by one in the salon last night are like living things – worlds of beauty. And what a joy to begin to learn which is a garden, which a café, which a prayer mat, which l'histoire de ses troupeaux and so on. My thoughts are full of carpets and Persia and Samarkand and the little rugs of Baluchistan.

Do you kill pigs where you are? It goes on here. Two were stuck yesterday and their horrid corpses were dissected in the kitchen. They are frightful things to watch *and* to smell. The worst of it is until their heads are cut off they are still so pig like. But we kill them outright. That is one comfort.

I am looking for signs of spring already. Under the espalier pear trees there are wonderful Xmas roses which I saw for the first time this year. They reminded me of Switzerland, and somebody found four primroses the other day. I have moods when I simply pine for the S. of France or somewhere like Majorka. *When* this time is over I shall make for the South or the East & never go North again.

My blue wool dress is in large holes. Those cashmir cardigans look as if rats have gnawed them. As to my fur coat – its like a wet London cat. The last time I was in the stable I caught one of the goats nibbling it. How are you off for clothes? Would you like brown corduroys? That big woman Miss Marston whom you took such a fancy to, wore them. She got them from Barkers – outsize – 35/- They are breeks and a smock & long plain coat. Very practical.

Write and tell me how you are will you? Dear Ida?

Our calf is still allowed to be with its Mother. I can't understand it. Its a huge creature now. We had great trouble with the mother who had to be massaged daily. Do you massage your cows? Will you tell me how your stable is kept? What is the condition of the floor. I'll tell you about ours in my next letter. It worries me.

With love from
K.M.[1]

MS BL. *MLM*, 225–6.

---

[1] This letter was not sent. KM died late on the evening of 9 January, the day Murry arrived to visit her at Fontainebleau.

INDEX OF RECIPIENTS

GENERAL INDEX

The following abbreviations are used: JMM-John Middleton Murry; KM-Katherine Mansfield; IB-Ida Baker